# INTRODUCTORY ECONOMICS
## COURSE COMPANION

# INTRODUCTORY ECONOMICS COURSE COMPANION

Barry Harrison

150th YEAR
M
MACMILLAN

First published 1993 by
THE MACMILLAN PRESS LTD
Houndmills, Basingstoke, Hampshire RG21 2XS
and London
Companies and representatives
throughout the world

ISBN 0–333–57913–5

A catalogue record for this book is available
from the British Library.

Copy-edited and typeset by Povey–Edmondson
Okehampton and Rochdale, England

Printed in Hong Kong

# CONTENTS

# ACKNOWLEDGEMENTS

The author and publishers are grateful to the following for permission to reproduce copyright material:

Barclays Bank plc for material on page 191.
*Daily Mirror* for extract on page 71.
*Economica* for Figure 28.5 form A. W. Phillips, 'The relationship between unemployment and the rate of change of money wages in the UK, 1861–1957', 1958.
*Financial Times* for extracts on pages 63, 198–9, 230–1.
*The Guardian* for extracts on pages 88 and 190.
The Controller of Her Majesty's Stationery Office for Tables 2.1, 17.1, 21.2, 27.2, 28.1 and 32.1 and Figures 2.1 and 2.2.
IEA for Table 2.3.
Longman Publishers plc for material on pages 13–15.
The Times Newspapers plc for material on page 187.
UNIDO for Table 30.7.
*Western Mail* for material on page 77.

They would also like to thank the following examination boards for permissions to reproduce examination questions, though the boards do not take any responsibility for the answers provided by the author:

Associated Examining Board
Joint Matriculation Board
Northern Ireland Schools Examination and
    Assessment Council
University of Cambridge Local School Examining
    Syndicate
University of London School Examining Board

Every effort has been made to contact all the copyright-holders, but if any have been inadvertently overlooked the publishers will be pleased to make the necessary arrangement at the first opportunity.

# *PREFACE*

This book is designed as a course companion for those studying 'A'-level Economics and equivalent courses. The aim is not to provide a substitute for a main course text. Rather the aim is to provide an introduction to the different topics in the syllabus, to identify the most common errors and to provide practice at answering questions so that understanding of the subject will be improved. It is hoped that by supplementing the information given in conventional textbooks economic awareness will be increased, and that this will be reflected in higher assignment marks throughout the course and in an improved examination performance.

Each chapter follows the same pattern. A topic summary provides the essential outline of the most important concepts, ideas and relationships associated with each topic on the syllabus. This will introduce readers to the subject-matter of the topic. The concise nature of the topic summaries will appeal to students who require more information on topics they have read about elsewhere, or who require a brief, but thorough, grounding in the topic before moving on to a more advanced treatment. The topic summaries are written so as to be accessible to students of all abilities.

Each chapter also contains detailed information on mistakes most commonly made, particularly by students new to the subject. Often basic concepts are mistaken for one another and the section 'Common Mistakes to Avoid' in each chapter identifies those concepts which are commonly confused and explains the differences between them.

In the section 'Questions and Answers' we give answers to typical examination questions. All types of examination question, multiple-choice, data response and essay, are included throughout the book and most of the questions are taken from past examination papers. Full and complete answers are given to each question and in total there are over 75 examination-type questions and answers. While I am grateful to the examination boards for permission to reproduce their questions, they are not necessarily in

agreement with the answers given here and they accept no responsibility for them.

Nevertheless, it is hoped that students will find the questions and answers helpful, but, remember, all examiners know that any particular question can often be answered in a variety of ways and no claim is made here that the answers given in this book are definitive. It is certainly not recommended that they be learned by rote in the hope that they reappear on an examination paper. The aim of including answers in this book is to show one way in which each of the questions can be answered and to give an indication of the standard required to achieve success in the examination. It is hoped that having seen examples of good work students will aim to achieve and better the standard set here.

In addition to examination-type questions and answers, this book contains over 220 'Review Questions and Answers' designed to probe and test understanding of each topic on the syllabus. The review questions are reproduced from the core textbook *Introductory Economics* (Barry Harrison, Charles Smith and Brinley Davies, Macmillan, 1992), and, while some of these questions were constructed by my co-authors of that book, the answers given here are my own work.

Many people have worked long and hard in the production of this book, and if I do not mention them all by name I am nevertheless grateful to them. As always, my wife Lea, and sons, Paul, Matthew and Simon, have provided a great deal of help, advice and support which all authors need. When I wrote my first book my eldest son had not started school and my youngest son was not even born. They are all now old enough to help with the humdrum chores around the house and while they might not always like sharing them, they are at least cheerful about doing them. Again I am grateful to the entire team at Macmillan but must make special mention of my publisher, Stephen Rutt, who has been a constant source of guidance and encouragement. I must also thank Keith Povey and his editorial team for removing many errors from my typescript and for transforming it into a version fit for the printer. Finally I have received helpful advice and comments on each chapter from Stan Goodman of Rickmansworth School, Hertfordshire, Phyllis Palmer of Dinnington Comprehensive School, Sheffield, and John Wigley of Haberdashers' Aske's School, Elstree. All of those mentioned above have suggested many improvements to the text, but as I have not always accepted their advice I am unable to implicate them in any errors or omissions that remain.

*Nottingham*             BARRY HARRISON

# AN INTRODUCTION TO STUDY SKILLS

Learning how to study effectively is an important skill to develop if **knowledge** and **understanding** of a subject are to grow. This introductory section sets out some general points of good practice.

## Reading and Note-taking

There are different reading techniques and which is most suitable depends on the nature of what you are reading and why you are reading it. The main techniques are easily summarised.

### Scanning

This is a technique where we simply focus on the main headings and sub-headings which are listed as an initial guide to the relevance of the material covered. In other words scanning is used to identify those sections which require more careful attention.

### Skimming

This technique involves reading material quickly and is useful when we are already familiar with a topic and simply require a different approach to a topic or a different set of examples. Using this technique it is often possible to skim two or three pages a minute.

### Detailed Reading

This is reading undertaken to build up knowledge and understanding of the subject. By comparison with the other techniques of reading described above, detailed reading is a slow process and requires far more concentration. It is important when reading in detail to adopt an analytical approach. You will derive greatest benefit from detailed reading when you question what you read. For example, when you read a particular argument try and identify the circumstances necessary for the argument to hold, try and think up examples to illustrate points you read about and so on.

### Note-taking

Compiling a set of notes is essential if you are to derive full benefit from the material you read. However notes should be just that, a summary of what you have read. There is sometimes a great temptation simply to rewrite what has been read. In fact this takes considerable time, leads to a copious set of notes that are less useful than the book from which they were taken and in no way improves understanding of the subject. Try to compile a set of notes which summarise in your own words what you have read.

### Writing an Assignment

During your course you will almost certainly be required to produce several assignments. In general it is important to complete work in good time. Rushed work seldom reflects an individual's ability. Before writing an assignment it is usually best to plan what you intend to do in the assignment and how it will be organised. Ideally the plan should cover the whole assignment. A plan should include only the amount of detail necessary for you to remember all of the points you intend to include in your assignment. Having completed your plan it is a good idea to refer to the title of your assignment and check that your plan actually covers all of the relevant material and provides a suitable answer to any questions posed.

## Preparing for the Examination

### Revision

How and when to revise are matters of individual judgement. However, for most people it is better to regard revision as an on-going process: something that begins when the course starts! Revision in this sense implies paying particular attention to those parts of the course you have difficulty with or which you do not fully understand. This is particularly important in a subject like economics where topics interrelate so that an understanding of one topic is necessary for an understanding of others. For example, economists use supply and demand techniques to explain the behaviour of markets. If these concepts are imperfectly understood it will be difficult to understand the behaviour of the different markets covered by the syllabus you are following.

A solid body of knowledge and understanding takes a considerable time to build up. It is not something that can be achieved in the few weeks before an examination. Final revision should be seen more as a consolidation phase when knowledge and understanding are strengthened. A useful idea before final revision begins is to draw up a revision plan. This should identify the specific times in the run up to the examination when different topics will be covered and understanding checked. One important point to remember is that revision will almost certainly take longer to complete than you anticipate. The further into your revision you go, the more difficult it will be to make progress. In other words be sure you begin revision early enough, so that you have sufficient time to cover the whole syllabus.

As part of your revision programme it is important to practise answering questions from past examination papers. Make sure you have plenty of practice at answering all of the different types of questions (multiple choice, data response, essay and short answer questions). If possible it is a good idea to have these marked by your teacher but this may not always be easy, especially if you are part of a large group. If it is not possible, ask your teacher for a few hints about the way different questions might be tackled and reassure yourself that you are thinking along the correct lines.

It is also useful to obtain the chief examiner's reports on past question papers. These give a good indication of what the chief examiner was looking for in the responses to the different questions, but also gives a guide to the standard required for success in the examination. Possibly of even more importance is that the reports provide information on the most common errors made by candidates in the examination. Few of us are immune from such errors. The more information you have on the mistakes most commonly made, the better your chances of success.

## In the Examination

When you are told to begin the examination it is important to read the question paper fully before you respond to any questions. Indeed it is a good idea to read the question paper more than once and think about what each question is asking you to do. Experience confirms that on a second reading, questions which seemed difficult are often easier than they appeared.

Before you begin your response to any question make a brief plan of what you will include in your answer. Pay particular attention to key words that indicate the type of approach required. Some of the more common key words are explained below.

**Briefly** or **Outline**   These words tell you that a sentence or a few sentences are all that is required for this part of the question. As your guide, look at the number of marks that are available for an answer to questions that begin with these words. Sometimes all that is required is a straightforward definition of a particular term or concept. At other times a little more explanation is required.

**Explain** or **Analyse**   These words ask you to demonstrate that you understand how concepts relate to one another and the assumptions that underpin a particular argument. For example, a phrase economists often use is *'other things equal'*. Being able to identify these other things and understanding what might happen if they do not remain equal is an analytical skill.

**Assess**, **Evaluate**, **Discuss** or **Examine** Questions which include these words require a balanced approach. *Reasoned judgements* must be made about different arguments and their possible validity assessed. Where appropriate it is important to consider advantages and disadvantages and your points must be supported by argument.

**Illustrate**   This simply means 'explain with examples'. Since you are asked to include examples in your explanation it is important that you do so. Failure to include examples will no doubt result in lost marks.

# CHAPTER 1
# *WHAT IS ECONOMICS?*

## Topic Summary

When you begin your course in economics, as well as your hopes for examination success you probably have hopes about what you will have learned by the end of the course. In one way or another the economy receives a great deal of coverage in the media and you will no doubt wish to understand such coverage. Typical headlines might read:

**'Sterling was weak against the dollar but gained ground against the Deutschmark'**

**'Unemployment rose again last month though the underlying trend is downwards'**

**'Britain's trade was in the red again with the biggest gap ever recorded between manufacturing exports and manufacturing imports'**

By the end of your course you will no doubt understand fully what each of these statements implies. But, much more important than this, you will have some idea of what causes these problems and your own opinions on how to deal with them. However to achieve this you must begin at the beginning, and in this chapter we aim to answer the question 'What is economics?'

In a nutshell, economics is about **the economic problem**. But what is 'the economic problem' and how can we suggest that there is only one economic problem? After all, we have mentioned several economic problems above: the exchange rate, the balance of payments, unemployment and inflation. We could add many more problems to this list without any difficulty at all if we wanted to, but the important point to stress is that all of these problems are in fact part of a much greater problem. It is this greater problem which economists refer to as 'the economic problem' and the entire study of economics stems from this central economic problem. It is therefore extremely important to understand exactly what is meant by 'the economic problem'.

## Scarcity

Scarcity is at the heart of the economic problem. However, by scarcity economists do not necessarily mean that something is rare or that there is not much of it. Instead, scarcity is defined as a situation that exists when **more of something is desired than is currently available**.

In this sense most of the goods and services we can think of are scarce. There is no doubt that for society as a whole there are many unsatisfied desires. Most people can think of material things they would like but cannot at present afford. A new car, a caravan, a second home, additional holidays, and so on, are examples that spring to mind. No matter how prosperous a country becomes the desires of society go on growing. In the UK there are now four times more cars on the roads than there were twenty years ago, but still the desire to possess even more cars is no closer to being satisfied! The existence of these **unsatisfied desires**, whatever form they take, is what economists mean by **scarcity**.

The question to ask is why countries are unable to satisfy all of their material desires. In fact goods and services are scarce because they are made from **resources** such as **land**, **labour** and **capital**. At any moment in time there is a limited supply of these resources, but there is no such limit on the desires of society for the output that these resources can produce. This means that some of society's desires will always be unsatisfied. This is one part of the economic problem.

## Choice

Because society cannot have all the goods and services it desires at any one time, it is forced to make choices. In other words, because of scarcity, society is forced to choose. In fact there are three fundamental choices which all societies must make. In summary these are:

**What output to produce.** Because resources are scarce, society cannot have all the goods and services it desires; it must therefore choose which goods and services will be produced.

**How to produce.** There are various ways of producing any given output. For example, it is often possible to substitute machinery for labour and society must therefore choose the way in which its factors are to be combined.

**For whom to produce.** Society must decide how its output is to be distributed among consumers. Will there be equal shares for all, or will some people have more output than others and, if so, how much more?

Choice is the second part of the economic problem, which can therefore be summed up as **scarcity** and **choice**.

## Opportunity Cost

Throughout your course you will find many references to the term **opportunity cost**. You will quickly realise that this is one of the most fundamental concepts in any study of economics. It is particularly relevant to decisions about production or consumption because there are **alternatives** to consider. How many alternative uses can you think of for timber and steel, for example? Or what about your weekly pocket money? How many alternative uses can you think of for that? The point to grasp is that, if resources are used to produce or consume one thing, we must do without the alternative good or service that could have been produced with the same resources or purchased with the same money. The alternative which is *forgone* is the opportunity cost of what is produced or consumed. For example, if the government, on behalf of society, chooses to build a new university, the opportunity cost of this might be a new hospital or a new housing estate.

Great care must be taken here. In this case the opportunity cost of the university is not the hospital and the housing estate. Society does not do without both of these. If, in order of preference, society would choose a university first, a hospital next and a housing estate last, then the opportunity cost of the university is the hospital, because this is what society will do without if it uses its resources to build a university. In practice, most of society's choices about the use of its resources do not mean choosing one thing in preference to another. They involve choosing more of one thing and having less of something else. One point to note in passing is

that economists often refer to opportunity cost as *real cost* to indicate the real sacrifices involved in making decisions about how resources are to be used. Simply remember that opportunity cost and real cost are different ways of saying the same thing.

## Production Possibility Curves

Sometimes opportunity cost is illustrated by means of a production possibility curve. A production possibility curve simply shows the different combinations of output that society can produce at any one time when all of its available resources are used or employed. For example, if we assume that society only produces two goods, good $X$ and good $Y$, we can illustrate a typical production possibility curve as in Figure 1.1.

Since a production possibility curve shows the maximum amount that can be produced from society's scarce resources, it follows that any point on the curve, such as $A$ or $B$, are points of full employment. Any point, inside the curve, such as point $C$, represent points at which not all of society's resources are fully employed. In other words there are unemployed resources in the economy.

It is clear from Figure 1.1 that, when the economy is at point $A$, it is producing 200 units of good $X$ and 615 units of good $Y$; whereas when the economy is at point $B$, it is producing 450 units of good $X$ and 340

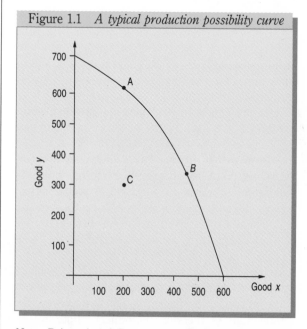

Figure 1.1    *A typical production possibility curve*

*Note*  Points $A$ and $B$ are points of full employment. At point $C$ there are unemployment resources.

units of good $Y$. We can see from this that if the economy is at point $A$, the opportunity cost of increasing the production of $X$ from 200 units to 450 units is 275 units of good $Y$. This is because the increased production of $X$ is only possible if the production of $Y$ is reduced by 275 units.

On the other hand if the economy is at point $C$, that is, currently producing 200 units of good $X$ and 250 units of good $Y$, it is possible to increase the production of both goods simultaneously. It is also possible to increase the production of one good without reducing production of the other. In other words when the economy is at point $C$, increased output has no opportunity cost. The reason is that at point $C$ there are unemployed resources which can be drawn into production.

## Economic Systems

Conventionally the discussion of economic systems focuses chiefly on **market economies** and **centrally planned economies**, though in its extreme form neither system exists anywhere in the world. Despite this the distinction is important because real world economies can be thought of as being more like one type of economic system and less like the other. In fact all economies are more properly termed **mixed economies** because they contain a mixture of both types of system. However, in recent years economies such as the Russian economy, which were regarded as largely centrally planned, have shifted dramatically towards market economies and away from central planning. The reasons for this are examined in the answer to Question 1 on pp. 3–5.

## Common Mistakes to Avoid

### Scarcity and Rarity

Take care to avoid confusing *scarcity* and *rarity*. Scarcity is measured relative to the amount of something which is desired. Rarity is measured relative to the amount of something which is available. Thus motor cars are scarce because society as a whole desires more of them than is currently available. However they are certainly not rare! On the other hand we might agree that an original Van Gogh painting is rare because there is only one original in existence.

## Questions and Answers

### Questions

1 (a) What problems have prompted several countries in Eastern Europe with centrally planned economies to make greater use of the price mechanism in directing economic activity?

   (b) Do these changes in Eastern Europe imply that a wholly free enterprise economy faces no problems in the task of resource allocation?

ULEAC, June 1991

2 Opportunity cost arises because:

   (1) society's wants exceed its ability to satisfy them,
   (2) resources are scarce and have alternative uses,
   (3) all goods consumed by society require scarce resources.

(A) 1, 2 and 3 are correct.
(B) 1 and 2 only are correct.
(C) 2 and 3 only are correct.
(D) 1 only is correct.
(E) 3 only is correct.

### Answers

1 (a) In the centrally planned economies of Eastern Europe there was a high degree of state ownership of the means of production which meant that the government, through its planning agency, had to plan the output of the different sectors of the economy. The collapse of these economies indicates that central planning operated inefficiently.

In the recent past we have learned a considerable amount about the planned economies of Eastern Europe and they are clearly struggling to overcome problems of inefficiency, poverty and pollution. A major case of these problems was that most resources were state owned and there was little in the way of private ownership. Most production was not therefore undertaken for profit and producers had little incentive to improve their product or the way it was produced.

Another source of inefficiency was that, once established, plans were difficult to alter. In these circumstances, if consumers demanded more of certain products and less of others, it was impossible to adjust production quickly and there were surpluses of some goods, shortages of others, and little prospect that the situation would improve. It is hard to imagine a more graphic example of inefficiency than this: an economy producing goods which people do not want, and simultaneously failing to produce enough of those goods which people do want, with no prospect of change!

Industry in the centrally planned economies of Eastern Europe also operated inefficiently for another reason. As part of the planning process, each production unit in the economy was assigned a target level of output. However, assigning target levels of output to individual factories and farms provided an incentive to underproduce. After all, any target that was met would most likely be increased when the plan was redrawn. This has been a major cause of poverty in the economies of Eastern Europe since the amount a country can consume is largely determined by the amount it produces.

In addition the economies of Eastern Europe directed vast amounts of resources towards military activities such as the production and development of armaments. If resources are devoted to military purposes, they are not available to produce goods and services the population might otherwise desire. Similarly drawing up the plan involved a considerable opportunity cost. Tens of thousands of officials were employed simply to gather data on resource availability, estimate the productive potential of factories and farms and decide the level of output each unit was to produce and, to a large extent, the way it was to be produced. The plan itself was so complex it required the aid of the most powerful computers. These resources could have been used to produce other goods and services, had they not been used for planning purposes.

However, it was not just in production that inefficiency was evident. The centrally planned economies also performed inefficiently in the distribution of output. Long food queues were a daily occurrence in many places and this represents a considerable waste of that most valuable resource, time. Moreover food queues are an indication that there is a shortage in the shops. However, in the planned economies of Eastern Europe this occurred when food was rotting in storage depots or in the fields because it was unharvested.

Centrally planned economies have also been criticised because of the degradation of the environment they allowed. Here again inefficiency in production has been a major cause of such environmental degradation. If waste materials, including toxic waste, are simply dumped into a river or lake, the disposal cost to the producer is zero since the waste

is not treated. However the creation of treatment plants requires resources which, because industry operated so inefficiently, the planners deemed could not be spared from other uses. The environment was therefore used as a resource which had no opportunity cost. In other words it was used as a free resource.

These are the major problems that have prompted the East European countries to move away from central planning and make greater use of the price mechanism in directing economic activity.

(b) There are clearly problems with central planning and these problems have led to the introduction of wide-ranging reforms aimed at creating a more decentralised economy with greater reliance on the market as a means of allocating resources.

Market economies have certain basic characteristics and in particular the government plays little part in the allocation of resources. Instead what is produced is decided by consumers and producers, with the latter being guided in their decisions by the profit motive. In other words, producers will supply those goods and services which offer the highest profit. This is only possible if individuals are permitted to own the means of production such as land and machinery. Therefore an important part of the reforms in the East European economies has been the return of certain assets to private ownership.

In free market economies resources are allocated through the price mechanism. Thus, when consumers buy a good or service, they are in effect casting a vote for the continued production of those goods and services. When particular goods or services become more popular, then more votes are cast for these than was previously the case and, as a result, their price rises. The higher price encourages producers to increase their output because by doing so they will earn higher profits. As a result, resources are diverted to the production of those goods and services which have become more popular with consumers.

The mechanism also works in reverse. When goods and services become less popular their price will fall. This reduces the profit from producing such goods. Producers will therefore supply less, thus releasing resources for the production of other goods and services.

A major advantage of the price mechanism is that it works automatically and does not require the vast bureaucracy that existed in centrally planned economies to allocate resources. Furthermore it ensures that the goods and services society demands are produced as efficiently and quickly as possible. If this were not the case, producers could improve their profits by increasing their efficiency.

Clearly some of the problems of central planning can be overcome by allowing a greater role for the price mechanism in the allocation of resources. However this does not imply that a wholly free enterprise economy faces no problems. One problem is that, because production is undertaken for profit, environmental considerations might again be neglected. The deforestation of the Amazon and Asian jungles in the quest for profit has led to environmental pollution and serious upheaval for those tribal societies who depend on the forest for survival.

Another problem with wholly free enterprise economies is that certain goods, known as demerit goods, will be produced when it is profitable to do so. An often quoted example is cigarettes. The illnesses cigarette smoking causes result in working days lost and this adversely affects the amount of goods and services the economy produces. In addition resources are used in the treatment of these illnesses which could be put to some alternative use if they were not required for health care.

A major problem with wholly free enterprise economies is that goods and services will only be produced if they are profitable. However, some goods confer substantial benefits on society but, by their very nature, can never be profitable. Public goods such as lighthouses and street-lighting have two distinct characteristic features: they are non-rival and non-excludable. They are non-rival because consumption by one person does not reduce the amount available for consumption by another person, and they are non-excludable because once provided it is impossible to restrict consumption to particular groups. Because of this, no-one would ever pay individually for a public good and such goods can therefore never be profitable. In other words in a free enterprise economy they would not be provided.

In addition merit goods, such as education and health care, which confer benefits on those who consume them and on society as a whole, would be underproduced in relation to the optimal level. In a wholly free enterprise economy, education and health care would only be provided for those who were prepared to pay. Inevitably some people would refuse to pay and in consequence would opt out of education and health care. Others would be unable to pay and some would economise on the amount they purchased. This would affect labour productivity because a healthy labour force loses fewer days through illness while a well-educated labour force is more adaptable to changes in demand or technology. The more productive the labour force the faster the standard of living improves.

It is clear that some of the problems of centrally planned economies can be alleviated by allowing a greater role for the price mechanism in the allocation of resources. However wholly free enterprise economies also have problems and this is why most economies in the world are mixed, that is, they contain elements of the centrally planned and the free enterprise economies.

**2** Opportunity cost is defined as *the next most desired alternative forgone*. The reason why an alternative is forgone is that the desires of society seem unlimited, while the ability to satisfy those desires is strictly limited by the availability of resources, the state of technology, the techniques of production, and so on. In other words resources are scarce and, since society cannot have all that it desires, it must choose which wants will be satisfied with its limited resources. Statement **1** is therefore correct.

Resources can be used to produce a whole range of goods and services. For example, everything which society produces requires labour. Labour can therefore be used in a variety of alternative ways and the same is true of society's other resources. If resources were specific and could only produce one particular good, then the opportunity cost of production would be zero because no alternative would be forgone. Statement **2** is therefore correct.

Not all goods consumed by society have an opportunity cost. Some are what economists term free goods. Such goods do not require the input of scarce resources. The most often quoted example of a free good is fresh air, but other examples include sand in the desert and ice at the north pole. In both of these cases there is no opportunity cost of production and increased consumption by one person does not necessitate a cut in consumption by another person. Statement **3** is therefore incorrect.

The key is B.

## REVIEW QUESTIONS AND ANSWERS

### Questions

1 Why is the 'economic problem' a problem?

2 Is the problem of scarcity in the UK greater now than it was in 1970?

3 Apply the concept of opportunity cost to:

(a) A student who stays in full-time education after the age of sixteen.

(b) A firm which borrows funds from a bank to buy a new machine.

(c) A government which finances increased spending on road construction by an increase in taxation.

(d) A home owner who carries out home improvements on a DIY basis in his or her spare time.

4 In what sense is the consumer sovereign in market economies?

5 In a market economy, how will the allocation of resources be affected by technological advances which significantly reduce the cost of producing a particular good?

6 What is 'mixed' in a mixed economy?

### Answers

1 The economic problem is a problem because it implies unsatisfied desires which compels society to make choices. All goods and services are produced from scarce resources which have alternative uses. Society is therefore forced to choose what goods and services will be produced, how they will be produced and for whom they will be produced.

2 The problem of scarcity cannot be quantified but it seems likely that there are at least as many unsatisfied desires in the UK now as there were twenty years ago. Of course the standard of living is higher, but in all societies, including the UK, it seems that as soon as one desire is satisfied another emerges.

3 (a) The opportunity cost of staying in education after the age of sixteen is the earnings forgone as a result of remaining in full time education.

(b) The opportunity cost here is the rate of interest that could have been earned, for example if funds had been deposited in a bank.

(c) In this case the opportunity cost is equal to the output that would otherwise have been produced if additional roads were not constructed. Since the value of the output forgone is exactly equal to the amount that would have been spent on it, the opportunity cost of additional road construction is also equal to the additional amount paid in taxation as a result of the road construction programme.

(d) The opportunity cost here is the alternative to which time might have been put. If the home owner would otherwise have done nothing, the opportunity cost would be nothing.

4 The consumer is sovereign in the sense that it is decisions by the consumer which dictate the pattern of production in a market economy. After all, if consumers do not buy products, producers will make no profits. We can be certain therefore they will produce those goods and services which consumers most desire.

5 A reduction in the cost of producing a particular good will, under normal circumstances, lead to a reduction in the price of that product. This will encourage consumption and persuade producers to increase their output.

6 The ownership of resources is mixed in a mixed economy. Some are owned by private individuals, but others are owned by the state and controlled by the government. For example, in the UK television sets are produced by privately owned businesses whereas law and order is provided through the state.

CHAPTER 2

# THE TOOLS OF ECONOMIC ANALYSIS

## Topic Summary

In this chapter we look briefly at the construction and interpretation of the different diagrammatic techniques most commonly used by economists.

## Graphs

Economists make great use of graphs to help interpret and illustrate economic data. A graph simply plots pairs of points or coordinates against a $y$ axis (vertical axis) and an $x$ axis (horizontal axis). Figure 2.1, which is derived from Table 2.1, illustrates a relationship between two variables, $x$ and $y$.

We can see from Table 2.1 that when $y$ is 5 $x$ is 40, and when $y$ is 4 $x$ is 50 and so on. Figure 2.1 simply plots the points given in Table 2.1. Graphs of this nature, as we shall see throughout this book, are widely used in economics.

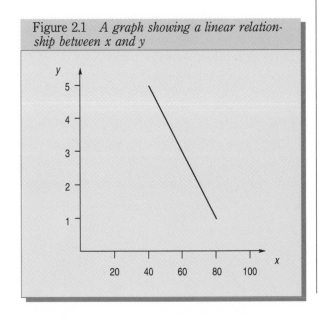

Figure 2.1 *A graph showing a linear relationship between x and y*

Table 2.1

| (y) | (x) |
|-----|-----|
| 1 | 80 |
| 2 | 70 |
| 3 | 60 |
| 4 | 50 |
| 5 | 40 |

## Bar Charts

Economists often use bar charts to illustrate data, particularly when making comparisons. For example, if we take a particular variable, let us call it $y$, we can use a bar chart to compare its value in different years and in different countries. Figure 2.2 which is based on Table 2.2, amply demonstrates the use of bar charts when making comparisons.

We can see that in year 1, $y$ was greatest in country A and lowest in country C. However, by the end of year 2 the situation had changed dramatically because of the growth of $y$ in country C. Even a glance at Figure 2.2 makes the changes in the value of $y$ between different countries clear.

## Pie Charts

Another diagram frequently used by economists is the pie chart. This is simply a circle divided up into segments to illustrate the proportionate value of the component parts of a particular aggregate. However, unless each segment gives the proportion of each of the components, it is often difficult to identify the relative size of the different components. On the other hand, if the respective proportions are given,

Figure 2.2  *A typical bar chart*

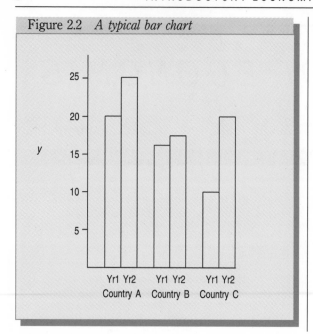

Table 2.2

| | y | |
|---|---|---|
| | Year 1 | Year 2 |
| Country A | 20 | 25 |
| Country B | 16 | 18 |
| Country C | 10 | 20 |

there seems little point in illustrating them in a pie chart! A pie chart is illustrated in Figure 2.3a on p. 9.

# REVIEW QUESTIONS AND ANSWERS

## Questions

1  Rather than using models would it be better if economists studied the real world as it actually operates when formulating theories?

2  Devise (1) positive and (2) normative statements about the following:

(a)  The comparative earnings of nurses and pop stars.
(b)  The level of unemployment.
(c)  The rate of inflation.
(d)  The housing shortage (see p. 47).

3  'Figures from the Institute of Economic Affairs (1991) show that in 1985 the numbers of newly qualified craftsmen, technicians and graduate engineers and technologists in the UK were 35,000, 28,000 and 15,000 respectively. In France the corresponding figures were 92,000, 30,000 and 16,000, while in Germany the figures were 120,000, 43,000 and 22,000'.

Summarise the statistical content of this quotation in tabular form, as a pie chart and as a bar chart. Which form is visually most effective?

## Answers

1  Economists do study the real world when formulating theories! All theories in economics begin with an observation of some event which the theory attempts to explain. The problem is testing theories because in the real world variables which affect economic behaviour often change concurrently and it is therefore difficult to identify the precise effect of a change in any single variable. To some extent models overcome this problem because we can then assume all variables, except those we wish to alter, are constant.

2  (a) (i) Nurses are more important than pop stars and therefore should earn more.
(ii) Those at the top of the earnings league in the nursing profession earn less than the most highly paid pop stars.
(b) (i) A high level of unemployment is undesirable.
(ii) Unemployment in the UK was over three million last year.
(c) (i) The rate of inflation in the UK is too high.
(ii) The UK has the lowest rate of inflation of any country in Europe.

(d) (i) Too many city centre properties have been converted into offices.

(ii) The increasing number of homeless people in the UK is evidence of a growing housing shortage.

**3**

Table 2.3

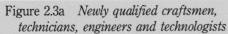

|  | Craftsmen | Technicians | Graduate engineers and technologists |
|---|---|---|---|
| UK | 35 000 | 28 000 | 15 000 |
| France | 92 000 | 30 000 | 16 000 |
| Germany | 120 000 | 3.000 | 22 000 |

*Source*: IEA, 1991.

Figure 2.3a  *Newly qualified craftsmen, technicians, engineers and technologists*

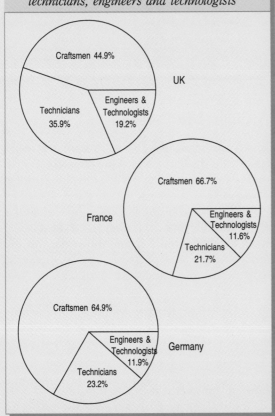

Figure 2.3b  *Newly qualified craftsmen, technicians, engineers and technologists*

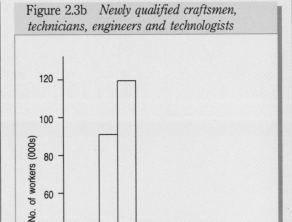

Which of the three statistical summaries is visually the most effective is a matter of opinion and partly depends on the purpose for which the data are to be used. Table 2.3 shows the actual numbers in each category, whereas Figure 2.3a shows the proportions in each category. For most people the relative size of each category is probably clearer in the bar chart.

# CHAPTER 3

# DEMAND, SUPPLY AND MARKET PRICE

## Topic Summary

To economists the term **demand** has a specific meaning. It is more than simply the desire to consume goods and services; it is the desire to buy something, backed up by the willingness and ability to pay for it.

## Demand

### A Change in Quantity Demanded

The basic law of demand is that for most goods and services the *quantity demanded* will vary inversely with price, that is, when price decreases, quantity demanded increases and vice versa. The operation of this law is easy to observe whether we consider the behaviour of an individual as the price of a good changes over a short period of time, or the quantity of a particular good or service demanded by all consumers as its price changes over a short period of time. Look at what happens during sale times, for example, when the prices of goods are marked down. But why do we stress the behaviour of demand over a short period of time? The answer is that this enables us to assume that all other influences which might affect demand are unchanged. In other words we can isolate the effects of price changes on quantity demanded. Figure 3.1 illustrates the basic relationship.

It is extremely important that you use the correct terminology when discussing movements along a demand curve. In Figure 3.1 we refer to a movement along the demand curve from *A* to *B* as an *increase in quantity demanded* or an *extension of demand*, and a movement from *B* to *A* as a *reduction in quantity demanded* or a *contraction of demand*. More is said about these important terms on pp. 12–13.

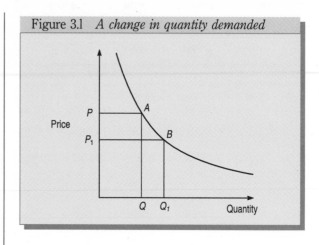

Figure 3.1 *A change in quantity demanded*

### A Change in Demand

In our analysis above it was stressed that demand curves are drawn on the assumption that all influences on demand other than price are unchanged. These other influences which affect demand are usually referred to as the **conditions of demand** or the **parameters of demand**. A change in any of these conditions of demand will cause the entire demand curve to *shift its position*. In Figure 3.2 a shift in the demand curve from *DD* to $D_1D_1$ is

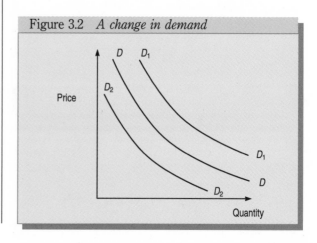

Figure 3.2 *A change in demand*

referred to as an **increase in demand** and a shift in the demand curve from *DD* to $D_2D_2$ is referred to as a **decrease in demand**.

## Supply

The basic law of supply is that for most goods and services the quantity supplied will vary directly with price, that is, when price per unit rises, quantity supplied falls and vice versa. There are two reasons for this. When price rises it becomes more profitable for those firms already producing the product to increase their output. Furthermore a rise in price encourages other firms to undertake production. For these reasons we find that more is supplied at a higher price than at a lower price, as Figure 3.3 shows.

### A Change in Quantity Supplied

We assume that all other things which might affect supply remain unchanged so that we can isolate the effects of price changes on quantity supplied, and again the same rules of terminology apply. A movement along the supply curve from *A* to *B* in Figure 3.3 is referred to as an **increase in quantity supplied** or an **extension of supply**, and a movement from *B* to *A* is referred to as a **reduction in quantity supplied** or a **contraction of supply**. More is said about these important terms on pp. 12–13.

### A Change in Supply

In our analysis above it was stressed that supply curves are drawn on the assumption that all influences which affect supply other than price are unchanged. These other factors which affect supply are usually referred to as the **conditions of supply** or the **parameters of supply**. A change in any of these conditions of supply will cause the entire supply curve to *shift its position*. In Figure 3.4 a shift in the supply curve from *SS* to $S_1S_1$ is referred to as an **increase in supply** and a shift in the supply curve from *SS* to $S_2S_2$ is referred to as a **decrease in supply**.

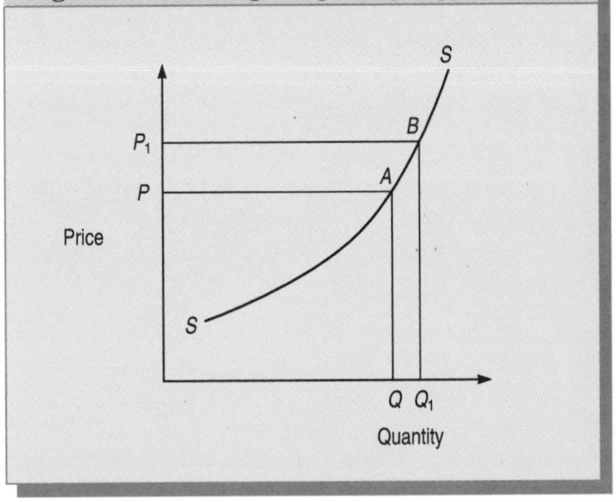

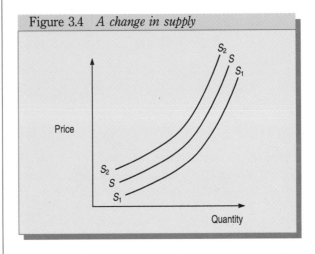

Figure 3.4   *A change in supply*

## Equilibrium Price and Quantity

In free markets prices are determined by the opposing forces of supply and demand and the *equilibrium* price and quantity exist when there is no tendency for price or quantity to change. In Figure 3.5, *P* is the equilibrium price and *Q* the equilibrium quantity. No other combination of price and quantity will be stable in this market.

Figure 3.3   *A change in quantity supplied*

Figure 3.5   *The equilibrium price and quantity*

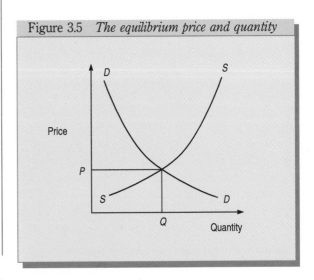

At any price above $P$ the quantity supplied will exceed the quantity demanded and price will fall. At any price below $P$ quantity demanded will exceed quantity supplied and price will rise. Once equilibrium is established there can be no change in price or quantity unless there is a shift in the demand curve and/or a shift in the supply curve.

## Elasticity

In this section we are concerned with four types of elasticity and the following symbols are used throughout:

$\Delta$ = change in
$Q$ = quantity
$P$ = price
$Y$ = income

**Price elasticity of demand** (usually referred to simply as elasticity of demand) is a measure of how responsive quantity demanded is to a change in price. It is calculated in the following way:

$$\frac{\Delta Q \times P}{Q \times \Delta P}$$

**Elasticity of supply** is a measure of how responsive quantity supplied is to a change in price. It is calculated in the following way:

$$\frac{\Delta Q \times P}{Q \times \Delta P}$$

**Income elasticity of demand** is a measure of the responsiveness of demand to a change in income. It is calculated in the following way:

$$\frac{\Delta Q \times Y}{Q \times \Delta Y}$$

**Cross elasticity of demand** is a measure of the responsiveness of demand for one good to a change in the price of another good. It is calculated in the following way:

$$\frac{\Delta Qa \times Pb}{Qa \times \Delta Pb}$$

In all cases, if the coefficient of elasticity is
  $> 1$, demand (supply) is said to be elastic;
  $< 1$, demand (supply) is said to be inelastic;
  $= 1$, demand (supply) is said to be in unity.

## Common Mistakes to Avoid

One of the most common mistakes made is to confuse movements *along a demand curve* with *shifts of a demand curve*. The difference is crucial because they each have different effects. The main point to remember is that demand curves are drawn on the assumption that all other things which affect demand, apart from price, are held constant. A movement along a demand curve can therefore *only be caused by a change in supply*, that is, *a shift of the supply curve*. Figure 3.6 illustrates this.

In Figure 3.6a $SS$ and $DD$ are the original supply and demand curves for a given manufacturing product. The equilibrium price is $P$ and the equilibrium quantity is $Q$. Subsequently an increase in costs of production shifts the supply curve to $S_1 S_1$. The new equilibrium position is established when price has increased to $P_1$ and the amount supplied and demanded has fallen to $Q_1$. However the im-

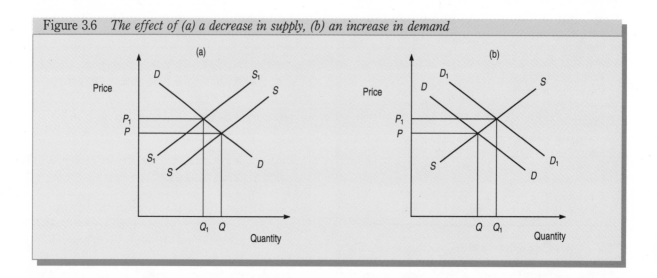

Figure 3.6    *The effect of (a) a decrease in supply, (b) an increase in demand*

portant point to note is that there has been no change in the position of the demand curve. There has therefore been a movement along the original demand curve, and in this case *quantity demanded has fallen* by $QQ_1$. A reduction in costs of production would have exactly the opposite effect and in this case there would be an *increase in the quantity demanded*.

In Figure 3.6b, *SS* and *DD* are again the original supply and demand curves for a given manufacturing product, and *P* and *Q* are the equilibrium price and quantity. Subsequently an increase in income shifts the demand curve to $D_1D_1$. The new equilibrium position is established when price has increased to $P_1$ and the amount supplied and demanded has increased to $Q_1$. In this case there has been an *increase in demand* and an *increase in the quantity supplied*. Notice that in both Figure 3.6a and 3.6b there has been an increase in price, but the *effect* on the equilibrium quantity is different because the *cause* of the price increase is different. A reduction in income has exactly the opposite effect.

The important point to grasp is that it is necessary to understand the cause of a price change before we can predict its effects. Furthermore, having identified the cause, you must take great care to ensure you use the correct terms when explaining these effects.

## Questions and Answers

### *Questions**

The data below give estimates of the elasticity of demand for selected foods in the UK. The figures in brackets are standard errors.

| Income elasticity of demand (1987) | |
| --- | --- |
| All foods: of which | 0.10 (0.03) |
| Beef and veal | 0.26 (0.03) |
| Margarine | −0.22 (0.08) |
| Fresh potatoes | −0.43 (0.08) |
| Fruit juices | 0.95 (0.18) |
| Bread | −0.18 (0.03) |

| Price elasticity of demand (1982–87) | |
| --- | --- |
| Beef and veal | −1.24 (0.26) |
| Bread | −0.25 (0.18) |
| Fresh potatoes | −0.14 (0.03) |
| Fruit juices | −0.65 (0.23) |
| Margarine | −0.37 (0.23) |

*The following questions and answers are taken from *British Economy Survey*, vol. 18, no. 2, Longman, 1989.

| Cross elasticities of demand for beef and veal, and pork (1980–87) | | |
| --- | --- | --- |
| Elasticity of demand for | With respect to the price of | |
| | beef and veal | pork |
| Beef and veal | −1.24 (0.26) | 0.10 (0.10) |
| Pork | 0.25 (0.25) | −1.86 (0.22) |

*Source*: 'Household Food Consumption Expenditure', *Annual Report of the Food Survey Committee*, 1987, HMSO.

1 Explain the phrase 'The figures in brackets are standard errors'.

2 What is meant by the terms (a) income elasticity of demand, (b) price elasticity of demand, (c) cross elasticity of demand?

3 Are the estimates of elasticity given here consistent with conventional demand theory?

4 How might these estimates of elasticity be used to predict future expenditure of consumers, and how accurate are these estimates likely to be?

### *Answers*

1 When statisticians calculate estimates of particular variables they also make predictions about how accurate these estimates are likely to be. The standard error of an estimate shows that there is only a 5 per cent probability, that is, a 1 in 20 chance, that the true value of the variable will not lie somewhere in the range given by its estimated value, plus or minus twice the standard error. Standard errors therefore provide a test on the reliability of statistical estimates.

2 (a) Income elasticity of demand for a good is a measure of the responsiveness of demand for that good to changes in income. It is usually measured by the formula:

$$\frac{\Delta Q_a}{Q_a} \div \frac{\Delta Y}{Y} = \frac{\Delta Q_a Y}{\Delta Y Q_a}$$

Where $Q_a$ is the amount demanded of good *a*, *Y* is income and $\Delta$ refers to a change in the variable it prefixes. In general, the greater the income elasticity of demand for a good, the greater the change in demand for that good following a change in income.

(b) Price elasticity of demand for a good is a measure of the responsiveness of quantity demanded for that good to changes in its price. It is usually measured by the formula:

$$\frac{\Delta Q_a}{Q_a} \div \frac{\Delta P_a}{P_a} = \frac{\Delta Q_a P_a}{Q_a \Delta P_a}$$

The variables are as previously defined with the exception of $P_a$ which refers to the price of good $a$. In general, the greater the price elasticity of demand for a good, the greater the change in the quantity demanded of that good following a change in its price.

(c) Cross price elasticity of demand for a good is a measure of the responsiveness of demand for that good, to a change in the price of another good. It is usually measured by the formula:

$$\frac{\Delta Q_a}{Q_a} \div \frac{\Delta P_b}{P_b} = \frac{\Delta Q_a P_b}{Q_a \Delta P_b}$$

The variables are as previously defined. In general, the greater the cross price elasticity demand for a good, the greater the change in demand for that good following a change in the price of another good.

**3** For all 'normal goods' the characteristic elasticity features are 'positive income elasticity of demand', and 'negative price elasticity of demand'. Not all of the goods listed in the table possess these characteristics. Normal goods have positive income elasticity of demand because, as income grows, more goods will tend to be demanded. However, in some cases, as income grows less of a particular good might be demanded. Such goods are referred to as 'inferior goods' since a rise in income persuades consumers to substitute more expensive goods for goods which have become cheaper in real terms because of the rise in income.

Examples of such goods are bread, fresh potatoes and margarine. All three are often cited as examples of inferior goods and it is easy to see the kind of substitutions that might take place as incomes rise. For example, as incomes rise it is likely that pre-packed potatoes will be substituted for fresh potatoes and so on.

Normal goods also possess negative price elasticity of demand. This implies that as the price of a good rises there is a reduction in the quantity of that good demanded. This is one of the laws of demand and it is this basic proposition that enables us to draw normal demand curves. All of the goods given in the table possess this characteristic and therefore all would have been expected to have normal demand curves during the period covered by the data.

In addition, the estimates of cross price elasticity of demand for beef and veal with respect to pork,

and vice versa, have the expected signs. Beef and veal might be considered substitutes for pork. Hence an increase in the price of beef and veal might be expected to cause an increase in demand for pork as consumers substitute pork for beef and veal.

The income elasticity of demand for 'all food' is relatively low at 0.10 since much the same quantity of food will be consumed whether income rises or falls. It might be possible to economise on the consumption of food when income falls, by cutting down on waste for example, but there is unlikely to be great scope for economies here. Equally a rise in income is unlikely to lead to an increase in the consumption of food, at least in a developed economy such as the UK. It seems likely therefore that rather than aggregate consumption of food changing as income changes, total spending on food changes because more expensive or less expensive food is consumed in response to a change in income.

The relatively low value of income elasticity of demand for beef and veal might seem somewhat surprising. It is possible that the income elasticity of demand for beef on its own would have a higher value since for many people on lower incomes beef is still something of a luxury good. As incomes rise such people will substitute beef, and probably to a lesser extent veal, for cheaper cuts of meat.

Of the products for which we have data, fruit juices have the largest income elasticity of demand. The implication is that as income rises by 1 per cent, total spending on fruit juices increases by 0.95 per cent. This implies an income elasticity of demand of almost unity and undoubtedly reflects a growing preference for fruit juices as income rises, compared with other kinds of soft drink which tend to contain additives, some of which are thought to have undesirable side-effects.

The price elasticity of demand for beef and veal is elastic, that is greater than 1. In such cases a change in price will lead to a more than proportional change in quantity demanded. With respect to beef and veal, one reason for this is that pork is perceived to be a substitute. Evidence of this is given in the data showing estimates of cross elasticity of demand for these products.

All of the other foods on which we are given data are price inelastic, that is, a change in price leads to a less than proportional change in quantity demanded. The low price elasticities of demand for bread and fresh potatoes in particular stem largely from the fact that these foods are considered necessities. The demand for fruit juices is also inelastic with respect to price. Fruit juices might be less of a necessity than bread and fresh potatoes, but consumers clearly have a strong preference for them and the inelastic demand probably reflects a perceived absence of close substitutes on the part of consumers.

In general, it is clear that the estimates of income elasticity and price elasticity that we are given are consistent with conventional economic theory.

**4** The data we are given is useful in predicting future consumer expenditure. However, on its own it is not enough. We also require estimates of how prices and incomes are expected to change. Over relatively short periods this is not a problem, since likely changes in prices and incomes can be estimated from raw material price increases, the level of wage settlements, changes in productivity, and so on. Given estimates of these, the data can be used to predict future consumer expenditure on the products listed. For example, if the price of bread is expected to rise by 5 per cent and incomes are expected to rise by 2 per cent over some period of time, and all other things remained unchanged, total expenditure on bread would rise by approximately 1.82 per cent of its current level. This is because the rise in the price of bread will lead to a fill in consumption of 1.25 per cent. In other words, the reaction to the price change alone would be such that 98.75 per cent of the current amount of bread purchased would be bought as 105 per cent of its current price. Furthermore the rise in income would lead to a fall in consumption of bread of 0.18 per cent. Multiplying this out we have:

$$98.75 \times 1.05 \times 0.982 \simeq 101.82$$

Given estimates of expected price changes for all goods it would be possible to predict expected future changes in consumer expenditure.

However, these predictions might not be entirely accurate. The values calculated for both income and price elasticities of demand are based on past trends, and this is not always a sound basis on which to make future predictions. There might be changes in tastes, or the emergence of new products which will influence expenditure patterns. For example, growing concern about the relationship between health and diet has exerted a powerful influence on the consumption of certain foodstuffs. In other words, future predictions are based on the assumption that all things remain equal. If they do not, predictions of future consumption expenditure will be less reliable.

Additionally, the estimates of elasticity might themselves be subject to a wide margin of error. Elasticity is an extremely difficult concept to measure. For example, if we attempt to measure price elasticity of demand for a commodity, it might be possible to observe a change in the price of that commodity and, in the following period, a change in the amount purchased. However, this does not necessarily imply a change in the quantity demanded unless we are certain that nothing other than price has changed. In the real world it is almost impossible to be completely certain that this is the case. Similar problems are apparent in the measurement of income elasticity of demand. If the estimates of elasticity are not accurate, predictions of future consumer expenditure derived from these will not be accurate.

A final problem is that estimates of price and income changes might not be accurate. This is especially likely when estimates refer to a longer time period. The shorter the time period to which estimates refer the greater their accuracy. Again if estimates of future changes in prices and incomes are not accurate, predictions based on them will not be accurate.

## REVIEW QUESTIONS AND ANSWERS

### Questions

1 Consider the following supply and demand schedules:

*The supply of and demand for lettuces in Borchester during August*

| Price (p) | Quantity demanded | Quantity supplied |
|---|---|---|
| 48 | 1000 | 16000 |
| 40 | 3600 | 12600 |
| 32 | 6000 | 10000 |
| 24 | 8000 | 6000 |
| 16 | 10000 | 4000 |
| 8 | 14000 | 2500 |

On graph paper, plot the supply and demand curves associated with these schedules, then answer the following:

(a) If market price were at a level of 40p, what would you expect to happen to price, and why?

(b) If market price were at a level of 16p, what would you expect to happen to price, and why?

(c) At what price would you expect the market to eventually settle, and why?

2 Use supply and demand analysis to predict the likely changes in the price and quantity of:

(a) tinned peaches after an increase in the price of tinned apricots;

(b) cream when there is a large fall in the price of strawberries;

(c) butter following publicity that consuming butter adversely affects health;

(d) beef following an epidemic which kills cattle;

(e) butter following a large increase in the price of cheese;

(f) flowers on the day before Mother's Day;

(g) ice cream during a hot summer;

(h) lamb when the price of wool rises considerably;

(i) cheese following an increase in the wages of dairy workers.

3 Why is a second-hand book generally cheaper than a brand new copy? Under what circumstances might a second-hand book attract a substantially higher price than a new one?

4 'An increase in price reduces quantity demanded, while a fall in demand reduces price.'

A non-economist might find this statement contradictory. By distinguishing between shifts of a demand curve and movements along a demand curve, explain the apparent contradiction.

5 Consider the following demand schedule:

| Price (pence) | Quantity (units) |
|---|---|
| 3 | 100 |
| 5 | 50 |
| 6 | 30 |

Calculate the price elasticity of demand for a change in price from:

(a) 3p to 5p;
(b) 5p to 3p;
(c) 5p to 6p;
(d) 6p to 5p;
(e) 3p to 6p;
(f) 6p to 3p.

Comment on your results.

6 A demand curve makes a parallel shift to the right. Has price elasticity of demand increased or decreased at each price? Explain your answer.

7 The Chancellor of the Exchequer is advised that the price elasticity of demand for milk is 1.2 for low income groups and 0.23 for high income groups. Why might this information help to lead to the conclusion that milk is a suitable item to be subsidised by the government?

# Answers

## 1

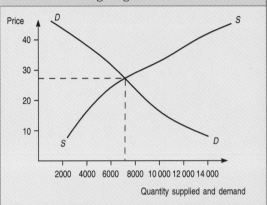

Figure 3.7 *Supply and demand for lettuce in Borchester during August*

(a) At a price of £0.40 supply exceeds demand and therefore the price of lettuce would fall.

(b) At a price of £0.16 demand exceeds supply and therefore the price of lettuce would rise.

(c) We are given insufficient information to enable us to determine precisely what the equilibrium price will be in this market, but the supply and demand schedules shown in Figure 3.7 suggest that a reasonable approximation would be £0.27. Why? Because at this price supply of lettuce during August equals demand for lettuce during August equals 7200 heads (approximately).

**2** Before we can predict the effect of any price change we must identify its cause. In some of the sub-sections of question 2 there are several possibilities depending on what assumptions we make about the cause of the initial price change. In each case it is necessary to assume that all other things remain equal. With these points in mind let us consider some of the alternatives.

(a) Assume the increase in the price of tinned apricots is caused by a reduction in supply. As the price of tinned apricots rises there will be a reduction in quantity demanded and consumers will increase their demand for substitutes such as tinned peaches. As demand for tinned peaches rises, the price of tinned peaches will rise.

(b) Assume the decrease in the price of strawberries is caused by an increase in supply. As the price of strawberries falls, the quantity demanded

will increase. Since strawberries and cream are jointly consumed, there will be an increase in the demand for cream and therefore the price of cream will rise.

(c) The demand for butter will fall and this will cause a reduction in the price of butter.

(d) The supply of beef will fall and therefore the price of beef will rise.

(e) Assume the increase in the price of cheese is caused by an increase in demand for cheese. The rise in the price of cheese will encourage an increase in production. Since milk and cheese are both produced from milk, it is possible, that as more milk is devoted to cheese production, less will be available for butter production. As the supply of butter falls the price of butter will rise.

(f) The demand for flowers will increase and therefore the price of flowers will rise.

(g) The demand for ice cream will increase and therefore the price of ice cream will rise.

(h) Assume the increase in the price of wool is caused by an increase in the demand for wool. As the price of wool rises, farmers will send fewer lambs for slaughter and therefore the supply of lamb will fall. In consequence the price of lamb will rise.

(i) An increase in the wages of dairy workers will increase the cost of producing cheese and this implies a reduction in the supply of cheese. In consequence the price of cheese will rise.

**3** At any given price consumers will, in general, prefer new books to secondhand books. This implies a greater demand at any given price for new books and this is the main factor explaining the higher price of new books compared to secondhand books. However, in some cases, books become collectors items, especially first editions. In such cases, the limited supply, coupled with the relatively high demand, results in secondhand books commanding a higher price than the most recent edition of the same book on sale in a book shop.

**4** This apparent paradox is easily explained using Figure 3.8.

Remember, a change in quantity demanded implies a movement *along* an existing demand curve while a change in demand implies a *shift* of the demand curve. A change in quantity demanded can only be caused by a change in supply. In this case there is a reduction in

Figure 3.8    *The effect of (a) a reduction in supply, (b) a reduction in demand*

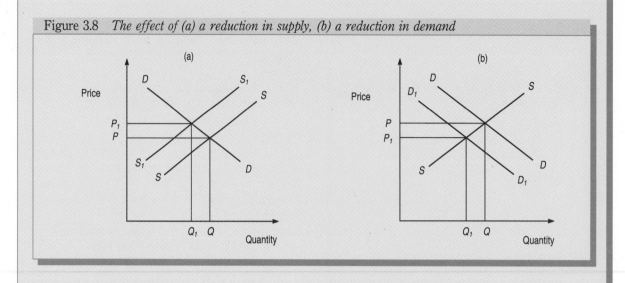

quantity demanded and therefore there has been a reduction in supply. This is illustrated in Figure 3.8a. *SS* is the original supply curve and *DD* the original demand curve, and *P* is the original equilibrium price. A reduction in supply shifts the supply curve *SS* to $S_1S_1$ and as price rises, there is a reduction in quantity demanded. The new equilibrium price is $P_1$.

A change in demand can only be caused by a change in at least one of the conditions of demand. In Figure 3.8b, *DD* and *SS* are the original supply and demand curves and the equilibrium price is again *P*. A fall in demand implies a shift of the whole demand curve closer to the origin, illustrated in this case by a shift to $D_1D_1$. The result is a reduction in the equilibrium price to $P_1$.

**5** The relevant elasticities of demand can be calculated by substituting in the formula $ED = \Delta Q/Q \times P/\Delta P$.

   (a) Ed = 0.75
   (b) Ed = 2.5
   (c) Ed = 2.0
   (d) Ed = 4.0
   (e) Ed = 0.7
   (f) Ed = 4.67

*Comments*

   (i) For a given price change, elasticity of demand is different if we consider a price fall rather than a price rise.

   (ii) Elasticity of demand varies along the entire length of the demand curve, being more elastic at higher prices than at lower prices for any given price change. There are only three exceptions to this rule, viz. when elasticity of demand is equal to zero, one or infinity.

   (iii) When elasticity of demand is elastic, that is, greater than 1, a price rise leads to a reduction in total revenue and a reduction in price leads to a rise in total revenue. When elasticity of demand is inelastic a price rise leads to a rise in total revenue and a reduction in price leads to a reduction in total revenue.

**6** When a demand curve makes a parallel shift to the right, elasticity of demand decreases at each and every price because any given change in price will now be associated with a smaller proportionate change in quantity demanded.

**7** Given these elasticity conditions, a subsidy might be justified on grounds of equity because if, as seems likely, the subsidy leads to a reduction in price, lower income groups will increase their consumption of milk by proportionately more than higher income groups.

CHAPTER 4

# *THE PRICE MECHANISM AND MARKET FAILURE*

## Topic Summary

In market economies resources are allocated through the **price mechanism** and the basic functions of price are to **ration** and **inform**. The rationing function is easy to understand. In market economies the problem of deciding how to allocate output to ultimate consumers is solved by allowing those who are willing and able to pay the market price to receive that output. Those unable or unwilling to pay receive nothing.

To understand how price informs it is useful to look at the way price mechanism works. Consider the market for a particular good, good X. Now if society's preferences change in favour of good X compared to other goods, the demand for good X will increase and (in most cases) so will the price of X. The increase in price therefore informs producers of a change in society's preferences. In response, firms will increase their output of good X because the higher price increases the profit available from producing X. A change in society's preferences away from good X would have exactly the opposite effect and would be quickly communicated to producers by a reduction in the price of good X.

Similarly a change in the conditions of supply would be quickly communicated to consumers of good X. For example, if technological progress makes possible the development of new and more productive machinery, the cost of producing good X will fall. At any given price, more will therefore be supplied than previously and we know from pp. 12–13 that this will cause a reduction in the price of good X. This price reduction informs consumers of the changed conditions in the market for good X. The opposite happens if there is a reduction in the supply of good X.

## *An Optimal Allocation of Resources*

When economists use the term **allocation of resources** they are simply referring to the allocation of resources to the different goods and services which society produces. An *optimal*, or *economically efficient* allocation of resources is said to exist when it is impossible to make one member of society better off without making at least one other member of society worse off by a reallocation of resources: in other words, by changing the quantities of the different goods and services produced.

It is often claimed that the free operation of the price mechanism will automatically lead to an optimal allocation of resources. The reasoning behind this view is simple. It is argued that price reflects the value consumers place on the last unit of a good they consume. It is further argued that price reflects the opportunity cost of producing the last unit because it reflects the additional cost the firm must pay to attract resources away from alternatives. Resources are allocated in the most efficient way when the value consumers place on the last unit they consume exactly equals the opportunity cost of production. Figure 4.1 is used to illustrate this point.

In Figure 4.1, *SS* and *DD* are the free market supply and demand schedules for a particular good and *P* is the equilibrium price. If the government fixed price above *P* there would be an inefficient allocation of resources because, at any price above *P*, consumers value additional units of this commodity more highly than they value additional units of alternative commodities. This must be so because they are prepared to pay an amount for additional units of this commodity that is greater than the amount necessary to attract resources away from

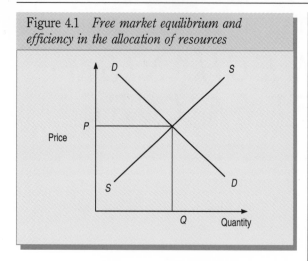

Figure 4.1  *Free market equilibrium and efficiency in the allocation of resources*

alternatives. Similarly, if the government fixed price below *P*, there would be an inefficient allocation of resources because, at any price less than *P*, consumers value additional units of alternative goods more highly than the last unit of this commodity consumed. This must be so because the amount they pay for the last unit they consume is less than the cost of attracting resources away from alternatives.

Despite the appealing logic of this argument one point must be stressed. The allocation of resources through the price mechanism partly depends on the distribution of income. If we change the distribution of income we will change the allocation of resources. If we argue that the operation of the price mechanism leads to an optimal allocation of resources we must assume that the distribution of income is also optimal. Given the differing views of society on the importance of equity this is quite an assumption!

Nevertheless it is clear from Figure 4.1 that at prices above *P* there is a market shortage of the commodity and when price is below *P* there is a market surplus of the commodity. In a free market shortages and surpluses are not sustainable. A surplus would lead to a fall in price until equilibrium is reached. In Figure 4.1, price will converge on *P* and at this point resources will be allocated in an optimal way because the value society places on the last unit of this product exactly equals its opportunity cost of production.

## Market Failure

Market failure is the term used to describe the circumstances when free markets fail to allocate resources in an optimal way. There are various reasons why markets might fail.

## Externalities

Externalities are the effects of production or consumption which fall on members of society other than the producer or consumer of some good or service. For example, if one person regularly smokes cigarettes in a room with non-smokers, the health of these non-smokers will be adversely affected because of passive smoking. The importance of externalities is discussed in the answer to question 1 on pp. 21–3. See also the next sub-section.

## Merit Goods and Demerit Goods

Merit goods are so called because they confer positive externalities on society. However, because free market prices do not include the effects of externalities, market prices would be greater than if prices did include the effects of positive externalities. Because of this, merit goods would be *under-provided* in relation to the optimum amount if they were supplied through the market. The most often quoted examples of merit goods are education and health care, which confer benefits on society as well as on those who consume them. (See the discussion of 'Common mistakes to avoid' below.) Demerit goods are exactly the opposite. They confer negative externalities on society and would be overconsumed in relation to the optimum amount if they were provided through the market. An often quoted example is cigarette smoking.

## Public Goods

Public goods confer benefits on society, but because of their characteristics they could never be provided through the market. The reasons for this are discussed in the answer to question 3 on p. 24. However it is important to realise that the absence of these goods is another source of market failure.

## Monopoly

The existence of monopoly, that is, a single supplier of a product, can cause markets to fail because a monopolist can restrict the amount of a product available for sale. Why this causes market failure is discussed on pp. 60–1.

## Common Mistakes to Avoid

### Private Costs, Externalities and Social Costs

The private cost of producing any good or service is simply the money cost of production. It therefore consists of such items as the cost of raw materials, labour, power to drive machinery and so on. However, acts of production or consumption sometimes generate externalities or spillover effects. When the value of these externalities is added to the private cost of production we have the full social cost of production.

### Public Goods and Merit Goods

Public goods are often confused with merit goods. Both confer positive externalities on the community and would therefore be underconsumed in relation to the optimal level if they were provided through the market. However, as we shall see in the answer to question 3 below, public goods have particular characteristics such that no individual consumer would ever pay for them. Because of this, public goods would never be provided through the market, that is, by the private sector. Merit goods, on the other hand, do not have these special characteristics and could therefore be provided through the market. However certain merit goods such as education up to age 18 and health care are provided free of charge to consumers in the UK because of the importance of the externalities associated with consumption of these goods.

## Questions and Answers

### Questions

1 Explain the terms 'external costs' and 'external benefits'. (30)

Examine the relevance of these concepts when considering a proposal to build a nuclear power station. (70)

ULEAC, June 1989

2 (a) Explain why the emission of pollution by a firm into the atmosphere or into a river may be economically inefficient. (13)

(b) Evaluate two ways of reducing any economic inefficiency caused by pollution. (12)

AEB June 1990

3 A pure public good is one which

1 if consumed by one person does not reduce the amount available for others
2 cannot be restricted in use to those willing to pay for it
3 can be efficiently provided by the market mechanisms

A 1, 2 and 3 are correct
B 1 and 2 only are correct
C 2 and 3 only are correct
D 1 only is correct
E 3 only is correct

ULEAC, January 1990

### Answers

1 Externalities are costs or benefits which stem from the activities of one individual or organisation but which affect other individuals or organisations who are not directly part of the original activity. In this sense externalities are the spillover effects of production or consumption.

An often quoted example of an external cost occurs when a chemical factory dumps its waste products into a river. As a result of toxic contamination fish in the river die and those who fish down river from the chemical plant are therefore denied an amenity they previously utilised. If the chemical producer were compelled to treat waste materials before discharging them into the river, the cost of producing chemicals would rise. Instead the chemical producer treats the river as a free resource and in consequence transfers part of the cost of chemical production to anglers who used to fish the river.

Externalities can often confer benefits on third parties. For example, individuals who vaccinate themselves against a contagious disease not only benefit themselves by eliminating the risk that they will catch the disease, they also confer a benefit on society since the risk that they will pass the disease on to others is also eliminated. Society benefits because there will be fewer working days lost through illness and costs of treatment will be avoided.

The existence of these externalities has implications for the allocation of resources in an economy. It is sometimes argued that the free operation of market forces will lead to an optimal allocation of resources. The reasoning behind this view is that price reflects the value consumers place on the last unit of a good they consume. But price also reflects the opportunity cost of producing the last unit because it reflects the additional cost the firm must pay to attract resources away from alternatives. Resources are allocated in the most efficient way when the value consumers place on the last unit they consume exactly equals its opportunity cost of production. Despite this, the existence of externalities can prevent free markets from achieving an optimal allocation of resources, as Figures 4.2 and 4.3 show.

In Figure 4.2 the demand curve $DD$ reflects only the private benefits from consuming nuclear energy and the supply curve $SS$ reflects only private costs of producing nuclear energy. If it included external benefits the demand curve would shift upwards to the right, for example to $D_1D_1$ and the equilibrium price would then increase to $P_1$. This implies a completely different allocation of resources, since consumers demand more of this commodity and prefer more resources to be competed away from alternatives. In a free market there would therefore be underconsumption of this commodity in relation to the optimum level.

In the case of a nuclear power station there are several positive externalities to consider and therefore the appropriate demand curve for nuclear energy is $D_1D_1$. A major benefit of constructing a nuclear power station is that it will create employment in the area where it is located. Construction workers will be required to build the power station, but even after completion it will provide employment because workers will be required to maintain and operate it. This will benefit the local economy generally as incomes rise and are (partly) spent in the local economy.

Once the power station is operational its benefits to society will be more widespread. A major benefit here is that greater reliance on nuclear power will reduce dependence on non-renewable sources of energy. In particular, coal-fired power stations have been major contributors to acid rain and global warming. Both of these impose costs on society. For example, acid rain is a major cause of dead lakes so that the social and recreational value of a lake is considerably diminished to users. However, global warming is potentially an even more serious problem and power stations which burn fossil fuels are the major UK contributor to global warming. The creation of nuclear power stations might therefore make a significant contribution to reducing environmental damage caused by burning fossil fuels.

Another benefit of creating nuclear power stations is that the cost of generating electricity is considerably less than that of generating electricity using fossil fuels. This would directly benefit all users of electricity since it implies lower energy prices. However there would also be an indirect benefit to society because lower energy prices imply lower input costs for industry and this might make a minor contribution to lowering inflation.

However, there are also potentially significant external costs associated with the generation of nuclear energy. In particular there are serious environmental and health risks to those who work in the power station or live in its vicinity. More generally in the case of a nuclear leak, radiation can contaminate vast areas, as the Chernobyl disaster of the 1980s demonstrated. In such cases whole communities might need to be evacuated and rehoused. Land that once provided food and recreation ceases to be available for these purposes, in some cases for many years. In the case of a nuclear accident, the cost of treating those unfortunate enough to suffer ill health are borne by society rather than being confined to those who generate electricity. The same is true of the cost of cleaning up the environment – where this is possible! Such cleaning up operations are financed by the taxpayer generally and can be relatively high. The loss of output due to illness imposes another cost on society. There are similar problems associated with the disposal of nuclear waste and with decommissioning a nuclear power station.

Again we can illustrate the effect of negative externalities on the allocation of resources diagrammatically, as in Figure 4.3.

In Figure 4.3 the supply curve $SS$ reflects only private costs of production. If it included the cost of externalities it would shift upwards to the left, for example to $S_1S_1$ and the equilibrium price would

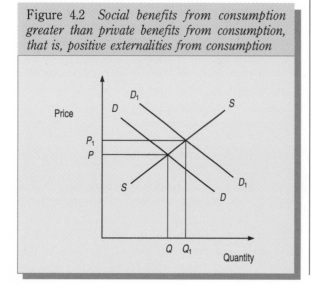

Figure 4.2 *Social benefits from consumption greater than private benefits from consumption, that is, positive externalities from consumption*

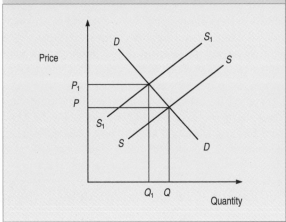

Figure 4.3 *The social cost of production greater than private costs of production, that is, negative externalities in production*

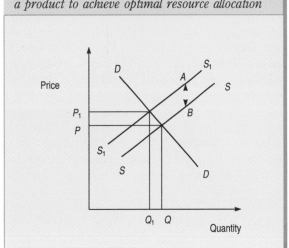

Figure 4.4 *The effect of placing a unit tax on a product to achieve optimal resource allocation*

then increase to $P_1$. Again this implies a different allocation of resources, since consumers demand less of this commodity and prefer resources to be used in the production of alternatives. In a free market there would therefore be overconsumption of this commodity in relation to the optimal level.

In the main the external costs associated with nuclear power generation are all potential costs. Nevertheless opting to generate more nuclear power is a high risk strategy and one which society favours less and less.

**2** (a) The answer to part (a) of Question 2 requires a discussion of why the existence of negative externalities can lead to an economically inefficient allocation of resources and has been discussed in the answer to Question 1 above.

(b) One way of reducing economic inefficiency caused by pollution is to tax the polluter in proportion to the amount of pollution generated. If we take the example of a factory which emits smoke pollution as a result of producing good X, those living in the vicinity of the factory experience a negative externality because the air around the factory is now polluted. The problem is illustrated in Figure 4.4.

*DD* is the demand for good $X$ and *SS* is the supply curve when only private costs of production are considered. If this market was free of any government interference, the equilibrium price would be $P$ and the equilibrium quantity Q. However, if $S_1S_1$ is the supply curve when the effect of pollution is considered then the economically efficient level of output is $Q_1$. One way of ensuring this level of output is produced is to place a tax on each unit of

X produced which is equal to the cost of the negative externality generated in production. In this case, if a tax per unit of *AB* is placed on the production of good $X$ the economically efficient level of output will fall to $Q_1$.

This approach to pollution regulation has much to commend it. Since the tax is levied on the amount of pollution generated, polluters have a clear incentive to cut down on the amount of pollution they generate by investing in cleaner technologies. Such a system of control is also relatively easy to administer. Firms simply pay a fee for each unit of pollution they discharge into the atmosphere. The difficulty, of course, is quantifying the cost of pollution and deciding on the appropriate rate of taxation. To achieve an economically efficient allocation of resources it is necessary to identify precisely the value of an externality. Economists are aware that it is extremely difficult to obtain an accurate evaluation of an externality, since those consulted might have a vested interest in overestimating or underestimating the value of the externality. Levying a tax which exceeds the value of the externality might lead to an allocation of resources which is inferior to that achieved by the market.

A different approach to the problem of pollution control is to place a limit on the amount of pollution a firm is allowed to emit. However here again, unless we know the precise value of the externality imposed on the community (and the community's demand for the product) there is no way of knowing what the economically efficient level of output is, and therefore what limit should be placed on the quantity of the product produced. If the limit is set too low, again it is possible that the allocation of resources will be inferior to the allocation achieved by the free market. However there are other problems with restricting the amount of output produced. In practice it is extremely difficult to monitor the regulations and there is likely to be widespread evasion, especially if the penalties are relatively low or if there is little risk of detection.

Another problem is that limits on pollution usually apply equally to all firms. This does not necessarily encourage efficiency in the allocation of resources because uniform limits might not give firms an incentive to develop cleaner technologies. It would be more efficient if those firms which could reduce pollution at a lower cost than other firms were assigned a lower pollution limit. This would provide low cost firms with an incentive to cut pollution because they would otherwise be compelled to cut their output and therefore their profits would fall. However, such an approach requires an accurate assessment of which firms have the lowest cost of reducing pollution. This would be very difficult to estimate since the most efficient firms have an obvious incentive to conceal their true level of efficiency. In any case, variable limits would be regarded as unfair and would almost certainly be resisted by industry.

**3** Pure public goods have two characteristics: they are **non-rival** in consumption and they are **non-excludable**. A good is non-rival when consumption by one person does not diminish the amount available for consumption by another person. An often quoted example is a lighthouse. Once constructed, a lighthouse can be used as a navigational aid by a ship's captain without diminishing its usefulness to others. Option 1 is therefore correct.

A good is non-excludable when it is either impossible or too expensive to prevent someone from consuming it. Again, if a lighthouse is constructed, it is impossible to prevent ships from using it as a navigational aid. Option 2 is therefore correct.

Because public goods are non-rival in consumption and non-excludable it is impossible to levy a charge for them. Who would pay to consume a public good when the amount available does not diminish with use, and non-payers cannot be prevented from consuming it? Of course no-one would pay individually for such a good and therefore in a free market firms would receive no revenue if they produced it. Because of this, public goods can never be provided through the market mechanism. Option 3 is therefore incorrect.

The key is therefore B.

## REVIEW QUESTIONS AND ANSWERS

### Questions

1 Give some examples of circumstances where 'rotas' and 'lotteries' are used to ration scarce resources.

2 Why do universities and other higher education institutions insist on certain 'A' level grades as an entry requirement? Could the student loan scheme be described as a movement towards using the price mechanism?

3 Examine the arguments for and against the use of the price mechanism as a means of overcoming traffic congestion at places such as the Severn Bridge.

4 During the Christmas shopping period of 1989 British Rail received some criticism when it increased its fares into certain cities on Saturday mornings in order to reduce overcrowding on trains. In what ways could this policy be criticised, and are these criticisms justified?

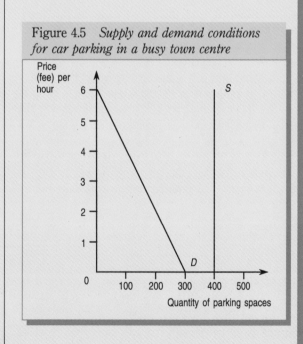

Figure 4.5   *Supply and demand conditions for car parking in a busy town centre*

5 Suppose the country is faced with a petrol shortage. What are the arguments for and against using the price mechanism to remove the shortage?

6 Figure 4.5 on page 24 shows the supply and demand conditions for car parking in the centre of a busy town.

(a) Why is it difficult in the circumstances shown for the city council to use market forces as a guide to what the price of car parking should be? What price would the council wish to charge in order to:

(i) encourage maximum use of the car park;
(ii) obtain maximum revenue?

(b) Suppose the demand for car parking spaces increases by 200 at each and every price. What price is the council now likely to charge? Explain your answer.

7 Public goods are non-rivalrous and non-excludable. Discuss the extent to which each of the following should be regarded as public goods.

(a) Radio and TV broadcasts.
(b) Secondary school places.
(c) University places.
(d) Hospital beds.
(e) Roads.

8 Why would the non-excludability of pure public goods make their provision an unattractive proposition for a profit-making entrepreneur?

9 Why might the social costs of a car journey exceed the private costs?

10 Why might the social costs of building a factory in an area of high unemployment be less than the private costs?

11 How would you decide whether to make a charge for a government service or to provide it free to the user?

## Answers

1 In cases where surgery is not considered urgent, rotas are used to ration hospital beds. Rotas are also used by local authorities to allocate housing. Some enterprising individuals have sold private housing by lottery, though this technique is usually used to sell tickets (which carry the chance of winning a prize) in order to raise funds for some other purposes such as a charity.

2 Setting entry requirements for institutions of higher education is a means of allocating the limited number of places available in such institutions. It might be argued that the student loan scheme is a move towards allocating university places through the price mechanism because students from poorer backgrounds who take out a loan will be obliged to pay interest on the loan. Students from wealthier backgrounds might not require a loan or might be better able to meet interest payments. On the other hand, student loans are available to all students with a university place and are at concessionary rates of interest which are *below* **market rates of interest.**

3 Setting a toll to overcome traffic congestion would be an effective means of reducing congestion on the Severn Bridge if the toll were set at a level high enough to deter use. It would also raise funds for the upkeep of the bridge. However, a disadvantage would be the possible congestion caused in other areas and the inefficiency caused by traffic taking a higher cost route to its destination to avoid the toll bridge.

4 British Rail might be criticised for simply attempting to increase profits as a result of increased demand for rail travel. On the other hand, there are only a limited number of spaces available on a train and therefore British Rail might argue that they were simply using the market mechanism to allocate the available spaces. This approach might well reduce congestion, but it might also be considered inequitable because those with lower incomes are likely to rely more heavily on rail transport and will therefore either cut journeys by proportionately more than other groups, or experience the greatest fall in real income as a result of the fare increase.

5 The price mechanism allocates resources on the basis of ability to pay rather than need. One important point in the case of petrol is that a rise in the price of this commodity will increase the distribution costs of industry and will therefore lead to an increase in prices generally.

**6** (a) In this case the council has a particular problem in using the price mechanism because there is no equilibrium between supply and demand. If the council wished to make a charge for car parking, it would be compelled to reduce the supply of car parking spaces.

(i) To encourage maximum use of the car park the council should make it freely available to motorists.

(ii) Maximum revenue is obtained by charging a price where elasticity of demand is equal to unity. In this case elasticity of demand is unity at the mid-point of the demand curve, that is, when price is £2.75 (approx.)

(b) [Hint: reproduce Figure 4.4 on graph paper and superimpose the new demand curve.] The price the council is likely to charge will depend on its aim. If it wishes to achieve maximum use of the car park and levy the highest charge it can, the maximum price it could charge is £2.50. On the other hand, revenue will now be maximised at the mid-point of the new demand curve, that is, at a price of £4.25.

**7** (a) Radio and television broadcasts are public goods because they are non-rival (consumption by one person does not diminish the amount available for others) and non-excludable (anyone with a receiver, and a satellite dish in the case of Sky, can pick up broadcasts).

In cases (b), (c), (d) and (e), it is possible to restrict consumption to certain groups and therefore the non-excludability condition is breached.

However, whether consumption by one person diminishes the amount available to others depends on several factors. For example, if there are empty hospital beds it is difficult to argue that admitting an additional patient will reduce the number of beds available to others.

**8** Any good which is non-excludable can never be profitable.

**9** Social costs will exceed private costs whenever there are externalities associated with production or consumption. Car use generates externalities such as pollution from exhausts which contributes to acid rain and global warming.

**10** The reduction in unemployment might be regarded as a positive externality because it will reduce the burden of supporting the unemployed and will lead to an increase in tax revenue.

**11** There are many considerations here. Government services are sometimes provided freely to consumers because they are public goods and it is impossible to make a charge for them. In other cases they are provided freely because of the benefits they confer on the community. Some services are provided free of charge on equity grounds. However, except in the case of public goods, providing a good free of charge will almost certainly lead to overconsumption in relation to the optimal amount and therefore a charge is sometimes made for goods provided through the state.

CHAPTER 5

# SOME APPLICATIONS OF PRICE THEORY

## Topic Summary

In Chapter 3 we saw how the interaction of supply and demand determines prices in free markets. However, in many markets supply and demand do not operate freely. There might be many possible reasons for this but, whatever the motive, any attempt by the government to influence price means that the market ceases to be 'free'. In other words, the market is no longer one in which demand and supply alone determine price.

## Maximum Prices

The government or its appointed agent might seek to establish a **maximum price** in the market, that is, a ceiling above which price will not be allowed to rise. One reason for this might be to redistribute income in favour of lower income groups. We can use our familiar demand and supply diagrams in Figure 5.1 to show what will happen in these circumstances.

Suppose the market illustrated in Figure 5.1 is a free market and supply and demand are initially in equilibrium at price $P$ and quantity $Q$. Now suppose that the government imposes a maximum price. How will this affect the market? In fact, if the maximum price is set *above* the existing equilibrium price P, there will be no effect. The market will already have reached its equilibrium and there will be no reason for price and quantity to change. However, if the maximum price is set *below* the free market equilibrium price, for example, at $P_1$, then price will have to fall from P to the new maximum $P_1$. We can see from Figure 5.1 that there will be a market shortage at price $P$, of $Q_1 - Q_2$ units.

Now if the market had remained free, any shortage would be removed by the price system. Remember, price acts as a signal to producers and consumers. But the important point here is that the market is not

Figure 5.1 *The effect of imposing a maximum price which is below the free market equilibrium price*

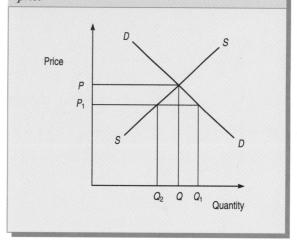

free! Price cannot rise above the maximum that has been set, $P_1$ in Figure 5.1. The shortage will therefore remain, and the price system will be unable to remove it. What non-price methods are available to allocate resources in this situation? There are several possibilities.

### Physical Rationing

The government or agency could issue vouchers to ration the limited supply amongst the greater number who wish to purchase the product. Rationing might at least ensure that those in greatest need receive some of the product. The government could also decide who should get more than the average amount. For example, if petrol were rationed, businesses might be given more vouchers than households, to ensure that products were transported around the country. Of course rationing has the disadvantage that it is costly to administer; vouchers have to be printed and distributed and so on. It also encourages the development of 'black markets'!

## First Come First Served

This method of allocating resources is often used when there are shortages. The limited supply is allocated to those who come first; this usually means those who are willing to queue the longest. In the 1980s and 1990s many countries in Eastern Europe suffered chronic shortages of meat and other food-stuffs because of price controls and queuing for many hours was a part of daily life for many households. In the UK, queues can be observed when tickets for major sporting events such as the FA cup final go on sale at the grounds of the two finalists. Unfortunately this means that other activities, such as production, are not taking place because of the time spent in the queues. In other words, this method of allocating resources might have a high *opportunity cost* in terms of lost output and wages.

## Ballots

The limited supply may be shared amongst the potential purchasers by means of a ballot. People may be issued with 'tickets' and a draw made to decide who is 'successful' and can have the product at the fixed price $P_1$. Again a ballot would be costly to administer. It could also be considered less fair than rationing since those unsuccessful in the ballot receive nothing at all, irrespective of their need.

## Minimum Prices

The government might seek to establish a minimum price in the market, that is, a floor below which price will not be allowed to fall. One reason for establishing minimum prices might be to protect the incomes of producers. Again we can use demand and supply diagrams to show what will happen in such circumstances.

In Figure 5.2, *SS* and *DD* are the original supply and demand conditions in a particular market. The initial equilibrium price and quantity are *P* and *Q* respectively. Suppose now that the government imposes a minimum price below which price will not be allowed to fall. If the minimum price is set below the equilibrium price *P*, there will be no reason for price to change. However, if the minimum price is

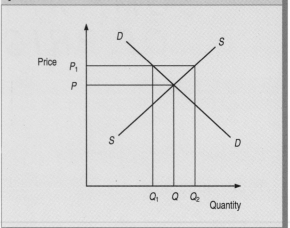

Figure 5.2 *The effect of imposing a minimum price which is above the free market equilibrium price*

set above the existing equilibrium price, for example at $P_1$, then price will be legally required to rise from *P* to the new minimum $P_1$. We can see from Figure 5.2 that at the higher price there will be excess supply of $Q_1 - Q_2$ units.

Again in a free market, any excess supply is eliminated by the price system. Price falls and thus simultaneously discourages production and encourages consumption. In the case of minimum price controls, to prevent price falling below the statutory minimum, the authorities must establish a purchasing agency to buy the excess at the statutory price $P_1$. In effect the demand curve for this product becomes perfectly elastic at the statutory minimum price $P_1$. The problem for the authorities is what to do with the surplus they accumulate through their intervention purchases. There are several possibilities.

## Destroy the Surplus

This technique is used in the case of certain agricultural commodities to preserve the market price. However it implies a waste of resources, since the high price encourages resources into the production of a commodity which is then destroyed.

## Export the Surplus

It might be possible to export the surplus. By selling the commodity abroad there is no reason why the domestic price should be disturbed. However, it might not always be possible to find an overseas buyer.

## Store the Commodity

It might be possible to store the commodity and release it onto the market when a reduction in supply forces the equilibrium price upwards. In other words buffer stocks could be used to stabilise price. The problem here is that it is usually expensive to store commodities and there is no guarantee that supply will fluctuate from one year to the next, making it possible to offload the surplus onto the market.

### Examples of Price Control

There are a number of well known examples of price control, including the following.

## Minimum Wage Legislation

Wages can be regarded as the 'price' of labour. For many years Wages Councils have set minimum wages for workers employed in certain industries. In terms of Figure 5.2 above, if the minimum wage ($P_1$) is set above the free market wage ($P$), then we will have excess supply, as shown in the diagram. In the case of the labour market, excess supply implies unemployment because more people are offering themselves for work than are demanded by employers.

## Common Agricultural Policy

The EC has a 'managed' market in agriculture. Rather than allow the free market, that is, supply and demand, to set prices, the Community institutions set guaranteed or minimum prices for the whole range of agricultural products within the Community. This attempt to set minimum prices is part of the Common Agricultural Policy (CAP) which is examined more fully on pp. 203–5.

## Black Markets

A black market is usually the result of setting a maximum or 'official' price for an item which is below the free market equilibrium price, as in Figure 5.1 above. This is often the case with tickets for the finals of major sporting events or for popular concerts.

## Rent Controls

Sometimes rents are fixed on private accommodation so as to limit the amount that can be charged by landlords. Rent controls are examined more fully in the answer to Question 1 below.

### Questions and Answers

### Questions

1  'Rent controls in the private sector of the housing market should be abolished.' Examine the economic arguments for and against this view.

ULEAC, AS Level, June 1990

2  The demand and supply schedules for a commodity are illustrated in Figure 5.3.

Figure 5.3

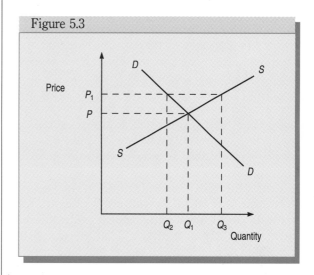

If the government wished to maintain a target price of $P_1$ by intervening in the market by buying or selling stocks it would:

A  buy quantity $Q_2Q_1$
B  sell quantity $Q_2Q_1$
C  buy quantity $Q_2Q_3$
D  sell quantity $Q_2Q_3$
AEB, June 1990

### Answers

1  There are limits on the rent which landlords can set for private accommodation in the United Kingdom. If a tenant appeals against a rent as being 'unfair', then a rent control officer can set what he or she regards as a 'fair' rent for property of that type, in that location.

Of course the rent control officer is not bound to fix a rent which is below the existing rent. He or she might recommend an increase in rent above the free market equilibrium! However, we are not much interested in this possibility because in these circumstances there would be an excess supply of accommodation and rents in general would fall. Rent control can therefore be taken to imply a reduction in rent below the free market equilibrium.

In the case of private accommodation there is a major advantage for those tenants fortunate enough to occupy a residence: landlords are prevented from charging rents above a maximum amount. This clearly redistributes income in favour of those tenants on a controlled rent. It is also possible for society to benefit from the existence of rent controls. It is sometimes argued that if rents increase this will be reflected in a higher rate of inflation and rising prices will encourage higher pay demands from the workforce. Rising prices and costs have several disadvantages and in particular make exports less competitive in world markets and imports relatively cheap in the home market. This will adversely affect the balance of payments and is likely to lead to rising unemployment. By helping to prevent rising prices, rent controls help avoid the emergence of these problems.

Rent controls have other potential advantages. If rents increase, more people will qualify for assistance through the DHSS and the higher expenditure might be financed through higher taxation, which is certainly a disadvantage for those paying it. Furthermore controlled rents might also have an advantage for landlords in so far as they know the maximum rent they can charge for a particular type of property in a particular location. This might be useful in making plans concerning their future income from rent. It will also be useful in making plans about whether to invest in other properties and make these available for rent or whether to dispose of existing properties.

However rent controls might also have serious adverse consequences. We can analyse one such adverse effect in terms of Figure 5.4.

In Figure 5.4, we illustrate the market for private rented accommodation. *SS* is the supply of private accommodation available for rent and *DD* is the demand for such accommodation. The equilibrium price is *P* and the amount of accommodation supplied and demanded is *Q*. Now if rent controls are applied in such a way that the rent is set below the free market price, for example at $P_1$, in Figure 5.4, then we will have excess demand for rented accommodation equal to $Q_1 - Q_2$. As long as rent controls

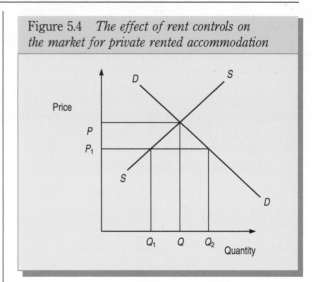

Figure 5.4   *The effect of rent controls on the market for private rented accommodation*

remain in force, this excess demand cannot be eliminated through the price mechanism. In other words, although rents are usually controlled so as to limit the amount tenants pay, if the rent is set too low the result will be a shortage of rented accommodation, that is, possible homelessness for some people!

Controlling rents might have other consequences. In particular the income of landlords will fall and as a result they are likely to invest less in the upkeep of property. The quality of the housing stock is therefore likely to deteriorate. Furthermore the falling incomes of landlords will encourage them to remove their property from the rental market and discourage other people from buying property to let out as private accommodation. Thus, in the longer term, the shortage of housing is likely to increase. Because of this there might be an increase in homelessness and increased pressure on the government to provide accommodation. Here again, if governments respond to this pressure with an increase in municipal house building, this will almost certainly mean higher levels of taxation.

The shortage of accommodation might lead to an increase in demand for private housing which could pull up house prices generally. This could be a source of inflation. Housing is one of the most important expenditures for the majority of people and an increase in the price of this might lead to demands for higher wages and through this further price rises for other products.

Another very serious consequence of controlling rents is that it might reduce mobility of labour. For an economy to be efficient it requires a labour force which is mobile occupationally and geographically.

Geographical mobility depends on the availability of suitable housing in different areas. Without this, geographical mobility will be seriously restricted. This is a very likely consequence because rent controls will be imposed more readily in areas where rents tend to rise more quickly than rents in other parts of the country. In these areas shortages of accommodation are likely to develop rapidly. By reducing geographical mobility of labour, rent controls might therefore reduce economic efficiency in general.

Some might argue that another disadvantage of rent controls is that their existence imposes an unnecessary opportunity cost on society. If controls were abolished and the property market were left to operate freely it can be argued that resources would be allocated more efficiently. The resources used to administer rent controls would then be available for an alternative use which might confer greater benefit on society.

Whether rent controls in the private sector should be abolished is a political decision. On grounds of equity it could be argued that rent controls should be retained. However, any form of price control implies an inefficient allocation of resources and it is likely that rent controls will reduce the quantity and quality of rented accommodation available.

**2** In the market illustrated in Figure 5.3 on p. 29 the free market equilibrium price is $P$ and the equilibrium quantity is $Q_1$. If the government wishes to maintain a target price of $P_1$, it must raise price above the free market equilibrium and this will have two effects. It will encourage producers to supply more but will simultaneously reduce the amount consumers wish to purchase. In fact at $P_1$ producers will supply $Q_3$ but consumers will only purchase $Q_2$. The market surplus at price $P_1$ will therefore be $Q_2Q_3$ and this is the amount the government must purchase if $P_1$ is to be maintained. The key is therefore C.

## REVIEW QUESTIONS AND ANSWERS

### Questions

**1** What conditions are necessary for a black market to exist?

**2** Figure 5.5 represents the market for a commodity where the demand curve is $D$ and which is supplied both by domestic producers whose supply curve is shown by $S_d$ and by a large number of producers in other countries whose supply curve ($S_w$) can be regarded as being horizontal at the world price, $P_w$. *OM* represents the output of domestic producers, and *MN* represents imports.

(a) Explain why the world supply curve is horizontal, and why it in effect imposes a ceiling price on domestic producers if there is free trade.
(b) Use Figure 5.6 to predict the effect of an import tariff on:
  (i) domestic output;
  (ii) imports;
  (iii) the price paid by consumers.
(c) Who benefits and who loses from a tariff?

**3** Why does the EC sometimes supply butter and cheese at a reduced price to certain targeted groups such as senior citizens?

**4** Use supply and demand curves to show how it can be predicted that as Russia moves towards a market economy queues for certain commodities might get shorter, but prices will rise.

Figure 5.5 *Horizontal world supply curve*

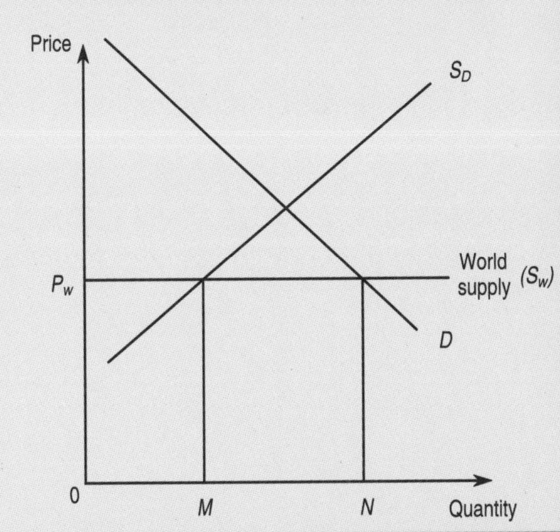

## Answers

1 The main condition for the existence of a black market is the existence of a maximum price which is below the free market equilibrium price. In these circumstances consumers will be willing to pay more than the maximum price for additional units of the product and sellers can therefore obtain higher rewards by selling on the black market.

2 (a) The world supply curve is horizontal because there are assumed to be many suppliers of this product located in different countries. The elastic supply curve imposes a ceiling price for this commodity because, if buyers are unable to purchase from one supplier at the ruling world price $P_w$, they will simply buy from another supplier. Any attempt to raise price by one supplier will simply result in a loss of sales to other suppliers.

(b) (i) A tariff is a tax on imports which can be expected to increase the price of imports by shifting the world supply curve vertically upwards by the amount of the tariff. In response consumers will demand more domestic output.

(ii) Since there has been no change in demand for the commodity and consumption of domestic output increases, it must follow that consumption of imports decreases.

(iii) Since the world supply curve shifts vertically upwards the price paid by consumers will rise.

(c) There might be many gainers and losers. For present purposes we identify only two. The most obvious gainer is the government since it receives revenue from the tariff. The most obvious loser is the consumer who pays the increased price! For more detail on gainers and losers see p. 180.

3 The main reason is to dispose of surplus commodities which are expensive to store and to cause as little disruption to the guaranteed minimum price as possible. This is achieved by restricting sales at reduced prices to certain groups such as those on low incomes. There are also social reasons in that butter and cheese are basic foodstuffs.

4 Figure 5.1 on p. 27 shows a market in which maximum prices are established. The former Soviet Union had a history of such price controls which established maximum prices for most goods. In Figure 5.1 there is a market shortage of $Q_1 - Q_2$ at the official price and queuing to obtain the product was an everyday occurrence. As price controls are lifted prices will rise and the familiar queue will become a thing of the past as supply and demand are brought into equilibrium. There are no queues in Figure 5.1 when price is $P$!

CHAPTER 6

# THE BASIS OF DEMAND

## Topic Summary

In this chapter we provide a theoretical underpinning for our assertion in earlier chapters that the quantity of a good varies inversely with its price.

## Utility

The word **utility** is used by economists to imply satisfaction from consumption. While there is no precise measure of satisfaction, it is clearly the motive for consumption. Furthermore economists assume that consumers act rationally and in so doing will adjust their purchases of goods and services so as to achieve maximum satisfaction; that is, they will aim to maximise total utility.

### The Law of Diminishing Marginal Utility

The law of diminishing marginal utility states that, as successive units of a good are consumed, each additional unit will add less and less to total satisfaction, that is, marginal utility falls as consumption increases. Now it can be shown that total utility is maximised when the ratio of marginal utility to price is equal for all goods consumed, that is, when $MU_a/P_a = MU_b/P_b = MU_n/P_n$ where $n$ is the $n$th good consumed. When this condition is attained the consumer is in equilibrium with respect to his (her) purchases because maximum total utility is achieved. For present purposes the important point to grasp is that, once equilibrium is achieved, a reduction in the price of one good will lead to an increase in the amount of that good consumed until equilibrium is restored. This provides justification for the downward sloping demand curve (inverse relationship between price and quantity demanded) assumed in Chapter 3.

## Income and Substitution Effects

A rise in real income will cause a rise in demand for most goods and services. Now, there are two ways in which real income can increase: either money income rises by more than prices rise, or prices fall by more than money income falls. The response of consumers to a change in real income is referred to as the **income effect**. However, when the relative prices of goods change, there will also be a **substitution effect**.

When the relative price of a good falls the substitution effect is simply the substitution of this good for other goods which are now relatively more expensive. The substitution effect is therefore always negative. (A fall in price encourages an increase in the amount demanded and vice versa.) Conversely for most goods and services the income effect is positive. (A decrease in prices implies an increase in real income and this encourages an increase in demand.) However, for some goods, usually of low quality, the income effect is negative; that is, demand falls as real income increases. Such goods are referred to as **inferior goods** because the rise in real income enables consumers to substitute goods of superior quality. An often quoted example is the substitution of better cuts of meat for relatively cheap offal, as income rises.

Normally, then, the income and substitution effects reinforce each other, encouraging the consumer to buy more of a good when its price falls. However, if the consumer considers the good to be inferior, the effects will work in opposite directions. The overall effect of any price change will therefore depend on which of the effects is the stronger. If the negative income effect is weak and the negative substitution effect predominates, more of a good will still be demanded as price falls – despite the negative income effect. However, if the negative income effect predominates, less will be demanded as the price of a good falls. Such cases are a special kind of inferior good and are referred to as **Giffen goods**.

## Common Mistakes to Avoid

An extremely common mistake is to confuse an indifference curve with a demand curve, probably because they usually have the same shape and are convex to the origin. In fact they are not the same thing, though they are related, because we can use indifference curves to derive an individual consumer's demand curve for a particular good. However an indifference curve shows different combinations of goods which give the same level of utility and therefore which leave the consumer indifferent about which combination is consumed. A demand curve, on the other hand, shows a relationship between price and quantity demanded for a particular good. The level of utility derived from consuming different amounts of this one good will vary all the way along the demand curve.

Another problem is in distinguishing between **Giffen goods** and **Veblen goods**. We have already seen that all inferior goods have negative income elasticity of demand and that Giffen goods are a special type of inferior good because they also have positive price elasticity of demand. In other words, for Giffen goods quantity demanded increases as price increases and vice versa. Veblen goods also have positive price elasticity of demand because they are purchased for ostentatious reasons, that is, they become more desirable as their price increases. However Veblen goods also have a positive income elasticity of demand and are not therefore Giffen goods.

## Questions and Answers

### Questions

**1** (a) What is meant by an inferior good?      (8)

(b) Use income and substitution effects to analyse the consequences of a substantial increase in bus fares in your country.   (17)
UCLES, Nov 1990

**2** The numerical value of the income elasticity of demand for an inferior good will be:

A   negative
B   zero
C   between zero and infinity
D   equal to unity
E   greater than unity
ULEAC, January 1991

**3** In Figure 6.1 $I_1$ and $I_2$ are indifference curves and $BL_1$ and $BL_2$ are budget lines.

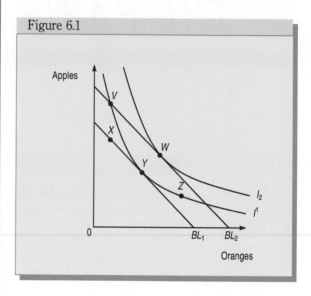

Figure 6.1

Which two points represent combinations which give equal utility?

(A)   V and W
(B)   W and Y
(C)   X and V
(D)   X and Z
(E)   Z and Y

### Answers

**1** (a) For most goods a rise in real income will lead to an increase in the quantity demanded. Such goods are referred to as normal goods and, since a rise in income will cause a rise in demand, they have positive income elasticity of demand. However, for certain goods an increase in real income will lead to a reduction in demand. Such goods are referred to as inferior goods and, since a rise in real income will lead to a reduction in demand, all inferior goods have negative income elasticity of demand. The diagrams in Figure 6.2 below are used to illustrate the relationship between income and demand for a normal good and for an inferior good.

Figure 6.2a illustrates a normal good because real income and demand are positively related. Figure 6.2b, on the other hand, illustrates an inferior good because income and demand are negatively related.

(b) The nature of inferior goods is such that when real income rises consumers prefer to substitute goods of a superior quality. Bus travel might be

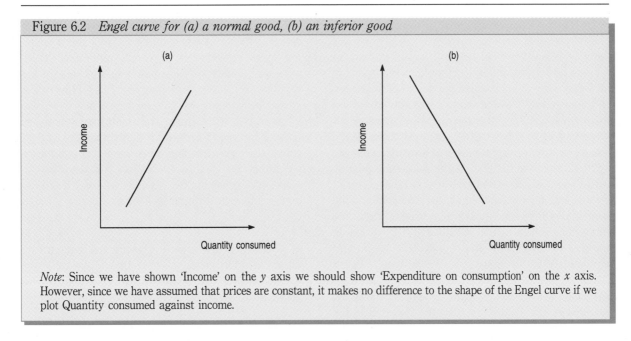

Figure 6.2    *Engel curve for (a) a normal good, (b) an inferior good*

(a)

Income

Quantity consumed

(b)

Income

Quantity consumed

*Note*: Since we have shown 'Income' on the $y$ axis we should show 'Expenditure on consumption' on the $x$ axis. However, since we have assumed that prices are constant, it makes no difference to the shape of the Engel curve if we plot Quantity consumed against income.

an inferior good because as real income rises more people tend to substitute private means of transport such as cars, rather than use public transport.

However, before we can make any firm judgement about whether bus travel is an inferior good, we need to analyse how the consumer's preference for bus travel changes as the price of bus travel changes. Figure 6.3 shows the amount of bus travel that can be purchased when the consumer's entire income is spent on bus travel ($OA$), the amount of private transport that can be purchased when the consumer's entire income is spent on other goods ($OB$) and all other attainable combinations when income is fully spent. $IC$ is an indifference curve which shows combinations of bus travel and private transport along which the consumer is indifferent. The equilibrium point is $X$, so that $OM$ of bus travel is consumed and $ON$ of all other goods.

Now if there is a substantial rise in bus fares and all other things remain equal, the budget line will shift from $AB$ to $A_1B$ in Figure 6.4 because the increase in bus fares implies a fall in real income. The consumer will then re-establish equilibrium on a lower indifference curve ($IC$, in Figure 6.4) at point Z.

Figure 6.3    *Consumer equilibrium*

B

N        X

0        M        A

All other goods

IC

Bus journies

Figure 6.4    *The income and substitution effects of an increase in bus fares*

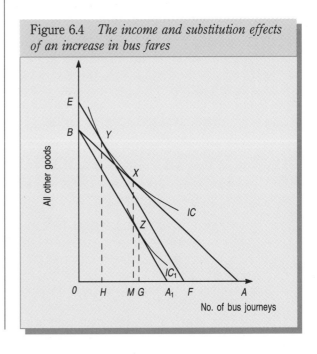

E

B        Y

X

All other goods

IC

Z

IC₁

0    H    M G    A₁    F        A

No. of bus journeys

At the new equilibrium point *Z*, the consumption of bus travel has fallen to *OH* compared with *ON* before the fare increase. Despite the fall in demand for bus travel we cannot conclude that bus travel is an inferior good. For normal goods, as well as most inferior goods, the reaction of consumers to an increase in price is to consume less. To ascertain what type of good bus travel is we must examine the income and substitution effects of the price change.

To do this assume that, at the same time relative prices changed, the consumer's real income increased by just sufficient to enable him (her) to remain on the original indifference curve *IC*. In this case the imaginary budget line would be *EF*, which is parallel to the actual budget line $A_1B$. In these circumstances the new equilibrium would be at point *Y*. The movement from *M* to *H* is therefore the substitution effect of the fare increase. However, for present purposes, we are more interested in the income effect of the price change. Since the movement from *M* to *H* is the substitution effect, the movement from *H* to *G* must be the income effect of the increase in bus fares. The final effect of the increase in bus fares is therefore an increase in the number of bus journeys made equal to *MG*. However, for present purposes the important point to note is that in this case the income effect is also *negative*. As real income falls, the number of bus journeys made increases. Bus travel is therefore an inferior good.

In practice it is extremely difficult to identify with certainty which goods are inferior goods and which are not. In recent years in the UK, as in many other advanced countries, there has been a decline in the number of people travelling by bus. This might partly be a result of fare increases but it is also likely to reflect the impact of rising money incomes on real income. There is no doubt that the greater convenience of travelling by car, whether simply for shopping or travelling backwards and forwards to work, has great appeal as income rises. If this is correct bus travel might well be an inferior good in the UK.

**2** The key is of course A. The characteristic feature of all inferior goods is that they have negative income elasticity of demand because as income rises demand falls and vice versa.

**3** All points on an indifference curve show combinations of different goods which give a consumer the same total utility. That is why the consumer is indifferent about which combination of goods purchased. The key is therefore E. All other options have one point which gives a higher level of utility than the other. Faced with such a choice the consumer would most certainly not be indifferent about which combination of goods was purchased.

## REVIEW QUESTIONS AND ANSWERS

### Questions

**1** The *paradox of value* was a problem which preoccupied many economists during the early stages of the development of economics as a social science. The question was posed along the following lines: why is it that water, which is essential to human life, is cheap, whereas diamonds, which are inessential, have a high price?

Distinguish carefully between total and marginal utility, and use this distinction to explain the paradox of value.

**2** Adam Smith stated that taxes should involve taxpayers in *equality of sacrifice*. Progressive taxes are related to the ability to pay, so that people on higher incomes pay a higher percentage rate of tax on each additional pound earned than do those on lower incomes. In what way does the law of diminishing mar-

ginal utility provide a justification for the use of progressive taxes?

**3** Refer to Table 6.1. Describe carefully how the marginal rate of substitution would alter as the consumer was asked to give up apples with pears being offered as a substitute. Explain *why* the marginal rate of substitution varies at different points along an indifference curve.

Table 6.1  *Combinations of apples and pears giving an equal level of utility*

| Pears | | Apples | Pears | | Apples |
|---|---|---|---|---|---|
| 10 | + | 0 | 4 | + | 15 |
| 9 | + | 1 | 3 | + | 22 |
| 8 | + | 2 | 2 | + | 32 |
| 7 | + | 4 | 1 | + | 58 |
| 6 | + | 7 | 0 | + | 85 |
| 5 | + | 10 | | | |

Figure 6.5  *Types of good*

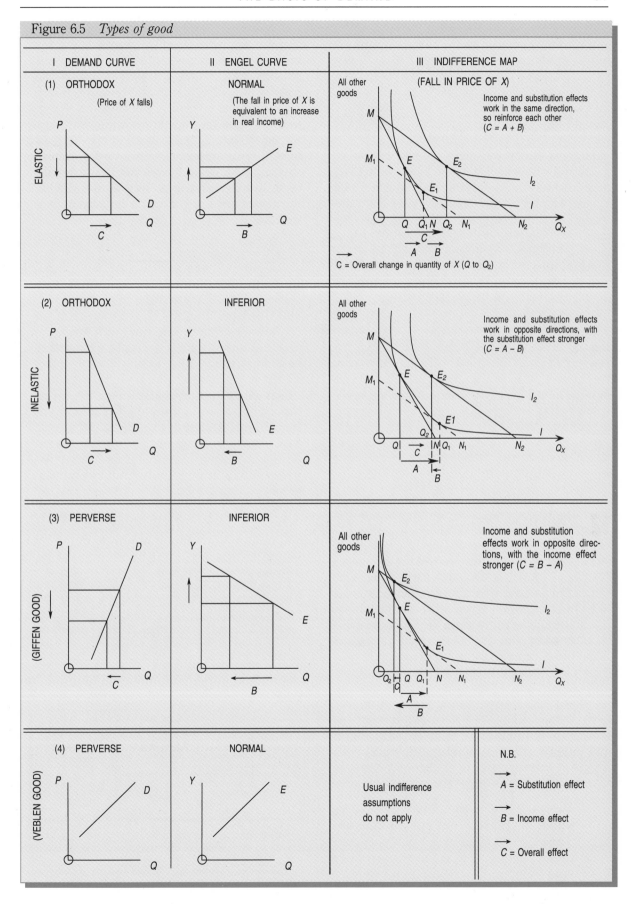

4  Carefully explain the following statements:

(a)  All Giffen goods, if they exist at all, are inferior, but not all inferior goods are Giffen goods.

(b)  A Rolls-Royce car might have a perverse demand curve, but it is not a Giffen good.

5  Examine Figure 6.5 and consider whether the demand curves and Engel curves shown there have positive or negative price and income elasticities of demand. Then complete Figure 6.6 by placing each of the following types of good in the appropriate cell of the matrix: orthodox–normal good; orthodox–inferior good; perverse–inferior ('Giffen') good; perverse–normal ('Veblen') good (we have filled in the first cell for you).

Figure 6.6  *Matrix box*

|  |  | PRICE ELASTICITY OF DEMAND | |
|  |  | NEGATIVE | POSITIVE |
| INCOME ELASTICITY OF DEMAND | POSITIVE | ORTHODOX-NORMAL GOOD | |
|  | NEGATIVE |  | |

## Answers

1  Total utility is simply the total amount of satisfaction gained from consuming a product. Marginal utility, on the other hand, is the additional utility gained from consuming one more unit of the product. Water, while essential to life, has a low marginal utility in the UK because it is so abundant. The first few drops are as precious as life itself, but the last few drops might be used only for watering house plants or cleaning windows. The total utility from consuming water is relatively high, but the marginal utility is relatively low and this explains why the price of water is relatively low. Diamonds, on the other hand, have a lower total utility than water, but a higher marginal utility. A diamond therefore commands a higher price than a glass of water.

2  The law of diminishing marginal utility tells us that the last few units of a good we consume give us less marginal utility than the first few units. If everybody paid the same amount in tax, for example £500, those on lower incomes would make a relatively greater sacrifice than those on higher incomes. Why? Because those on higher incomes consume more than those on lower incomes. The marginal utility of the last few units they consume will therefore be lower than the marginal utility of the last few units consumed by those on lower incomes. To achieve equality of sacrifice in terms of marginal utility forgone, it is therefore necessary for those on higher incomes to pay a higher percentage of their income in taxation.

3  The marginal rate of substitution changes because, as more of a good is consumed, marginal utility declines. It follows that as more pears (or any other good) are consumed, each additional unit is worth fewer and fewer apples (or any other good) in exchange.

4  (a)  All inferior goods have a negative income elasticity of demand. However Giffen goods are a special case of inferior good because they also have a positive price elasticity of demand, that is, an upward sloping demand curve. All other inferior goods have negative price elasticity of demand, that is, normal downward sloping demand curves.

(b)  It is sometimes argued that the demand for Rolls-Royce cars is upward sloping because, as their price rises, they become more desirable for ostentatious reasons. Any upward sloping demand curve will have positive price elasticity of demand, but goods such as Rolls-Royce cars will also have positive income elasticity of demand and cannot therefore be a Giffen good.

5

Figure 6.7

|  |  | PRICE ELASTICITY OF DEMAND | |
|  |  | NEGATIVE | POSITIVE |
| INCOME ELASTICITY OF DEMAND GOOD | POSITIVE | ORTHODOX–NORMAL GOOD | VEBLEN GOOD |
|  | NEGATIVE | ORTHODOX–INFERIOR GIFFEN | PERVERSE–INFERIOR GOOD |

# CHAPTER 7

# *THE LAWS OF RETURNS*

## Topic Summary

The laws of returns explain the behaviour of output as the input of a variable factor changes. This, as we shall see in the next chapter, has an important bearing on the firm's costs of production.

## Changes in Productivity

A change in productivity occurs when there is **a change in output per unit of input**. It is very rare in modern economies for productivity to fall and so we tend to focus on increases in productivity and in particular on increasing the productivity of labour. An increase in the productivity of labour occurs when there is an increase in output *per man hour* or *per man day*. A different way of saying the same thing is to say that the average output of the labour force increases.

The way in which changes in the number of workers employed changes output and productivity is usually explained by the **law of variable proportions**. This is discussed below but first we must distinguish between the *short run* and the *long run* in production.

## The Short Run and the Long Run

In economics the short run and the long run are not specific time periods such as a month or a year. Instead they relate to the length of time required to change the input of factors of production. In particular, during the short run it is only possible to change the input of variable factors. If, at any point in time, there is at least one factor of production whose input cannot be increased, then the firm is operating in the short run. In other words, the short run is a period during which there is at least one fixed factor of production. The long run, on the other hand, is a period of time during which there are no fixed factors of production.

## The Law of Variable Proportions

The effect on output of changing the input of variable factors can be explained in terms of the law of variable proportions. This law can be broken down into two component laws. These are the *law of increasing returns* and the *law of diminishing returns*. We take each in turn.

**The Law of Increasing Returns** This states that, as more units of a variable factor are added to a fixed factor, output will at first rise *more than proportionately*. When this happens we say that the firm experiences *increasing returns*.

**The Law of Diminishing Returns** This law states that, as more units of a variable factor are added to a fixed factor, there will come a point when output will rise *less than proportionately*. When this happens we say that the firm experiences *diminishing returns*.

## Average and Marginal Product

When discussing the law of variable proportions or its component laws we often make use of the concepts of *marginal product* and *average product*. These are measured with respect to a specific type of input, usually labour. The marginal product of labour is simply the change in total product when one more worker is employed. The average product of labour, on the other hand, is simply total output divided by the number of workers employed.

## Returns and the Division of Labour

The laws of returns discussed above are widely known. However we have not yet explained what causes increasing and diminishing returns. In fact increasing returns are due to increased scope for *division of labour* as more workers are recruited. The major advantage of the division of labour is that it makes possible an increase in productivity, that is, a higher average product. For this to happen marginal product must be greater than the existing average product, as Table 7.1 demonstrates.

Table 7.1

| No. of workers | Total product | Marginal product | Average product |
|---|---|---|---|
| 1 | 2 | 2 | 2 |
| 2 | 5 | 3 | 2.5 |
| 3 | 12 | 7 | 4 |
| 4 | 20 | 8 | 5 |
| 5 | 24 | 4 | 4.8 |

As soon as marginal product falls below the existing average product, productivity falls. This occurs after the employment of the fourth worker in Table 7.1. When productivity falls as a result of employing more workers this is simply an indication of the fact that there is a limit to the gains from specialisation given that the firm has at least one fixed factor of production. In other words falling productivity simply indicates that the combination of factors of production used has become less favourable.

## Returns to Scale

In the long run there are no fixed factors of production. When firms change the input of all factors of production we say that there has been a change in the scale of production. When an increase in the input of all factors of production leads to a *more than proportional* increase in output, we say that the firm has experienced **economies of scale**. For example, if the firm increases the scale of production, that is, the input of all factors of production, by 10 per cent, the firm has experienced economies of scale. On the other hand, when an increase in the input of all factors of production leads to a *less than proportional* increase in total output, we say that the firm experiences **diseconomies of scale**.

For simplicity economies of scale are sometimes defined as an increase in the scale of production that leads to a fall in the average cost of producing each unit. Diseconomies of scale, on the other hand, are defined as an increase in the scale of production that leads to an increase in the average cost of producing each unit.

## Reasons for Economies of Scale

There are several reasons why firms might experience economies of scale as they grow. The main ones are summarised below.

### Technical Economies

These are increases in productivity which result from changes in the technical process of production made possible as a result of an increase in the scale of production. We can identify several technical economies of scale:

**Increased Specialisation**    The larger the size of the firm, the greater the opportunities for specialisation. Specialisation results in an increase in productivity for a variety of reasons, such as that it facilitates increased division of labour and the use of specialist machinery.

**Better Linkage of Processes**    Products often require two or more separate processes in producing the finished item. Suppose a product needs two types of machine, machine A capable of producing a maximum output per hour of 20 units, and machine B capable of producing a maximum hourly output of 15 units. A firm that possesses only one of each machine has a maximum hourly output of 15 units. However, for an average 15 minutes per hour machine A is not used. The firm therefore has unused or excess capacity. Now if the firm expands its output to 60 units per hour (assuming it can sell the additional output) there need not be any idle machine time, that is, excess capacity is eliminated. The firm will simply use three of machine A (3 × 20 units per hour) with four of machine B (4 × 15 units per hour). Here again it is clear that productivity will increase when output is expanded.

**Indivisibilities**    It will always be possible for firms to increase productivity by using more efficient capital. For example, if two machines perform exactly the same function but one machine produces twice as much per hour as the other, productivity can be increased by using the more efficient machine. However the capital equipment which is most efficient is often large and expensive. In many cases it will be indivisible in the sense that smaller versions are not available. For example, a nuclear power station cannot be scaled down. Only as the firm's output grows will it be able to afford and use these large, more productive, items of capital equipment. At relatively low levels of output such indivisible units of capital equipment would be underutilised and firms would again be operating with excess capacity.

**Increased Dimensions**   A well-known mathematical relationship tells us that, if we double the surface area of a container, the cubic capacity increases ninefold! This explains the increasing use of juggernauts to transport goods across land and supertankers to transport oil over the sea.

## Marketing Economies

As well as the above technical economies, a firm that grows in size might also benefit from a number of marketing economies.

**Economies of Bulk Purchases**   Firms which are large can buy in bulk, gaining 'discounts' on raw materials and other items purchased as inputs. This gives large firms a considerable advantage over smaller firms which cannot buy in bulk.

**Economies of Bulk Dstribution**   Firms which are large can use their own distribution fleets, such as heavy goods vehicles, bulk containers and so on, to transport their product to buyers. This in itself would give them an advantage over smaller firms but they also gain another advantage: as the size of containers and transport vehicles rises, the cost per unit transported falls. It is many times cheaper to transport a barrel of oil from the Gulf using a fully laden supertanker with a carrying capacity of some 500 000 tonnes, than it is to use a tanker with a carrying capacity of only 50 000 tonnes for example.

## Financial Economies

Larger firms can often obtain finance more cheaply and easily than smaller firms. Banks and other financial institutions might consider larger firms less risky and be more willing to lend, and at lower rates of interest than might be available to smaller firms.

These are some of the major reasons why a firm might experience economies of scale as the size of output rises. However it is possible that beyond a certain level of output further increases in scale might lead to diseconomies of scale. These might occur for several reasons.

## Diseconomies of Scale

### Managerial Difficulties

The complexity of managing large organisations is thought to be a major reason for diseconomies of scale. Large organisations have several departments, and controlling and coordinating each department so that costly errors are avoided, work is not duplicated, and so on, is a difficult task. It is possible that smaller organisations are managed more efficiently and, if this is correct, larger organisations might experience diseconomies of scale as capacity grows beyond a certain point.

### X-Inefficiency

This is a vague term but at its simplest level it implies that human inputs rarely operate with maximum efficiency unless there are powerful incentives for them to do so. Despite the vague nature of the term, X-inefficiency is thought to vary directly with the level of competition firms face and the scale of their operations. In large organisations, X-inefficiency might be caused by low morale, perhaps because individuals feel they have little influence on the decisions of management. Large organisations certainly experience higher levels of absenteeism than smaller firms and it is often suggested that this is indicative of low morale.

### Higher Input Costs

As firms grow they require more and more inputs. It is possible that in some cases the increased demand for inputs will result in higher input prices. In addition manufacturing firms will almost certainly place orders for inputs with the lowest cost supplier. However, as they increased their scale of production, they might be forced to place orders with higher cost suppliers because of the inability of lower cost suppliers to meet their needs in full. Again this would force up average costs of production as output increased.

### Marketing Diseconomies

When a firm grows and acquires a large market share it may be necessary to increase its marketing expenditures by a relatively large amount in order to gain even a small increase in market share. For example, if a firm has a market share of 25 per cent, even if it doubles its advertising expenditure it is unlikely to increase its market share by a hundred per cent. Similarly, if a firm attempts to supply small retail outlets in remote areas, its distribution costs will be relatively high, that is, average distribution costs will increase.

## Mergers and Acquisitions

A **merger** occurs when two or more firms join together by mutual agreement, while an **acquisition** or takeover occurs when one firm acquires a majority of the equity, that is, 51 per cent plus of the voting share capital, of another firm. Sometimes management of a company will advise their shareholders to accept the takeover bid of another company but when they do not, the takeover bid is regarded as *hostile*. Figure 7.1 shows the extent of integration, that is, mergers and acquisitions, in the UK in the late 1980s and early 1990s.

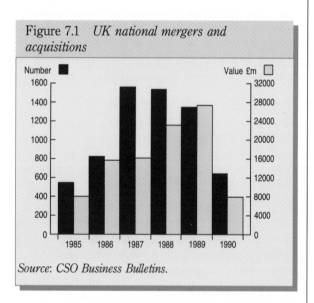

Figure 7.1   *UK national mergers and acquisitions*

*Source*: CSO Business Bulletins.

## Motives for Integration

**Economies of Scale**   Increased size might enable firms to gain economies of scale. This is particularly important in the UK, as well as other EC countries, because of the increased size of the market made possible by the competition of the Single Market in 1992 (see p. 211). Firms might prefer integration to

internal growth because they acquire existing good-will and brand loyalty. When a firm grows internally it must persuade consumers to switch brands and may provoke retaliation from other producers. Acquiring an existing firm therefore involves less risk and may also give the acquiring firm prime sites. This is especially important when retail sites are acquired.

**Diversification**   Firms might integrate in order to diversity into different areas of production as a means of reducing business risk. In the event of a reduction in demand for one product, firms are not forced to close as long as sales of other products continue. Here again external growth might be preferable to diversification through internal growth because the latter implies an increase in supply which might lead to falling prices. In these circumstances diversification might adversely affect profits.

**Rationalisation**   When an industry is contracting, firms might integrate in order to carry out a planned reduction of capacity and concentrate production in the most efficient plants.

**Asset Stripping**   One firm sometimes acquires another firm with the intention of selling off parts of its acquisition at a profit. This can only happen when a firm's equity is undervalued, perhaps because of incompetent management or because management have pursued a low dividend policy in order to finance growth. For whatever reason, when the component parts of an organisation can be sold at a higher price than the firm as a whole, asset stripping becomes possible.

## Common Mistakes to Avoid

Great care must be taken to distinguish between an increase in productivity that has occurred because of an increase in the scale of production, and an increase in productivity that has occurred as a result of an increase in the use of variable factors only. Increasing returns and diminishing returns refer to short run changes in output; that is, changes in output when the firm has at least one fixed factor. Economies and diseconomies of scale refer to long run changes in output; that is, changes in output when there are no fixed factors.

Sometimes internal economies of scale are confused with external economies of scale. Internal economies of scale apply to the individual firm and, if they exist, they are experienced as the individual firm grows. External economies of scale, on the other hand, are experienced by all firms in an industry as the industry grows. They are particularly common when an industry is localised. The problem arises partly because of the convention adopted by writers of textbooks (including this one) of simply using the term 'economies of scale' without specifying whether we are referring to internal or external economies. In fact, used on its own, the term 'economies of scale' is usually taken to imply internal economies of scale.

Another very common mistake made by many candidates in the examination room is to write a general answer to any question of scale. Questions on economies of scale are sometimes quite specific. For example, Question 1 below asks about economies of scale in retailing. It is well known that almost any question on economies of scale will be attempted by a majority of candidates, but not all candidates score well. A disappointing number seem to misread the question and provide a general answer covering all aspects of economies of scale without relating their points to the specific issues raised in the question.

## Questions and Answers

### Questions

1 (a) Comment on the cost advantages which large supermarkets have over small retailers. (12)
(b) Given the advantages you describe account for the continued existence of small retailers. (13)
UCLES, Nov/Dec 1990

2 A bus company replaced its original fleet of vehicles, each with a crew of two, with an equal number of one-man operated vehicles with the same capacity. As a result, the company produced the same passenger/mile output at a lower unit cost. This was because it benefited from:

A economies of scale
B an extension of the principle of division of labour
C higher labour productivity
D rationalisation of maintenance
AEB, June 1991

### Answers

1 (a) Economies of scale are generally thought of as the advantages firms gain from the higher levels of output that are made possible by an increase in capacity. In particular, higher levels of output can often lead to lower average costs of production so that as output grows the cost per unit falls. It is this which provides the incentive for firms to grow and exploit economies of scale.

In many industries there is considerable scope for economies of scale, and retailing is no exception. Increasing size makes possible a higher degree of specialisation. It is well known that greater specialisation can often lead to an increase in productivity and through this to a reduction in average cost. For example, in the grocery trade we find small independent retail outlets owned and run by a single person. There is little scope for specialisation in such organisations but in the case of large grocery retail chains such as Sainsburys and Tesco a high degree of specialisation is possible among staff. It is economic to train staff to perform various roles and to employ specialist staff, both of which can have a profound effect on productivity. For example, the employment of specialist buyers with detailed knowledge of market conditions can result in considerable savings to larger firms. This is particularly important in retailing, since a major cost is buying in products for sale to the public.

Another advantage larger retailers have over smaller retailers is that their higher turnover makes it possible to fully utilise expensive items of capital which would be underutilised in smaller retail outlets and which are not available as smaller, cheaper units. For example, the larger supermarkets use electronic point of sale (EPOS) equipment to deduct items from stock as their sale is registered at the checkout. This removes the periodic need to employ staff for stocktaking. The problem for smaller retail outlets is that their turnover is often insufficient to make economic use of an EPOS system.

Larger retailers have a clear advantage over small retailers with respect to purchases of goods for sale to customers because they can negotiate bulk discounts. The largest firms place the largest orders and can therefore negotiate the greatest discounts. The size of such discounts are not publicised (for obvious reasons) but the largest firms can sometimes negotiate discounts in excess of 50 per cent on their purchases. Smaller firms find it more difficult to negotiate discounts because of the relatively small size of their order.

Similarly large retailers have an advantage over smaller retailers in the storage of goods. It is well known that if we double the surface area of a cube we increase its volume eightfold. Large firms, with larger warehouses, gain an advantage over smaller firms because the average cost of storage will be smaller, assuming, of course, storage space is fully utilised. Similarly insurance charges against fire and theft do not rise proportionately with the volume of goods stored and here again larger retailers have a cost advantage over smaller retailers.

(b) Clearly large retailers have many advantages over smaller retailers and yet smaller retailers are common. There are many possible reasons for this. Many small retailers survive because they purchase end-of-range products from manufacturers (and from larger retailers in some cases). In such cases the volume of goods would be too small to be of any interest to larger retailers. This is true in the case of carpets, for example, and many small independent retailers survive alongside such giants as Allied Carpets. Similarly many small retailers buy 'slight seconds' in clothing, pottery and so on, which they sell on market stalls.

In some cases the nature of the product is such that small retailers survive. This is true in the case of jewellery, for example, where small independent retailers are common and thrive because they provide variety and personal service. The same is true in clothing and, despite the existence of large groups specialising in menswear, bespoke tailors, who produce hand made suits, are increasingly common. Large chains, such as the Burton Group, cannot provide the same personal service and their product is perceived by consumers to be different from that provided by a bespoke tailor.

Personal service is also common in the grocery trade. Small retailers will often stock particular products if requested to do so by customers. They also offer other services such as the delivery of groceries, which is clearly important for the elderly and the housebound. They often stay open until quite late to cater for marginal trade where consumers require this kind of convenience. Smaller retailers frequently offer credit to regular customers and are often more accessible than larger supermarkets for those who do not possess a car. Similarly smaller retailers often satisfy a small local market, perhaps on a housing estate or in a small village. They may also offer regular customers credit and are often open longer hours than major supermarkets. In such cases it is more convenient to patronise the smaller retailer, especially when only a few low value items are required.

It is often suggested that small firms continue to survive because of the attraction for many people of being self-employed. In retailing there are no significant barriers to entry and therefore, once an individual or small group of individuals have raised sufficient funds, there is nothing to stop them entering the retail trade. Some household names, such as Sainsburys and Boots, started off as small independent retailers, but grew as they exploited the available economies of scale. The absence of barriers to entry, coupled with the desire to be self-employed, are undoubtedly important factors explaining the existence of small independent retailers alongside large supermarkets.

Clearly there are many reasons why small retailers continue to survive despite the cost advantages that larger retailers have. Different factors will be responsible in different cases. However it is also possible to exaggerate the cost advantages that larger retailers have. In particular, smaller retailers often club together as a voluntary chain to gain economies from purchasing and advertising. For example, two well-known chains are Mace and VG, which buy in bulk, but then distribute the goods among small independent grocers.

**2** There has been no change in the scale of production. The bus company has simply replaced its fleet of buses with another fleet of buses and left its passenger carrying capacity unchanged. Option A is therefore not correct.

There has been no increase in the division of labour. On the contrary, since the buses are now one-man operated there has been a reduction in specialisation because the same person must now take fares and drive the bus. Option B is therefore incorrect.

The same work is now performed by fewer workers using the same amount of capital and this implies an increase in the productivity of labour. Option C is therefore the key.

Option D is incorrect because the same number of buses must be maintained and we are given no indication that any kind of rationalisation in maintenance has taken place.

## REVIEW QUESTIONS AND ANSWERS

### Questions

1  Why do firms experience increasing returns as they employ additional units of a variable factor?

2  What is the difference between increasing returns to scale and increasing returns?

Question 3 is based on the following matrix which shows the output available when different combinations of capital and labour are employed

|               |   | 1  | 2  | 3   | 4   |
|---------------|---|----|----|-----|-----|
| Units of      | 4 | 40 | 80 | 120 | 160 |
| Labour        | 3 | 36 | 72 | 108 | 144 |
|               | 2 | 30 | 60 | 90  | 120 |
|               | 1 | 20 | 40 | 60  | 80  |

Units of capital

3  Does the firm illustrated above experience:

(a)  Increasing, diminishing or constant marginal returns to labour?

(b)  Increasing, diminishing or constant marginal returns to capital?

(c)  Economies or diseconomies of scale?

4  What economies of scale might exist in retailing?

5  What type of integration is involved in each of the following cases?

(a)  A publisher takes over a papermill.

(b)  A tobacco company amalgamates with a manufacturer of potato crisps.

(c)  A tyre manufacturer amalgamates with a car producer.

Question 6 is based on Table 7.2 which shows how output varies when an increasing amount of labour is used with a fixed amount of other factors.

Table 7.2  *Output variation with increasing amounts of labour and fixed amounts of other factors*

| No. of workers | Total product | Average product | Marginal product |
|----------------|---------------|-----------------|------------------|
| 1 | 1  | – | – |
| 2 | 3  | – | – |
| 3 | 8  | – | – |
| 4 | 20 | – | – |
| 5 | 30 | – | – |
| 6 | 36 | – | – |
| 7 | 40 | – | – |

6  Complete Table 7.2 and then identify the point at which:

(a)  diminishing average returns are experienced;

(b)  diminishing marginal returns are experienced.

### Answers

1  The main reason why firms experience increasing returns is that, up to certain limits, employing additional units of a variable factor increases the scope for specialisation.

2  Strictly increasing returns to scale occur when a change in the input of all factors of production leads to a more than proportionate change in output. Firms can only therefore experience economies of scale in the long run. Increasing returns, on the other hand, occur when there is at least one fixed factor and a firm increases the input of a variable factor. Increasing returns therefore occur in the short run.

**3** (a) The firm experiences diminishing marginal returns to labour because, as the input of labour increases and the input of capital is constant, the marginal product of labour falls.

(b) The firm experiences constant marginal returns to capital because, as the input of capital increases and the input of labour is constant, the marginal product of capital is constant.

(c) The firm experiences economies of scale because as the input of capital and labour increase there is a more than proportional increase in output.

**4** Economies from bulk buying, increased scope for specialisation and ability to use indivisible units of capital are major sources of economies of scale in retailing.

**5** (a) Vertical integration backwards.

(b) Conglomerate merger.

(c) Vertical integration forwards for the tyre manufacturer but backwards for the car producer.

**6**

| No of workers | Total product | Average product | Marginal product |
|---|---|---|---|
| 1 | 1 | 1.0 | 1 |
| 2 | 3 | 1.5 | 2 |
| 3 | 8 | 2.67 | 5 |
| 4 | 20 | 5.0 | 12 |
| 5 | 30 | 6.0 | 10 |
| 6 | 36 | 6.0 | 6 |
| 7 | 40 | 6.7 | 4 |

(a) Diminishing marginal returns set in after the employment of the fourth worker.

(b) Diminishing average returns are experienced after the employment of the sixth worker.

# CHAPTER 8

# COSTS AND REVENUE

## Topic Summary

In this chapter we look at the behaviour of costs as output changes. Our analysis builds on the ground covered in the previous chapter and will form an integral part of our analysis of the behaviour of firms covered in Chapters 10–13.

## Costs in the Short Run

In the short run there are two types of cost: **direct** or **variable cost**, and **indirect, overhead** or **fixed cost**.

### Direct Costs

Direct costs are those which **vary directly with output**. They are therefore sometimes known as variable costs. If a firm produces more output it will need more raw materials and it will use more energy (electricity, gas, oil, and so on) in production. It might also require more labour. Clearly when the firm increases the input of these factors of production it will incur higher total costs. It is for this reason that such costs are called direct costs.

### Indirect Costs

Indirect costs do not vary directly with output; this is why they are sometimes known as fixed costs. They are *fixed, or constant,* as output changes. A firm might be able to produce more output in the same building and by using the same machinery. The associated costs such as rent and the cost of capital equipment might therefore be unchanged or fixed, despite increases in output.

*Average total costs (ATC)* Average total cost is the total cost per unit of production. We simply divide total cost (*TC*) by total output (*Q*). Thus:

$$\frac{ATC = TC}{Q} = \frac{TFC + TVC}{Q}$$

that is, $ATC = AFC + AVC$.

## Marginal Cost (MC)

Marginal cost is the addition to total cost from producing an extra unit of output. Since there is no change in fixed costs, marginal cost is the increase in total variable cost from producing an extra unit.

## Costs and Returns

The law of variable proportions has a crucial effect on the behaviour of costs in the short run. For example, when the firm experiences increasing marginal returns as the input of labour increases, the change in total output exceeds the change in total labour costs. This implies that marginal costs fall as output increases. The opposite occurs when the firm experiences diminishing marginal returns. Moreover, when marginal cost is less than average cost, average cost will be falling; and when marginal cost is greater than average cost, average cost will be rising.

## Costs in the Long Run

The long run is the time period required to bring about a change in the input of all factors of production. In the long run therefore all factors of production are variable and the amount of each factor of production used can be varied so as to achieve any combination of inputs the firm requires. If we assume firms aim to maximise profits, factor inputs will be varied so as to achieve the *least cost combination*.

Since there are no fixed factors in the long run, the law of variable proportions does not apply. Nevertheless, if firms experience economies of scale as output expands, average costs will fall in the long run. However, beyond some level of output, it is likely that economies of scale will give way to diseconomies of scale and if this happens long run average costs will rise.

## Revenue

Revenue is simply the return firms receive from sales. For purposes of analysis it is useful to distinguish between **total revenue**, **average revenue** and **marginal revenue**.

## Total Revenue (TR)

Total revenue is simply the amount received by the firm from the sale of its output. If the price is £5 per unit, and the firm sells 10 units, then its total revenue is £5 × 10 = £50.

## Average Revenue (AR)

Average revenue is simply the average amount received by the firm from the sale of each unit of output. As with any average, we simply divide the total by the number of units. Thus we have:

$$\text{Average Revenue} = \frac{\text{Total Revenue}}{\text{Total Output}}$$

i.e. $AR = \dfrac{TR}{Q}$

i.e. $AR = \dfrac{P \times Q}{Q} = P$

The average revenue is therefore the price of the product provided that the firm sells all its output at the same price. If we want to find the average revenue from any given level of sales we simply look at the demand curve. In Figure 8.1, the firm sold 100 units at a price of £4 which is exactly the same as average revenue. Similarly the price, or average revenue, when the firm sells 120 units in Figure 8.1 is £3.50. In other words, the demand curve is the average revenue curve. It tells us the price, or revenue per unit, the firm receives when it sells any given quantity of output.

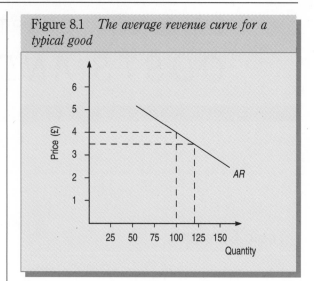

Figure 8.1    *The average revenue curve for a typical good*

## Marginal Revenue (MR)

Marginal revenue is the addition to total revenue gained from selling an extra unit of output. Suppose 5 units can be sold at a price of £100 per unit and 6 units at £90 per unit. The total revenue from 5 units would then be £500, and from 6 units £540, so that the addition to total revenue, that is marginal revenue, from selling the sixth unit would be £40.

## Common Mistakes to Avoid

The short run average cost curve and the long run average cost curve are a common source of confusion. At any moment in time a firm will be producing along a short run average cost curve. However, in the long run, capacity can be adjusted and the firm will then move on to another short run average cost curve. The long run average cost curve simply shows the minimum cost of producing any given level of output that can be achieved by adjusting capacity.

## Questions and Answers

### Questions

1   (a)  Distinguish between a firm's fixed costs and its variable costs                                      (6)
    (b)  Why is it that a firm will continue production so long as its average revenue exceeds its average variable cost?                        (7)

(c) Why do industries in which firms have very high fixed costs tend to be oligopolistic or monopolistic? (12)

UCLES, Nov/Dec 1990

**2** If a firm's average total costs of production are falling, then its marginal costs of production must be

A   above its average total costs
B   below its average total costs
C   constant
D   falling

AEB, June 1991

## Answers

**1** (a) Fixed costs, as their name suggests, are those costs which do not vary with output and represent the cost of employing fixed factors of production. Fixed costs are easily identified because they are incurred even if the firm produces no output. Such costs include rent on premises (or mortgage repayment), insurance charges, the cost of purchasing and installing machinery and so on. However, while total fixed costs do not vary with output, average fixed costs fall continuously as output expands because we are dividing the same total fixed costs by a larger and larger output.

Variable costs, on the other hand, vary directly with output. The more a firm produces the greater the total variable costs it incurs. Variable costs are the costs of employing variable factors of production and include such costs as raw materials, power to drive machinery and direct labour. It is normally assumed that firms initially experience increasing returns as output expands and therefore average variable costs at first fall. However, with the onset of diminishing returns, average variable costs will rise as output expands.

(b) The distinction between fixed costs and variable costs is important because, if average revenue is just sufficient for the firm to cover its average variable costs, it is neither better off nor worse off if it undertakes production. If average revenue equals average variable costs, then total revenue must equal total variable costs and the firm would make a loss equal to its fixed costs of production whether it undertook production or not. It follows that, if total revenue exceeds total variable costs, the firm is better off if it undertakes production. Of course if average revenue is less than average total costs of production the firm will make a loss, but it will make a smaller loss than if it ceases

production altogether, since by continuing in production it will make a contribution to its fixed costs. On the other hand, if average revenue is less than average variable cost, the firm will make a smaller loss if it ceases production altogether because its total loss will then only be equal to its fixed costs of production. The problem can be illustrated diagrammatically as in Figure 8.2.

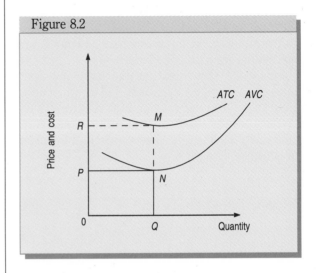

Figure 8.2

In Figure 8.2 *AVC* is the average variable cost and *ATC* is the average total cost. If the firm's product sells at a price of *OP*, the firm will just cover its total variable cost if it produces *OQ*. In other words, total revenue = total variable cost = *OPNQ*. In this case the total loss the firm makes if it produces *OQ* is equal to the total fixed cost (total cost minus total variable cost) = *PRMN*, so the firm makes exactly the same loss whether it undertakes production or not. At any price greater than *OP* the firm can make a contribution to its fixed costs. Indeed at prices above minimum *ATC* profits are earned.

It seems clear that the firm will remain in production if average revenue is at least sufficient to cover its average variable costs of production. Of course in the long run all costs must be covered, but since in the long run all costs are variable the statement is true whether we consider the short run or the long run.

(c) A monopolistic industry is one where a single firm dominates the market while in oligopolistic markets a small number of large scale producers dominate the market. One reason for the tendency towards large scale production in some industries is that firms have relatively high fixed costs of production. This is true in the case of railways, the supply of electricity, the production of motor vehicles, chemicals, and so on. In such cases large production runs are necessary to spread the average fixed cost of production. For example, the design and development of a new motor vehicle along with the cost of re-tooling and setting up the production line involves car producers in hundreds of millions of pounds of expenditure even before a single car is produced. This implies relatively high fixed costs of production and therefore large scale production runs are necessary to reduce the average fixed cost so as to bring the final cost of the car within the budget of a sufficiently large group of consumers. Figure 8.3 is used to illustrate the importance of this.

Figure 8.3 shows that, as the level of output increases, average fixed costs fall continuously. However, it is clear that only at relatively high levels of output have average fixed costs fallen sufficiently to bring the product within the budget of potential consumers.

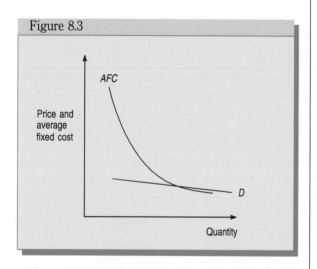

Figure 8.3

This explains why, in certain cases, large scale sales are important, but it does not necessarily explain why monopolistic or oligopolistic industries emerge. In fact, because the optimum size of the firm is very large, a single firm or a few firms can quite effectively meet total demand. Any new firm wanting to enter the market would have to undertake production on a similar scale to those firms already in the market in order to be competitive. For many firms the relatively high fixed costs represent a formidable entry barrier and in any case entering the industry is a high risk strategy because it implies a substantial increase in total output and cut-throat competition between giants. The price of the product would clearly fall and might leave all firms unable to cover their variable costs of production. Relatively high fixed costs therefore make it inevitable that an industry will either be monopolistic or oligopolistic.

**2** The behaviour of a firm's average total cost is largely dictated by the behaviour of its marginal cost. If marginal cost is above the existing average total cost, then average total cost must rise. Option A is therefore incorrect.

The opposite is also true. If marginal cost is below the existing average total cost, then average total cost must fall. Option B is therefore correct.

If marginal cost is constant at all levels of output, it is true that average total cost will fall because of falling average fixed cost. However it is not true that, if average total cost is falling, marginal cost must be constant. Option C is therefore incorrect.

It is also true that if marginal cost is falling total average cost will be falling. However, even if marginal cost is rising, as long as it is less than the existing average, average total cost will fall. Option D is therefore incorrect.

Key: B.

# REVIEW QUESTIONS AND ANSWERS

## Questions

1 Draw a graph to illustrate the relationship between long run and short run average costs for a firm experiencing constant returns to scale at all outputs.

2 Calculate *MC, AVC* and total fixed costs for the data below:

| Output | Total cost |
|--------|------------|
| 0 | 20 |
| 1 | 25 |
| 2 | 30 |
| 3 | 35 |
| 4 | 40 |
| 5 | 45 |
| 6 | 50 |
| 7 | 55 |
| 8 | 60 |

3 If, for a particular firm, *AVC* and *AR* are constant at £80 and £90 respectively, calculate the break-even level of output if total fixed costs are:

(a) £4000
(b) £2000
(c) zero

4 A market research survey suggests that a reduction from £500 to £480 in the price of a particular make of mountain bike would lead to an increase in the quantity sold from 30 to 33 per week. It is estimated that total profit would then be maintained at £3000 per week. On the basis of this data calculate:

(a) The price elasticity of demand for the bike.
(b) the average total cost per bike at a weekly output of:
  (i) 30 units;
  (ii) 33 units.
(c) If the price elasticity of demand was in fact −0.5, and assuming the same cost data as above, what effect would the price reduction have on total profit?

5 You are planning the introduction of a new airline service between London and Manchester and are faced with the following costs per flight:

| | |
|---|---|
| Fuel charges | £2000 |
| Interest and depreciation | £500 |
| Insurance | £1000 |
| Landing charges | £500 |
| Labour | £900 |

(a) From the above data distinguish between fixed and variable costs, giving reasons for your choice.
(b) Given a maximum seating capacity of 55 persons per aircraft, what is the minimum price per seat which you must charge to avoid making a loss?

6 A firm finds that over the range of output from 0 to 100 tonnes total physical product is given by the following formula:

$$TPP = 5 \times E$$

where *TPP* is total physical product (in tonnes per time period) and *E* is the number of workers employed on a production line. Draw a graph showing the marginal and average physical product of the first 20 persons employed on the production line. What sort of path would be followed by the graphs showing the marginal and average costs of production?

## Answers

1

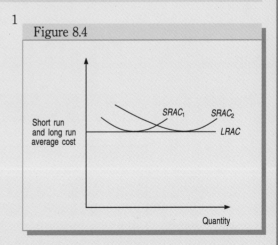

Figure 8.4

*Notes*: $SRAC_1$ and $SRAC_2$ are short run average cost curves and *LRAC* is the long run average cost curve. The long run average cost curve is horizontal because the firm experiences constant returns to scale all levels of output. Note that we have assumed in this case that fixed costs are insignificant. If they were significant *LRAC* might fall as output increased, though the effect of falling average fixed costs on *LRAC* would become less and less significant at higher levels of output.

**2** Since marginal cost is constant at all levels of output, $MC = AVC = £5$.

**3** The break-even level of output occurs when $TC = TR$.

(a) Let $q$ equal the amount produced and sold. Now when fixed costs are £4000 we have

$$£4000 + £80(Q) = £90(Q)$$
$$\therefore £4000 = £(10)\,Q$$
$$\therefore Q = 400$$

(b) When fixed costs equal £2000 we have £2000 = £10 $(Q)$ and therefore $Q = 20$.

(c) When there are no fixed costs there is no break-even level of output because revenue exceeds costs at all levels of output.

**4** (a) Ed $\Delta Q/Q \times P/\Delta P = 3/30 \times 500/20 = 2.5$

(b) (i)  Profit equals total revenue minus total cost.

When weekly output is 30 units, £3000 = £500 (30) − $TC$

$$TC = £15\,000 - £3000 = £12\,000$$
$$ATC = £12\,000/30 = £400$$

(ii) When weekly output is 33 units, $TC = £480\,(33) - £3000$

$$TC = £15\,840 - £3000 = £12\,840$$
$$ATC = £12\,840/33 = £389.09$$

(c) Ped =     −0.5 = %$\Delta Q$/%$\Delta P$
$$\therefore \Delta Q/4\% = -0.5$$
$$\therefore \Delta Q = 2\%$$

Following the price reduction the new level of output will be $30 \times 1.02 = 30.6$, that is, an increase of 2 per cent. Of course in practice it is impossible to sell 0.6 of a mountain bike and so we must calculate the effect on profit over some convenient period, such as 5 weeks. In the original situation profit over a 5 week period would be £15 000. In the new situation the total number of bikes sold over the 5 week period would be $30.6 \times 5 = 153$. Total revenue would therefore be $153 \times £480 = £73\,440$ and total cost would be equal to $£12\,000 \times 5 = £60\,000$. This implies a total weekly profit of £13 440/5 = £2688.

**5** (a) It would seem reasonable to treat insurance, interest and depreciation as fixed costs since these costs would be incurred whether aircraft took off or not. Fuel and landing charges are clearly variable costs, but labour is ambiguous. Economists usually distinguish between direct labour and indirect labour. The former is a variable cost because the input of direct labour varies directly with output, but the latter is a fixed cost. Since we are not given any information on the type of labour used we could argue that fixed costs are £2400 or £1500 and variable costs are therefore either £3400 or £2500.

(b) The total cost of the flight is £4900. Dividing this by 55 gives £89.09, which is the minimum price required to break even – assuming all seats on the aircraft are filled!

**6** Figure 8.5

If we assume that the firm has no fixed costs then the graph showing average and marginal costs would be a straight line and would be parallel to the graphs of the average and marginal physical product curves.

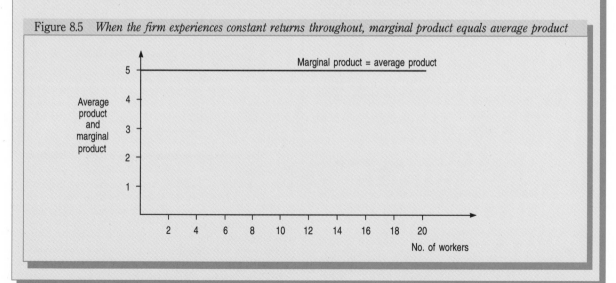

Figure 8.5   *When the firm experiences constant returns throughout, marginal product equals average product*

# CHAPTER 9
# THE FINANCE OF INDUSTRY

## Topic Summary

All firms need to raise finance. Broadly long term finance is required to start a business and to finance its growth, while short term finance is necessary to bridge the gap between purchase of materials which are turned into output, and receipt of revenue from the sale of goods. The very survival of a firm depends on ensuring that inflows of funds are at least sufficient to meet maturing liabilities, that is, debts which are due for repayment.

## Share Capital

The shareholders are the owners of a company and there are two basic types of share, **ordinary** and **preference**. Shareholders own shares, or parts of a company, and the amount owned depends on the number of shares held. However, while shareholders own a company, they do not necessarily control the day-to-day activities of the company. Control is in the hands of salaried managers and, unless these are also shareholders, **ownership** and **control** are vested in different groups. The implications of this are discussed more fully in Chapter 15.

*Ordinary shares* carry voting rights (one vote per share) at the AGM at which the board of directors is elected. In return they receive a dividend in years when profits permit payment of one. However, before ordinary shareholders receive any dividend, the company's creditors and preference shareholders must be paid. In addition, if a company is wound up, all other obligations are settled before ordinary shareholders receive any kind of reimbursement.

*Preference shares* carry a maximum rate of dividend but no guarantee of a minimum rate. They are referred to as preference shares because the full dividend is paid on these before the ordinary shareholders receive any dividend and because, in the event of liquidation, the full face value of the preference shares is refunded before the ordinary shareholders receive any reimbursement. The lower

risk undertaken by the preference shareholders is reflected in the fact that they carry no voting rights at the AGM.

## Debenture Stock

Debentures are long term loans to a company and are secured against particular company assets, such as buildings, which are sold to reimburse debenture holders in the event that a company is wound up. The company must meet annual interest payments on debenture stock or this is precisely what will happen! In other words, if debenture holders do not receive interest due, they can force the company to sell off assets to meet such interest payments.

## The Banks

Banks provide finance in a variety of forms:

*Overdrafts* are an important source of finance for most firms. They are flexible in the sense that interest is only paid on the day to day amount an account is overdrawn.

*Discounting bills of exchange* is an increasingly important source of short term finance. Bills of exchange are simply IOUs given as a credit note in exchange for goods. These IOUs can be sold at a discount, that is, for an amount less than their maturity value. Banks are often willing to do this, but bills will also be discounted by other institutions, particularly when they have been *accepted* or endorsed by a bank, because the bank then accepts responsibility for repayment in the event of default by the debtor.

## Regional Assistance

For many years the government has provided finance to firms which locate in certain assisted areas. During the 1980s most assistance was in the form of a

**Regional Development Grant (RDG)**. This was a subsidy on capital investment and was paid only if certain conditions, relating mainly to the creation of new jobs or the safeguarding of existing jobs, were satisfied. Payment of RDG has now ceased, although existing commitments under the scheme will be met in full until they have run their course.

The nature of regional assistance has now changed. Whereas RDG was available automatically if certain criteria were satisfied, this is no longer the case and **Regional Selective Assistance (RSA)** is now discretionary. RSA is a grant towards capital or training costs and is available for projects which;

- are likely to be financially viable,
- create or safeguard jobs,
- benefit the local or national economy,
- would not proceed without government money.

Two new **Regional Enterprise Grants** have also been introduced and are available to firms employing fewer than 25 people. An *investment grant* of 15 per cent up to a maximum of £15 000 is now available towards the costs of fixed assets. Additionally an *innovation grant* of 50 per cent up to a maximum of £25 000 is available to support product and process development.

## REVIEW QUESTIONS AND ANSWERS

### Questions

1  What is the difference between an ordinary share and a preference share?

2  Does a debenture holder own part of a joint 'stock company'?

3  Why is the gearing ratio important to firms?

4  What is 'exchanged' on the Stock Exchange?

5  Is ploughing back profit a costless source of finance for firms?

### Answers

3 Firms which have a high gearing ratio have a relatively high debt to share capital ratio, that is, they have relatively high debt obligations and must generate sufficient funds annually to meet interest payments, or face closure. However such firms might also have unstable equity (ordinary share) prices and might therefore be vulnerable to takeover. The high gearing ratio means that, in years when company profits are low, the return to ordinary shareholders will be low because of the need to meet interest payments and this may depress equity prices.

4 Shares in joint stock companies and loan stock issued by companies, local authorities and central government are exchanged for money, that is, they are bought and sold by Stock Exchange dealers.

| 1 | Ordinary shares | Preference shares |
|---|---|---|
| (i) | Carry voting rights at the AGM | Carry no voting rights |
| (ii) | Holders receive dividend after all preference shareholders have received full payment | Holders receive dividend up to a stated maximum before ordinary shareholders receive anything |
| (iii) | In the event of liquidation holders are the last group to receive any reimbursement on shareholding | In the event of liquidation holders receive the full face value of their shareholding before ordinary shareholders receive anything |

2 No. Debenture holders are simply creditors of the company. In other words, they simply lend the company money and are entitled to full annual payment of interest. If a company cannot pay interest on its debts the creditors can call in a receiver to recover their funds by selling company assets.

5 No. If a firm uses its own funds to finance investment, and this is easily the most important source of finance for most firms, interest is forgone on the funds used. There is therefore an *opportunity cost* to consider with internal finance.

# CHAPTER 10

# *PERFECT COMPETITION*

## Topic Summary

### Assumptions of Perfect Competition

Perfect competition is one particular market form based on several assumptions. Many of these assumptions are unlikely to exist in the real world, but, as we shall see on p. 57, perfect competition is important to economists because it leads to a particular pattern of resource allocation. The main assumptions of perfect competition are:

- There are **large numbers of buyers and sellers** in the market, each so small that individually they cannot influence market price.
- There is no product differentiation and all products are regarded as **perfect substitutes for each other**.
- Buyers and sellers are **well informed** about prices charged by producers.
- There are **no long run barriers** to the entry of firms into the market or their exit from the market.
- Producers aim to **maximise profit**.

The assumptions of perfect competition ensure that individual firms have no influence over market price and perceive their demand curve to be perfectly elastic at the ruling market price. If one firm attempted to raise price above that charged by other firms, consumers would buy from alternative suppliers. On the other hand, firms have no incentive to lower price, since they can sell their entire output at the existing market price. In other words the firm in perfect competition is a **price-taker**.

## A Note on Profit

Profit is often thought of as the difference between total revenue and total cost. However economists find it useful to identify **normal profit** as the cost

of the entrepreneur and if anything less than normal profit is earned in the long run the entrepreneur will leave the industry. Anything less than normal profit is referred to as a **loss** and anything in excess of normal profit is referred to as **supernormal profit**.

## Short Run Equilibrium: Supernormal Profit

In Figure 10.1 (on the following page) market supply and market demand are represented by *SS* and *DD* respectively. The market price is therefore *OP*. The firm perceives its own demand curve to be perfectly elastic at this price and produces where marginal cost (*MC*) equals marginal revenue (*MR*) so as to maximise profit. Profits are maximised when *MC* = *MR* because if *MC* > *MR* the last unit produced adds more to cost than to revenue, so profits fall. Conversely if *MC* < *MR* the last unit produced adds more to revenue than to costs so profits rise.

Note that, because the individual firm perceives its demand curve to be perfectly elastic at the ruling market price, marginal revenue always equals average revenue in perfect competition. The firm simply adjusts output so as to equate marginal cost with marginal revenue and in Figure 10.1 this implies an output of *OQ*. Total cost is given by the area *ORSQ* and total revenue is given by the area *OPTQ* so the firm earns supernormal profit of *RPTS*. We shall see later that these supernormal profits will be competed away in the long run.

## Short Run Equilibrium: Loss situation

In Figure 10.2 market supply and market demand are represented by *SS* and *DD* respectively and market price is *OP*. The firm adjusts output so as to equate marginal cost with marginal revenue and therefore produces *OQ*. Total cost is given by the area *ORSQ* and total revenue is given by the area

Figure 10.1   *Short run equilibrium in perfect competition: the firm earns supernormal profit*

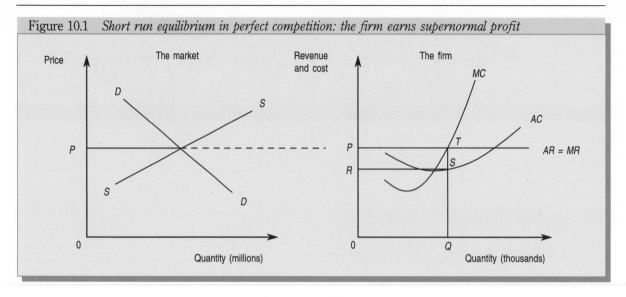

*OPTQ*. The firm therefore makes a loss of *RPTS*. However, losses cannot continue indefinitely and in the long run some firms will be forced to leave the industry.

## Long Run Equilibrium

We have seen that firms might make supernormal profits or a loss in the short run, but in the long run the assumptions of perfect competition ensure that all firms earn only normal profit. The existence of supernormal profits will attract other firms into the industry in the long run and, as market supply increases, price falls and it will go on falling until firms are earning only normal profit. Exactly the opposite happens in the case of a loss. Firms leave the industry in the long run. As a consequence market supply falls, price rises and goes on rising until those firms which remain in the industry earn only normal profit. Figure 10.3 shows the long run equilibrium of the firm in perfect competition.

The adjustment from short run supernormal profit to long run normal profit is easy to understand, but the adjustment from short run loss to long run normal profit is more difficult. Remember, from p. 49, that firms must cover their fixed costs whether they undertake production or not and will therefore remain in the industry in the short run only if they can *at least* cover their variable costs. Firms which cannot cover their variable costs will leave the industry immediately and in the long run any firm unable to cover total costs will cease production and withdraw from the industry.

Figure 10.2   *Short run equilibrium in perfect competition: the firm makes a loss*

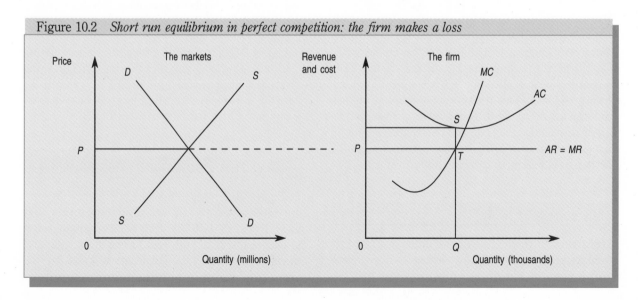

Figure 10.3   *Long run equilibrium in perfect competition: the firm earns normal profit*

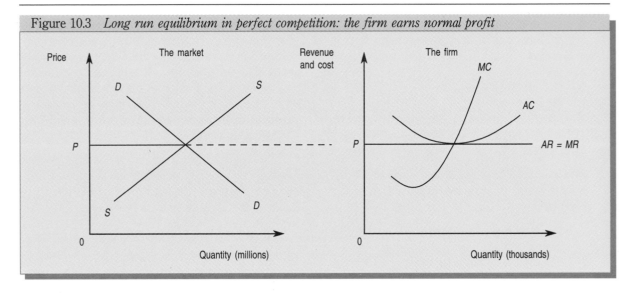

## Common Mistakes to Avoid

One very common source of confusion concerns the *accountants'* interpretation of profit and the *economists'* interpretation of profit. Intuitively it seems that profit is a residual, the amount left over after all accounting costs (raw materials, labour, premises and so on) have been met. This is indeed how accountants treat profit. However economists have coined the concept of *normal profit* as the long run cost of the entrepreneur. This is important because, since normal profit is treated as a cost of production, it is included in all cost schedules. Therefore to the economist normal profit is earned when a firm breaks even, whereas to the accountant no profit is earned when the firm breaks even because profit is treated as a residual rather than a cost of production.

Another very common source of confusion concerns **the aims of the firm**. In perfect competition it is assumed that firms aim to maximise profit. This aim never changes. Now in the long run in perfect competition the firm is forced to the point at which its average cost is reduced to a minimum, but it does not aim to achieve minimum average cost. It simply aims to maximise profit. In the long run the entry and exit of other firms forces any individual firm to move along its average cost curve so as to preserve the equality between marginal cost and marginal revenue as market price changes.

Another point to be aware of is the difference between allocative efficiency and productive efficiency. **Allocative efficiency** implies that resources are allocated in such a way that it is impossible to make one member of society better off by a reallocation of resources without simulta-

neously making at least one other member of society worse off. Now allocative efficiency occurs when marginal cost is equal to price. Remember, marginal cost is the cost of producing an additional unit. It therefore measures the opportunity cost of production because it can be thought of as the cost of attracting resources away from alternatives. On the other hand the price consumers are willing to pay for a product measures the value they place on it. When consumers pay an amount for the last unit they consume which exactly equals its opportunity cost of production, allocative efficiency exists.

**Productive efficiency** exists when a given output cannot be produced in a cheaper way by using an alternative technology or by reorganising the way in which factors of production are used. Firms are producing at their most efficient level when average cost is at a minimum.

Economists are more concerned with allocative efficiency, than productive efficiency which is of more interest to managers and engineers. Nevertheless the two are often confused, especially since, under perfect competition, allocative efficiency and technical efficiency coincide in the long run.

## Questions and Answers

### Questions

1  A perfectly competitive firm's marginal cost curve represents:

   (1)  the marginal variable costs of the product
   (2)  the marginal utility of the product

(3)  the firm's supply curve for the product
(4)  the least cost of production for any level of output

A    (1), (2) and (3) only
B    (1) and (3) only
C    (2) and (4) only
D    (4) only
E    (1) and (4) only
JMB, 1991

**2**  Which of the following features will confirm that a firm is operating under conditions of perfect competition?

A    Marginal cost cuts average cost at its lowest point
B    The firm does not advertise
C    Marginal revenue equals average revenue
D    The firm always produces at the optimum
E    Normal profits are earned
ULEAC, Jan 1991

## Answers

**1**  Marginal cost is the change in total cost when output changes by a single unit. Marginal cost is therefore unrelated to fixed cost and is determined entirely by the change in a firm's variable cost, that is, the firm's marginal variable cost. Option 1 is therefore correct. Marginal utility is the change in satisfaction a consumer experiences when consumption of a product changes by one unit. In other words, marginal utility is unrelated to marginal cost and so option 2 is incorrect.

Firms in perfect competition produce where marginal cost equals marginal revenue. However, in perfect competition, because the firm faces a perfectly elastic demand curve, marginal revenue always equals price. As price rises the firm will simply increase output until marginal cost again equals price. In perfect competition the firm's marginal cost

above its average variable cost curve is therefore its short run supply curve and option 3 is correct.

Firms in perfect competition aim to maximise profit. They do not aim to minimise costs. In the long run it is true that profit maximisation coincides with cost minimisation, but firms never *aim* to minimise costs. Option 4 is therefore incorrect.

The key is therefore B.

**2**  The relationship between marginal cost and average cost is a mathematical one and for all firms marginal cost will cut average cost at the lowest point on the average cost curve. Option A is incorrect.

In perfect competition there is no product differentiation so that an individual firm will never advertise its own product. However all firms might participate in collective advertising aimed at increasing demand for the product in general. Option B is therefore not correct.

In perfect competition the individual firm can sell as much as it wishes at the ruling market price. It therefore perceives its demand curve to be perfectly elastic at the ruling market price so that marginal revenue will always equal average revenue. This can only be true under perfect competition because in no other market structure will firms perceive their demand curve to be perfectly elastic at the ruling market price. Option C is therefore correct.

Firms produce at the optimum level when average cost is at a minimum. In the short run in perfect competition firms will either earn supernormal profit, in which case they will be operating above minimum average cost, or they will accept a loss, in which case they will be operating below minimum average cost. Only in the long run will they operate at the optimum level and therefore option D is incorrect.

In the long run firms in perfect competition earn only normal profit. However the same is true of firms in monopolistic competition and option E is therefore incorrect.

The key is C.

# REVIEW QUESTIONS AND ANSWERS

## Questions

1   Define and distinguish between the following terms: firm, industry and market.

2   Explain how economists distinguish between the *short run* **and** *long run*. Why are these concepts important to the theory of perfect competition?

3   Explain why a firm which is making losses in the short run might *increase* its output in the long run while the output of the industry *falls*.

4   Why are there no significant economies of scale in perfect competition?

## Answers

1   A firm is a unit of ownership. An industry consists of all firms engaged in producing the same output or using the same processes. A market is any arrangement or set of arrangements which brings buyers and sellers of a particular product into contact.

2   During the short run firms employ both fixed and variable factors. The long run is the time period required to bring about a change in the input of all factors of production and therefore in the long run there are no fixed factors of production. The distinction is important in perfect competition (and all other market structures) because it is argued that firms will cease production in the short run if revenue is insufficient to cover variable costs of production (see p. 49).

3   In Figure 10.4 *SS* and *DD* are the initial market supply and demand conditions. The market price is *P* and the firm's equilibrium output is *Q*. At this price and output the firm is making a loss of *PRST*. In the long run, as firms leave the industry market supply shifts to $S_1S_1$ and price rises to $P_1$. At the higher price the firm's equilibrium output has increased to $Q_1$. In other words firms that remain in the industry produce more, but total market supply falls.

4   If there were significant economies of scale firms would grow so as to exploit these economies. However, as firms grow, they acquire market power and a major assumption of perfect competition is that firms have no market power, that is, they are unable, by their own actions, to influence market price.

Figure 10.4   *The adjustment from short run loss to long run equilibrium in perfect competition*

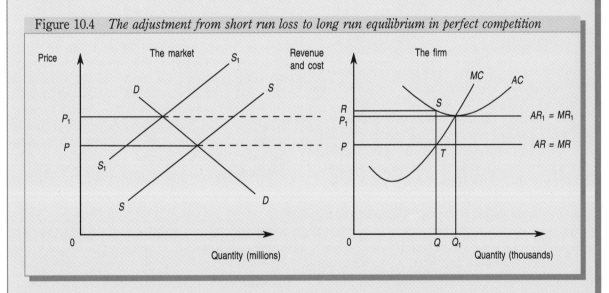

# CHAPTER 11

# *MONOPOLY*

## Topic Summary

A monopoly exists when supply of a particular good or service is in the hands of a single supplier, either a single firm (*pure monopoly*) or a group of firms who jointly coordinate their marketing plans (*a cartel*). By controlling supply a monopolist can influence price. However a monopolist lacks complete market power because of an inability to control demand. A monopolist can therefore either fix price and allow demand to determine output, or fix output and allow demand to determine price.

It is normally argued that monopolies will use their market power to drive up the price of their product so as to earn supernormal profit. However, if a monopoly is able to earn supernormal profit in the long run, there must be barriers which prevent the entry of new firms which would otherwise compete away supernormal profits.

## Barriers to Entry

*Legal barriers*  In the case of nationalised industries the state grants sole right of supply and this is undoubtedly the most complete barrier to entry.

*Natural monopoly*  A natural monopoly exists when production requires relatively high fixed investment so that the entire market is most efficiently supplied by a single firm. The classic example of a natural monopoly is electricity distribution, since it would be wasteful to have two national grids!

*Control of retail outlets*  The distribution of certain products requires a particular type of retail outlet and control of these can give a firm monopoly power. For example, many pubs are owned by the breweries and many filling stations are owned by the petrol majors.

*Control of raw materials*  In some cases a single supplier might control the supply of a particular raw material input. South Africa has a virtual monopoly of the world's supply of diamonds and most of the world's nitrates come from Chile.

*Cartels*  Producers might agree to coordinate their marketing activities so as to act as a single producer. Each firm party to the agreement accepts a quota on its output and in this way firms jointly restrict market supply to drive up price.

## The Monopolist's Equilibrium Output

The monopolist's demand curve is the market demand curve and like all normal demand curves it shows an **inverse relationship between price and quantity demanded**. Because of this, marginal revenue will always be less than average revenue under monopoly. For example, if the monopolist sells 1 unit for £100 but is forced to reduce price to £99 in order to increase sales to 2 units, average revenue will be £99 but marginal revenue will be £98, that is, $(2 \times £99) - £100$.

Although marginal revenue is less than average revenue under monopoly, the equilibrium condition remains the same as under perfect competition; that is, profit is maximised when marginal cost equals marginal revenue. In Figure 11.1 the equilibrium price and output combination of the monopolist is *OP* and *OQ* respectively and this results in supernormal profit of *PRST*. Of course these supernormal profits can only continue in the long run if, as we have seen, there are barriers which restrict the entry of new firms.

## Perfect Competition and Monopoly Compared

### Resource Allocation

We have seen on p. 57 that an optimum allocation of resources exists when price equals marginal cost. However, a glance at Figure 11.1 will confirm that a monopolist will never produce where marginal cost equals price because this will yield less profit than

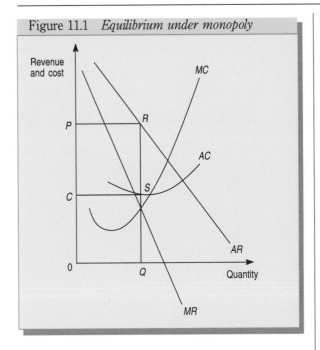

Figure 11.1 *Equilibrium under monopoly*

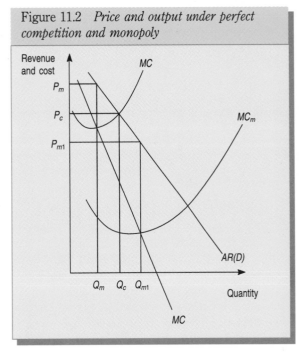

Figure 11.2 *Price and output under perfect competition and monopoly*

when marginal cost is equated with marginal revenue. Indeed, under monopoly, price will always be greater than marginal cost and therefore consumers value additional units of the monopolist's product more highly than they value alternatives (because they are prepared to pay an amount for additional units of the monopolist's product which is greater than the amount required to compete resources away from alternatives). In other words, it is argued that the allocation of resources is inferior under monopoly compared with perfect competition.

## Price and Output

In Figure 11.2, $AR(D)$ is the average revenue curve of a monopolist and the demand curve for the industry's product. The marginal revenue curve refers to the monopolist. Remember, while the market demand curve is downward sloping under perfect competition, the individual firm perceives its $AR$ and $MR$ curves to be horizontal at the ruling market price. $MC$ is the combined marginal cost curves of all firms in a perfectly competitive industry and in this sense could also represent the marginal cost curve for a monopolist.

Under perfect competition the marginal cost curve above the average variable cost curve is the firm's short run supply curve. It follows in terms of Figure 11.2 that equilibrium for the perfectly competitive industry occurs at price $P_c$ and $Q_c$. This compares with an equilibrium price and output under monopoly of $P_m$ and $Q_m$ respectively. It therefore seems

that price will be greater and output lower under monopoly than under perfect competition.

However, if a monopolist gains economies of scale, it is unrealistic to assume the same marginal cost curve as for a perfectly competitive industry. In fact, if economies of scale are significant enough, output will be greater and price lower under monopoly than under perfect competition. In Figure 11.2, $MC_m$ is the marginal cost curve of a monopolist and the equilibrium price and output in this case is $P_{m1}$ and $Q_{m1}$ respectively. Note that despite this the allocation of resources under monopoly is still sub-optimal because marginal cost is not equated with price. Nevertheless, although it is possible to improve the allocation of resources achieved under monopoly, it remains true that the allocation achieved under monopoly might be superior to that achieved under perfect competition because of the benefits of economies of scale!

## Research and Development

It is sometimes argued that competition will provide an incentive to invest in R&D as a means of acquiring a competitive advantage over rival firms. In fact there is no evidence that competition will necessarily have this effect. After all, many advances which result from successful R&D will be copied by rival firms and even patents only give limited protection since they can often by circumvented by producing similar designs or processes. On the other hand, we could argue that the supernormal profits of monopoly will provide the funds to finance R&D while the protected market ensures that successful R&D will lower costs and so raise the profits of the monopolist, thus providing the incentive to invest in R&D. It is certainly true that the pharmaceutical industry, which is dominated by very large scale producers, has a proven track record of successful R&D expenditure.

## Market Stability

Because a monopolist is the sole supplier in an industry it is argued that the response of supply to a change in demand will be more measured than might be the case when there are a number of competitive suppliers. For example, in competitive conditions an increase in demand might lead all firms in the industry to expand output and encourage the entry of other firms. This might lead to large swings in output, which would not happen under monopoly. It is argued that society benefits from market stability because large swings in output imply large swings in incomes and employment.

## Regulating Monopoly

Despite the points made above it remains true that monopolies sometimes have considerable influence on the price charged for particular products and have an obvious incentive to stifle the emergence of competition. Because of the possible abuse of monopoly power all advanced economies, including the UK, have some form of policy on monopoly. In the USA there is an outright ban on monopolies, but in the UK there is a case-by-case approach which aims to achieve the advantages of size but avoid the abuses of monopoly.

## Monopolies and Mergers Commission

The government has set up a Monopolies and Mergers Commission to investigate the behaviour of monopolistic firms which are referred for its consideration either by the Secretary of State for Industry or the Director General of Fair Trading. However most of its work in this area is now concerned with investigating proposed mergers which might create or strengthen the dominance of a firm in the market. In the course of its investigations the Commission can request any information from the firms under investigation that it thinks

relevant and in its report it has the power to make recommendations. In the case of a monopoly it might recommend that a firm discontinue certain practices and, in the extreme, that a firm be broken into competing units. Merger reports might indicate that the Commission feels a particular merger might operate in favour of, or against, the public interest.

One area of criticism is that the Commission has no teeth in so far as its recommendations are not automatically implemented. Implementation requires the **Secretary of State to lay Orders before Parliament** before recommendations are given the force of law. The criticism is that on many occasions the Secretary of State has chosen to ignore the Commission's recommendations, for reasons that are not always apparent.

## Taxing Monopoly Profits

It could be argued, that since supernormal profits result from a monopoly abusing its market power, one solution to the problem is to tax away supernormal profits. This would remove the incentive for a monopoly to abuse its power. However it is extremely difficult to identify the amount of profit which is supernormal and in any case taxing profits more heavily would simultaneously reduce the amount of funds available for investment and the incentive to undertake investment – something which is counter to the policy aims of all governments.

## Deregulation

Current policy in the advanced economies is to open markets up to competition by removing the legal barriers which prevent competition. Deregulation is discussed more fully on p. 224.

## Common Mistakes to Avoid

It is frequently thought that a monopolist will always charge the highest possible price for his (her) product. In fact the highest possible price exists when only a single unit is sold! No monopolist would ever restrict output to this level. In fact conventional theories of the firm normally assume that monopolists aim to maximise profits and charge whatever price is consistent with achieving this aim. It might well be that the price charged is above the minimum necessary to cover cost (including normal profit) but it is most certainly not the highest possible price!

Another area of difficulty is deciding whether monopolists produce where demand is elastic or inelastic. In fact profit maximising monopolists will always produce where demand is elastic because marginal revenue will only be positive when demand is elastic (see p. 18). Since marginal cost can never be negative, profit maximising monopolists must always produce where demand is elastic.

## Questions and Answers

### Questions

1 'If there was ever one phrase that outlived its relevance almost before it left the mouths of those who used it, "small is beautiful" must be it. As a catchphrase signalling the demise of the corporate giant and the rise of the little man, it was the most overused one in business life in the early 1980s.

The past few years have rendered the term meaningless as the biggest companies in a wide range of industries from food and drink manufacturing to domestic appliances gobbled up or elbowed out smaller and weaker companies.

During the past few weeks alone, big acquisitions in elevator manufacturing, pumps, power station equipment and printer machinery have tilted market power towards the bigger and tougher company. The merger process has indeed gathered pace over the past three years.

In engineering, clever specialist manufacturers will always survive. But the best of the bigger companies are becoming larger through acquisition and joint ventures. They are seeking control of more markets and broadening product ranges in order to offer the customer complete services and systems.'

(*Source*: Adapted from N. Garnett, 'The relentless drive for size', *The Financial Times*, 24 August 1988.)

(a) Why might the author suggest that 'in engineering, clever specialist manufacturers will always survive' (line 19)?
(5 marks)

(b) Analyse possible alternative motives in the trend towards acquisition. (5 marks)

(c) What are the implications for consumers of this trend towards acquisition? (5 marks)

(d) If a government is concerned about mergers, what policies can it pursue in order to preserve and promote competition?
(5 marks)

ULEAC, June 1991

2 Figure 11.3 shows the revenue and cost curves of a monopolist.

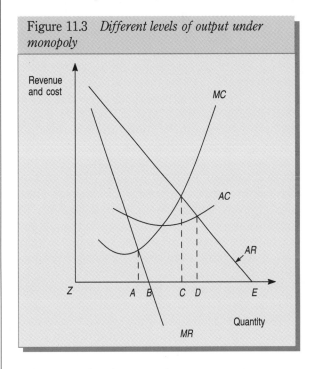

Figure 11.3 *Different levels of output under monopoly*

If the monopolist changes from an objective of profit maximisation to an objective of sales revenue maximisation, the equilibrium level of output will increase by:

A  ZA
B  ZB
C  ZC
D  ZD
E  ZE

3 For a profit maximising monopolist with positive costs in equilibrium,

1  marginal revenue is always positive
2  demand is elastic
3  Price always equals average cost
A  1, 2 and 3
B  1 and 2 only
C  2 and 3 only
D  1 only
E  3 only
ULEAC, January 1992

## Answers

**1** (a) In engineering clever specialist manufacturers will always survive because of the nature of the product they produce. Work of a specialist nature will tend to be produced in small firms because it will often serve a small market where mass production would be inappropriate. In other words, the work of specialist engineers will be tailored to the individual requirements of their clients. In such circumstances large firms cannot compete.

(b) The trend towards acquisition partly reflects the increased availability of economies of scale brought about by technological advances. When these become available firms will grow to exploit them because they lead to lower average costs and confer significant advantages on larger firms.

However it is also clear that acquisition reflects a quest for growth for other reasons. The creation of the Single Market in Europe will increase competition in manufacturing (and in services) and smaller firms will be at a considerable disadvantage. Acquisition might therefore be strategic and reflect a desire for survival in an increasingly competitive environment.

The desire to increase profit by increasing market domination is also a likely reason for the trend towards acquisition. As firms grow they acquire more power to stifle the growth of new entrants, partly because of the cost advantages available to larger firms, but they also acquire more influence over market price and can use this influence to increase profits. We are given some evidence in the text that firms might be concerned to restrict the growth of new entrants because we are told that firms are 'seeking control of more markets and broadening product ranges in order to offer the customer complete services and systems'.

(c) The implications for the consumer of the trend towards acquisition partly depends on the motives behind the trend. If firms aim to increase profits by using their influence to force up market price, income will be redistributed away from consumers in favour of producers. This is clearly not in the interests of consumers. On the other hand, if larger scale production leads to economies of scale and these are passed on to the consumer in the form of lower prices the consumer will gain.

Again it might be argued that, if the trend towards acquisition implies a reduction in competition because there are fewer firms in the industry, this will operate to the detriment of consumers. One way in which this would happen is that less competition might lead to higher prices, but another factor to consider is that less competition might imply a reduction in the range of products available to consumers. On the other hand, it might be argued that competition in markets dominated by a few large firms is more fierce than when there are many firms in the market. This might be so, but competition among larger firms does not always take the form of price competition, which is likely to be most important to consumers.

One way in which consumers might gain is through increased expenditure on research and development, which might lead to cost and price reductions but might also increase the range of products coming onto the market.

Smaller firms often provide more in the way of consumer service by catering for individual consumer requirements. Larger firms are broadening their own product ranges but the total range available to consumers might actually fall as smaller firms are eliminated. Again this would operate to the detriment of consumers.

(d) Various policies are available to government to control mergers. One policy option is to prohibit all mergers which create a firm which satisfies more than a given percentage of the total market. Such an approach would clearly protect the consumer from the emergence of monopolies through acquisition. However it would also deny consumers the possible benefits of a merger which creates a large scale producer. An additional consideration for the authorities is that, if acquisitions which create firms of more than a particular size are prohibited, domestic firms might be unable to compete with larger scale producers abroad, with the result that UK exports of that firm's product would fall and imports would increase. This is detrimental to the balance of payments and might also cause unemployment in the domestic economy.

A different approach is for the authorities to adopt a case-by-case approach as they do in the UK. This is a time consuming process which must be financed by the taxpayer, but it is designed to ensure that the benefits of a merger are gained while the possible abuses of monopoly power are avoided.

It is sometimes suggested that, if mergers lead to consumer exploitation and excessive profits for firms, the way to deal with this is to tax excess profits. In practice it is difficult to identify excess profits and it is generally conceded that higher rates of taxation have a disincentive effect on investment. If this is the case there will be an adverse effect on the consumer and on the economy. A lower level of investment would reduce the ability of domestic firms to compete internationally while it would also reduce the ability of firms to take advantage of the latest technological advances.

**2** For any producer, total revenue is maximised whenever marginal revenue is zero. Again this is a mathematical relationship but it should be clear that, when marginal revenue is zero, very small changes in sales will leave total revenue unchanged. Option A is therefore correct.

If the firm produces where marginal cost equals average cost it will minimise average cost but it will certainly not maximise sales revenue. Option B is therefore incorrect.

If all firms in the economy produce where marginal cost equals average revenue this will achieve an optimum allocation of resources but it will not maximise sales revenue for any individual firm. Option C is therefore incorrect.

If the firm produces where average cost equals average revenue it will earn only normal profit. Here again this strategy will not maximise sales revenue and so option D is incorrect.

If the firm produces at point E it will maximise sales but since average revenue is zero total revenue will also be zero. Option E is therefore incorrect.

The key is A.

**3** A profit maximising monopolist will always produce where marginal cost equals marginal revenue. Since the monopolist has positive costs in equilibrium, marginal cost will be positive and therefore marginal revenue must also be positive. Option 1 is correct.

Demand is elastic whenever a fall in price leads to an increase in total revenue. This condition is satisfied whenever marginal revenue is positive because marginal revenue is the addition to total revenue when output increases by one unit. Option 2 is therefore correct.

It is usually conceded that monopolists will earn supernormal profit and this implies that price will exceed average cost. It is only under exceptional circumstances that price will equal average cost. Option 3 is therefore incorrect.

The key is B.

## REVIEW QUESTIONS AND ANSWERS

### Questions

1 British Gas is a monopoly. Why, then, does it spend so much money on television advertising?

2 Is it possible for a monopoly to make losses?

3 Make a list of the advantages and disadvantages of monopolies. Are monopolies necessarily undesirable?

4 Compare the effects on a monopolist of a specific tax on its output and a lump-sum tax on its profits.

5 Why are patents granted to manufacturers who develop new products or techniques? Do patents restrict or encourage competition?

### Answers

1 British Gas has a monopoly in the supply of gas in the UK. However it does not have a monopoly in the supply of energy and in fact faces stiff competition, especially from the electricity generating boards such as Powergen. It is because of competition in the supply of energy that British Gas advertises its products on television and elsewhere.

2 No private sector firm can make losses indefinitely and survive. However all firms, whether they have a monopoly or not, may be prepared to accept a short run loss as long as they are able to cover their variable costs of production (see p. 49).

**3**

| Advantages | Disadvantages |
|---|---|
| (i) Possibility of economies of scale leading to lower prices than would exist in competitive markets | Possibility that monopolies will use their market power to restrict supply and drive up prices above levels that would exist in competitive markets. |
| (ii) As the sole supplier of a product, monopolies are likely to possess more complete knowledge of market demand than is available to any individual firm in a competitive market | In competitive markets changes in demand or supply can cause price fluctuations which might lead to further changes in output. |
| (iii) Monopolists have an incentive to improve design, delivery and quality of their product because this will increase their supernormal profits | There is a welfare loss under monopoly because marginal cost is not equated with price. In addition monopolists will rarely produce at minimum average cost and might have no incentive to improve the quality of their product. |

The advantages which monopoly might confer on society are potentially significant and if the abuses of monopoly power can be constrained, there might very well be a net benefit to society from monopoly.

**4** A specific tax on the output of a monopolist implies that a fixed rate tax is levied on each unit produced. This will shift the marginal cost curve upwards at each point by the full amount of the tax. The equilibrium output will therefore fall.

A lump sum tax on profits, on the other hand, implies that the same amount of tax is paid whatever level of profit is earned. It will therefore have no effect on the equilibrium output of the monopolist. It is worth noting that, if a tax is levied as a fixed percentage of profit so that the amount of tax paid rises as profit rises, there will still be no effect on the price or output of the monopolist.

# CHAPTER 12
# PRICE DISCRIMINATION

## Topic Summary

Price discrimination involves charging different consumers different prices for the same product, or the same consumer different prices for the same product. Although there are different types of price discrimination, they all require certain conditions to be met. These are briefly summarised below

## Conditions Necessary for Price Discrimination

### Monopoly Control

Supply of the product must be controlled by a monopolist. By definition, price discrimination implies that some consumers obtain the product at a lower price than other consumers. If supply is not controlled by a monopolist those consumers offered the higher price would obtain the product from an alternative supplier.

### Separation of Consumers

There must be clearly identifiable groups of consumers who are prepared to pay different prices for the product. Furthermore those consumers who buy the product at the lower price must be unable to resell to those consumers who buy the product at the higher price. In other words there must be no *seepage* between markets. Sometimes markets are separated by distance so that it is not economic for consumers to buy in the lower priced market and resell in the higher priced market. The most often quoted example of this is *dumping* in international trade when a firm sells products more cheaply in the world market than in the domestic market. The EC practices this when it disposes of its agricultural surpluses outside the EC. Seepage is prevented by controlling the re-

entry of food imports. Sometimes markets are separated by time as in the case of peak rates and off-peak rates for travel, telephone calls and electricity consumption. Sometimes there is separation by type of consumer, as with discounts offered to students and the unemployed.

## Different Elasticities of Demand

The conditions above make price discrimination possible but they do not necessarily make it profitable. In fact price discrimination will only be profitable when there are different elasticities of demand in the different markets in which the product is sold. It can be shown that, if price elasticity of demand is equal in different markets at any given price, marginal revenue will also be equal at that price. Since the monopolist maximises profit when marginal revenue equals marginal cost, it follows that profits cannot be increased by charging different prices.

## Types of Price Discrimination

Economists find it convenient to identify three classes of price discrimination: first degree, second degree and third degree. We consider each in turn.

## First Degree Price Discrimination

First degree price discrimination is the most complete form of discrimination because it involves paying a different price for each unit consumed. The aim of the monopolist is to charge exactly what the market will bear for each unit sold and in so doing remove completely any consumer surplus. In the real world first degree price discrimination is unlikely to exist because to practise it the monopolist requires perfect knowledge of every individual consumer's demand for the product.

## Second Degree Price Discrimination

Second degree price discrimination occurs when a consumer is charged different prices for the first few units consumed than for subsequent amounts consumed or when there are peak rates and off peak rates.

## Third Degree Price Discrimination

Third degree price discrimination occurs when at least two markets can be clearly identified by the monopolist. Figure 12.1 illustrates the way in which the monopolist fixes the equilibrium output and then divides this between two markets, *A* and *B*.

The average and marginal revenue curves in markets *A* and *B* are added together to obtain the total average and marginal revenue conditions facing the monopolist at each and every price. The monopolist simply equates marginal revenue in the combined market with marginal cost to obtain the profit maximising level of output. This is then divided between markets *A* and *B* so as to equate marginal revenue in each market with marginal cost. Note that the monopolist can only maximise profit when marginal revenue in each market is equal. For example, if marginal revenue in market *A* exceeded marginal revenue in market *B* the monopolist could increase profit by reducing sales in market *B* and diverting output to market *A*. This would increase profit because the last unit sold in market *A* adds more to revenue than the last unit sold in market *B*. It follows that profit can only be maximised when marginal revenue is equal in all markets.

## Common Mistakes to Avoid

Probably the most frequent source of confusion concerning **price discrimination** is distinguishing it from **price differences** associated with slight differences in the nature of the product. For example, the existence of first class and second class travel on British Rail does not imply price discrimination for rail users. First class and second class travel are different products and we would expect this to be reflected in some difference in prices. However the existence of discounts for students and senior citizens compared to other rail travellers is price discrimination because different rail users are paying different prices for the same product.

Similarly the existence of different prices for a good or service does not necessarily imply price discrimination. The most obvious reason for price differences is in fact competition between different suppliers. Price discrimination requires the same firm to charge different prices for the same product so that different consumers pay a different price, or the same consumer pays different prices per unit for different amounts of the product.

## Questions and Answers

### Question

1   A recent newspaper report stated that a Japanese businessman had been fined for going to Taiwan to purchase Japanese manufactured goods, reimporting them to Japan and selling

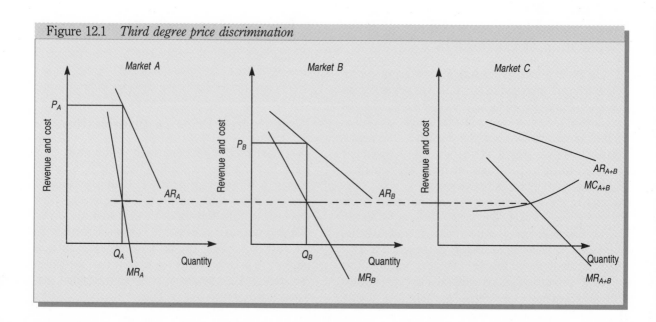

Figure 12.1   *Third degree price discrimination*

them at a price below the current market price. His offence was to breach the practice of price discrimination.

(a) Explain what price discrimination is and the circumstances necessary for it to be both successful and profitable. (10)

(b) How did the actions of the Japanese businessman affect the practice of price discrimination? (5)

(c) Who benefits and who loses as a result of the actions of the Japanese businessman? (10)

UCLES, November 1991

2 Which of the following is an example of price discrimination?

(1) A reduction at the turnstile for a child to watch a football match compared with the entrance fee paid by an adult.

(2) Bulk discounts on purchases of goods compared with the price paid for small amounts.

(3) A seat in a second-class compartment of a train compared with a seat in a first-class compartment.

(A) 1, 2 and 3
(B) 1 and 2 only
(C) 2 and 3 only
(D) 1 only
(E) 3 only.

## Answers

1 (a) Price discrimination exists when consumers in different markets are charged different prices for the same product. However not all cases of such differential pricing are examples of price discrimination. Suppliers might charge different prices when there are differences in the cost of supplying different consumers. In these circumstances there is no discrimination because it is the motive behind price differences that determines whether discrimination is taking place. In short, price discrimination exists when suppliers are charging different prices simply to increase profits.

Price discrimination is only possible when separate markets exist for a product, when different classes of consumer are charged different prices for a product, or where individual consumers are prepared to pay different prices per unit for different amounts of a product. For price discrimination to be possible three conditions must be satisfied:

- supply of the product must be controlled by a monopolist;
- there must be separate markets and the monopolist must possess knowledge of the demand for the product in different markets;
- resale of the product must be impossible.

Control of supply by a monopolist is essential because, if there are many suppliers of the product, competition among firms will prevent price discrimination. Furthermore knowledge of consumer demand is necessary, otherwise the monopolist will be unaware of the opportunity for price discrimination. Finally it must be impossible for consumers to buy the product at the lower price and then resell to other consumers who pay the higher price.

The conditions above make price discrimination possible but they do not necessarily imply that price discrimination will be profitable. Price discrimination will always be profitable when an individual consumer is prepared to pay different prices for the product because the monopolist will be able to reduce consumer surplus. However, when there are different markets, price discrimination can only be profitable if the elasticity of demand for the product is different in each market. If elasticity of demand was identical at each and every price, marginal revenue would be identical at each and every price and, because profit maximisation implies that marginal cost is equated with marginal revenue, the monopolist would maximise profits by charging a common price.

(b) It is not clear from the example we are given why the Japanese businessman was guilty of any kind of discrimination. By buying in one market and selling in another he acted more as an arbitrageur than one guilty of price discrimination. We are not told that he charged different consumers different prices. The implication is that, having purchased the product, he sold this in a single market at a uniform price. The fact that the price he charged was below the current market price is not discrimination!

Nevertheless the information we are given does contain evidence of price discrimination. We are told that the businessman bought a Japanese product in Taiwan that had been exported at a price below the current market price in the Japanese market. If this were not the case, how could the businessman undercut the price charged for the product in the Japanese market? It would seem that the exporting firm, by charging higher prices in the domestic market, was guilty of price discrimination rather than the businessman. However, even here we cannot be certain. It is possible that domestic sales are subject to some form of taxation from which exports are exempt. This would explain why it was cheaper to buy abroad. In these circumstances the businessman's actions might be regarded as unfair competition.

(c) One obvious gainer from the actions of the Japanese businessman is the businessman himself! There are costs involved in his actions, in particular the cost of purchasing goods in Taiwan and shipping them to Japan. For this to be profitable the businessman must be able to sell at a profit in the Japanese market.

A section of Japanese consumers also gain because of the businessman's action. Those consumers who buy from the Japanese businessman are able to obtain at a lower price a product from abroad which is identical to that produced for the domestic market. This clearly improves the standard of living of those consumers who purchase the good imported from Taiwan because it implies that they are able to increase their total utility.

The economy of Taiwan also gains because of the businessman's actions. By re-exporting to Japan they add value to the product they import and this has a favourable effect on the balance of payments. It also creates employment in Taiwan and no doubt adds to government revenue through increased tax yields.

There are also losers from the businessman's action. The Japanese manufacturing firm loses sales in the domestic market. Clearly demand for the product exceeds the amount supplied by domestic sources at the existing price. It is therefore reasonable to assume that many consumers who purchase the good imported from Taiwan would purchase from a domestic supplier if the imported substitute were not available. If Japanese manufacturers are selling to Taiwan at lower prices than they are offering in the domestic market, then the lost sales to imports from Taiwan imply lower sales revenue and lower profits for domestic suppliers than would otherwise be earned.

Just as the actions of the businessman might benefit the economy of Taiwan there will be a reciprocal loss to the Japanese economy. The value added in Taiwan implies an increase in net imports which adversely affects the Japanese balance of payments. Similarly lower sales from domestic suppliers might adversely affect employment in Japan and imply lost tax revenue to the Japanese government.

**2** Price discrimination occurs when consumers pay different prices for the same product or when the same consumer pays different prices for the same product. Option 1 is correct because different consumers pay different prices for the same product. Option 2 is also correct. In this case either different consumers, or the same consumer, will pay different prices for the same good depending on the amount bought. However, option 3 is clearly incorrect. In this case different consumers purchase a different product.

The key is B.

## REVIEW QUESTIONS AND ANSWERS

### Questions

1  Consider whether or not each of the following is a case of price discrimination. Give your reasons in each case, and for each instance of price discrimination, state how the conditions (such as avoiding separation between markets) have been achieved:

(a)  The Ford Motor Company offers a fleet of Ford Fiestas to the British School of Motoring at a substantial discount.

(b)  Industrial users of electricity are charged a different price to domestic users.

(c)  Business travellers flying from London to Madrid by scheduled air services pay higher prices than holidaymakers on a package deal.

(d)  A concert is advertised with seats at no fewer than *nine* different prices.

(e)  Surplus butter from the EC is sold cheaply to Russia, and is given away to British senior citizens.

(f)  Parents pay different contributions towards their children's university education, depending on income.

Question 2 is based on the following article:

## A Large Beef About Oxo

Are you paying too much for Oxo cubes? It has come out in a court case that Brooke Bond's export price for Oxo cubes is 42 per cent cheaper than shops in Britain pay. On the face it that should mean that a packet of Oxo selling at around 38p in your local shop should cost only 22p.

Brooke Bond could not explain its double pricing because all its experts are busy giving evidence at the trial.

The defendants are accused of trying to buy Oxo at the cheaper export price in order to sell it in Britain at a profit.

Surely the real crime is that firms operate such two-faced pricing systems in the first place.

I look forward to hearing Brooke Bond's explanation when its experts can spare me the time.

*Source*: *Daily Mirror* (28 October 1987).

(a) How does your knowledge of price discrimination enable you to analyse the behaviour of Brooke Bond with respect to the pricing of Oxo cubes?

(b) One of the conditions for price discrimination to exist is a 'separation of markets' with no 'seepage' between markets.
   (i) Explain how this condition seems to have broken down in the Oxo case.
   (ii) Would you agree that the continuation of price discrimination partly depends on consumer ignorance?
   (iii) Suggest why the company appears to be willing to go to the expense of a court case in order to maintain separate markets.

(c) Apart from the condition referred to in (b), how are the other conditions for price discrimination likely to apply to Oxo?

(d) What possible reasons might Brooke Bond put forward to try to justify their pricing policy, and how might these differ from an economist's analysis of the matter?

## Answers

**1** (a) Discounts offered for bulk purchases are an example of price discrimination. One buyer obtains the product at a lower average price than another buyer.

(b) This is another example of price discrimination. Different buyers purchase an identical product but pay different prices.

(c) This is not price discrimination. Scheduled flights have preference over package flights in terms of flight departures (delays on package flights are frequent and often lengthy) and in terms of in-flight provisions for passengers.

(d) Whether this is price discrimination or not depends on why different prices are charged. If different prices are charged for different seats there is no discrimination. On the other hand, if different prices reflect concessions made to different groups such as pensioners, the unemployed and students, this is clearly price discrimination.

(e) This is clearly a case of price discrimination because purchasers in the EC pay a higher price than Russian consumers and British senior citizens, who receive butter free of charge.

(f) If parents are required to pay a portion of their son's or daughter's university fees which is related to their income, this would indeed be price discrimination because parents would effectively be charged a different price for their son's or daughter's university education. However at present this does not happen in the UK. At present parents with a relatively high combined income simply have responsibility for making a contribution towards their child's grant. This is not price discrimination because in this case parents are not purchasing anything.

**2** (a) Brooke Bond are selling Oxo cubes in the domestic market at a higher price than consumers pay abroad. The aim is probably to increase profits and the higher price in the domestic market probably reflects a lower elasticity of demand than in export markets.

(b) (i) The information we are given indicates that an attempt has been made by a buyer or buyers to purchase Oxo cubes in the cheaper export market and resell them in the more expensive domestic market. Presumably the Oxo cubes would have been sold in the domestic market at a price below that which Brooke Bond charges domestic consumers.

(ii) In this case it would seem that consumer ignorance was an important barrier preventing seepage between markets. However, since Brooke Bond is taking action in the courts, there might also be some legal barrier preventing purchase and resale. In general the continuation of price discrimination requires the fulfilment of certain conditions, one of which is the existence of barriers which prevent seepage between markets. Consumer ignorance is one possible barrier, but it is not the only one and is by no means a necessary condition for the continuation of price discrimination.

(iii) Brooke Bond clearly believe the ending of price discrimination will adversely affect profits. The fact that they are seeking action through the courts to maintain the practice indicates this, but might also indicate that some legal regulation has been breached by the buyer's actions.

(c) Brooke Bond has a monopoly over the supply of Oxo cubes and if there is greater competition from substitutes in export markets the elasticity of demand for Oxo cubes will differ between the domestic market and the export market.

(d) The most obvious reason Brooke Bond might use to justify its policy of price discrimination is that competition in the international market forces prices down to levels at which the company simply breaks even and realises a profit from its domestic operations. It might even argue that additional export sales make possible economies of scale and, in the absence of these, prices might even be higher in the domestic market. Depending on the levels of profit actually earned, an economist might interpret Brooke Bond's action as simply exploiting its monopoly position to increase its own profits.

## CHAPTER 13

# *IMPERFECT COMPETITION*

## Topic Summary

### *Product Differentiation*

Competition is said to be imperfect when products are **differentiated** in some way. Products are differentiated either because they are **real** or **imaginary** differences between them. Real differences might be based on the use of different additives to produce a product or on slight differences in design. Imaginary differences are created through **advertising** which highlights some desirable, though indefinable quality a product purports to possess but which is not possessed by other products. In the case of real differences between products, advertising is used to reinforce differentiation.

### *Monopolistic Competition*

#### Assumptions

Monopolistic competition exists when certain conditions are satisfied. In summary these are:

- There are **many sellers** of a slightly differentiated product.
- There are **many buyers** each so small they have no individual ability to influence price.
- No single firm dominates the market, but each individual firm is **large enough to influence market supply and therefore market price**.
- In the long run firms are **free to enter or leave** the industry.

In such markets there will clearly be *competition* between firms since they produce only a slightly differentiated product. However it is important to note that there is also an element of *monopoly*: each firm has a monopoly over its own brand of the product.

### Equilibrium

Because of product differentiation, the firm in monopolistic competition will face a downward sloping demand curve for its product. If it increases price it will lose some, but not all, of its customers. Brand loyalty ensures it will retain some of its customers. Similarly by reducing price it will be able to increase sales. This implies that, as in pure monopoly, average revenue and marginal revenue will fall as sales increase. It also implies that the firm's marginal revenue curve will lie below its average revenue curve. Short run equilibrium under monopolistic competition is therefore identical to monopoly equilibrium and is illustrated in Figure 13.1.

The firm maximises profit when it equates *MC* with *MR*. It will therefore produce *OQ* units and charge a price of *OP* per unit. However, if we subtract total cost (*OTSQ*) from total revenue

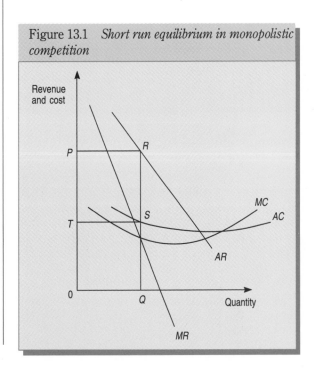

Figure 13.1   *Short run equilibrium in monopolistic competition*

(*OPRQ*), it is clear that the firm is earning supernormal profit equal to *PRST*.

Because there are no long run barriers to entry, the existence of supernormal profit will attract other firms into the industry. As more firms enter the industry, the demand for any individual firm's product will fall and its average revenue curve will therefore shift to the left. Demand for the firm's product will also become more elastic at any given price because consumers now have a wider range of products to choose from. The extent of the firm's monopoly power therefore decreases as the number of firms entering the industry increases. In fact firms will go on entering the industry until supernormal profits have been competed away and all firms earn only normal profit. This is illustrated in Figure 13.2.

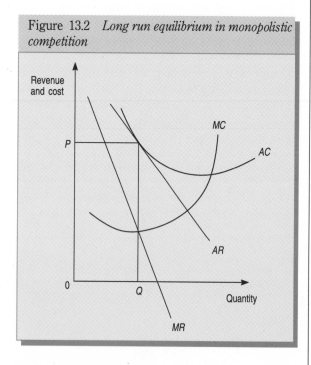

Figure 13.2 *Long run equilibrium in monopolistic competition*

In Figure 13.2 the firm is maximising profit when price is *OP* and output is *OQ* because at this price and output combination marginal cost is equal to marginal revenue. However, at the equilibrium price and output, the firm's average cost curve is just tangential to its average revenue curve and therefore, when the firm is in equilibrium, total revenue equals total cost, that is, the firm earns only normal profit. This is just sufficient to attract other firms into the industry. When normal profits are earned the industry is therefore in long run equilibrium.

## Oligopoly

Oligopoly is usually referred to as **competition among the few**. Of course the term 'few' cannot be interpreted unambiguously. We cannot say five is few but six is not! However the crucial point in oligopolistic markets is that the number of sellers is so small that the market is characterised by **interdependence**. In other words, each firm produces a significant part of total market supply and therefore any decision to adjust its price or its output will have repercussions on other firms in the industry.

The model of oligopoly is usually generalised so that there are several producers of a slightly differentiated product. Such markets are easy to identify. Petrol, car tyres, motor vehicle production and so on are all examples of oligopolistic markets. However economists sometimes distinguish **perfect oligopoly** in which there is no product differentiation, from **imperfect oligopoly**, as described above. They also identify a special case of oligopoly, **duopoly**, in which there are only two producers. In this chapter we stick to the general case.

## Price Stability in Oligopoly

One feature of oligopolistic markets that attracts attention is their **relative price stability**. It is sometimes alleged that, once established, prices in oligopolistic markets will remain fixed for relatively long periods. Furthermore, when prices do change, all firms in the industry adjust prices either **simultaneously** or in **quick succession**. There are several possible reasons for this but the three most commonly suggested are the **kinked demand curve**, **price leadership** and **collusion**. We examine each in turn.

### The Kinked Demand Curve

In oligopolistic markets, the entire supply of a product consists of the output of a few large scale producers. Because of this, oligopolistic markets are characterised by a high degree of interdependence between producers. Any decision by one firm to adjust its output will affect all other firms because of its impact on market price. In forming price and output policies, therefore, each firm must consider how its rivals will react to any change.

Oligopolistic behaviour has therefore been likened to a game of chess. Before making any move it is necessary to consider how an opponent will react. This idea underpins the notion that oligopolists consider their demand curve to be *kinked* at the ruling market price. If we assume that there is no change in costs of production or demand for the product, if one firm raises price it will do so in isolation. Other firms have no incentive to increase price because they will gain consumers from the firm which does raise its price. For a price increase a firm's demand curve will therefore be relatively elastic. On the other hand, if one firm reduces price all other firms will be forced to match the price cut to avoid losing customers. For a price cut, therefore, the individual firm faces a relatively inelastic demand curve. This approach implies that each firm perceives its own demand curve to be kinked at the ruling market price' as shown in Figure 13.3.

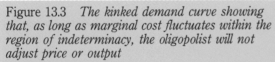

Figure 13.3 *The kinked demand curve showing that, as long as marginal cost fluctuates within the region of indeterminacy, the oligopolist will not adjust price or output*

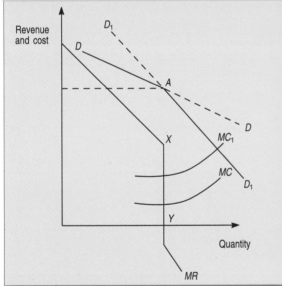

In Figure 13.3, *DD* is the appropriate demand curve for a price rise, and $D_1D_1$ is the appropriate demand curve for a price reduction. The kink at the ruling market price, *P*, gives the oligopolist a perceived demand curve of $DAD_1$. Because the oligopolist is simultaneously at a common point on two demand curves, the associated marginal revenue curve will be discontinuous and will be indeterminate at the kink in the demand curve. Even if costs of production change, so long as marginal cost remains

within the *region of indeterminacy*, *XY*, the oligopolist has no incentive to change price or output.

The implications of this analysis can be further extended. If costs move out of the region of indeterminacy it is likely that oligopolists will adjust prices and possibly output. However, if costs are rising for one firm, they are likely to be rising for all firms and by equal amounts. After all, since firms produce a similar product they are likely to use similar techniques. All that will happen when costs increase is that all firms will increase prices simultaneously or at least in reasonably quick succession. Consequently a new price will be established and each oligopolist will perceive their demand curve to be kinked at the new market price.

Despite its obvious appeal, it is important to note that the kinked demand curve is not a complete theory of oligopolistic behaviour. It simply explains why prices might be stable, but tells us nothing about how those prices are established in the first place. Other theories of oligopoly have more to say on this issue.

## Price Leadership

Another approach to oligopolistic behaviour is that a *price-leader* exists. This firm leads the way in initiating a price change and other firms simply follow suit. In the case of **dominant firm price leadership** the largest firm in the industry performs the leadership role. Other firms in the industry accept the power of the dominant producer to influence market supply and price, and simply follow any changes this firm initiates. A different approach is **barometric price leadership**, when firms in the industry accept that one firm interprets changes in supply and demand conditions more accurately than other firms and simply follow changes initiated by the barometric leader.

Again this gives a possible explanation of price stability in ologopolistic markets, but it also provides a more complete theory of oligopoly. Prices are stable because they are established by the leader and other firms simply react passively to any changes the leader initiates. This is a more complete theory of oligopoly because we can identify the way in which prices might be set in oligopolistic markets. The leader is able to act in the same way a monopolist would act because there is no fear of competition. The leader therefore simply adjusts price and output so as to maximise profit and other firms charge the same price as the leader and adjust their output so as to preserve this price.

## Collusion

A third approach stresses that, because there are only a few producers in oligopolistic markets it is relatively easy for firms to *collude* over price and output decisions. The highest degree of collusion exists when firms form a *cartel*. In this case firms agree on a common price and accept output quotas to ensure that the agreed price is maintained. Here again we have a possible explanation of price stability and a more complete theory of oligopolistic behaviour than is offered by the kinked demand curve. Prices are stable because they are fixed by agreement. In the case of a cartel the combined marginal cost of all producers is equated with the overall marginal revenue curve to give the profit maximising price and output for the cartel as a whole, and then the output is divided into quotas which are allocated to members according to some agreed formula.

Most cartels are illegal in the UK because the aim is clearly to establish higher prices than would exist in competitive conditions. Economists also argue that, since cartels effectively function as a monopoly, there is an implied efficiency loss which occurs whenever price is not equated with marginal cost (see p. 57). However, unlike the case of pure monopoly, there is no possibility of an offsetting gain in productive efficiency through the realisation of economies of scale.

## Common Mistakes to Avoid

It will be recalled from p. 75 that in the long run, under conditions of monopolistic competition, the firm earns only normal profit. However it must not be inferred from this that monopolistic competition is as efficient a market form as perfect competition. Remember, in monopolistic competition each firm has a monopoly over the supply of its own brand. Even in the long run each firm therefore faces a downward sloping demand curve for its own product and in maximising profit it will never equate price with marginal cost as occurs in perfect competition in the long run. As in pure monopoly there is a welfare loss associated with monopolistic competition.

It is also important not to confuse price leadership with the existence of a cartel where there is a formal agreement among firms to charge a common price for their product. In the case of *price leadership*, firms choose to follow the leader and are perfectly free to pursue a different policy at any time. In neither case

of price leadership, is there an agreement, tacit or otherwise, to follow all courses of action initiated by the leader, nor is there any exchange of information between managers about price and output changes or other marketing strategies. There is certainly no agreement to accept a quota which fixes each firm's output. All of these are characteristic features of a *cartel*.

## Questions and Answers

### Questions

1  Which of the following distinguishes perfect competition from monopolistic competition?

   A   A large number of firms in the industry
   B   No barriers against firms entering or leaving the industry
   C   Many buyers of the product or service
   D   Small firms, in relation to the size of the industry
   E   A homogeneous product or service
   ULEAC, June 1991

2  In oligopolistic markets the existence of a kinked demand curve implies that

   1   Firms avoid competition between each other.
   2   Prices do not change unless costs of production change.
   3   Oligopolists are aware of a high degree of interdependence between them
   A   1, 2 and 3
   B   1 and 2 only
   C   2 and 3 only
   D   1 only
   E   3 only

### Answers

**1** Both perfect competition and monopolistic competition assume the industry consists of a large number of small firms. This implies an absence of significant economies of scale so that no firm grows to a size where it can dominate the market. Option A is incorrect.

Both market forms also assume there are no barriers to entry or exit. It is this assumption which ensures that in both markets firms only earn normal profit in the long run. Option B is incorrect.

In both markets there are many buyers of the product or service, which implies that no single buyer can influence price. Option C is incorrect.

Similarly, as explained above, firms remain so small they are unable by their individual actions to exert any influence on market price. Because of this we can assume away any possibility of retaliation by other firms if one firm changes its price. Other firms will not retaliate because they will be unaffected! Option D is incorrect.

In perfect competition a homogeneous product or service is supplied, whereas in monopolistic competition each firm has a monopoly over its own brand of the product. This is what distinguishes perfect competition from monopolistic competition. Option E is correct.

The key is E.

**2** In oligopolistic markets the existence of a kinked demand curve implies an absence of price competition between two rival firms but it most certainly does not imply a total absence of competition. Indeed oligopolistic markets are often characterised by a high degree of non-price competition between firms. Option 1 is correct.

The theory of the kinked demand curve does not imply that the only influence on price is costs of production. It is quite possible that a change in demand for the product, independently of any change in costs of production, will result in a change in oligopolistic prices. Option 2 is correct.

If firms perceive their demand curve to be kinked at the ruling market price, this implies the existence of a high degree of interdependence between them. They believe that if they raise the price of the product they will do so in isolation and will therefore lose sales to rival firms. On the other hand, they believe that if they cut the price of their product other firms will be obliged to match the price cut to avoid a loss of sales. It is such interdependence which gives rise to the possibility of a kinked demand curve and therefore option 3 is correct.

The key is E.

## REVIEW QUESTIONS AND ANSWERS

### Questions

Question 1 is based on the following extract:

# Oil price tumbles – 14 dollars a barrel

### By GEORGE SIVELL, City Editor

NORTH SEA oil prices fell below 14 dollars a barrel yesterday for the first time since the 1986 oil crisis. At one stage yesterday a barrel of North Sea crude could have been had for as little as 13.85 dollars, a fall of a dollar on the day.

Concern in the City over the oil price has mounted in the past few days as it has become clear that the relatively mild European winter and continued strong production by the Opec cartel have left oil stocks at the highest level for five years.

Opec production is now estimated at just below 17 million barrels a day for January and just above for February.

These levels are still within the agreement which was rolled over at the December Opec meeting but the pressure still remains on prices because certain states are coming under pressure to offer discounts to their main customers.

Such has been the level of discounting that prices on the oil markets are now four dollars adrift of the official Opec price of 18 dollars a barrel.

Prices have held to an average 18 dollars over the past year but dipped to just below 16 dollars in mid-December on dismay that Opec had failed to agree firmer production quotas or pricing controls.

Opec is not due to meet again until June and in the meantime Saudi Arabia, which took up any production slack, has complicated matters by abandoning its role as a swing producer.

Before the oil price crisis of 1986 the Saudis would always cut output when production accelerated and prices weakened.

But Saudi Arabia actually increased production from an estimated four million barrels in January to 4.3 million barrels in February.

"March is going to be a very severe test for the oil market," said one analyst last night.

**Source:** *Western Mail*, 3 March 1988.

(a) On what grounds would the extract lead to the conclusion that oil is not bought and sold in a perfect market?

(b) Saudi Arabia is described in the extract as a 'swing producer'. Explain this term, and describe how the abandoning of this role destabilises oil prices.

(c) Describe the effects on the price and output of oil of the events of August 1990 when Iraq invaded Kuwait.

2 Since *excess capacity* is a prediction of the theory of monopolistic competition, does it necessarily follow that society would benefit from a reduction in the number of firms in such a market?

3 Under monopolistic competition price taking does not occur. Explain why it is nevertheless likely that firms will have only very limited control over the market clearing price.

4 It can be argued that the banking industry, which was once very oligopolistic and collusive in the UK, is now much more competitive. What factors have influenced this trend?

5 Is collusion between firms necessarily undesirable?

6 Describe and account for differences in expenditure on advertising between industries.

## Answers

1 (a) There is clear evidence in the extract we are given that the oil market is not perfect. We are told in the second paragraph that oil stocks are at least influenced by a cartel. In perfect competition it is assumed that there are many suppliers of a product who act independently. We are further told in the fourth paragraph that certain OPEC members are under pressure from buyers to offer a discount on oil sales. Again under perfect competition each buyer is so small that they are unable to influence the price of the product. Later we are told that Saudi Arabia is a 'swing producer', that is, a supplier which heavily influences the market supply. This is yet another breach of the assumptions of perfect competition.

(b) A swing producer is a supplier which adjusts its output in response to changes in market demand for a product so as to preserve an agreed market price. By abandoning this role

Saudi Arabia is free to adjust its output of oil so as to achieve its own aims. We are told in the extract that Saudi Arabia increased its output at a time when there was already a surplus of oil on the market and this explains why the price of oil tumbled to 14 dollars a barrel.

(c) Kuwait was a major exporter of oil before the Gulf War. Immediately after Iraq invaded Kuwait, exports from Iraq and Kuwait were cut off and the world supply of oil fell. The price of oil inevitably increased but not by as much as was feared. There are several reasons for this. For example, Saudi Arabia and several other OPEC members increased their output, President Bush released the strategic oil reserves onto the American market and the Gulf War did not, as was feared at one stage, spread throughout the Arab world.

2 Firms in monopolistic competition will always cease production at a point where average cost is still falling and will therefore always operate with excess capacity. However fewer firms will not necessarily result in firms increasing their output and moving to the point of minimum average cost. A reduction in the number of firms implies an increase in monopoly power for those firms remaining in the industry. Because of this, the reduction in competition might actually increase inefficiency!

3 Firms in monopolistically competitive markets have only limited, if any, ability to influence market price because individually they produce such a small part of total market supply.

4 Deregulation of the banking industry has outlawed collusion in banking and increased the number of firms offering banking services. There has also been an increase in the number of foreign banks establishing premises in the UK. Another factor has been the reduction in the cost of banking activities, in particular the cost of clearing cheques, made possible by technological advances.

5 Collusion, by ensuring price stability, might have beneficial effects on society. It ensures long run supply of the product and might guarantee the existence of smaller producers who might otherwise be forced out of the market.

6 Differences in advertising expenditures largely reflect different degrees of competition in different markets.

## CHAPTER 14
# *LABOUR*

## Topic Summary

As a factor of production, labour refers to the input of human effort. The value of this input is quite substantial, and even in a developed economy such as the UK, labour costs account for well over 50 per cent of the total value of output produced.

## *Division of Labour*

Division of labour refers to **specialisation of labour**. This might imply specialisation in a particular occupation, but increasingly labour now specialises in the performance of a particular task or small group of tasks within an occupation. Division of labour is common in all sectors of industry: primary, secondary and tertiary alike.

### The Advantages of Specialisation

Specialisation is so common because it **facilitates an increase in productivity**. There are several reasons for this but in general the main reason is that specialisation makes possible the use of more specialised capital equipment. Without specialisation of labour, investment in specialised units of capital would be uneconomic because they would not be in use continuously throughout the working day. Without continuous use, the average cost of such capital equipment would be prohibitive. It is also true that when workers specialise less time is wasted, since they are not moving from job to job. In addition it is easier to train workers since they only perform a narrow range of tasks and by their repeating the same tasks throughout the working day the speed at which they perform these tasks is likely to increase.

For whatever reasons productivity increases, the fact that it does confers a major benefit on society. Strictly an increase in productivity implies an increase in output from a given amount of input. When productivity increases, therefore, society is using its resources more efficiently and, as we shall see on

p. 220, this is one of the sources of **economic growth**.

### The Disadvantages of Specialisation

Despite the advantage of raising productivity, increased division of labour also has certain disadvantages. For the majority of workers there is no doubt that **increased productivity implies increased boredom**. On the other hand, higher productivity has led to higher real wages. For individual firms (and the economy as a whole) a more serious problem is that if a small group of key workers are absent from work, for example because of illness or strike action, production can be seriously disrupted and in some cases can grind to a halt.

## *Mobility of Labour*

There are two broad types of mobility: *geographical* and *occupational*. Geographical mobility refers to the movement of a factor of production from one location to another, whereas occupational mobility refers to a factor of production changing its occupation. Both types of mobility are important if an economy is to operate efficiently. Consumer demand and technology are constantly changing, and without a mobile labour force it is impossible to respond fully to these changes.

### Population

Population growth is important to economists because it affects the future supply of labour and the future demands on a nation's (or the world's) resources.

### The Labour Supply

Many factors determine the potential labour supply to an economy. The main factors can be summarised as follows:

**Size of Population**   Other things being equal, the larger a nation's population, the larger its potential supply of labour. Population size depends on the *birth rate* **and the** *death rate* **plus** *net migration*, that is, *emigration minus immigration*.

**Population Age Structure**   An economy with a large proportion of people at or above retirement age and/or a large proportion under school leaving age will tend to have a smaller labour supply, though as children mature they will add to the labour supply. As well as the age structure of the population, the minimum school leaving age and the age of retirement have important effects on the supply of labour.

**Population Sex Structure**   In all countries men are more likely to seek paid employment than women. There are many possible reasons for this. In Moslem countries religious principles prevent most women from entering the labour market. In other countries women often withdraw from the labour market to raise a family. For whatever reason, if the sex structure of a nation's population is more heavily biased in favour of women than men, then, if all other things are equal, the labour supply will be smaller than if men outnumber women.

**Standard Working Week**   The labour supply is usually measured in number of hours per week. The number of hours worked per day, length of the working week and the number of public holidays per year will all therefore influence the supply of labour.

## UK Population Trends

The UK population exhibits certain characteristics that are common to most developed countries: a declining birth rate (number of live births per thousand of population) and a declining death rate (number of deaths per thousand of population). The decline in the birth rate is relatively slight from year to year, whereas the decline in the death rate is more marked. If the birth rate continues to decline it will ultimately lead to a falling population, but at present the decline in the birth rate is so slight that the focus of attention is the increasing average age of the population.

In general an ageing population might have several effects:

● An ageing population implies an increase in the **dependency ratio**, that is, the ratio of the

working population to total population. A rising dependency ratio implies that the working population will have to support a larger number of non-working people. In a developed economy like the UK this implies that the *standard of living* (output per head – see p. 105) will rise less quickly than it would have done if the population had remained static.

● An ageing population will cause changes in the pattern of demand for different goods and services. For example, more demands will be made on the health services and on the social services. There will be an increased demand for sheltered accommodation, and so on.

● It is usually very difficult for younger people to save out of current income. Personal sector saving tends to be undertaken by other groups and it seems reasonable to suggest that an ageing population will be associated with an increase in personal sector saving. Additional saving will make possible a higher level of investment and might increase productivity.

● An ageing population is a less mobile population both geographically and occupationally. However the effect of this is difficult to ascertain. In the UK the main reason for the increase in the average age of the population is that there has been an increase in life expectancy, that is, those of retirement age and over now live longer. Since those in this group are not part of the labour force, a reduction in their mobility has no relevance!

## The Optimum Population

An optimum population is said to exist when *average product is at a maximum*. If the population is less than the optimum, a nation is said to be underpopulated and if it is greater than the optimum it is said to be overpopulated. These concepts are illustrated in Figure 14.1. The optimum size of population in this case is *ON*.

Many factors determine the optimum population and it is not a static concept. An increase in the capital stock, or the skills the labour force possess, will increase the optimum population. Discoveries of raw materials such as oil in the North Sea will also affect what is considered an optimum population. However, in modern economies the most important factor is undoubtedly technological progress. In particular, greater technological progress, by increasing the productivity of labour, will increase the optimum population.

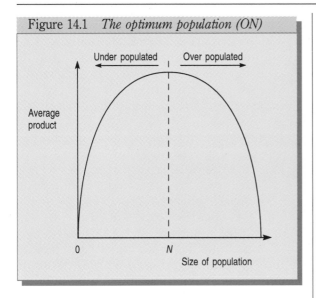

Figure 14.1   *The optimum population (ON)*

Under populated | Over populated

Average product

0          N

Size of population

## Increasing Participation of Women in the Labour Force

Women now constitute over one third of the total labour force and the number is rising. At the start of the 1970s only 43 per cent of females in the working age groups participated in the labour market. By the 1990s this figure had risen to over 60 per cent. There are many reasons for the increasing participation of women in the UK labour market, including the following:

### Changes in Social Prejudice

Increasingly the prejudice against women participating fully in the labour market has diminished. In consequence women are more active seekers of employment than they might have been years ago. To some extent this reflects the labour shortages which characterised the 1950s and 1960s. Shortages of labour increasingly drew more women into paid employment and this established the pattern for the future.

### Changes in the Structure of Industry

The decline of the industrial base in recent years, coupled with the expansion of the service sector, has increased the number of opportunities for women to participate in the labour market.

## The Rise of Part-time Jobs

Many women prefer to combine employment with running a home and organising a family. The growth in the number of part-time jobs in the UK has increased the opportunity for this and women have responded by taking up most of the opportunities for part-time employment. It is estimated that, between 1951 and 1990, part-time employment as a percentage of total employment increased from 4 per cent to 27 per cent and that, in 1990, 88 per cent of all part-time workers were women.

## Rising Real Income

In post-war years there has been a considerable rise in real income and this has increased the sacrifice involved in not obtaining employment. It seems reasonable to suggest that, as the opportunity cost of non-participation in the labour market has increased, so the number of job seekers has increased. Because of the relatively low participation of women, the increase in the number of females seeking employment has been more significant than the increase in the number of males seeking employment.

## Tax Advantages

In 1988, the tax laws were changed to allow women to be taxed independently of their husbands. For many women this increased the attractiveness of paid employment because it reduced the risk of joint income pushing the family into a higher tax bracket. The effect was therefore to increase disposable income from employment for at least some married women.

## Common Mistakes to Avoid

A very common mistake is to confuse **working population** with the **numbers in the working age groups**. They are not the same! The working population consists of those in paid employment (full-time or part-time), the self-employed, those in the armed forces and those registered as unemployed. The working age groups consist of all females between the ages of 16 and 60, and all males between the ages of 16 and 65. There will be clear differences between these totals because of those in full-time education, the unemployed, those who work full-time as a homemaker, pensioners, those who do full-time voluntary work, and so on.

It is also important to distinguish between the **growth rate** of the population and the **natural rate of increase** of the population. The natural increase in population is measured by the difference between the live birth rate and the death rate.

Crude birth rate = number of births per annum per thousand of the population.

Crude death rate = number of deaths per annum per thousand of the population.

Natural rate of increase = birth rate – death rate.

If we allow for net migration (emigration minus immigration), the growth rate of the population can be set out as:

Growth rate = birth rate – death rate + net migration.

## Questions and Answers

### Questions

1   The data in this question are concerned with the projections made in 1986 of the populations of Northern Ireland (NI), the United Kingdom (UK) and the Republic of Ireland (RI) for the three years 1991, 1996 and 2001.

(a)   Given that the data suggest that the proportion of the population who are of working age in the Republic of Ireland is going to increase over the period 1991–2001, explain why an increase in employment levels may not result in a reduction in unemployment rates.

(b)   Throughout the period shown, evidence (not given here) suggests that birth rates in the Republic of Ireland will exceed death rates. How then can the statistics point to a fall in population size?

(c)   The projected age distribution of the UK population shown in Table 1 forecasts a decline in the proportion of the population who are of pensionable age and over and an increase in the proportion under school leaving age. How then can it be that the median age of the population is projected to increase by 1.7 years in a period of only 10 years?

(d)   It has been suggested that, whilst in 1991 the population of Northern Ireland lay somewhere between that of the United Kingdom and the Republic of Ireland in its demographic characteristics, by the year 2001 it will resemble the United Kingdom population less than the Republic of Ireland population does. To what extent do the data support this view?

(e)   The results of the 1991 Censuses of Population in both the United Kingdom and the

Table 14.1   *Projected population sizes and percentage age distributions*

|  | 1991 | | | 1996 | | | 2001 | | |
|---|---|---|---|---|---|---|---|---|---|
| *Age group* | *NI* | *UK* | *RI* | *NI* | *UK* | *RI* | *NI* | *UK* | *RI* |
| Under school leaving age | 26.5 | 20.4 | 27.0 | 26.4 | 21.3 | 24.6 | 25.7 | 21.6 | 22.8 |
| Working age | 59.1 | 61.3 | 59.9 | 59.2 | 60.5 | 62.2 | 60.0 | 60.4 | 63.8 |
| Pensionable age and over | 14.4 | 18.3 | 13.1 | 14.4 | 18.2 | 13.2 | 14.3 | 18.0 | 13.4 |
| Population (millions) | 1.61 | 57.5 | 3.54 | 1.65 | 58.3 | 3.50 | 1.68 | 59.0 | 3.49 |
| Median age (years) | 30.3 | 35.8 | 29.3 | 31.3 | 36.4 | 31.5 | 32.4 | 37.5 | 33.4 |

*Notes*:

(i)   In 1986, the school leaving age in the Republic of Ireland was 15 years, one year below that in the United Kingdom. Pensionable ages were the same (65 years for males and 60 years for females). It is assumed in these projections that there will be no changes prior to 2001.

(ii)   The median age is that which divides the population in half, in that 50 per cent are younger than it and 50 per cent older.

Republic of Ireland are almost certainly going to lead to the projections shown in Table 1 being revised. As an economist, what factors do you think should be taken into account when determining the frequency of censuses?

NISEAC, June 1991

**2** Which of the following is (are) usually suggested as an advantage of the division of labour?

1  It makes greater use of machinery possible.
2  It encourages the preservation of craftsmanship.
3  It increases the size of the market.

A  1, 2 and 3
B  1 and 2 only
C  2 and 3 only
D  1 only
E  3 only

## Answers

**1** (a) The rate of unemployment is measured as the percentage of the working population who are registered as unemployed. The working population consists of those in employment, including the self-employed, those in the armed forces and those registered as unemployed. The data we are given show that for the Republic of Ireland the percentage of the population in the working age group is expected to rise from 59.9 per cent in 1991 to 63.8 per cent in 2001. This represents an increase of about 136 110 people in the working age group. Unless employment increases by at least this number between 1991 and 2001, the rate of unemployment in Northern Ireland will increase.

(b) Population growth is affected by only three factors: the live birth rate, the death rate and net migration, that is, emigration minus immigration. In the Republic of Ireland between 1991 and 2001, the birth rate is expected to exceed the death rate and therefore the natural rate of increase in population is expected to be positive. In these circumstances the growth rate of population can only be negative if emigration exceeds immigration by an amount greater than the absolute difference between the number of live births and the number of deaths per year.

(c) The data we are given show that for the UK the proportion of the population of pensionable age and over is forecast to fall, while the proportion under school leaving age is forecast to rise. If all other things remained equal, these changes would tend to reduce the median of the UK population as the absolute numbers under school leaving age

increased relative to the absolute number of retirement age and over. The forecast increase in the median age of the UK population therefore implies that there is an expected increase in life expectancy. In other words, although the proportion of the UK population of retirement age and over is expected to fall, the average age of those in this group is expected to rise.

(d) A full comparison of demographic characteristics is impossible from the information we are given. It is not easy to see from the data why the population of Northern Ireland might lie somewhere between the population of the UK and the Republic of Ireland. The proportion of the population under school leaving age in Northern Ireland is less than the proportion in this age group in both the UK and the Republic of Ireland. The same is true of the proportion of the population of working age and of pensionable age and over. Only the median age of Northern Ireland's population compared to the median age of the population of the other two countries lends support to the view that in 1991 the population of Northern Ireland lies somewhere between that of the UK and the Republic of Ireland in terms of its demographic characteristics.

In 1991, the demographic characteristics of Northern Ireland closely resembled those of the Republic of Ireland. Although the situation is expected to change by 2001, there is little evidence that the demographic characteristics of Northern Ireland will resemble the characteristics of the UK less closely than the Republic of Ireland does. The proportion of the population in the under school leaving age group in Northern Ireland is expected to exceed the proportion in this group for the UK by 4.1 percentage points. The position of the Republic of Ireland for the same group is closer to the UK and only exceeds the UK by 1.2 percentage points. However in both other groupings the population of Northern Ireland more closely resembles the population of the UK than the Republic of Ireland does. Indeed the proportion of the population in the working age groups for Northern Ireland is expected to be only 0.4 percentage points behind the UK, whereas the proportion in this group for the Republic of Ireland is expected to exceed the UK by 3.4 percentage points!

If we consider those of pensionable age and over, the population of Northern Ireland is again expected to be closer to the UK than the Republic of Ireland is expected to be. Admittedly there is expected to be only 0.9 percentage points between the proportion of the population in this group in Northern Ireland and the proportion of the population in this group in the Republic of Ireland, but the difference between

Northern Ireland and the UK is still smaller than the difference between the Republic of Ireland and the UK. Again only the expected median age lends support to the assertion that the demographic characteristics of the population of Northern Ireland in 2001 will resemble the UK population less than the population of the Republic of Ireland does.

(e) In determining the frequency with which a census should be carried out there are two broad considerations. On the one hand, the more frequently a census is carried out, the more accurate the information it will contain. This is important in forecasting future demand for most goods and services, especially those provided through the public sector where investment is financed from tax revenues. On the other hand, the more frequently a census is carried out, the greater the cost involved in gathering information. The opportunity cost to society must therefore be considered. This boils down to an optimisation problem and the solution would be where the gains to society from more accurate information are equal to the cost of gathering this information. If the cost of gathering information is less than the benefits of possessing such information, the allocation of resources could be improved by increasing the frequency with which a census is carried out and vice versa.

2 When production is broken down into a small number of repetitive tasks there are far greater opportunities for the substitution of capital for labour. Option 1 is therefore correct.

Option 2 is incorrect because greater and greater specialisation implies a decline in craftsmanship. Workers simply perform a series of repetitive tasks.

Specialisation makes greater levels of output pssible but this does not increase the size of the market. On the contrary, the size of the market limits the scope for specialisation. Unless large scale sales are possible large scale production is uneconomic. Option 3 is therefore incorrect.

The key is D.

## REVIEW QUESTIONS AND ANSWERS

### Questions

1  How does the degree of specialisation affect productivity?

2  In what ways, if any, might the mobility of labour be affected by (i) the introduction of a National Curriculum in UK schools, (ii) an increased tendency for people to buy their own homes, with a corresponding reduction in the size of the privately rented housing sector?

3  The more specialised a factor of production the higher its productivity, but the lower its mobility. Why is this?

4  How would you assess whether Britain was overpopulated or underpopulated?

5  Why might (a) companies producing goods and services, and (b) local and central government, be interested in whether future trends will show an expanding, declining, or ageing population?

6  For what reasons might some of the less prosperous regions of the UK find that they have even fewer 15–19 year olds than other areas during the 1990s? What problems might they face as a result?

7  Analyse the arguments for and against someone who reaches the age of 18 in the year 2000 leaving school for a mechanical apprenticeship rather than going to university to read for a degree.

### Answers

1  The greater the degree of specialisation, the greater the productivity of any factor production. In the case of labour there are many reasons for this. For example, specialisation of labour makes greater use of machinery possible and reduces the time required for training.

2 (i) The National Curriculum aims to ensure a more broadly based education in schools and to raise educational standards. The more broadly based curriculum might increase the number of students studying sciences and through this the number of entrants into science based courses such as engineering. The National Curriculum will therefore make possible a wider career choice

at sixteen plus and if it raises educational standards this might increase occupational mobility.

(ii) It is usually argued that a reduction in the number of rented properties available will reduce geographical mobility of labour. On the other hand, the majority of families are property owners and the numbers are rising. It could therefore be argued that a decline in the availability of rented accommodation and an increased tendency for people to buy their homes makes sale and repurchase of private property easier, and in so doing encourages geographical mobility of labour.

3 As a factor of production becomes more specialised it concentrates on a narrower and narrower range of activities. Its occupational mobility therefore falls but, because of increased specialisation, its productivity increases.

4 Overpopulation and underpopulation are assessed against the optimum population. This is the population level at which average product per head is at a maximum. In order to decide whether Britain is overpopulated or underpopulated, it is necessary to estimate the optimum population of Britain and then compare the actual population against this estimate. In fact estimates of the optimum population are likely to be subject to a wide margin of error and in any case will change quickly because of technological change. Perhaps all that can be done is to assess whether there are labour shortages and whether these are likely to continue in the future. Here again estimates of possible future labour shortages are likely to be subject to a wide margin of error which will increase the further into the future predictions stretch.

5 (a) Private companies would be interested in population projections because they would indicate which goods and services are likely to experience an increase in demand in the future and which are likely to experience a reduction in demand. This would influence their planning and investment decisions.

(b) In general future population trends give a guide to future demands on the nation's resources. Such projections are of particular importance to central and local government because it is usually necessary to plan public sector investment many years ahead. Population trends will give a guide to future demand for school places, hospital beds, road and rail links (infrastructure) and so on.

6 Younger people are geographically the most mobile section of the community. In less prosperous areas prospects of future employment and career development are poor and therefore younger sections of the community move to other areas and, by taking their families with them, contribute to a further net reduction in the labour market entrants in the poorer regions. This exacerbates the problems of such areas because it increases the average age of the population in these areas and discourages new business investment.

7 The problem is to weigh the opportunity cost of a university education against full-time employment. Loss of earnings while studying full-time is an important consideration which must be balanced against future earnings. In general the earnings of graduates are greater than the earnings of non-graduates. However, many graduates find it difficult to obtain employment after graduation and some undergraduates fail to graduate. This implies the existence of risk, which must be considered. Another factor to consider is employment prospects after completion of a mechanical apprenticeship. Here again risk is important and even qualified engineers sometimes experience unemployment. Apart from financial considerations many people derive other benefits from a university education. Some people derive pleasure from further study for its own sake. At 18 this is perhaps not such an important consideration as it once was. Institutions of higher education have an 'open access policy' which actively aims to encourage applications from mature students, so that the opportunity to participate in higher education is available long after the age of 18 has been attained.

CHAPTER 15
# ENTERPRISE

## Topic Summary

Of all factors of production the entrepreneur is the most difficult to define. It is usually argued that the **entrepreneur** is the individual who bears the *uninsurable risks of production*. In this sense the entrepreneur is regarded as a true **capitalist**, that is, one who risks his or her funds in the pursuit of profit from some productive activity. However, the entrepreneur is also regarded as an **organiser** and a **decision-taker**. In this sense the entrepreneur's role is to decide what the factors of production will produce, how they will be combined, how the product will be marketed and so on. The entrepreneur might also be an **innovator** who recognises an opportunity for profit from the inventions of others.

Beyond this little can be said by way of obtaining a precise definition of the entrepreneur. Economic theory has so far largely ignored the way in which the entrepreneur initiates, carries on and brings to a successful conclusion some productive activity. Neither is there any agreement on whether the entrepreneur is an individual or might constitute a group of people such as a family. It is sometimes argued that the functions of the entrepreneur are split as in public companies, where the management and ownership responsibilities, the traditional functions of the entrepreneur, are carried out by salaried personnel and shareholders respectively.

## Characteristics of the Entrepreneur

Despite these problems with identifying a functional definition of the entrepreneur, it is often argued that the entrepreneur will possess certain characteristics that will set him or her apart from other factors of production. These are easily summarised.

### Greater Occupational Mobility

Whatever it is an entrepreneur does, there seems no reason why the skills and abilities should be specific to one firm or one industry. The ability to organise, to recognise and exploit opportunities for profit, the ability to take decisions and bear risks, all of which are associated with the entrepreneur, are not industry-specific. Because of this it is likely that entrepreneurial talent, displayed by an individual in one organisation or industry, will draw that individual into other industries where entrepreneurial talent can again be displayed. Richard Branson is often regarded as one who possesses entrepreneurial talent and he has certainly proved that his abilities are equally well suited to running a chain of record shops or running an international airline.

### Indeterminate Reward

There is a view that the risk an entrepreneur takes stems from the fact that the entrepreneur supplies **risk capital**, that is, an entrepreneur invests his or her own funds in an organisation. Since he is a risk-taker, an entrepreneur's income is likely to be directly derived from profits of the organisation. Unlike other factor incomes, profit cannot be fixed in advance of production: it is the residual amount left over after all other factor incomes have been paid.

### More Variable Income

Moreover, because an entrepreneur sometimes risks personal funds in a business venture, he or she has a vested interest in the success of that business venture. The more successful the business, the greater the return to the entrepreneur. Failure implies that an entrepreneur might lose the value of the funds invested, whereas there is no fixed limit on the return from a successful business. In any event, whether a business succeeds or fails, for most businesses the level of profit earned fluctuates with the level of economic activity. During periods of buoyant economic activity, when the economy is booming, profits will tend to rise, whereas, during a recession, when economic activity is depressed, profits will tend to fall. In consequence it can be argued that no other factor income will fluctuate as widely as the return to the entrepreneur.

## The Divorce of Ownership and Control

In most Western economies large business organisations are owned by shareholders who literally own a share of an organisation. These organisations are known as joint stock companies. The shares in public companies can be transferred from one shareholder to another almost without restriction, whereas in private companies there are usually restrictions to prevent the transfer of shares to parties other than those approved by existing shareholders. The reason for this is that in public companies the shareholders appoint salaried managers to run the company on their behalf, whereas in private companies the shareholders wish to retain control themselves.

In public companies the divorce of ownership from control raises the issue of what aims the company will pursue. Obviously the owners will require a rate of return on their investments in the company which they consider satisfactory and this implies that the company must aim at a minimum profit. They have some power to ensure this because they elect a board of directors annually and it is this group that decides company policy. However achieving a minimum level of profit allows ample scope for the board of directors to pursue other aims.

Traditionally economic theory has assumed that firms aim to **maximise profit**. Companies might well pursue this aim. However profit maximisation is a risky strategy since it means altering price and output levels as market conditions change. This might antagonise customers who find that frequent price changes make it difficult for them to plan their own purchase requirements. It is also a risky strategy because, if successful, it might encourage other firms to enter the industry if profits are high enough and in these circumstances increased competition might well depress profits for existing producers.

If managers were also the owners of companies these risks might be perceived differently. After all, entrepreneurs are risk-takers and the threat of competition might well encourage a policy of profit maximisation. However, because salaried managers are not usually also company owners, they might consider an alternative policy. One alternative frequently suggested is a policy of **sales maximisation**. This might be an attractive policy, for various reasons. As sales increase, market share is likely to increase and this will give a company more security against the emergence of competitors. The company's long term survival prospects, and therefore the job security of its managers, might therefore be enhanced by a policy of sales maximisation.

There are other factors to consider. Since it is impossible to know for certain what level of profit would be earned under a policy of profit maximisation, it could be argued that shareholders have no way of knowing whether managers are maximising profit or not. For them, the important consideration is whether they find the return on their investment satisfactory. They are more likely to do so when market share is increasing rather than when it is static, or even shrinking. However, perhaps the most important consideration of all is that the salaries of managers are most frequently thought to be related to market share rather than profit. The larger the organisation, the more complex it is to manage. If salary is indeed linked with company size, managers might have a vested interest in maximising sales and growth rather than profits.

## REVIEW QUESTIONS AND ANSWERS

### Questions

1  Explain how a public limited company forms part of the private sector of the industry.

2  To what extent could a registered charity such as the RSPCA be regarded as an enterprise? Who carries out the functions of the entrepreneur within such an organisation?

3  If a company devotes resources to sponsoring a symphony concert, is this a sign that the firm is not maximising profits? In what way could it be argued that such sponsorship has a direct link with profitability?

4  Consider the article in Figure 15.1, which appeared in the *Guardian*:

   (a)  To what extent does this article reinforce the view that there is a divorce between ownership and control?
   (b)  Many school pupils now take part in 'enterprise' activities. Is it possible to learn how to be enterprising?

5  Is entrepreneurship possible within large organisations? Suppose you were employed by a multinational car manufacturer. What opportunities might there be for you to display the characteristics of entrepreneurship?

Figure 15.1   *What motivates tycoons*

The British Psychological Society hears what motivates tycoons, and the risks in moving staff

# Entrepreneurs' spur to success

**Chris Mihill**
**Medical Correspondent**

Tycoons who founded multi-million pound empires are more likely to be poorly educated, come from deprived backgrounds and have had mothers with strong personalities, a study of successful people has found.

The personality of entrepreneurs is significantly different from that of senior managers and company chairmen who worked their way up the corporate ladder.

A unique study of what motivates elite businessmen and the forces that shaped their drive has been carried out by a mature PhD student, Reg Jennings, which involved detailed interviews with some of the richest and most powerful business people in this country and the United States.

The four-year study consisted of an analysis of self-reported characteristics of 19 entrepreneurs and 22 managers, two of whom were women.

The entrepreneurs included Lord Young, the former Trade and Industry secretary, George Davies of Next, businessman Owen Oyston, publisher Eddie Shah, Gerald Ronson of the Heron group, financier Peter de Savary, and Jeffrey Archer.

The managers included Anthony Pilkington of Pilkington glass, Lord McAlpine, Julian Smith of W H Smith, Sir Adrian Cadbury of Cadbury Schweppes, Sam Whitbread of the brewing firm, and Denis Thatcher.

Mr Jennings, of Lancaster University, told the annual meeting of the British Psychological Society in Bournemouth at the weekend that the hardest part was getting access to the people. Once he had done so, they were happy to talk, although reluctant to fill in personality questionnaires.

An analysis of their characteristics found the entrepreneurs had higher reserves of energy, were more creative thinkers, more risk-seeking, but becoming bored with routine. They were more likely to attribute their success to luck.

They also strongly believed their early years of poverty had shaped their ambition, and, in particular, that their mothers had been a strong influence.

Mr Jennings said the entrepreneurs "gave not a damn for education," usually having left school at 15. The managers had usually been to the best schools.

The entrepreneurs sought excitement and saw adversity as a challenge.

Lord Young said: "I spent a very miserable year in 1973 when I thought I was rich and didn't know what to do. Very luckily for me the 1974 bank crash wiped me out and I woke up one morning full of the joys of spring because I knew what I had to do."

One tycoon said being Jewish in a poor area and being beaten up nearly every day of his school life had acted as the spur to prove himself.

Owen Oyston, Peter de Savary and Jeffrey Archer all said their mothers had influenced them strongly.

Mr Oyston commented: "I was ill for years at school. My mother was the driving force. She created in me an uneasiness about not working and the pressure for me to really prove to the world what I had in me."

By contrast, Denis Thatcher said: "As a businessman I am still, and always have been, the professional director. The decision-maker, yes, but not with the flair of the real entrepreneur."

*Source: Guardian*, 15.4.91.

## Answers

**1** The public sector consists of those organisations which are state owned and which are controlled by central or local government either directly, as with the armed forces, or through their agent, as with the nationalised industries. Public companies do not fall into this category because in general they are owned by private individuals. The exceptions are registered charities and trusts.

**2** An enterprise is usually defined as an organisation and in particular a business organisation. The RSPCA is a registered charity rather than a business organisation and its ultimate aims differ radically from those of a business organisation. It has no product to sell and therefore does not aim to maximise profit or market share. Nevertheless it does aim to maximise donations and holds fund raising events to achieve this. It also actively advertises its work to encourage donations from the public. Like most organisations it has limited availability of funds and no doubt aims to place the funds at its disposal where they will achieve maximum benefit in preventing cruelty to animals. In this sense the RSPCA is clearly an enterprise.

**3** Sponsorship of events such as a symphony concert might well be done for altruistic motives. If this is the case it might well be true that a firm is not maximising profits. However, before we can be sure, we need to know the amount of sponsorship money involved, the total sponsorship budget, how much exposure the firm received as a result of its sponsorship and so on. In many cases there is no doubt that sponsorship is used as a means of advertising a firm and its products. In this sense there is a direct link between sponsorship and profitability.

**4** (a) The article we are given provides some information on the personal backgrounds of managers and entrepreneurs but it provides little evidence of a divorce between management as a decision-taking function and risk-seeking as an entrepreneurial function. Those individuals referred to as 'managers' in the passage are decision-takers on behalf of their employer. The traditional view of the entrepreneur is one who recognises profitable opportunities and is willing to risk personal funds backing his or her view. The distinction is clear in Dennis Thatcher's statement when he admits to being a decision-taker, 'but not with the flair of the real entrepreneur'.

(b) It is probably true that schools and other educational establishments can teach individuals to be more enterprising, but it is doubtful whether it is possible to teach an individual to be enterprising. The passage we are given indicates that entrepreneurs are 'risk-seekers' who become 'bored by routine'. They apparently have 'higher reservers of energy' than others. These are personality traits that cannot be taught in schools or learned from a book. Similarly they 'strongly believed their early years of poverty had shaped their ambition, and, in particular, that their mothers had been a strong influence'. Again these influences cannot be taught.

Despite this it is possible to teach individuals some aspects of the 'enterprise culture'. There are skills involved in time management and in seeking out profitable opportunities. It is also possible to teach the use of decision-making techniques such as discounted cash flow techniques (see pp. 123–4). Similarly it is possible to teach other techniques used in business, such as profit and loss accounting and advertising as well as the various sources of finance available to a business. Furthermore, in many schools, enterprise activities frequently involve running a 'business' and the experience this provides will no doubt aid individuals to be 'enterprising'.

**5** Many large organisations are owned or controlled by individuals classed as entrepreneurs. Richard Branson's Virgin Atlantic is an often quoted example. However in large organisations there is generally less scope for entrepreneurship because of the divorce between ownership and control. The largest organisations are the joint stock companies, and it is the shareholders who bear the risks of business failure while salaried managers exercise control. Entrepreneurship is clearly an essential ingredient of any business organisation but it is difficult for one person to finance the largest organisations and so different groups carry out the different functions of the entrepreneur. Whether there is scope to exercise an entrepreneurial role in a large multinational organisation partly depends on the qualities an individual possesses and on the position that person occupies within the organisation. The person who is responsible for a particular overseas market might play more of an entrepreneurial (though not necessarily more important) role than a shopfloor worker.

# CHAPTER 16
# LAND AND CAPITAL

## Topic Summary

Economists define land to include the surface area of the planet, including seas, lakes, rivers and the mountains. It also includes all ores and mineral deposits as well as fish in the seas, lakes and rivers, wildlife in the woods, and so on.

Capital, on the other hand, is any asset which is created for use in production. Because of this capital goods are often referred to as *producer goods.*. For convenience economists distinguish between *fixed capital* which is durable and is used time and again in the production process, and *circulating capital* which can only be used once. Circulating capital consists of such items as raw materials, semi-finished goods, finished goods held in stock and so on.

## Characteristics of Land

As a factor of production land has certain characteristic features, some of which are also common to other factors of production.

### Zero Cost of Production

Since land is regarded as a **free gift of nature** it has no cost of production. It is not created by the efforts of any living individual. It is true that human effort can improve the quality of land and its resources, but its actual creation is not the result of any human input. This characteristic is not unique to land. Unskilled labour also has zero cost of production.

## Mobility of Land

Land is perfectly **immobile geographically** in the short run and the long run. It is impossible to move Mount Kilimanjaro or the North Sea to a different location. Other factors of production might be immobile in the short run, but no other factor of production is geographically immobile in the long run to the same extent as land. Again in the short run we might expect land to be **occupationally immobile**. It takes time to convert arable land to building land. However, even in the long run, some parts of land might be occupationally immobile. What else could the North Sea or the peaks of the Himalayas be used for except fishing and mountaineering?

## The Accumulation of Capital

The accumulation of capital depends on abstention from current consumption, which is the phrase most often used to describe the *sacrifice* involved in capital accumulation. Abstention from current consumption implies that in order to accumulate capital it is necessary for the community to save. Remember, a nation only has limited resources and if these are fully employed, and more of these are devoted to producing goods and services for current consumption, less will be available for producing capital goods. When the community saves, resources are released from current consumption and these resources are then available for the production of capital goods. Saving therefore makes capital accumulation possible but it does not guarantee that it will take place. Capital accumulation, as we shall see in Chapter 21, is determined by many factors. All we are saying here is that without saving there is no possibility of capital accumulation.

## Common Mistakes to Avoid

**Land** and **working capital** can sometimes be confused. Land is not just the surface area of the globe. It is defined by economists to include all natural unexploited resources. Thus economists would classify oil in the ground as land, but oil in a pipeline on its way to the refinery would be classified as working capital.

Money and capital are also frequently confused and it is common for people to refer to money as capital. In fact, as we shall see in Chapter 23, money is simply a claim to assets. Money is clearly important in creating the conditions necessary for specialisation. In this sense it is probably the most important invention of all time! However it is not a factor of production. Capital has quite a specific definition. It is any asset which has been created entirely for use in production. Money does not satisfy this definition and is therefore not capital.

## REVIEW QUESTIONS AND ANSWERS

### Questions

1 Is land a renewable or non-renewable resource? Explain your answer.

2 The Bible tells us to turn 'swords into ploughshares', and there is much talk nowadays of the 'peace dividend'. What are the practical problems involved in such changes, and how can they be illustrated by the use of a production possibility curve?

3 Is a screwdriver an example of fixed or working capital?

### Answers

1 Land is usually defined as 'all the free gifts of nature'. Land therefore includes the surface area of the planet and all its contents such as minerals, ores, forests, the fish in the sea and so on. Given this definition, land is partly a renewable resource and partly a non-renewable resource. For example, we can plant more forests, impose a quota on fish catches to conserve stocks and so on. On the other hand, once minerals and ores have been extracted they cannot be replaced.

2 Turning swords into plough shares implies changing one type of physical asset into capital equipment. The problem is that a great deal of capital is specific and cannot be converted into other uses. In the short run, specific items of capital are completely immobile geographically and it is literally impossible to convert a sword into a ploughshare. However, in the long run, resources can be diverted away from the production of one type of good and can instead be used to produce capital equipment or some consumer good. This is what the term 'peace dividend'

implies. The end of the 'cold war' has released resources away from the production of military equipment and these resources can now be put to other purposes.

No doubt you will recognise this as an example of opportunity cost. Scarce resources have alternative uses. In the present context, if they are used to produce capital equipment the opportunity cost of this is the consumer goods that might otherwise have been produced. We can see from Figure 16.1 that, as fewer and fewer resources are devoted to the production of capital goods, more and more consumer goods can be produced. However, as more of one good is produced the opportunity cost increases because of diminishing returns.

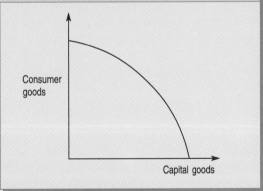

Figure 16.1 *A production possibility curve showing the opportunity cost of consumer goods in terms of capital goods*

3 A screwdriver is an item of fixed capital. Its form does not change, no matter how many times it is used in the course of producing output. Working capital has no fixed form. Raw materials, for example, become semi-finished products and then finished products. These are all examples of circulating capital.

CHAPTER 17

# THE DISTRIBUTION OF FACTOR INCOMES

## Topic Summary

### The Marginal Productivity Theory

One approach adopted by economists to analyse the distribution of factor incomes is in terms of the **marginal productivity theory**. For convenience we concentrate in this chapter on the case of labour but the marginal productivity theory is equally easily applied to other factor markets. In the case of labour the basic question to answer is why some workers, such as footballers, stockbrokers and accountants, earn significantly higher incomes compared to other workers such as cleaners, nurses and typists.

The marginal productivity theory is based on the assumption that there is **perfect competition in the factor and product markets**. In the labour market this implies that workers are price-takers. They accept the wage rate as given and therefore the firm can recruit as many workers as it wishes at the ruling wage rate. Furthermore each worker is regarded as **homogeneous** and therefore all workers are equally efficient. Perfect competition in the product market implies that the firm sells its entire output at the ruling market price and simply adjusts output so as to equate marginal revenue with marginal cost.

The marginal productivity theory predicts that a firm will go on employing additional units of labour until the marginal cost of employing the last worker exactly equals the marginal revenue of that worker. This is simply a restatement of the **profit maximisation condition**, that marginal cost is equated with marginal revenue, first mentioned on p. 55. However, our aim here is to identify the equilibrium number of workers, not the equilibrium level of output.

## The Marginal Productivity Theory Under Perfect Competition

Perfect competition in the product market implies that the individual firm is powerless to influence the price at which it sells its product. It simply accepts the market price as given and adjusts output so as to equate marginal revenue with marginal cost. By focusing on the effect of changes in output on the demand for factor inputs, in this case labour, we can identify the firm's demand for labour curve. This is our starting point for an analysis of wage determination under conditions of perfect competition.

The contribution of the last worker employed to the firm's revenue is referred to as marginal revenue product. When there is perfect competition in the product market this is equal to marginal physical product multiplied by the price at which the product is sold. In symbols we can write

$$MRP_L = MPP_L \times P$$

Where $MRP_L$ is the marginal revenue product of labour, $MPP_L$ is the marginal physical product of labour and $P$ is the price of the product.

In general we would expect the marginal revenue product of labour to rise at first and subsequently to fall as more workers are employed. We know from p. 40 that as firms employ more workers there will be increased scope for specialisation and therefore the firm will experience increasing returns to labour, that is, marginal physical product will at first rise. However, beyond a certain level of employment, increasing returns will give way to diminishing returns, that is, marginal physical product will fall. Since changes in the output of an individual firm have no effect on market price of the product, it follows that marginal revenue product will vary directly with marginal physical product.

Because we have assumed that the firm can recruit as many workers as it wishes at the ruling market wage rate, the wage rate is perceived to be *constant* and therefore the marginal cost of labour equals the average cost of labour. The firm simply follows the profit maximising condition and equates marginal cost with marginal revenue product to obtain its required input of labour. Figure 17.1 is used to illustrate this.

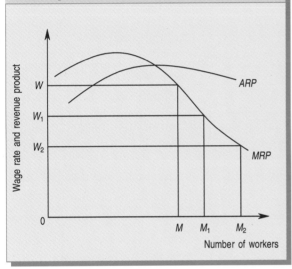

Figure 17.1  *The effect of changes in the wage rate on the number of workers employed when there is perfect competition in the labour market and the product market*

In Figure 17.1, *MRP* is the marginal revenue product of labour and *ARP* is the associated average revenue product of labour. If the wage rate is *OW*, the firm will employ *OM* workers, because this is where marginal cost equals marginal revenue. If the wage rate is $OW_1$ the firm will employ $OM_1$ workers, at $OW_2$ the firm will employ $OM_2$ workers and so on. In other words, the firm's *MRP* curve below its *ARP* curve is its demand for labour curve! Given the *MRP* curve, we can read off how many workers will be demanded at any given wage rate.

## Criticisms of the Marginal Revenue Productivity Theory

1   The marginal productivity theory under conditions of perfect competition is a partial theory of wage determination. It enables us to derive the firm's demand for labour curve but it takes the wage rate as given. It tells us nothing about how the wage rate is determined.

2   In the real world firms do not operate in perfectly competitive markets. In particular the supply or workers to an organisation is unlikely to be perfectly elastic. Indeed in some cases wages are negotiated by powerful trade unions.

3   The marginal revenue productivity theory is based on the assumption that firms aim to maximise profit, but organisations in the public sector, for example, might not always aim to maximise profit. Furthermore, as we have seen on p. 87, firms might pursue other goals.

4   Even if firms do aim to maximise profit they are unlikely to possess the precise knowledge of marginal revenue and marginal cost to enable them to adjust employment so as to equate marginal revenue with marginal cost.

## The Market Theory of Wages

### The Demand for Labour

Although the marginal productivity theory was originally conceived as a theory of income distribution under conditions of perfect competition, our analysis of wages is easily adapted to the more realistic conditions of the real world.

In the product market under imperfect competition the firm must reduce the price of its product in order to increase sales. In this case marginal revenue product will rise less steeply and fall more steeply than under perfect competition because the fall in price as sales increase will reduce the effect of increasing returns on marginal revenue product, whereas it will increase the effect of diminishing returns on marginal revenue product. However the general shape of the marginal revenue product curve is unchanged whether we consider perfect competition in the product market or imperfect competition in the product market. We can therefore assume that, in the real world, the demand for labour by an individual firm will be inversely related to the wage rate. Furthermore, by summing horizontally, or adding together, each individual firm's demand for labour curve we can derive a market demand for labour curve.

### The Supply of Labour

In the real world the market supply of labour increases as the wage rate increases. The main reason for this is that as the wage rate increases workers will be attracted away from alternative occupations.

## Determination of the Wage Rate

The market theory of wages explains wage determination as the result of the interaction of supply and demand for labour as illustrated in Figure 17.2.

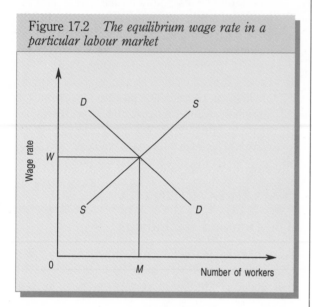

Figure 17.2   *The equilibrium wage rate in a particular labour market*

In Figure 17.2, *SS* and *DD* are the free market supply and demand curves for labour. The equilibrium wage is *OW* and *OM* workers are employed at the equilibrium wage. Once equilibrium is established in this labour market there will be no reason for either the wage rate or the number of workers employed to change unless there is a prior change in the conditions of supply and/or demand.

## Changes in the Demand for Labour

We can identify two broad reasons why the demand for labour might change; each is summarised below.

- If the demand for the product which labour produces changes, there will be a change in the demand for labour in the same direction. If all other things remain equal, an increase in demand for the product will cause an increase in the price of the product. As price rises, marginal revenue product will rise and the whole *MRP* curve will shift vertically upwards at any given level of employment.
- If the marginal product of labour changes, the demand for labour will change in the same

direction. If all other things remain equal, an increase in productivity will increase marginal revenue product because at any given level of employment the firm will now have a greater volume of output to sell. Again the effect of an increase in productivity will therefore be to shift the firm's *MRP* curve vertically upwards at any given level of employment.

The effect of a change in demand for labour is illustrated in Figure 17.3.

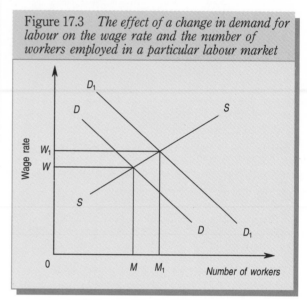

Figure 17.3   *The effect of a change in demand for labour on the wage rate and the number of workers employed in a particular labour market*

In Figure 17.3, *SS* is the supply curve of labour to an industry. If *DD* is the initial demand curve for labour then a shift in the demand curve to $D_1D_1$ represents an increase in the demand for labour. On the other hand, if $D_1D_1$ is the initial demand curve for labour then a shift in the demand curve to *DD* represents an decrease in the demand for labour. It is clear that an increase in the demand for labour will result in an increase in the wage rate (from *W* to $W_1$) and an increase in the number of workers employed (from *M* to $M_1$) while a reduction in the demand for labour will result in a reduction in the wage rate (from $W_1$ to *W*) and a reduction in the number of workers employed (from $M_1$ to *M*).

## Changes in the Supply of Labour

A major factor affecting the supply of labour to an occupation is the existence of *barriers to entry*. These might take many forms and the removal or erection of barriers to entry will affect the supply of labour to an occupation. For example, if one of the professional organisations, such as the Institute of Chartered Accountants, raises its entry requirements, over time this will reduce the supply of chartered accountants. On the other hand, if the ability of a trade union to enforce a closed shop is removed this will increase the supply of labour because firms will be able to employ both union and non-union workers.

Measures to improve mobility of labour will also affect the supply of labour. Increased provision of training schemes will increase the occupational mobility of labour and, through this, the supply of labour. Similarly measures to increase geographical mobility will increase the supply of labour.

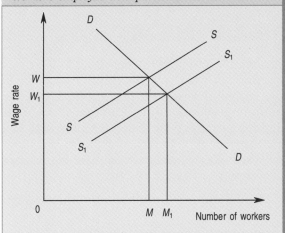

Figure 17.4 *The effect of a change in the supply of labour on the wage rate and the number of workers employed in a particular labour market*

In Figure 17.4, *DD* is the demand curve for labour to an industry. If *SS* is the initial supply curve for labour then a shift in the supply curve to $S_1S_1$ represents an increase in the supply for labour. On the other hand, if $S_1S$ is the initial supply curve for labour then a shift in the supply curve to *SS* represents a decrease in the supply for labour. It is clear that an increase in the supply for labour will result in a decrease in the wage rate (from *W* to $W_1$) and an increase in the number of workers employed (from *M* to $M_1$) while a reduction in the supply of labour will result in an increase in the wage rate (from $W_1$ to *W*) and a reduction in the number of workers employed (from $M_1$ to *M*).

## The Effect of a Union

For many workers wages are negotiated between their trade union and representatives of their employ-

er. The ability of a union to influence the pay and conditions of its members depends on several factors. Here we take the simplest case, where the union controls the entire supply of labour to an employer. In these circumstances a union has considerable ability to fix wages but it must be aware that any increase in wages might affect the number of workers employed. Figure 17.5 is used as a basis for illustration.

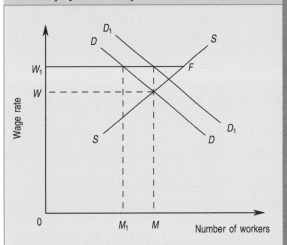

Figure 17.5 *The effect of a union on wages and employment in a particular labour market*

In Figure 17.5, *SS* and *DD* are the free market supply and demand curves for a particular type of labour. The equilibrium wage is *OW* and *OM* workers are employed. Now if a union demands a wage increase of $WW_1$ and refuses to supply any workers at a wage below $OW_1$, the supply of labour curve is now effectively given by $W_1FS$. The new equilibrium is $OW_1$, but if all other things remain equal the number of workers employed in the industry will fall to $OM_1$.

It is doubtful whether this reduction in employment will be acceptable to the union. To obtain the higher wage and yet simultaneously avoid any redundancies among its members, the union must persuade employers in the industry to increase their demand for labour. In Figure 17.5, if demand for labour shifts to $D_1D_1$ the union will achieve its objective of a higher wage without any reduction in the numbers employed.

There are various options available to the union. One solution is for the union to *increase productivity* of the workforce. If all other things remain equal an increase in productivity will increase marginal revenue productivity, and this in turn will cause an increase in the demand for labour. It is for this reason that pay awards are sometimes linked to changes in working practices or the introduction of new equipment.

A different strategy is to persuade an employer to finance the pay award by raising the price of the product. Again, if all other things remain equal this will increase the marginal revenue productivity of labour and therefore the demand for labour will increase. The ability of the union to persuade employers to increase product prices will partly depend on the elasticity of demand for the products. The union of course cannot control this.

A longer term strategy is for the union to insist on longer periods of training before workers are qualified to enter an occupation. If successful this will cause a reduction in the supply of qualified workers and, as we we have seen on p. 95, as the supply of workers falls, the wage rate will rise.

## Elasticity of Demand for Labour

A crucial determinant of the effect of a change in supply of labour on the wage rate and the numbers employed is the elasticity of demand for labour. There are three main factors which influence elasticity of demand for labour in a particular occupation.

### Elasticity of Demand for the Product

The elasticity of demand for labour is directly related to the elasticity of demand for the product that labour produces. If demand for a good is relatively elastic, then a change in the price of that good will cause a proportionately greater change in quantity demanded. If the increase in price is caused by an increase in wages, as the quantity of the product demanded falls, there will also be a proportionately greater fall in the quantity of labour demanded.

### Labour Costs as a Proportion of Total Costs

The elasticity of demand for labour is directly related to the proportion of total costs which are made up of labour costs. When labour costs account for a small proportion of total costs, then even a relatively large increase in labour costs will cause only a relatively small change in total costs. In such cases the effect of an increase in labour costs on the final price of the product will be relatively small and therefore the

effect on the demand for labour will also be relatively small.

## The Substitutability of Capital for Labour

The elasticity of demand for labour is directly related to the ease with which capital can be substituted for labour. When capital and labour are close substitutes, even a relatively small increase in labour costs might cause a more than proportionate reduction in the amount of labour demanded. The more labour costs increase, the more elastic will be the demand for labour because it will become more and more economic to substitute capital for labour.

## Elasticity of Supply of Labour

Just as the elasticity of demand for labour is important in identifying the effect of a change in the supply of labour on the wage rate and the numbers employed, so the elasticity of supply is important in identifying the effect on the wage rate and the numbers employed of a change in demand for labour. We can summarise the main determinants of elasticity of supply of labour to a particular occupation.

### Length of Training

Elasticity of supply will vary directly with the length of training required for entry to an occupation. Some occupations, such as doctors and architects, require a lengthy period of training and so have a relatively low elasticity of supply. Other occupations, such as window cleaners and builders labourers, require little or no training and so have a relatively elastic supply.

### Natural Ability

Elasticity of supply will vary directly with the degree of natural ability required to enter an occupation. In some cases, such as footballers and actors, it is easy to recognise the high degree of natural ability required to enter an occupation. However, a high degree of natural ability is also required to become an accountant or solicitor. When a high degree of natural ability is required by an occupation, elasticity of supply will be lower.

## Mobility of Labour

Elasticity of supply will vary directly with the degree of mobility of labour. The more occupationally and geographically mobile the labour force, the more elastic the supply of labour to an occupation.

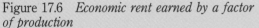

## Economic Rent

Economic rent is the surplus a factor of production earns over and above its **transfer earnings**. Transfer earnings are the minimum reward necessary to keep a factor of production in its present occupation. For any factor of production, if actual earnings fall below transfer earnings then that factor of production will transfer to its next most well paid occupation. The concept of economic rent is illustrated in Figure 17.6.

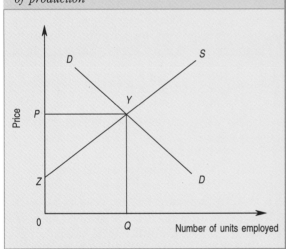

Figure 17.6 *Economic rent earned by a factor of production*

In Figure 17.6, *ZS* and *DD* are the supply and demand conditions for a factor of production. The equilibrium price is *OP* and the quantity employed in equilibrium is *OQ*. However only the last unit of this factor employed receives its transfer earnings. Every other unit would be willing to work for an amount less than *OP*. Apart from the last unit employed, every other unit of this factor receives economic rent and the total amount of economic rent earned is equal to the area *PYZ*.

The amount of economic rent earned by any factor of production is determined crucially by its elasticity of supply. When elasticity of supply is perfectly elastic, the entire earnings of a factor of production are transfer earnings and no economic rent is earned. At the other extreme, when the elasticity of supply of a factor of production is perfectly inelastic it has no transfer earnings and therefore its total earnings, whatever they happen to be, consist of economic rent.

It is important to note that any factor of production can earn economic rent. For example, it is likely that the earnings of most soccer stars consist of economic rent. Similarly, since normal profit can be regarded as the opportunity cost of the entrepreneur, the supernormal profit of the monopolist consists of economic rent. In the case of capital, the earnings of circulating capital might be close to its transfer earnings but this is unlikely to be true of a great deal of fixed capital which is likely to have few, if any, alternative uses!

## Profit

Profit is the **reward to the entrepreneur**. Normal profit is the minimum acceptable reward if the entrepreneur is to remain in the industry in the long run. Normal profit is therefore a cost of production, but in practice, because normal profit is a vague concept that cannot be measured, profit is treated as a residual, that is, the amount left over after all other costs of production have been met.

There are various ways in which profit can be measured, depending on the purpose for which profitability statistics are required.

### Profit as a Residual

The simplest measure of profit is simply total revenue minus total cost. Thus if total revenue is £1m and total cost is £0.8m, profit is £200 000.

### Profit as a Percentage of Turnover

Profit is sometimes expressed as a percentage of turnover or total revenue. Thus, if total profit is £200 000 and total revenue is £1m, profit as a percentage of turnover is £0.2m/£1m = 20 per cent.

### Profit as a Return on Capital

Profit is sometimes expressed as a percentage return on capital assets. Thus, if total profit is £200 000 and the value of capital employed is £2m, the return on capital employed is £0.2m/£2m = 10 per cent.

## Common Mistakes to Avoid

A common mistake, frequently made in examinations, concerns the **marginal cost of employing an additional worker**. Remember, the marginal cost of an additional worker is simply the change in the total wage bill when one more worker is employed. For example, if a firm employs 10 workers at a wage of £300 per worker and, in order to attract one more worker it is necessary to increase wages to £310, the marginal cost of the last worker is $(£310 \times 11) - (£310 \times 10) = £410$. In other words the marginal cost of the last worker is £410 – not £310!

Sometimes there is confusion over the *accountant*'s notion of profit and the *economist*'s notion of profit. To the economist, normal profit is a cost of production. It is the minimum acceptable return to the entrepreneur for bearing the uninsurable risks of production. Anything in excess of normal profit is supernormal profit. To the accountant, profit is simply the difference between total cost and total revenue. Accountants have no use for the concept of normal profit and in their calculations they do not even recognise its existence!

Economic rent, as we have seen on p. 97, is the amount a factor of production earns over and above its transfer earnings. However not all economic rent will be earned in the long run. Sometimes economic rent disappears in the long run. For example, the supernormal profit earned by firms in perfect competition in the short run is economic rent which disappears in the long run. Such economic rent is referred to as *quasi-rent*.

## Questions and Answers

### Questions

1 Outline the factors which determine the structure of wages in the economy. Explain whether or not there are any economic reasons why, despite equal pay legislation, on average women are paid less than men in Britain.

JMB, 1991

2 A trade union is likely to be in a favourable position to influence wages when its members

 1  are employed in relatively few production plants
 2  work in production systems where capital costs are a high proportion of total costs
 3  are employed making products which the employers sell in competitive markets

A  1, 2 and 3 are correct
B  1 and 2 only are correct
C  2 and 3 only are correct
D  1 only is correct
E  3 only is correct

ULEAC, Jan 1992

3 A rise in wages in a particular industry would be likely to produce unemployment in conditions where

 1  the supply of alternative factors is elastic
 2  labour costs form a high proportion of total costs
 3  the marginal cost of labour rises above marginal revenue product

A  1,2 and 3 correct
B  1 and 2 only correct
C  2 and 3 only correct
D  1 only correct

AEB, June 1991

### Answers

**1** The structure of wages in an economy refers to the existing pattern of wage differentials between workers in different occupations. Some groups, such as coal face workers in mining receive relatively high wages while others, such as agricultural workers, receive relatively low wages. The differences are accounted for by differences in the conditions of supply and demand in the different labour markets.

It is normally argued that the demand for labour will be inversely related to the wage rate. One reason for this is that, after a certain level of employment, each additional worker will make a smaller and smaller contribution to total revenue because of diminishing returns. Because of this, in any given occupation, firms will be willing to employ more workers only if the wage rate falls as employment increases.

On the other hand, the supply of labour to an occupation will vary directly with the wage rate. As the wage rate rises in an occupation, more and more workers will offer themselves for employment in that occupation. The reason is simple. As the wage rate in one occupation rises relative to other occupations, workers will be attracted away from lower paid occupations.

The implication is that, in any particular labour market, and for the labour market as a whole, supply and demand curves will be the normal shape. Figure

17.7 shows a typical labour market where *DD* is the demand for labour and *SS* the supply of labour. In this market the equilibrium wage rate is *OW* and *OM* workers will be employed at this wage rate.

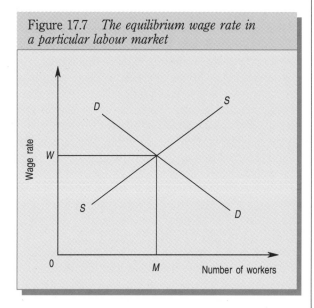

Figure 17.7 *The equilibrium wage rate in a particular labour market*

This explains how the wage rate is determined in a typical labour market, but it does not explain the structure of wages within an economy. In fact the structure of wages is determined by differences in the conditions of supply and demand in different labour markets. In particular there are considerable differences in the elasticity of demand and supply for different groups of workers. If we consider two distinct labour markets, for surgeons and for window cleaners, the importance of differences in the elasticity of supply and demand will be apparent.

In the case of surgeons a specialist skill is sold on the labour market. Society places a tremendous value on this skill. After all, the surgeon saves lives and eases pain and suffering, all of which society is prepared to pay dearly for. Furthermore there are no substitutes available for the surgeon's skill so that demand for surgeons is relatively inelastic. Supply will also be relatively inelastic. It requires a relatively high minimum level of academic ability, a cool head under pressure and a steady hand to become a surgeon. Even if someone does possess these skills, it takes several years to train as a surgeon. The supply of surgeons will therefore be relatively inelastic.

This contrasts markedly with the market for window cleaners. For most people a window cleaner is a convenience which saves many people having to perform a tedious and thankless chore. However having someone else clean our windows is hardly a necessity and if the price rose significantly many people would simply clean their own windows. The demand for window cleaners is therefore relatively elastic.

Similarly window cleaning is classed as unskilled work, which implies that it is possible for almost anyone to undertake the work after only the briefest amount of training. There are certainly no entry requirements, though to clean some windows a head for heights is necessary!

We can illustrate the effect of different elasticities of supply and demand on wages in different labour markets. In Figure 17.8, $S_sS_s$ and $D_sD_s$ represent the supply and demand conditions for surgeons, while $S_wS_w$ and $D_wD_w$ represent the supply and demand conditions for window cleaners. Note the relatively inelastic demand for surgeons compared with window cleaners, representing the greater value society places on the work of surgeons compared to window cleaners. The supply of surgeons is also relatively inelastic compared with the supply of window cleaners because of the time taken to acquire the skills of a surgeon compared with window cleaning, where little or no training is necessary.

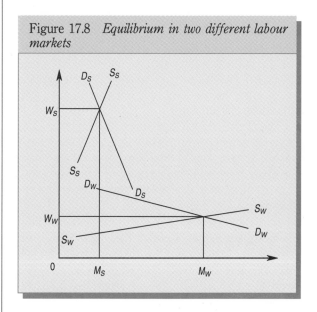

Figure 17.8 *Equilibrium in two different labour markets*

The inevitable result of these supply and demand conditions is the relatively high reward received by surgeons ($W_s$) and the relatively low reward received by window cleaners ($W_w$). More generally, differences in supply and demand conditions in each of the different labour markets largely explain the structure of wages in the economy.

In the real world other factors might also affect the wage received by certain groups. In particular it is sometimes alleged that discrimination might affect the wages of women and ethnic minorities. It is difficult to be certain about the extent of this but there is no doubt that on average in the UK female earnings are about one third less than male earnings. However this does not necessarily imply discrimination and the difference in average earnings can be explained, at least partly, by economic reasons.

Typically the marginal productivity in occupations dominated by female workers is below that in occupations dominated by male workers. This is mainly due to the fact that women tend to work in labour-intensive occupations where the impact of capital, and especially changes in technology, have little effect on the productivity of labour. Workers who are able to work with modern equipment are able to raise productivity compared with other groups and so are able to secure higher pay awards.

Investment in human capital is also an explanatory factor accounting for the pay differential between male and female workers. On average women undertake less training than men and their relatively poor performance in the pay league therefore partly reflects a differential between skilled and unskilled workers. There might be many reasons why women undertake less training than men, but the fact that they do adversely affects their pay. There might also be an indirect effect. Men are more likely to be promoted into better paid positions, again perhaps reflecting a higher level of training compared with their female counterparts.

The problem of low pay might be compounded for married women who have historically been less mobile geographically than men. Again there might be many reasons for this, not all of them economic, but the effect is to depress the pay of women in the labour market because lack of mobility prevents them from moving to better paid jobs. Family commitments often restrict the opportunity for women to participate fully in the labour market. We therefore find that most part-time jobs, which tend to carry a relatively low wage, are filled by women.

Another possible factor accounting for the relatively low pay of women is the fact that a smaller proportion of women are members of a trade union than male workers. In addition, many of those who are union members belong to unions which are relatively weak, such as those in clothing and retailing. The effect of trade unions on the proportion of national income going to labour is unclear but powerful unions might be able to affect the distribution of labour's share of national income.

**2** If workers are employed in relatively few production plants they will be in a stronger bargaining position than when they are employed in a relatively large number of production plants. There are many possible reasons for this. In large organisations there is likely to be greater scope for specialisation and economies of scale which will tend to reduce labour costs as a proportion of total costs. We explain the importance of this in the next paragraph. The first statement is therefore correct.

When capital costs form a large proportion of total costs then, by definition, labour costs form a small proportion of total costs. In such cases an increase in labour costs has a relatively small effect on total costs. This is a relatively favourable situation for a trade union because it implies that an increase in wages has a relatively small effect on final price. The second statement is therefore correct.

When products are sold in competitive markets a small increase in price might adversely affect sales. In such a case a trade union has less ability to influence the wages of its members. Statement 3 is therefore incorrect.

The key is B. Statements 1 and 2 only are correct.

**3** When the supply of factors of production is elastic it will be relatively easy to substitute capital for labour. An increase in wages in these circumstances will almost certainly lead to unemployment of labour. The first statement is therefore correct.

When labour costs form a high proportion of total costs, a rise in labour costs will cause a relatively large rise in the price of the product. In consequence, quantity demanded will fall and fewer workers will be required to produce the product. The second statement is therefore correct.

When a wage increase results in the marginal cost of labour rising above the marginal revenue product of labour, the firm will be employing too many workers for profit maximisation. The effect of a wage increase in such circumstances will be to reduce the numbers employed. The third statement is therefore correct.

The key is A. Statements 1, 2 and 3 are all correct.

## REVIEW QUESTIONS AND ANSWERS

### Questions

1 Why is the productivity of the average American worker likely to be higher than that of a worker in Russia?

2 A trade union negotiates a wage rate which is greater than marginal revenue product. Use a diagram to illustrate that not all members of the union can expect to benefit from this in the long run. How might an increase in productivity alter this diagram?

3 For a time in the late 1970s and early 1980s some airlines stopped training new pilots. Use supply and demand analysis to predict how the wages of pilots subsequently altered during times of increased economic activity.

4 Are the promoters of a recital by Pavarotti able to pay the artist high wages because of the high ticket prices they can charge for admission, or are they forced to charge high ticket prices because of the artist's ability to command high fees?

5 Explain why land prices are much higher in New York City than on the plains of the American mid-west.

Figure 17.9 *Lorenz curves of income earned and earners*

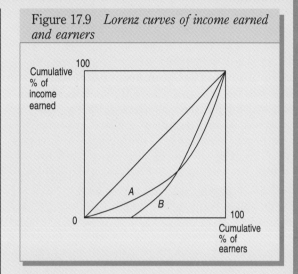

6 Examine the two Lorenz curves A and B in Figure 17.9.

Which of these Lorenz curves shows a more unequal distribution of income? Carefully justify your answer.

7 A person inherits £50,000 and uses it to buy a shop. At the end of the first financial year an accountant finds that sales receipts were £40,000 and costs were £36,000 and reports

Table 17.1 *Male and female earnings and employment*

|  | 1973 | | | 1988 | | |
|---|---|---|---|---|---|---|
| Occupational group | Female–male differential* | Proportion of female employment† | Male earnings, as % of average male earnings‡ | Female–male differential* | Proportion of female employment† | Male earnings as % of average male earnings‡ |
| Clerical and related | 70.7 | 49.0 | 103.6 | 80.2 | 59.2 | 109.0 |
| Selling | 46.0 | 7.8 | 111.5 | 55.9 | 8.4 | 127.3 |
| Catering, cleaning, etc. | 72.4 | 14.5 | 76.3 | 82.5 | 12.5 | 77.4 |
| Materials processing: excluding metals | 63.1 | 3.9 | 95.9 | 68.4 | 2.2 | 94.8 |
| Making and reparing: excluding metal, electrical | 58.5 | 8.4 | 104.8 | 66.2 | 6.4 | 98.6 |
| Processing, making and repairing: metal, electrical | 61.5 | 4.1 | 105.9 | 69.6 | 2.0 | 104.1 |
| Repetitive assembling and related | 61.2 | 10.6 | 100.7 | 72.8 | 8.2 | 93.5 |
| Transport operating, storage and related | 70.5 | 1.6 | 89.7 | 79.9 | 1.1 | 87.9 |
| All identified occupations | 65.7 | 100.0 | 100.0 | 79.1 | 100.0 | 100.0 |

*Notes*: *Average hourly earnings (excluding overtime pay and overtime hours) of adult women in full-time employment as percentage of average hourly earnings of adult men in full-time employment.
† Females in occupational group as % of all females in identified occupations.
‡ Male hourly earnings in occupational group as % of average male earnings in all identified occupations.

*Source*: Department of Employment.

that profits were therefore £4,000. Explain why an economist might not agree that this represents a true picture of the shop's profitability.

8  Suppose that a local firm were negotiating a wage deal with a trade union, and asked you as an economist for advice. Write a report showing how economic theory might be relevant to the negotiations.

9  Examine the figures in Table 17.1 (on p. 101).

(a) What are the difficulties involving comparing male and female wages?

(b) Why do women tend to have inferior pay to men? Are these reasons purely economic?

(c) can legislation improve the wages of women? Does the data support the view that the Equal Pay Act of 1970 has been effective?

## Answers

1  There are many reasons for the differences in productivity. The main factor is undoubtedly that workers in the USA work with more advanced and efficient capital equipment than their counterparts in Russia. Workers in the USA are also likely to be better educated, better fed and generally healthier than workers in Russia. Motivational factors might also be important. For example workers in the USA are more likely to receive bonus payments as a reward for increasing productivity than are workers in Russia.

2  In Figure 17.10, $MRP$ represents the firm's initial marginal revenue product curve. The existing wage rate is $OW$ and in equilibrium the profit maximising firm employs $OM$ workers.

If a trade union is able to negotiate a wage increase above the rate currently paid, for example, to $W_1$, and all other things remain equal, the number of workers employed will fall to $OM_1$. However, if the union is also able to increase productivity, then $MRP$ will shift to $MRP_1$. In this case the union might be able to negotiate a wage increase of $WW_2$ with no reduction in the number of workers employed.

3  In Figure 17.11, $SS$ and $DD$ are the original supply and demand curves for airline pilots. The original wage rate for airline pilots is therefore $W$.

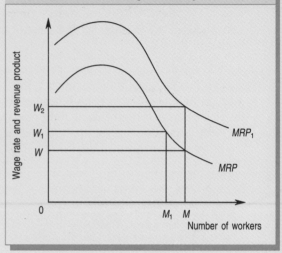

Figure 17.10   *The effect of a wage increase on the number of workers employed with and without an increase in productivity*

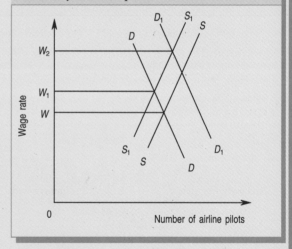

Figure 17.11   *The effect on the wage rates of pilots of a change in supply and a change in demand for airline pilots*

A reduction in the number of airline pilots trained will, over time, result in a shift in the supply curve to $S_1S_1$. If all other things remained equal this would cause an increase in the wages of pilots to $W_1$. However, if increased economic activity also leads to an increase in air travel, perhaps because more people take holidays abroad as a result of increased prosperity, the demand for pilots will increase, shown by the shift in the demand curve to $D_1D_1$, and wages will rise to $W_2$.

**4** The ticket prices for a Pavarotti concert, like all other prices, are determined by supply and demand. The demand to see an artist like Pavarotti is such that demand for tickets to see any of his concerts will be relatively high, whereas the number of places will be limited. Consequently ticket prices will be relatively high. The same reasoning explains the ability of Pavarotti to command the fees he does.

**5** The explanation is simple. Sites in New York City command higher prices than sites on the plains of the mid-west because there is a higher demand at any given price for such sites. In turn, the higher demand is explained by the fact that New York City offers access to millions of consumers, whereas the plains of the mid west are more remote. Sales would therefore be greater for a firm located in New York City and this explains the difference in site values.

**6** Curve B shows a more unequal distribution of income than curve A because curve B shows that a greater proportion of the population earn a smaller percentage of total income than illustrated by curve A.

**7** An economist would also consider the opportunity cost of using the £50 000 inheritance. For example, it might have been deposited in a building society, in which case it would earn interest. In using the money to buy a shop, interest is forgone and this is why an economist and an accountant would have different views on the level of profit earned in the first year.

**8** There are many factors that might be considered here. Local conditions in the labour market would be relevant to a trade union, especially if there was a labour market shortage. Another factor that might be highlighted is the willingness of the workforce in cooperating with the introduction of new equipment or changed working practices aimed at increasing productivity. When productivity increases, firms can increase the wage rate without necessarily increasing their costs of production. A trade union might also stress the level of profit earned by the organisation since the last pay award and the contribution of union members in raising profit. Changes in the cost of living in the area might also be relevant, especially when this exceeds the national average, as it might do in London and the south east. These points could be linked to the potential loss of workers to rival firms or other parts of the country if pay demands are not met.

**9** (a) A major problem with such comparisons is that differences in pay are often based on differences in the type of work performed. In addition, comparisons of this nature take average wages and this might mask considerable differences between workers in one organisation compared with workers in another organisation.

(b) There are many possible reasons. Women often seek part-time employment to coincide with school hours. They are often more willing to accept employment in the low paid jobs because they are not the main household earner and have often sacrificed their own careers so as to run a home and raise a family. They often lack strong union representation. These are clearly economic factors accounting for wage differences but discrimination might also account for differences in pay. Women might very well be discriminated against when applying for more highly paid jobs or when there are opportunities for promotion. They might also be discriminated against if employers are less willing to train female workers because they fear they will withdraw from the labour market to raise a family. In fact many women now combine a career with an active family life and it is hoped that this kind of discrimination will disappear.

(c) There is no doubt that equal pay legislation can improve the position of women by making it illegal to offer different rates of pay for the same work purely because of gender differences. The narrowing of the female differential in the table we are given clearly indicates that the relative position of women has improved between 1973 and 1988. However the existence of the differential suggests that discrimination still exists. If this is correct the most effective long term solution is to change attitudes.

CHAPTER 18

# NATIONAL INCOME AND ITS MEASUREMENT

## Topic Summary

National income statistics provide a summary of a nation's economic activity. This information is necessary for the formulation and implementation of economic policy as well as in determining quotas, such as contributions to the EC budget, and the allocation of economic aid to less developed countries.

## Defining National Income

At its simplest, national income is a measure of output produced in a given period, usually one year. The main official measure of national income in the UK is **gross national product** (GNP). However, this is not the value of output produced within the UK. The total value of output using resources located within the UK is **gross domestic product** (GDP). The difference between GNP and GDP is due to income paid on resources owned by residents of one country, but which are located in another country. Such incomes are referred to as **property income** because they are derived from the ownership of property. They take the form of interest rent, and dividends and the difference between inflows and outflows is referred to as **net property income paid abroad**.

Despite the fact that GNP is the main official measure of national income, the term 'national income', is usually taken to refer to **net national product** (NNP). The difference between GNP and NNP is depreciation of capital. Deducting depreciation simply recognises the fact that not all of the capital equipment which is produced in a given period adds to the nation's stock of capital. Some is used to replace capital that has become obsolete over the accounting period.

## Measuring the National Income

### The Income Method

This approach to calculating national income is based on the fact that the value of goods and services produced must be exactly equal to the value of incomes paid to the factors of production which have produced them. Factor incomes consist of income from employment, income from self-employment, interest, rent and profit. Again we must add net property income from abroad to obtain GNP and deduct depreciation to obtain NNP. The main problem with computing national income in this way is the need to avoid including **transfer payments**. These are simply payments made as part of a redistribution of income rather than as payment to a factor of production in return for its contribution to output. Transfer payments include pensions and social security payments to the unemployed.

### The Expenditure Method

The expenditure method of calculating national income is based on the fact that whatever is produced must either be sold or added to stock. All that is necessary is to add up the value of final expenditures on domestic output plus any domestic output which is added to stock or consists of work in progress. We have stressed the importance of domestic output because some expenditure of UK residents will be on **imports**, including imports of raw materials and other components. Since national income is defined as national output, expenditure on imports must be deducted from total expenditure when calculating national income.

This calculation will yield GDP. However not all expenditure undertaken by residents is paid to the factors of production, some is paid to the government in the form of **taxation**. To obtain the amount received by the factors of production we simply deduct from final expenditure the amount paid in indirect taxation and add on any government **subsidies**. This is because subsidies reduce the market price of goods and services so that the amount received by the factors of production exceeds the market price paid by consumers by the amount of the subsidy.

After these adjustments have been made we have *GDP at factor cost*. If we add on *net property income from abroad* we have GNP at factor cost and deducting *depreciation* from this aggregate gives NNP.

A possible problem with this approach is to ensure that we distinguish between a change in the value of stock due to a rise in prices, which does not add to national income, and a change in the value of stock caused by a change in the amount of stock held, which does add to national income.

## The Output Method

When national income is measured by the output method we simply add the value of all goods and services produced within the UK to yield GDP at *market prices*. Again, if we wish to obtain GDP at *factor cost* we simply *deduct* indirect taxes and *add on* subsidies. Adding net property income from abroad gives GNP at factor cost and deducting depreciation gives NNP.

The main problem with this approach to calculating national income is the need to avoid **double counting**, that is, counting the same output twice. For example, if we include the total output of the steel industry and the total output of the coal industry we will be including the value of the coal used to produce steel twice. To avoid double counting we must either add the final value of output or the value added at each stage of production.

## *Changes in Real GNP*

Nominal GNP is simply GNP at current market prices, whereas real GNP refers to the *volume* of output produced (plus net property income from abroad). The main causes of a change in nominal GNP are changes in the prices of goods and services due to inflation and changes in the volume of output a nation produces. To measure changes in real GNP we need to eliminate the effect of inflation on nominal GNP. To do this we measure GNP **at constant prices**. This simply means that we reduce nominal GNP in the

ratio that prices have increased between the two years that we wish to compare. The following example illustrates the general principles involved. (Note that an index of prices simply shows the percentage increase in prices of a specified basket of goods and services – see Chapter 27.)

| Year | Nominal GNP (£m) | Index of prices |
|------|------------------|-----------------|
| 1    | 300 000          | 100             |
| 2    | 350 000          | 110             |

To change nominal GNP in year 2 to GNP at constant year 1 prices we simply reduce nominal GNP in year 2 in the ratio that prices have increased between year 1 and year 2. Thus we have:

$$£350\,000 \times 100/110 = £318\,181.8\text{m (approx)}.$$

From this we can calculate the percentage increase in real income. Thus we have:

$$(£18\,181.8\text{m} - £300\,000\text{m}) \times 100 = 6 \text{ per cent}$$
$$\text{(approx)}.$$

## *Problems with Comparing the Standard of Living*

The most common measure of the standard of living is *GNP per head* or *GNP per capita*. This statistic is the basis of most official comparisons of the standard of living, whether we compare one year with another year or one country with another country. Despite its widespread use, there are several limitations of using per capita GNP for purposes of comparison.

### Inflation

When comparing the standard of living at different points in time it is important to ensure that we use GNP at constant prices rather than GNP at current prices. If we did not, then comparisons of GNP per capita would be misleading. For example, if there was a rise in prices but no change in population, using nominal GNP to compare living standards implies that the standard of living would increase each time prices increased!

### The Distribution of Income

If there is an increase in per capita GNP at constant prices, this does not necessarily imply that for most people the standard of living has increased. For example, if the distribution of income becomes less equal, then the increase in per capita GNP at constant prices might imply that a relatively small number of people have significantly higher real incomes while for the majority of the population real income is either unchanged or only slightly changed.

## Leisure Time

An important determinant of living standards is the availability if leisure time. Even when per capita income at constant prices between two periods or two countries is constant, the standard of living will differ if there has been a change in the numbers of hours worked or the number of annual holidays awarded to the workforce. This is a particular problem when making comparisons between developed countries and less developed countries because the latter are usually characterised by vast inequalities in the distribution of income.

## Composition of Output

Changes in per capita income might inaccurately reflect changes in living standards because there have been important changes in the range of goods and services produced. For example, in recent years the 'peace dividend' has released resources from the production of military equipment which are now available for the production of goods and services which more directly affect the standard of living. In other words, although the value per capita income may not change between two periods, the standard of living may differ if the composition of output changes. Similarly, if there are differences in the composition of output between two countries, per capita income will not necessarily provide a reliable indicator of living standards.

## Externalities

All measures of GNP per capita are based on market prices but these omit all externalities. If society loses the use of some amenity as a result of production or consumption then the measured value of GNP per capita will underestimate its true value. For example, if a chemical factory dumps its toxic waste into a river and kills all the fish, then those who use the river, such as anglers, bear part of the cost of production. In other words, if negative externalities increase, an increase in per capita GNP at constant prices does not necessarily imply that the standard

of living has increased. Similarly, if there are differences in the level of externalities imposed on the population in different countries, comparisons of per capita income will give a misleading indicator of relative living standards.

## Self-provided Commodities

When there are differences in the volume of output provided on a 'do it yourself' basis comparisons of per capita income will give an inaccurate estimate of the standard of living. Anyone painting their own house or growing their own vegetables produces an output which is unrecorded in estimates of GNP. Where there are differences in the amount of work undertaken on a DIY basis, either from one year to the next or from one country to another, comparisons of per capita income will distort the true difference in the standard of living.

## The Underground Economy

A great deal of economic activity is unrecorded because those involved do not declare their earnings so as to avoid payment of taxes. The existence of the underground economy reduces the accuracy of GNP statistics and adds to the problem of making meaningful comparisons of per capita income. For example, if the size of the underground economy changes from one period to the next or differs between countries, comparing per capita income will not accurately reflect relative living standards.

## Common Mistakes to Avoid

GDP and GNP are frequently confused. The former is simply the value of output produced within a nation's borders. It takes no account of the ownership of resources used in production. GNP, on the other hand, measures the value of incomes received by a nation's population. The difference between these two aggregates is explained on p. 104.

Another general problem is to recognise **which activities make a contribution to measured national income**. In general, an activity makes a contribution to measured national income if we can identify an output, an expenditure and an income. For example, if someone cleans their own windows, an output is produced but there is no expenditure on this output and certainly no income is received from supplying it. On the other hand, if a window cleaner is employed the same output is produced but now we can also identify an expenditure (the householder pays the window cleaner) and an income is received (the householder's expenditure is the window cleaner's income). There are exceptions to this rule – for example, an estimate is included of the rental value of owner-occupied dwellings – but, in general, the rule is reliable.

## Questions and Answers

### Questions

1  (a)  Distinguish between the cost of living and the standard of living.
   (b)  Examine the factors likely to improve the standard of living either in the UK or in a country of your choice over the next ten years.
   ULEAC, January 1992

Questions 2 and 3 are based on the following information about different aggregates for an economy during the course of a particular year.

|  | £m |
|---|---|
| Consumers' expenditure | 3500 |
| Gross investment | 500 |
| Government final expenditure | 950 |
| Taxes | 375 |
| Subsidies | 100 |
| Imports | 175 |
| Exports | 250 |
| Net property income from abroad | 20 |
| Depreciation | 190 |

The following options apply to questions 2 and 3 below.

A  £5045m
B  £5025m
C  £4855m
D  £4770
E  £4580

2  Which one of the above options gives the value of GNP at market prices?

3  Which one of the above options gives the value of net national product?

### Answers

1  (a)  The cost of living refers to the quantity of goods and services which can be purchased with a given amount of money. If we take a typical basket of goods, then, as the price of those goods in the basket rises, the purchasing power of money will fall. In this sense, there has been an increase in the cost of living because goods and services now cost more. In the UK, the Index of Retail Prices is sometimes referred to as the 'cost of living index' because it measures changes in the price of a specific basket of goods and services which are bought regularly by the average household.

The standard of living is a vague concept bound up with notions of the quality of life. Economists attempt to measure the standard of living in various ways, such as the number of qualified doctors per head of population or the amount of income the average family spends on food. However, it is recognised that the most important determinant of the standard of living is the level of consumption achieved by the average family. As an approximation to this, economists rely on GNP per head, or per capita income as a measure of the standard of living. Despite its limitations such as the fact that it takes no account of inequality in the distribution of income and wealth, GNP per capita does provide a reasonable approximation to the standard of living. After all, the higher GNP per capita the lower the proportion of income that is devoted to basic necessities, and the greater the proportion that can be devoted to other areas that affect the quality of life, such as health care.

(b)  In the UK, a major factor that is expected to increase living standards over the next ten years and beyond is the completion of the Single European Market in 1992. The main effect of this was to liberalise trade within the EC. Over time this will increase the scope for competition, specialisation and trade within Europe and the UK, along with all other EC countries, will benefit from this. The Cecchini Report estimated that the benefits of creating a single market might be as high as 5 per cent of Community GDP. To the extent that the UK shares in these gains, living standards in the UK will rise.

In the 1980s the UK, along with many other countries, introduced policies of privatisation and deregulation. The former returned public sector assets, such as the electricity generating boards, to the private sector, while the latter opened up markets to competition by removing legal barriers which prevented the emergence of competition. Both policies are expected to encourage increased productivity into the future. There is already some evidence that, because privatised industries place more emphasis on profit than public sector organisations, there has been an increase in productivity. Similarly it has been argued that, by encouraging competition, deregulation has led to increased efficiency. The gains from privatisation and deregulation will continue into the future as firms are forced to seek further improvements in efficiency. They will certainly have a favourable effect on living standards over the next ten years.

One major development that will have an important effect on living standards in the UK is the end of the 'cold war' and the 'peace dividend' released as a result. It is now no longer thought necessary to maintain such high levels of expenditure on the armed forces and therefore more resources will be available for the production of those goods and services which are directly consumed by the population. Of course, whether the end of the 'cold war' will result in a higher level of consumption depends on whether the resources released are put to some productive use!

Another factor that will have an important bearing on the standard of living in the UK is the rate at which output in the rest of the world grows. The UK is an open economy and if the world, and in particular Europe, is in recession the demand for UK exports will be depressed and this will reduce output and employment in the UK. If world output is rising rapidly, demand for UK output will increase and this will have a positive effect on the standard of living over the next ten years. To some extent, therefore, the growth of living standards in the UK over the next ten years will depend on developments in the rest of the world, and in particular Europe, since this is the UK's major export market.

Over the next ten years the output of oil from the North Sea will decline and therefore the UK will become more dependent on imports of oil. The implication is that to maintain the same levels of oil consumption it will be necessary to cut back on imports of other goods and services, or to increase exports. In both cases there will be an adverse effect on the standard of living because of the implied cut in domestic consumption. It might be possible to economise on the consumption of oil, and to some extent the standard of living in the UK over the next ten years depends on this. The greater the reduction in oil consumption, the lower the negative effect of declining North Sea output on the standard of living.

Another important factor that affects future living standards is investment, which increases the size of the capital stock. In this context it is important to distinguish between capital widening and capital deepening. The former refers to an increase in the size of the capital stock during a period of rising population such that the amount of capital per worker is unchanged. In these circumstances the standard of living is unlikely to increase because productivity is unlikely to change. On the other hand, capital deepening occurs when the rate of investment is such that there is an increase in the stock of capital per worker. Given the productivity of capital, this will make possible an increase in output per head and will therefore lead to an improvement in living standards. After all, the more we produce per head, the more we can consume per head! In the UK, as in any other country, if investment outstrips population growth, the standard of living will rise. However, even if the ratio of capital to population is constant, if technological progress is rapid the standard of living may improve because of the higher productivity derived from investing in the latest technologies.

Productivity is also influenced by the efficiency with which the labour market functions. In this context education and training of the labour force are important determinants of future productivity. The UK has implemented a series of educational reforms and training initiatives throughout the 1980s and into the 1990s which will no doubt have some influence on productivity and living standards. It is also recognised that taxation, and in particular rates of income tax, can have an important effect on incentives. If there is a connection, then if the government achieves its aim of reducing income tax there will be a favourable impact on living standards over the next ten years.

Despite the importance attached to levels of material consumption it is increasingly recognised that other factors make an important contribution to living standards. In recent years the impact of externalities on the environment has attracted increasing attention. We are now very aware of the effect of sulphur dioxide emissions by motor vehicle exhausts and power stations which burn fossil fuels. Sulphur dioxide emissions are a major cause of acid rain which pollutes rivers, lakes and forests. The environment is an important amenity and its loss imposes a cost on society which must be set against any gains from increased output. Past emissions of sulphur dioxide, and other pollutants such as CFCs, by the UK and other countries, will continue to have a negative effect on living standards over the next ten years through their detrimental effect on health. However, if action is taken now to reduce atmospheric pollution by UK based firms, this will cause a reduction in living standards over the next ten years in the UK because it will increase the production costs of firms in the UK and this implies a reduction in real income. The major benefits of such a policy would occur in the longer term. Given the increased awareness of environmental issues it seems likely that the UK, along with many other countries, will enact legislation designed to reduce pollution. The effect on living standards will depend on how severe this legislation is.

Clearly there are many factors that will influence the standard of living in the UK over the next ten years. Any action which affects the allocation of resources or the growth of productivity will affect the standard of living. However, there are also many non-quantifiable variables that have an important bearing on living standards. Such factors as the increased availability of leisure time, improved medical knowledge and the incidence of negative externalities are all important determinants of the 'quality of life'. Progress in all of these areas is expected in the UK over the next ten years and this will have a favourable effect on the standard of living.

**2** GNP = GDP + net property income from abroad.

= C + I + G + X − M + net property income from abroad

= £3500m + £500 + £950 + £250m − £175m + £20m

= £5045m

Option A is correct.

**3** NNP = GNP at market prices − taxes + subsidies − depreciation

= £5045m − £375m + £100m − £190m

= £4580

Option E is correct.

---

# REVIEW QUESTIONS AND ANSWERS

## Questions

**1** When will GNP > GDP?

**2** Can personal disposable income ever be greater than GNP?

**3** You are given the following information about a particular economy.

| Year | Nominal income (£m) | Index of prices |
|------|---------------------|-----------------|
| 1 | 100 000 | 100 |
| 2 | 120 000 | 110 |

What has happened to real income over the period shown?

**4** Which of the following are transfer payments?

(a) A soldier's pay while serving abroad?
(b) A gambler's winnings?
(c) A student's grant?
(d) A son's earnings while employed in his father's business?

**5** The following data refer to the UK economy in 1984 (all figures are in £m)

| | |
|---|---|
| Income from employment | 180342 |
| Depreciation | 38371 |
| Total domestic expenditure at market prices | 391470 |
| Rent | 18937 |
| Net property income from abroad | 3304 |
| Exports | 91736 |
| Imports | 91852 |
| Taxes on expenditure | 52578 |
| Subsidies | 7797 |

(a) What is meant by the term 'total domestic expenditure at market prices'?
(b) What is the value of (i) GDP at market prices; (ii) GNP at market prices; (iii) NNP at factor cost?

**6** Why are leisure time and externalities important in estimating the standard of living?

**7** Apart from estimates of *per capita* income, how else might we compare living standards of people in different countries?

## Answers

**1** GNP = GDP + net property income from abroad. When net property income from abroad is positive, that is, when property income paid abroad is less than property income received from abroad, GNP will be greater than GDP.

**2** Personal disposable income is simply GNP + transfer payments − direct taxes and national insurance contributions. Personal disposable income will therefore be greater than GNP if transfer payments are greater than direct taxation and social security contributions. This implies that the government borrows to finance transfer payments.

**3** In year 2 national income at year 1 prices is £120 000m × 100/110 = £109 090.9m. Real income has increased by about 9.1 per cent, that is, the percentage change in national income at constant prices.

**4** A transfer payment is simply a transfer of income from one party to another which is not made in respect of any economic activity. On this definition a gambler's winnings and a student's grant are transfer payments.

**5** (a) Total domestic expenditure is simply total spending by domestic residents on domestic output. It therefore excludes import expenditure and earnings from exports.

(b) (i) £391 354m (ii) £394 658m
(iii) £311 506m.

**6** Most estimates of the standard of living simply take the average income per head as a guide to the average level of consumption. However the number of hours worked also affects the standard of living. If the average income in two countries is the same but one country has twice as much leisure time as the other, the standard of living will differ because leisure time has value. Similarly, if the average income in two countries is identical but one country has relatively little pollution compared to the other, the standard of living will again differ because of differences in the quality of life associated with a lower level of pollution.

**7** Sometimes estimates of the number of doctors per head or levels of literacy are used. Sometimes an estimate of the number of hours of work required to earn sufficient to buy a given basket of goods is used. Sometimes the extent of home ownership is used. These are important indicators of the standard of living but the most widely used measure is still per capita income.

# CHAPTER 19

# THE DETERMINATION OF NATIONAL INCOME

## Topic Summary

In chapter 18 the emphasis was on measuring national income. In this chapter and Chapter 20 we examine one model of income determination. The model is sometimes referred to as the **Keynesian model** after the economist, John Maynard Keynes, who created the model.

## The Two-sector Model

For simplicity it is usual to consider how national income is determined in an economy which consists only of **firms** and **households**. In this economy total spending will consist of spending by the households on consumption (C) and spending by firms on investment (I). That part of income which households do not spend is saving (S). Let us consider each in turn.

## Consumption

It is usually argued that consumption expenditure has two components: an **autonomous component** and an **induced component**. Autonomous consumption spending represents the basic minimum that consumers will spend on such items as food and clothing. This basic minimum is completely inelastic with respect to income. Induced consumption spending represents consumption that is determined by changes in income. In other words, a rise in income induces a rise in consumption expenditure and vice versa.

Because there is an autonomous and an induced component of consumption, the consumption function is usually expressed in the form

$$C = a + bY$$

where $a$ and $b$ are constants.

The extent to which consumption changes as a result of an increase in income is determined by the value of $b$. In fact $b$ is referred to as the **marginal propensity to consume** (MPC) which is given by the formula:

$$MPC = \Delta C / \Delta Y$$

where: $\Delta C$ = change in consumption and $\Delta Y$ = change in income. We shall see later that the marginal propensity to consume plays an important part in our analysis of income determination.

## Investment

In the real world there are many factors that influence the rate at which firms invest and we consider these in Chapter 21. In the present chapter and Chapter 20, we make an important distinction between **planned investment** and **unplanned investment**. Planned investment, as the term suggests, is simply the amount firms plan to invest during the next period. For simplicity we assume that this is exogenous, that is, it is unrelated to changes in income and can therefore be treated as a constant. However additions to stock are also classed as investment and the amount that will be added to stock in the following period cannot be determined beforehand since in part it depends on the amount firms sell. When actual or realised investment is greater than planned investment then unplanned investment has occurred.

## Saving

Saving is that part of income which is not spent on consumption by households. We noted earlier that the consumption function is given by

$$C = a + bY$$

and therefore the savings function is given by

$$S = -a + (1-b)Y$$

Note that, whenever $a$ is greater than $(1-b)Y$, saving will be negative; economists refer to this as **dissaving**.

Since $b$ is the marginal propensity to consume $(1-b)$ must be the **marginal propensity to save** (MPS), that is, the rate at which savings change as income changes. The marginal propensity to save is given by the formula

$$MPS = \Delta S/\Delta Y$$

## Leakages and Injections

In the simplest models of the circular flow of income all income earned by households is spent on consumption and all output produced by firms is for consumption by households. This, of course, is a highly unrealistic abstraction from the real world, but it does enable us to classify any expenditures other than consumption expenditures by households as *injections* into the circular flow of income, and any incomes paid out by firms which are not spent on consumption as *leakages*. In the two-sector model of the economy there is one injection, investment, and one leakage, saving.

## The Equilibrium Level of Income

The equilibrium level of national income exists when there is no tendency for income to change. Equilibrium can only exist when planned output by firms **exactly equals** planned expenditure. If planned expenditure exceeds planned output there will be **unplanned disinvestment** in stocks. On the other hand, if planned output is greater than planned expenditure, there will be **unplanned investment** in stocks and firms will cut back on the amount they produce in the following period. In other words, in this model of income determination, output adjusts to demand, that is, **output is demand determined**. If planned aggregate demand exceeds planned aggregate supply, firms will adjust their plans and output will go on rising until planned output is brought into equality with planned expenditure. The opposite occurs if planned aggregate demand is less than planned aggregate supply. In this case firms will revise their plans downwards and output will go on

falling until planned output is again brought into equality with planned expenditure.

The economy will also be in equilibrium when *planned injections* are equal to *planned leakages*. It is easy to show, using simple algebra, that realised saving will always equal realised investment:

$$Y = C + I$$
$$Y = C + S$$
$$I \equiv S$$

However this equality does not imply that planned savings always equal planned investment. In fact planned savings will only equal planned investment when the economy is in equilibrium. Consider what will happen if planned investment is greater than planned savings. In these circumstances planned output will be greater than planned expenditure and output will therefore rise in the following period. Alternatively if planned investment is less than planned saving, planned output will be less than planned expenditure and output will fall in the following period. Only when planned investment equals planned savings will income be in equilibrium. This is illustrated in Figure 19.1.

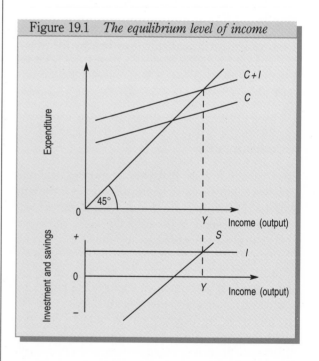

Figure 19.1   *The equilibrium level of income*

In the upper part of Figure 19.1, the 45° line shows all points of equality between realised expenditure and realised output. The graphs $C$ and $C + I$ show the levels of planned expenditure for consumption (C), and consumption plus investment ($C + I$), respectively. It is clear that $OY$ is the equilibrium level of income because only at $OY$ does planned expenditure equal planned output. At any level of income less than $OY$, planned expenditure is greater than planned output and therefore output will rise. On the other hand, at any level of income greater than $OY$ planned expenditure is less than planned output and therefore output will fall.

In the lower part of Figure 19.1, $I$ shows planned investment at all levels of income and $S$ shows planned savings at all levels of income. Again it is clear that $OY$ is the equilibrium level of income. At any other level of income planned expenditure is either greater than or less than planned output so that output will be changing so as to bring them into equality.

## A Numerical Example

Let us assume that in a particular economy we have the following values:

$$C = £200m + 0.8Y$$
$$I = £500m$$

From these values we can derive the equilibrium level of income:

| | or in equilibrium $I = S$ |
|---|---|
| $Y = C + I$ | |
| $Y = £200m + 0.8Y + £500m$ | $£500m = -(£200 + 0.2Y)$ |
| $0.2Y = £700m$ | $£700m = 0.2Y$ |
| $Y = £3500m$ | $Y = £3500m$ |

## The Multiplier

It is interesting to see what will happen to the equilibrium level of income in the above example if planned investment increases from £500m to £600m. Now we have:

| | or in equilibrium $I = S$ |
|---|---|
| $Y = C + I$ | |
| $Y = £200m + 0.8Y + £600m$ | $£600m = -(£200 + 0.2Y)$ |
| $0.2Y = £800m$ | $£800m = 0.2Y$ |
| $Y = £4000m$ | $Y = £4000m$ |

In other words an increase in investment of £100m leads to a fivefold increase in income! Why is this? Note that the $MPC$ is 0.8, so that, when investment increases by £100m, income will rise by £100m and households will spend 80 per cent of this, that is, £80m, on consumer goods. This implies a further increase in income of £80m and households will spend 80 per cent of this, that is, £64m, on consumer goods, etc.

In fact, following the increase in investment, we can easily calculate the eventual increase in income through the multiplier. It can be shown that the multiplier is equal to

$1/MRL$, where $MRL$ is the marginal rate of leakage. In this case saving is the only leakage and therefore this general formula for the multiplier reduces to $1/MPS$ in a two-sector economy. In our example we have

$$k = 1/MPS = 1/0.2 = 5$$

where $k = $ the multiplier. Given that the value of the multiplier is 5, if investment increases by £100m, income will rise by 5 x £100m, that is, by £500m.

## Common Mistakes to Avoid

One possible problem arises because of the labelling of the **Keynesian cross** or 45° diagram illustrated in the upper part of Figure 19.1 on. The $x$ axis is labelled Income (output). This reflects the fact that we are concerned with national income and therefore the incomes received by the factors of production are equal to the value of the output they produce. Hence income = output.

A more serious problem arises over the interpretation of **planned and realised values**. Planned values are simply what the different sectors of the economy *plan* to spend and produce. Realised values are the amounts that the different sectors *actually* spend and produce. Now there is no reason why planned values should always equal realised values. For example, if consumers change their attitudes and decide to increase the amount they save, firms will be left with unsold goods which they had previously planned to sell. However the important point to note is that, if the plans of any sector (households or firms) are not achieved, these sectors will revise their plans for the next period. In fact plans will be continually revised until they are achieved, in which case planned and realised vales will coincide and the economy will be in equilibrium.

## Questions and Answers

### Questions

1   In a closed economy with no government activity the level of national income rose by £100m as a result of an increase in autonomous injec-

tions of £40m. The marginal propensity to consume in that economy must have been

A   2.5
B   1.66
C   0.6
D   0.4

JMB, June 1991

**2** We are given the following information about planned saving at different levels of income in an economy:

| Income (£) | 500m | 600m | 700m | 800m | 900m |
|---|---|---|---|---|---|
| Saving (£) | −10 | 0 | 10 | 20 | 30 |

We can conclude that in this economy the marginal and average propensities to save are:

| | MPS | APS |
|---|---|---|
| A | constant | falls with income |
| B | constant | constant |
| C | constant | rises with income |
| D | rises with income | constant |
| E | rises with income | rises with income |

**3** Figure 19.2 shows the consumption function of a country.

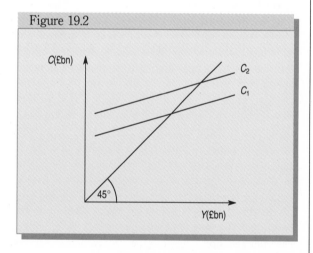

Figure 19.2

What could cause the consumption function to shift upwards from $C_1$ to $C_2$?

A   a rise in interest rates
B   a increase in direct taxation
C   the introduction of a 50 per cent deposit for the purchase of goods on credit

D   the expectation of an increase in indirect taxation

## Answers

**1** In general, the multiplier can be expressed in the form $k = \Delta Y/\Delta J$, where $k$ = the multiplier;

$\Delta Y$ = change in income
$\Delta J$ = change in autonomous injections

Substituting the information we are given tells us that in this case the value of the multiplier is 2.5. Now we know that in a closed economy with no government activity $k = 1/1 - MPC = 1/MPS$ and by rearranging this we have $MPS = 1/2.5$. This gives a value of 0.4 for the $MPS$, which implies that $MPC = 0.6$. The key is therefore C.

**2** For each change in income of £100, savings rises by £10. The MPS will therefore be constant at 0.1. However, as income rises, the proportion of income saved increases. For example, £20/£800 = 0.25, £30/£900 = 0.133 and so on. This implies that the MPS rises as income rises. The key is therefore C.

**3** Figure 19.2 shows that when the consumption function shifts from $C_1$ to $C_2$ consumption expenditure increases at all levels of income. Question 3 asks us to identify the cause of this.

An increase in interest rates would reduce consumer spending. For example, those with mortgages would have a lower disposable income and the cost of credit would increase, so reducing demand for many consumer durables. Option A is therefore incorrect.

Again an increase in direct taxation would reduce disposable income and consumption would fall. Option B is therefore incorrect.

The introduction of a minimum 50 per cent deposit for goods bought on credit would mean that many potential consumers would need to increase their savings in order to acquire the deposit. This implies a cut in consumption and therefore option C is incorrect.

An increase in indirect taxation such as value added tax would increase the prices of those goods and services on which tax is levied. The expectation of an increase in indirect taxation would therefore encourage consumers to bring forward their decisions on purchases. Option D is therefore correct.

The key is option D.

# REVIEW QUESTIONS AND ANSWERS

## Questions

1 A hypothetical two-sector economy is initially in equilibrium, with $MPS = APS = 0.25Y$ and investment is £100m. Subsequently $MPS$ falls to $0.2Y$.

   (a) Construct a graph to show the original equilibrium level of income and the new equilibrium level of income after the fall in $MPS$.

   (b) Why is there no change in investment in response to the decline in planned saving?

2 In a hypothetical economy which is initially in equilibrium, the consumption function is:

$$C = 100 + 0.8Y$$

where $C$ denotes consumption and $Y$ income. The level of investment is 100. Why is 600 not an equilibrium level of income? What is the actual equilibrium level of income?

3 The data below relate to a hypothetical economy for which column '$n$' shows the values of the variables when a state of equilibrium has been attained

|  | Weeks | | | | |
|---|---|---|---|---|---|
|  | 1 | 2 | 3 | 4 | '$n$' |
| Income (= output) | 200 | 180 | 164 | 151.2 | 100 |
| *Exante* investment | 20 | 20 | 20 | 20 | 20 |
| *Exante* savings | 40 | 36 | 32.8 | 30.2 | 20 |
| Consumption goods produced | 180 | 160 | 144 | 131.2 | 80 |
| Consumption goods demanded | 160 | 144 | 131.2 | 130 | 80 |
| *Exante* savings minus *exante* investment | 20 | 16 | 12.8 | 10.2 | 0 |

   (a) Calculate the MPC and MPS.
   (b) Explain the process of ajustment which is taking place.
   (c) What conditions are necessary for equilibrium to be attained?

## Answers

1 (a)

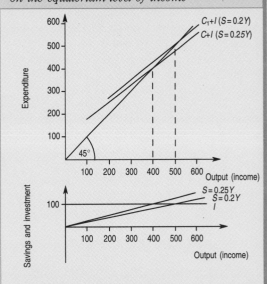

Figure 19.3 *The effect of a change in the MPS on the equilibrium level of income*

(b) The simple answer is that in the Keynesian model investment is assumed to be exogenous and therefore is unrelated to the level of income. However, in terms of the model, when planned saving falls to $0.2Y$ the equilibrium income rises to £500m; there is no change in the absolute level of savings which is constant at £100m. Since in equilibrium planned savings equal planned investment, this implies that investment will also be constant at £100m.

2 The equilibrium level of income occurs when planned output equals planned expenditure.
In equilibrium $Y = C + I$

$$Y = 100 + 0.8Y + 100$$
$$0.2Y = 200$$
$$Y = 1000$$

OR

In equilibrium $I = S$

$$100 = 0.2Y$$
$$Y = 1000$$

600 cannot be an equilibrium level of income because planned expenditure exceeds planned output at this level of income. This implies an unplanned reduction in stocks and as a consequence firms will increase output.

**3** (a) The MPS can be calculated by dividing the change in saving ($\Delta S$) by the change in income ($\Delta Y$) for any relevant pair of values. For example, $40/200 = 0.2 = 36/180$ and so on.

(b) The process of adjustment illustrated is the multiplier process in a two sector economy. In period 1, planned expenditure is less than planned output, so that firms cut back on the amount they produce in period 2. Here again planned expenditure exceeds planned output, so that firms again cut back on the amount they produce. This process continues until planned expenditure is brought into equality with planned output. The eventual change in income is a multiple of planned savings, hence the term 'multiplier process'.

(c) Equilibrium exists when planned expenditure equals planned output. In a two-sector economy this occurs when planned saving equals planned investment.

# CHAPTER 20

# NATIONAL INCOME DETERMINATION: THE FOUR-SECTOR ECONOMY

## Topic Summary

In the four-sector model of income determination we introduce the **government sector** and the **international sector**. In such an economy the equilibrium level of income occurs when planned expenditure equals planned output and in notation we can write

$$Y = C + I + G + X - M$$

where $Y$ = national income,
$C$ = consumption expenditure,
$G$ = direct government expenditure on goods and services,
$X$ = exports, that is, foreign expenditure on UK output,
$M$ = imports, that is, UK expenditure on foreign output.

We can also show that equilibrium occurs when planned injections = planned leakages.

We know that planned spending = $C + I + G + X - M$. We also know that income ( = output) = $C + S + T$.

This implies that $C + I + G + X - M = C + S + T$, that is,

$$I + G + X = S + T + M$$
(injections) = (leakages)

We can illustrate the equilibrium level of income diagrammatically, as in Figure 20.1

In the upper part of Figure 20.1, $AD$ represents aggregate demand or total planned expenditure at different levels of income. Again the 45° line shows all points of equality between planned expenditure

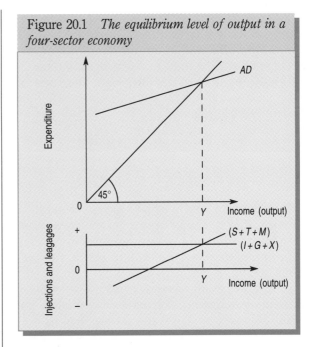

Figure 20.1 *The equilibrium level of output in a four-sector economy*

and planned output. $OY$ is therefore the equilibrium level of income. At any level of income less than $OY$, planned expenditure will exceed planned output. In this case firms will experience an unplanned reduction in stock and will therefore increase output in the following period. At any level of output greater than $OY$, firms will experience an unplanned increase in stock and will consequently cut back output in the following period. The economy can therefore only be in equilibrium when national income is equal to $OY$.

In the lower part of Figure 20.1, equilibrium is illustrated in terms of equality between planned injections ($I + G + X$) and planned leakages ($S + T + M$). Again it is clear that at any level of income less than $OY$ planned injections are greater than planned leakages, so that output will rise and at any level of income greater than $OY$ planned injections are less than planned leakages, so that output will fall.

## The Multiplier

In Chapter 19 we saw that the multiplier was equal to $1/MPS$. In the **extended Keynesian model** discussed in this chapter the multiplier is given by $1/MRL$, where $MRL$ is the marginal rate of leakage from gross income. In the full Keynesian model we must take account of the **marginal propensity to import** (MPM) which is the proportion of any increase in income which is spent on imports, and the **marginal rate of taxation** (MRT) which is the proportion of any increase in income which is paid in taxation. Thus, if we have the following values, $MPS = 0.2Yd$, $MRT = 0.25$ and $MPM = 0.125Yd$, the marginal rate of leakage from gross income is $0.25(0.8) + 0.2 + 0.125(0.8) = 0.5$. The value of the multiplier in this economy would therefore be equal to $1/0.5 = 2$.

## The Balanced Budget Multiplier

The balanced budget multiplier shows the effect on income of equal change in taxation and government expenditure. It can be demonstrated that in this case the multiplier has a value of 1, so that income will increase by an amount which exactly equals the increase in government expenditure. For example, assume government expenditure and taxation are both increased by £1000 and the marginal propensity to consume ($c$) equals 0.8. Now for $\Delta G$ we have:

$$\frac{\Delta Y}{\Delta G} = \frac{1}{1-c} \text{ that is } \frac{\Delta Y}{£1000} = \frac{1}{0.2}$$

$$\text{that is} \quad \Delta Y = £5000.$$

The effect of an increase in taxation on income occurs because the reduction in disposable income causes a reduction in consumption spending. For an increase in taxation we have:

$$\frac{\Delta Y}{\Delta T} = \frac{-c\Delta T}{1-c}, \text{ that is, } \frac{\Delta Y}{£1000} = \frac{-0.8}{0.2}$$

$$\text{that is} \quad \Delta Y = -£4000.$$

In other words, a simultaneous increase in government expenditure and taxation will result in a final increase in income equal to the increase in government spending, that is, the balanced budget multiplier is 1.

## Common Mistakes to Avoid

When calculating the multiplier in a four sector economy it is crucial to stress **the importance of gross income** in calculating the marginal rate of leakage. When we have taxation to consider we cannot simply add together the marginal propensity to save (MPS), the marginal rate of taxation (MRT) the marginal propensity to import (MPM) to derive the marginal rate of leakage because MPS and MPM are marginal rate of leakages from *net income*, whereas MRT is the rate of leakage from *gross income*. If MPS and MRT are expressed as functions of disposable income, that is, functions of net income, to obtain the multiplier we must convert these values to functions of gross income, as described above. However, take care when reading a question because MPS and MPM are sometimes given as functions of gross income, in which case they can simply be added together to obtain MRL. The difference is easy to identify. If variables are expressed as functions of $Yd$, they are functions of net income. If they are expressed as functions of $Y$, they are functions of gross income.

When an open economy with government is in equilibrium we know that planned leakages equal planned injections. However this does not imply that the balances of each individual sector must necessarily be equal. In other words, equilibrium does not require that $I = S$, $G = T$ and $X = M$. This condition might exist, but all that is required for equilibrium is that the sum of planned injections equals the sum of planned leakages.

## Questions and Answers

### Questions

1  (a)  Examine the factors which influence the size of the national income multiplier.     (40)
   (b)  Distinguish between the different multiplier effects of
        (i)   an increase in social security payments,     (30)
        (ii)  a cut in the top rate of income tax. (30)
ULEAC, Jan 1992

2

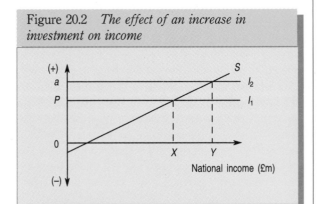

Figure 20.2   *The effect of an increase in investment on income*

In Figure 20.2, *S* is the savings function and $I_1$ and $I_2$ are different levels of investment. If investment increases from $I_1$ to $I_2$ the value of the marginal propensity to consume is represented by

A   *XY/PQ*
B   *PQ/XY*
C   *(XY/PQ) − 1*
D   *1 − (PQ/XY)*
E   *1 − (XY/PQ)*
ULEAC, Jan 1991

## Answers

**1** (a) The national income multiplier is simply the ratio of the change in income to the change in injections which brought it about. It can be written as:

$$k = \Delta Y / \Delta J$$

where $\Delta Y$ is the final income, $\Delta J$ is the change in injections and $k$ is the multiplier. It can be shown that the multiplier will always be greater than 1 and therefore a given change in injections will always result in a more than proportional change in income.

An injection is an autonomous change in expenditure and the multiplier effect occurs because any initial change in injections results in a more than proportional change in output and factor incomes. For example, if there is an increase in injections, perhaps because investment increases, output and factor incomes will rise. As factor incomes rise, expenditure will rise and this will generate a further round of increases in output and incomes. However this process will not go on indefinitely because each successive change in expenditure will be less than

the previous change. After all, for the economy as a whole, part of any increase in income will be paid in taxation, part will be saved and part will be spent on imports. In each case part of the income paid out will not be returned to domestic producers in the form of expenditures and so will not contribute to any subsequent rise in income.

When injections fall the opposite occurs: income falls, causing a reduction in expenditure and a further reduction in income. At each stage the reduction expenditure is less than the reduction in income because the reduction in income leads to a cut in savings, taxation and import expenditure, none of which contributed to income anyway.

The multiplier effect can easily be illustrated. For example, if we assume that the marginal rate of leakage is 0.5, then we know that half of any increase in injections will be spent on additional consumption and half will leave the circular flow of income as a leakage. If we further assume that autonomous investment increases by £100m, we can represent the eventual change in income as the sum of a series diminishing to infinity. The first few terms in this series are

$$£100m + £50m + £25m + \ldots\ldots = £200m$$

The first term (£100m) is the initial change in injections and the subsequent terms are the induced changes in consumption that result from the increase in income. In this case the multiplier has a value of 2, that is $\Delta Y / \Delta J = £200m/£100m = 2$.

The eventual change in income following a change in injections will depend on the size of the multiplier and this, in turn, depends on the rate at which income is withdrawn from the circular flow at each stage. The rate of withdrawal is the sum of the marginal propensity to save, the marginal rate of taxation and the marginal propensity to import. The greater the rate of withdrawal, the smaller the size of the multiplier because the smaller the proportion of income returned to producers following an increase in income, and vice versa. This is easily demonstrated since the value of the multiplier is equal to $1/MRL$ where *MRL* is the marginal rate of leakage from the circular flow of income. Thus if $MRL = 0.4$, the value of the multiplier is 2.5. If $MRL = 0.5$, the value of the multiplier is 2 and so on.

The size of the marginal propensity to save will depend on many factors. For example, a rise in the rate of interest might encourage an increase in saving. If this happens the value of the multiplier will fall. A change in expectations might also have an effect. If there is a widely held view that inflation will rise in the future, this might encourage an increase in present consumption which implies a reduction in the marginal propensity to save. In this case the value of the multiplier would rise. Another factor to consider is that in the initial stages of a recession there is some evidence that those in employment increase the amount they save to bolster consumption in the event of redundancy. In other words, the onset of recession might be associated with a rise in the marginal propensity to save and therefore with a fall in the value of the multiplier.

The rate of taxation is another major determinant of the size of the multiplier. Taxation is a leakage from the circular flow of income and therefore the greater the amount paid in taxation, the smaller the proportion of income that is returned to producers and therefore the smaller the value of the multiplier.

Import expenditure is another important leakage from the circular flow of income and the greater the marginal propensity to import, the smaller the value of the multiplier. There are several factors that might influence demand for imports and in the UK the marginal propensity to import is thought to be relatively high, perhaps as great as 30 per cent. In the case of the UK, foreign competitors often have an advantage in terms of design, delivery, after sales service and so on. A change in any of these factors will change the marginal propensity to import and therefore the value of the multiplier will change.

(b) (i) Social security payments are a transfer payment; that is, they represent transfers of income from some members of society to other members of society. The recipients of transfer payments experience an increase in disposable income and, depending on their marginal propensity to consume, will spend part of this increase in disposable income. The proportion of disposable income spent on domestic output will generate an increase in national income and, as noted above in the answer to part (a), if all other things remain equal, the final change in income will depend on the marginal rate of leakage.

However all other things might not remain equal and the net effect of a change in transfer payments depends partly on how these transfer payments are financed. If they are financed by an increase in taxation then there will be an offsetting reduction in expenditure. In this case the net effect of the increase in social security payments depends on the marginal propensity to consume of those who receive transfer payments relative to the marginal propensity to consume of those who pay higher taxes. In fact, because those in receipt of social security payments are likely to be on lower incomes

than taxpayers, it is likely that the former will be greater than the latter, so that national income will rise.

On the other hand, if transfer payments are financed by an increase in government borrowing the effect on national income will be greater. Because those in receipt of social security payments will be on lower incomes they will have a relatively high marginal propensity to consume. When the government finances increased social security payments by borrowing it simply increases the disposable income of those receiving social security payments by using the community's savings. Since savings are not part of the circular flow of income, the net effect of the increase in social security payments is determined entirely by the proportion of social security payments which is spent. Because this is likely to be relatively high, the effect on national income will also be relatively high.

(ii) The effect on national income of a cut in the top rate of income tax is likely to be less than the effect of an increase in social security payments. When there is a cut in taxation there is an increase in the disposable income of taxpayers. In consequence there will be an increase in expenditure and the size of this increase will depend on the marginal propensity to consume domestic output of those whose tax has been cut. In fact it seems reasonable to assume that those who pay the highest rate of taxation will have a higher marginal propensity to save than other groups in society. Because of this a relatively large proportion of any reduction in the top rate of income tax will be saved. The multiplier effect of a cut in income tax might therefore be relatively low. It will certainly be less than the multiplier effect of an increase in **social** security payments, where the majority of the increase in disposable income will be spent.

Another factor to consider is the proportion of income spent on imports and goods which are themselves taxed. Those on higher incomes are likely to spend relatively more on imported goods and services than those on lower incomes. Many imports, such as new cars, automatic washing machines, holidays abroad and so on are outside the budget of many of those who receive social security payments. If, as seems likely, a relatively large proportion of any cut in the top rate of income tax is spent on imports compared with an increase in social security payments the multiplier effect of the former will be smaller than the multiplier effect of the latter.

Similarly there are likely to be differences in the type of good that those who pay the top rate of income tax consume compared with those who receive social security payments. Specifically, those in receipt of social security payments might consume relatively more goods, such as food, which are not subject to VAT, compared with those who pay the top rate of income tax. To the extent that this is correct the multiplier effect of an increase in social security payments will be greater than the multiplier effect of a cut in the top rate of income tax.

**2** In a closed economy without government the marginal propensity to consume equals $1 - MPS$. In turn $MPS$ is equal to $\Delta S/\Delta Y$ where $\Delta S$ = change in savings and $\Delta Y$ = change in income. In this case $\Delta S = PQ$ and $\Delta Y = XY$. $MPC$ is therefore equal to $1 - (PQ/XY)$. The key is therefore $D$.

# REVIEW QUESTIONS AND ANSWERS

## Questions

**1** Explain the difference between an *endogenous* variable and an *exogenous* variable. Using examples from the national income model outlined in this chapter, distinguish between endogenous variables and exogenous variables.

**2** How is the equilibrium level of national income determined in a closed economy?

**3** The following data refer to a hypothetical economy:

Consumption = 100 + 0.8$Yd$
Investment = 150
Government = 200
Exports = 200
Taxation = 0.2$Y$
Imports = 0.05$Yd$

where $Y$ is the level of national income.
   (a) Find the equilibrium level of national income, using both the aggregate-demand and injections-leakages approaches. Illustrate your answer with the appropriate graphs.
   (b) Is there a budget surplus or budget deficit at the equilibrium level of income?
   (c) Is the balance of trade in deficit or surplus at the equilibrium level of income?
   (d) What is the value of the multiplier in this economy?
   (e) If exports increase to 250, what is the new equilibrium level of income?
   (f) In the original situation, if the government introduced transfer payments by 200, what is the new equilibrium level of income?

**4** Why is the balanced budget multiplier equal to 1?

## Answers

**1** An endogenous variable is a variable determined from within the system. With respect to national income an endogenous variable is one which varies directly with national income such as consumption, savings, taxation and imports. By contrast an exogenous variable is a variable that is determined outside the system. In the case of national income determination this implies that an exogenous variable is one that is unrelated to changes in national income. In the model of income determination outlined in this chapter the endogenous variables are consumption (though this often has an exogenous component), saving, taxation and import expenditure. The exogenous variables are investment, government expenditure on goods and services and export expenditure.

**2** The equilibrium level of national income exists when planned expenditure is equal to planned output. If the plans of the different sectors in the economy are not realised they will adjust the amount they plan to spend and produce until all plans are achieved.

**3** (a)  In equilibrium
$$Y = C + I + G + X - M$$
$$Y = 100 + 0.8Yd + 150 + 200 + 200 - 0.05Yd$$
$$Y = 650 + 0.8Y(1 - 0.2) + 0.05Y(1 - 0.2)$$
$$Y = 650 + 0.64Y - 0.04Y$$
$$0.4Y = 650$$
$$Y = 1625$$

OR

In equilibrium
$$I + G + X = S + T + M$$
$$150 + 200 + 200 = -100 + 0.2Yd + 0.2y + 0.05Yd$$
$$650 = 0.2Y(1 - 0.2) + 0.2Y + 0.05Y(1 - 0.2)$$
$$650 = 0.16Y + 0.2Y + 0.04Y$$
$$650 = 0.4Y$$
$$Y = 1625$$

(b) The state of the budget is given by $G - T$. In this case we have:

$G - T = 200 - 0.2Y = 200 - 325$. The budget surplus is therefore 125.

(c) The balance of trade is given by $X - M$. In this case we have:

$$X - M = 200 - 0.05Yd$$
$$= 200 - 0.05[0.8(1625)]$$
$$= 200 - 65$$
$$= 135.$$

The balance of trade surplus is therefore 135.

(d)  $k = 1/MRL$
  $MRL = MPS + MRT + MPM.$
  $MPS = 0.2(0.8)$
    $= 0.16.$
  $MRT = 0.2$
  $MPM = 0.05(0.8) = 0.04.$
  $MRL = 0.16 + 0.2 + 0.04$
    $= 0.4.$
    $k = 1/MRL = 1/0.4 = 2.5.$

(e)  $\Delta Y = k\Delta X$
  $\Delta Y = 2.5(250)$
  $\Delta Y = 625$
  $Y = 2250$

[You can easily check this by substitution in (a) above.]

(f) Government spending only adds directly to national income when it is spent on goods and services. Transfer payments are simply transfers of income from one group to another. They add to disposable income but they do not add directly to national income. However any increase in spending by those who are in receipt of transfer payments will add to national income because this will represent additional spending on goods and services. In this case disposable income rises by 200 and consumers will spend 80 per cent of this, that is, 160, on output. National income will therefore rise by $k \times 160 = 400.$

**4** The balanced budget multiplier is equal to 1 because any increase in government spending on goods and services leads to an increase in national income. However an equivalent increase in taxation does not lead to an equivalent reduction in national income because part of any increase in taxation will be financed by a reduction in saving. To the extent that this happens we are simply replacing one leakage with another leakage and the net effect on national income of this is zero. Only that part of taxation which is financed by a cut in expenditures reduces national income.

# CHAPTER 21

# *INVESTMENT*

## Topic Summary

Investment is the creation of real physical assets whose only function is to make possible further production. Investment is therefore a *flow* and the greater this flow the greater the change in the capital stock. As we shall see in Chapter 36, it is usually argued that increases in the capital stock are a major source of improved living standards. Economists are therefore very interested in what determines the flow of investment.

## *Discounting to Present Value*

Discounting to present value (DPV) is a technique used to assess the **present value of a stream of income received in the future** and/or **a stream of costs paid in the future**. DPV is important because the returns on investment usually accrue over several years into the future. However the costs of the investment will normally be met early on in its life. The problem is that a pound received now is worth more than a pound received in the future if only because it could be placed in a bank deposit, on which interest would be earned. Similarly costs incurred earlier in a project's life are greater in real terms than the same costs incurred later in the project's life. We therefore need a technique for comparing future revenues with present and future costs.

Discounting to present value can be thought of as the opposite of interest rate compounding. For example, if £100 is invested for two years at a rate of interest of 10 per cent per annum, the value of the investment will rise to £110 (£100 × 1.1) after one year and to £121 (£110 × 1.1) after two years. This is the same as £100 × (1.1)$^2$. Similarly, if we are offered £121 in two years' time, we can use our interest rate of 10 per cent as a discount rate to calculate the *present value* of £121 in two years' time. In this case we have £121/(1.1)$^2$ = £100.

We can see the importance of this if we consider the following example. Assume a firm is considering buying a machine for £250 000 and it will pay for it in full immediately. Assume further that the machine has a life expectancy of three years, after which its scrap value is expected to be £10 000. The net annual returns, that is, the annual returns after all operating costs have been met, are expected to be:

| | |
|---|---|
| Year 1 | £100 000 |
| Year 2 | £90 000 |
| Year 3 | £70 000 |

If we simply subtract the cost of the machine from the expected net returns, the investment looks profitable, that is, (£100 000 + £90 000 + £70 000 + 10 000) − £250 000 = £20 000. However the cost of the machine is incurred **now**, whereas the returns accrue **in the future**. If the appropriate rate of discount is 10 per cent, we can use this to obtain the present value of future returns. Thus we have:

$$\text{DPV} = \frac{£100000}{(1.1)} + \frac{£90000}{(1.1)^2} + \frac{£70000}{(1.1)^3} + \frac{£10000}{(1.1)^3}$$

$$= £225\,394.$$

Once we reduce future returns to present value we can see that in this case buying the machine would not be profitable.

DPV techniques are clearly superior to simply adding together expected returns and subtracting this from costs when deriving an estimate of expected profit. However there are major problems with DPV techniques. It is extremely difficult to estimate future returns and this becomes more difficult the further into the future we look. It is easier to estimate the return on a project with a life of one year than on a project with a life of ten years. In addition there are problems associated with selecting an appropriate rate of discount. Instead of using a discount rate of 10 per cent in the example above, if we use a discount rate of 4 per cent, purchasing the machine would be expected to yield a small profit of £483.6 when discounted to present value. The choice of discount rate can therefore affect the expected profitability of an asset. To a large extent estimating future returns and selecting a discount rate are matters of guesswork. Nevertheless this approach is at least more scientific than making no attempt to estimate the present value of future returns.

## Theories of Investment

### The Accelerator

This theory of investment relates changes in investment to changes in the level of economic activity. It seems intuitively obvious that there should be a relationship between investment and real GNP because in order to produce a greater amount of output firms will require a higher level of investment. However the accelerator indicates that changes in GNP might have a *more than proportional* impact on the rate of investment. An example will make this clear. Assume a capital–output ratio of 2:1; that is, to produce one unit of output per period the firm requires two units of capital, that each unit of capital has a life expectancy of five years and that every year 5 per cent of the capital stock is replaced. Given these assumptions, we can see in Table 21.1 the effect of changes in demand for final output on the rate of investment.

In year 1 we are in equilibrium with the capital stock equal to twice the rate of output. However in year 2 demand increases and therefore to produce the higher level of output the firm increases investment. But the rate at which investment increases is much higher than the rate at which output rises. In fact output rises by 10 per cent whereas total investment rises by 200 per cent. In year 3 the rate at which investment increases is again above the rate at which

output rises but in year 4 the level of investment actually falls, despite the fact that output is constant. In year 5 the fall in demand for final output results in a further fall in investment demand. Indeed in year 5 the portion of the capital stock that depreciates is not even replaced.

Of all the components of GNP, fixed investment is the most unstable element. The accelerator provides a possible explanation as to why investment demand might fluctuate markedly between periods. However, there are many possible reasons why the accelerator might not operate in the mechanical way outlined here. We have assumed that firms are willing and able to respond to increases in demand for their products. This might not be correct, for several reasons:

- The first response of any firm which experiences an increase in demand for its product will almost certainly be to run down stocks of finished goods rather than increase capacity.
- If firms have excess or unused capacity, an increase in demand will be met by using existing plant and machinery rather than by an increase in investment.
- Firms might not consider any increase in sales to be permanent. If they do not they are unlikely to increase fixed investment. Instead they are likely to meet increased demand by lengthening waiting lists or introducing overtime or shift working.
- Firms might not be readily able to alter investment plans because they might be constrained by lack of available plant, such as greater factory space. Similarly they might be unable to obtain additional supplies of capital, especially when resources are fully employed or they are dependent on an overseas supplier.
- Over time technological progress will increase the efficiency of capital so that it may be possible

| Table 21.1 | | | | | | |
|---|---|---|---|---|---|---|
| *Year* | *Sales* | *Existing capital* | *Required capital* | *Replacement investment* | *Net investment* | *Total investment* |
| 1 | 1000 | 2000 | 2000 | 100 | 0 | 100 |
| 2 | 1100 | 2000 | 2200 | 100 | 200 | 300 |
| 3 | 1250 | 2200 | 2500 | 100 | 300 | 400 |
| 4 | 1250 | 2500 | 2500 | 100 | 0 | 100 |
| 5 | 1200 | 2500 | 2400 | 0 | −100 | 0 |

to increase output without increasing the rate of investment.

- Changes in the rate of interest may lower the profitability of investment from one period to the next. If interest rates rise an increase in sales may not be sufficient to persuade firms to increase their investment in fixed assets, and vice versa.

Despite this, changes in the rate of investment are related to changes in GNP. However the relationship is unlikely to be of the magnitude illustrated in Table 21.1 and may, at certain times, be quite weak.

## The Marginal Efficiency of Investment

The DPV technique outlined on p. 123 might be useful for an individual firm in assessing the expected profit from additional investment, but it does not explain the determination of investment in the economy. However the **marginal efficiency of investment** adopts a different approach to derive a theory of aggregate investment. In this case we estimate future returns but then identify the rate of discount that reduces the present value of these future returns to equality with the cost of additional capital. In other words, we need to identify the rate of discount which makes the present value of expected future returns exactly equal to the cost of investment. The rate of discount which does this is the marginal efficiency of investment. If the rate of discount which achieves this is greater than the existing rate of interest, then, if all other things remain equal, additional investment will be profitable. If the rate of discount which achieves this is less than the existing rate of interest, then, if all other things remain equal, additional investment will be unprofitable.

A major problem with this approach is identifying the cost of additional capital. There will be considerable differences in the nature and type of assets bought and therefore considerable differences in their price. We therefore take the market rate of interest as our estimate of the cost of capital. In this situation the equilibrium rate of investment occurs when the discount rate is equal to the market rate of interest.

We can construct a hypothetical marginal efficiency of investment (MEI) schedule, as shown in Figure 21.1. In general the marginal efficiency of investment falls as the rate of investment increases. One reason for this is that firms will exploit the most profitable investment opportunities first and there-

fore, as investment increases, the present value of future returns will fall because of diminishing returns. Additionally, as investment increases, a greater volume of final output will be produced and, if all other things remain equal, the price of final output will therefore fall. As the price of final output falls the expected value of future returns will fall.

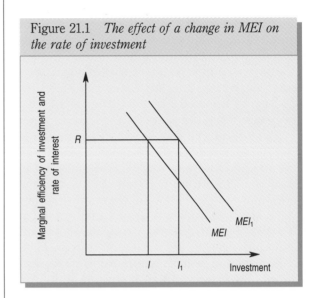

Figure 21.1 *The effect of a change in MEI on the rate of investment*

In Figure 21.1 the market rate of interest is $R$ and *MEI* is the initial marginal efficiency of investment schedule. The equilibrium rate of investment is $I$. Once this rate of investment is reached there will be no tendency to change unless there is a change in the rate of interest or a change in the productivity of capital. For example, if the rate of interest rises the rate of investment will fall, and vice versa. An increase in technological progress will shift the *MEI* schedule to $MEI_1$ and the new equilibrium rate of investment will be $I_1$.

Again there are problems with the MEI as a theory of investment. In particular it is extremely difficult to predict future returns and future rates of interest. A great many investment decisions are long term and changes in the rate of interest will change the cost of capital so that investment that might appear profitable at one rate of interest might not be profitable at a higher rate of interest. Firms may not always be prepared to invest if they suspect interest rates may rise before their investment projects are completed. Similarly it is difficult to estimate future returns, especially when these accrue in the long term, and the MEI schedule is therefore grounded in uncertainty. The less certain firms are of future returns, the less willing they will be to undertake investment projects at any given rate of interest.

## Cost–Benefit Analysis

Cost–benefit analysis is a technique used to assess the costs and benefits of large scale investment projects such as the construction of the Channel Tunnel. It is commonly used in the public sector where investment projects frequently confer benefits on society which are difficult to quantify. For example, constructing a bypass around a major town benefits road users since they complete their journeys more quickly, but it also benefits town residents since there will be less congestion around the main streets, probably fewer accidents, less damage to the foundations of buildings, a reduction in exhaust fumes and so on.

One problem with cost–benefit analysis is identifying all of the relevant costs and benefits. This is an extremely difficult task. Another problem is how to value all of the relevant costs and benefits including externalities. In the example, above what money value would we place on a reduction in road use in the town? Having identified and valued all relevant costs and benefits, they must be discounted to present value to facilitate comparison. We have seen on pp. 124–5 the problems associated with DPV techniques and the same considerations apply here.

One point to note in the case of public sector investments is that, if a cost–benefit analysis predicts an excess of benefits over costs, this does not imply that a project should go ahead. It simply implies that society would benefit if the project went ahead. Whether the project actually goes ahead is a political decision. The public sector has limited resources and politicians must decide how these are allocated. Cost–benefit analysis is simply an aid to decision taking.

## Common Mistakes to Avoid

The **accelerator** and the **multiplier** are frequently confused. Remember, from p. 113, that the multiplier is used to calculate the eventual change in income following a change in injections. The accelerator coefficient shows the change in investment that results from a change in income. Of course the two concepts are related. For example, an increase in income will, through the accelerator, generate a more than proportional change in the rate of investment. In turn, an increase in investment will, through the multiplier, generate an increase in income and so on. However this process will not go on indefinitely and at some stage the growth of national income will be insufficient to generate an accelerator effect.

There is a great deal of confusion over the difference between the **marginal efficiency of capital** and the **marginal efficiency of investment**. In fact the concepts are related, but the marginal efficiency of investment is a flow concept and relates to the short run, whereas the marginal efficiency of capital is a stock concept and relates to the long run. Remember, net investment is the rate at which the capital stock is increasing. In the short run the equilibrium rate of investment is given by the point on the MEI schedule where the marginal efficiency of investment is equal to the rate of interest. In the long run the equilibrium level of the nation's capital stock is given by the point on the MEC schedule where the marginal efficiency of capital is equal to the rate of interest.

## Questions and Answers

### Questions

1  The accelerator theory suggests that the level of net investment depends on changes in the level of national income. These changes might not occur in practice because:

1  business expectations of profit may be very pessimistic,
2  firms may have considerable spare capacity,
3  the rate of interest may be too low.
A  1, 2 and 3 are correct
B  1 and 2 only are correct
C  2 and 3 only are correct
D  1 only is correct
AEB, Nov 1990

2  Ways in which government policy may be used to shift the marginal efficiency of capital schedule to the right include:

(1) increasing depreciation allowances set against tax liabilities of firms,
(2) reducing the supply of money,
(3) increasing investment grants to industry,
(4) raising the rate of interest.
A  (1), (2) and (3) only are correct
B  (1) and (3) only are correct
C  (2) and (4) only are correct
D  (4) only is correct
E  (1) and 4 only are correct
JMB, 1990

3  In economic theory which of the following is NOT regarded as 'investment'?

A The purchase of stocks of raw materials

B Construction of new factories and ware-houses

C The building of a Channel Tunnel

D The purchase of shares on the Stock Exchange

E Training programmes for school leavers

ULEAC, Jan 1990

## Answers

**1** Profit is an important goal of firms in the private sector. Even if national income is rising, firms will not be persuaded to increase their rate of investment unless they expect investment to be profitable. They may not, for example, if their expectation is that the increase in national income is only temporary. Option 1 is therefore correct.

If firms have considerable spare capacity then output can be increased without increasing the rate of investment. In these circumstances the accelerator may not respond as national income rises. Option 2 is therefore correct.

A low rate of interest would tend to encourage greater investment. There might be several reasons for this. For example, at low rates of interest the cost of borrowing funds will be relatively low and, in many cases, this will reduce the cost of capital for firms. At low rates of interest demand for many consumer durables will be relatively high and this will increase the expectation of profit. This implies that low rates of interest would tend to encourage the accelerator effect. Option 3 is therefore incorrect.

The key is therefore B.

**2** If all other things remained equal, increasing depreciation allowances to set against the tax liabilities of firms would increase the expected net return on capital assets because it would reduce the amount paid in tax. The marginal efficiency of capital schedule would therefore shift to the right if depreciation allowances were increased. Option 1 is therefore correct.

If there was a reduction in the supply of money, in the short run at least, this would reduce demand for many goods and services because individuals and organisations would, on average, have less money to spend. This would tend to reduce the expected return on capital assets and would therefore tend to shift the MEC schedule to the left. Option 2 is therefore not correct.

An increase in investment grants to industry would tend to reduce the supply price of capital and therefore at any given rate of interest more capital would be demanded than previously. In other words the marginal efficiency of capital schedule would shift to the right. Option 3 is therefore correct.

When we construct the marginal efficiency of capital schedule we equate the rate of interest with the rate of discount which reduces expected future returns on capital assets to the supply price of capital assets. An increase in the rate of interest would lead to an upward movement along the marginal efficiency of capital schedule. It would not cause a shift of the schedule and therefore option 4 is not correct.

The key is therefore B.

**3** Economists define investment as the flow of expenditures devoted to increasing or maintaining the capital stock, plus additions to stock and work in progress. Raw materials are additions to stock and so option A is regarded as investment.

The construction of new houses and factories is regarded as fixed investment. They add to or maintain the nation's stock of capital and so option B is regarded as investment.

The construction of a Channel Tunnel would add to the nation's infrastructure and so option C is regarded as investment.

The purchase of shares on the Stock Exchange simply represents the transfer of assets from one owner to a new owner. There is no increase in the capital stock and therefore option D is not regarded as investment.

Training programmes for school leavers represents investment in human capital. Option E is therefore regarded as investment.

The key is therefore D.

# REVIEW QUESTIONS AND ANSWERS

## Questions

1  At a market rate of interest of zero, would the level of business investment be infinite?

2  (a) Using economic analysis and the information in Table 21.2, how might you explain observed changes in net fixed investment?

(b) What other factors may have influenced the level of net fixed investment in the period shown?

3  The data below refers to a hypothetical investment project with a life of two years and no final resale value.

Cash flow year 1        £1035
Cash flow year 2        £1058
Supply price of project    £1600

If the market rate of interest is 15 per cent, determine the viability of the project by estimating:

(a)  the present value of the cashflows.
(b)  the net present value of the project;

How would your appraisal be affected by a rise in the rate of interest to 25 per cent?

## Answers

1  The equilibrium rate of investment occurs when the marginal rate of return on investment is exactly equal to the marginal cost of capital. At zero rate of interest investment would continue up to the point at which the marginal rate of return on investment was zero.

2  (a) Net fixed investment refers to additions to the stock of capital. It is therefore investment net of depreciation and excludes additions to stock and work in progress. In general the behaviour of net investment follows the behaviour of GNP at constant prices with a lag of one year. In other words, if GNP at constant prices rises, net investment rises the following year and vice versa. This is illustrated in Figure 21.2.

The response of investment to changes in GNP is variable but the data lend support to the notion that there is an accelerator effect associated with changes in real GNP. The variable response of investment to changes in real GNP might also indicate that changes in expectations are important in determining investment decisions.

Table 21.2  *Investment and GNP, 1978–88*

| Year prices | GNP at 1985 prices | Gross investment at 1985 prices | | Net fixed investment at 1985 | |
|---|---|---|---|---|---|
| | (£b) | (£b) | (% of GNP) | (£b) | (% of GNP) |
| 1978 | 322.2 | 54.9 | 17.0 | 20.6 | 6.3 |
| 1979 | 331.8 | 56.4 | 17.0 | 21.3 | 6.4 |
| 1980 | 322.4 | 53.4 | 16.6 | 17.0 | 5.3 |
| 1981 | 320.1 | 48.3 | 15.1 | 10.7 | 3.3 |
| 1982 | 325.8 | 50.9 | 15.6 | 12.2 | 3.7 |
| 1983 | 338.8 | 53.5 | 15.8 | 13.6 | 4.0 |
| 1984 | 347.3 | 58.1 | 16.7 | 17.1 | 5.2 |
| 1986 | 358.1 | 60.3 | 16.8 | 18.5 | 5.0 |
| 1987 | 390.1 | 66.9 | 17.1 | 23.2 | 5.9 |
| 1988 | 406.7 | 75.7 | 18.6 | 29.8 | 7.3 |

*Source*: HMSO, UK National Accounts (1989).

Figure 21.2   *The behaviour of investment and GDP*

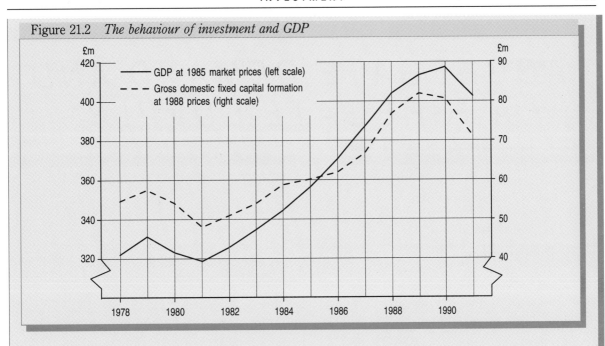

(b) Net fixed investment is influenced by a host of factors, such as changes in labour productivity and technological progress. However, the major factor influencing investment is expectations of future demand for output. If the expected return on investment increases, the rate of investment will increase.

**3** (a) Given a market rate of interest of 15 per cent, we can estimate the present value of future returns on the project. Thus:

$$PV = \frac{£1035}{(1.15)} + \frac{£1058}{(1.15)^2} = £900 + £800 = £1700.$$

(b) Given that the present supply price of the project is £1600, this project will yield an expected profit with a net present value of £100.

If the rate of interest increased to 25 per cent, the present value of future returns would fall to

$$PV = \frac{£1035}{(1.25)} + \frac{£1058}{(1.25)^2} = £828 + £677.12 = £1505.12$$

The net present value of the project now yields a loss of £98.88.

## CHAPTER 22

# AGGREGATE DEMAND AND AGGREGATE SUPPLY

## Topic Summary

In Chapters 19 and 20 it was assumed that the price level was fixed so that any change in national income implied a change in only real national income. It was also assumed that real national income responded passively to changes in aggregate demand. These are major assumptions and a more modern view of the macro economy is that changes in aggregate demand might have a short term effect on real national income, but in the long term lead only to changes in the price level. This implies the existence of supply-side constraints in the economy and it is therefore no longer feasible to assume that aggregate supply simply responds passively to changes in aggregate demand. This chapter addresses these issues.

## The Aggregate Demand Curve

As we have seen in Chapter 20, aggregate demand shows total expenditure in an economy over some period of time. In this chapter it is argued that at lower prices aggregate demand will be greater than at higher prices. The aggregate demand (AD) curve therefore shows an **inverse relationship** between quantity demanded and the average price level. This is illustrated in Figure 22.1.

There might be several reasons why, as the average price level falls, aggregate demand increases. One reason is that, as the price level falls, the purchasing power of money rises. In consequence this will persuade firms and consumers to increase their spending. Another reason is that, as the average price level falls, exports become more competitive, so that foreigners will tend to buy more, while imports will become less competitive, so that domestic residents will turn to domestic substitutes.

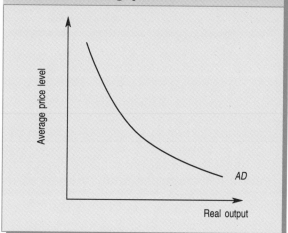

Figure 22.1 *The aggregate demand curve showing that the demand for real output is inversely related to the average price level*

## The Aggregate Supply Curve

Aggregate supply (AS) is the amount firms are willing to supply at different prices over some given period of time. However, while this statement is always true, there are important differences between the aggregate supply curve in the short run and the aggregate supply curve in the long run.

### Aggregate Supply in the Short Run

In the short run as prices rise firms will supply more. Again there might be many reasons for this, but one important reason is that, as prices rise, the profits available from production rise. Since firms produce for profit they will supply more as the average price level rises. It is also likely that, as the price level rises, less efficient producers who cannot make a profit at lower prices will be able to do so at higher prices. For both of these reasons aggregate supply will vary directly with the average price level, as illustrated in Figure 22.2, where $AS_S$ is the short run aggregate supply curve.

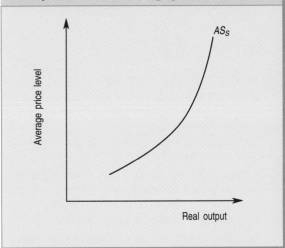

Figure 22.2 *The aggregate supply curve showing that in the short run the supply of real output is directly related to the average price level*

Despite the fact that output rises as the price level increases, there is a limit on the amount that can be produced at any point in time. This limit is reached when resources are fully employed in an economy. At this point the short run aggregate supply curve will become vertical.

## Aggregate Supply in the Long Run

It is now widely believed that in the long run aggregate supply is not influenced by changes in the price level. Instead aggregate supply in the long run is determined by **real factors** (as opposed to monetary factors) such as the size of the labour force and the skills it possesses, the size of the capital stock, technological progress which increases the productivity of capital, and so on. If this is correct it implies that in the long run the aggregate supply curve will be *vertical*, or *inelastic*, with respect to the average price level. In the long run the equilibrium level of output is referred to as *the natural rate* and in the long run this is regarded as the full employment level of income. In Figure 22.3, $AS_L$ is the long run aggregate supply curve and $Y_N$ is the natural rate of output.

## Short Run and Long Run Equilibrium

In Figure 22.3, $AD$ is the initial aggregate demand curve, $AS_S$ is the initial short run aggregate supply curve and $AS_L$ is the long run aggregate supply curve. The economy is initially in long run equilibrium with the average price level at P and output at the natural rate $Y_N$. Assume that the economy has been in equilibrium at this price and output combination for a considerable period of time and that no change in price or output is expected in the future.

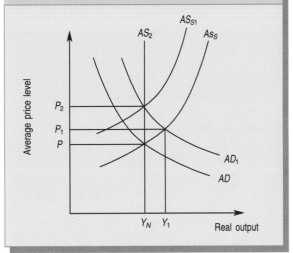

Figure 22.3 *The effect of an increase in aggregate demand on the price level and the level of real output in the short run and the long run*

Now assume that aggregate demand increases to $AD_1$, perhaps because of an autonomous increase in demand for exports. This increase in aggregate demand will cause the price level to rise and, as producers increase their output, we move up the short run aggregate supply curve until equilibrium is established with price at $P_1$ and output at $Y_1$. However the economy is not in long run equilibrium because trade unions will have negotiated pay awards for their members on the assumption that the average price level would not change from $P$. At the higher price level they will require higher wages to preserve their real income. When pay agreements are reached, the higher wage settlements will increase firms' costs of production at any given price level. This will shift the short run aggregate supply curve to $AS_{S1}$. Long run equilibrium is restored when output returns to the natural rate $Y_N$ and in this case the average price level has risen to $P_2$. (You might like to explain how long run equilibrium is restored following an autonomous increase in costs, perhaps because of a rise in oil prices.)

## Common Mistakes

In Chapters 19 and 20 we analysed aggregate demand on the assumption that there was no change in the price of goods and services. In other words we assumed that the average price level was constant. It was this assumption which allowed us to draw the aggregate demand curve in such a way that, as expenditure increased, real output increased. If prices are constant, an increase in domestic expenditure is only possible if domestic output increases. However, in the **real world**, prices are not constant and in this chapter we have analysed aggregate demand in the context that the price level can change. In particular the aggregate demand shows how the demand for real output changes as the price level changes.

There is also some confusion over the **nature of the aggregate supply curve** and economists are themselves by no means in agreement on this. In particular the notion of a vertical long run aggregate supply curve and the assumption of a natural rate of output are contested by many economists, who argue that the short run and long run aggregate supply curve are one and the same. They argue that the supply curve varies directly with the average price level and only becomes vertical at the point of full employment. They further argue that there is no natural rate of unemployment and that there is no reason why the full employment level of output should not also be the equilibrium level of output. Despite this it is fair to say that most economists now accept the notion of a natural rate of output and the notion of a long run aggregate supply curve that is vertical at the natural rate.

## Questions and Answers

### Questions

1 'Whether an expansion of aggregate demand increases employment, or the price level, depends upon the nature of aggregate supply.' Discuss

AEB, June 1991

2 If there is an upward shift in the aggregate supply curve, given a downward sloping aggregate demand curve, then it is likely that:

1    prices will rise
2    production will fall
3    unemployment will rise

A    1, 2 and 3 all correct
B    1 and 2 only correct
C    2 and 3 only correct
D    1 only correct
E    3 only correct

ULEAC, Jan 1990

### Answers

The answer to question 1 has been partly covered on p. 131. Consequently there is some overlap between the answer to this question and material covered in these pages.

1 Aggregate demand equals total expenditure in an economy over some given period of time. It is argued that, if all other things remain equal, aggregate demand will vary inversely with the average price level. In other words, as the price of output falls a greater amount will be demanded.

There may be several reasons why, as the average price level falls, aggregate demand increases. One reason is that, as the price level falls, the purchasing power of money rises. In consequence this will persuade firms and consumers to increase their spending. Another reason is that, as the average price level falls, exports will become more competitive, so that foreigners will tend to buy more, while imports will become less competitive, so that domestic residents will turn to domestic substitutes.

Aggregate supply is the amount firms are willing to supply at different prices over some given period of time. However, while this statement is always true, some economists believe that there are important differences between the aggregate supply curve in the short run and the aggregate supply curve in the long run.

All economists agree that in the short run, as prices rise, firms will supply more. Again there may be many reasons for this but one important reason is that, as firms expand output, they will experience diminishing returns and in consequence costs of production will rise. An increase in the price level is therefore necessary to persuade firms to increase their output. It is also likely that, as the price level rises, less efficient producers who cannot make a profit at lower prices will do so at higher prices. For both of these reasons aggregate supply will (usually) vary directly with the average price level.

Despite the fact that output rises as the price level increases, there is a limit on the amount that can be produced at any point in time. This limit is reached when resources are fully employed in an economy. At this point the short run aggregate supply curve will become vertical and output will cease to vary with the price level. Conversely at relatively low levels of output the short run aggregate supply curve might be relatively elastic. In such circumstances firms are likely to be operating with unused capacity and when they expand output they are unlikely to experience significant diminishing returns.

In Figure 22.4, aggregate demand and aggregate supply are initially represented by $AD$ and $AS$, respectively. Given these aggregate supply and aggregate demand conditions, the equilibrium price level is $P$ and the equilibrium level of output is $Y$.

Now whether an increase in aggregate demand affects employment, the price level or a combination of both, in the short run at least, depends on the nature of the aggregate supply curve. In Figure 22.4(a), aggregate supply is relatively elastic as aggregate demand increases from $AD$ to $AD_1$. In this case the increase in aggregate demand leads mainly to a rise in output from $Y$ to $Y_1$ and hence an increase in employment, but has little effect on the price level. In Figure 22.4(b), the increase in aggregate demand again leads to an increase in output, from $Y$ to $Y_1$, and employment, but in these circumstances there is also a significant rise in the price level, from $P$ to $P_1$. In Figure 22.4(c), the economy is initially at the full employment level of output $Y_F$ with the price level at $P$. In this case an increase in aggregate demand leads entirely to an increase in the price, from $P$ to $P_1$, since no increase in output beyond the full employment level is possible.

Some economists regard the adjustment to an increase in aggregate demand outlined in Figure 22.4 as permanent; that is, a short run and long run equilibrium. If this is so, it is clear that whether an increase in aggregate demand leads to an increase in employment or an increase in the price level does indeed depend on the nature of the aggregate supply curve. However it is now widely believed that, in the long run, aggregate supply is not influenced by changes in the price level. Instead aggregate supply in the long run is determined by real factors (as opposed to monetary factors) such as the size of the labour force and the skills it possesses, the size of the capital stock, technological progress which increases the productivity of capital, and so on. If this is correct it implies that in the long run the aggregate supply curve will be vertical, or inelastic, with respect to the average price level. This implies that the adjustments to an increase in aggregate demand outlined in Figure 22.4 are only short run adjustments. In the long run the equilibrium level of output is referred to as the natural rate and in the long run this is regarded as the full employment level of income.

In Figure 22.5, $AD$ is the initial aggregate demand curve, $AS_S$ is the initial short run aggregate supply curve and $AS_L$ is the long run aggregate supply curve. The economy is initially in long run equilibrium with the average price level at $P$ and output at the natural rate $Y_N$. Assume that the economy has been in equilibrium at this price and output combination for a considerable period of time and that no change in price or output is expected in the future.

Figure 22.4   *The effect of an increase in aggregate demand on the price level and the level of real output*

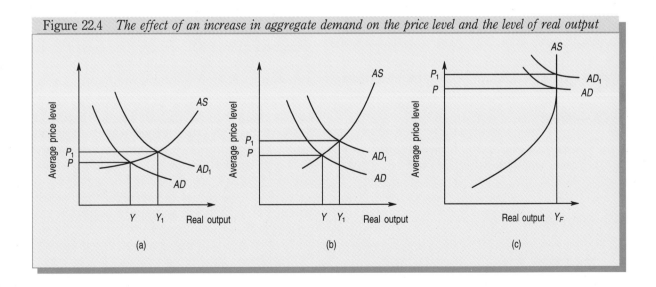

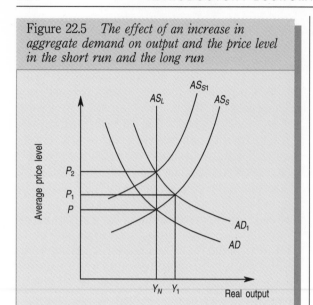

Figure 22.5   *The effect of an increase in aggregate demand on output and the price level in the short run and the long run*

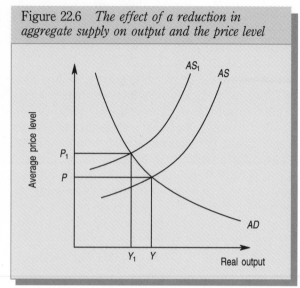

Figure 22.6   *The effect of a reduction in aggregate supply on output and the price level*

Again as aggregate demand increases to $AD_1$ the price level rises and, as producers increase their output, we move up the short run aggregate supply curve until equilibrium is established, with price at $P_1$ and output at $Y_1$. However the economy is not in long run equilibrium because trade unions will have negotiated pay awards for their members on the assumption that the average price level would not change from $P$. At the higher price level they will require higher wages to preserve their real income. When pay agreements are reached, the higher wage settlements will increase firms' costs of production at any given price level. This will shift the short run aggregate supply curve to $AS_{S1}$. Long run equilibrium is restored when output returns to the natural rate $Y_N$ and in this case the average price level has risen to $P_2$.

If this view of the economy is correct, the effect of an increase in aggregate demand on employment and the price level depends on whether we consider the short run or the long run. In the short run an increase in employment and/or the price level are possible following an increase in aggregate demand, but in the long run the effect of an increase in aggregate demand falls entirely on the price level.

**2** The simplest way to answer this question is to draw the appropriate diagram, which we have done in Figure 22.6

Note that, since the question specifically refers to an upward movement in the aggregate supply curve, we need only confine our analysis to the short run. In Figure 22.6, $AD$ is the aggregate demand curve and $AS$ is the initial aggregate supply curve. The original equilibrium is therefore given by price level $P$ and real output $Y$. The upward shift in aggregate supply implies a movement of the aggregate supply curve to $AS_1$.

It is clear that, at the new equilibrium between aggregate supply and aggregate demand, the price level is higher at $P_1$. Option 1 is therefore correct. It is equally clear that at the new equilibrium real output has fallen to $Y_1$ and therefore options 2 and 3 are also correct. (Note that a lower level of output implies a lower level of employment.)

The key is therefore A.

## REVIEW QUESTIONS AND ANSWERS

### Questions

1  What will be the effect on aggregate demand of each of the following? Assume all other things remain equal in each case.

   (a) A strike in the docks which prevents the loading and unloading of exports and imports.
   (b) Technological advances which improve the productivity of capital.
   (c) A decrease in the expected rate of inflation.
   (d) A budget deficit.

2  How would the slope of the aggregate demand curve in an economy differ if the real balance effect was (i) relatively strong; (ii) relatively weak?

3  Is the natural rate of output the full employment level of output (i) in the short run; (ii) in the long run?

4  When will the output of an economy be at the natural rate?

5  Show diagrammatically what effect an unanticipated increase in exports would have on price and output in an economy in the short run and the long run.

6  What effect will each of the following have on the price level of an economy?

   (a) An unanticipated increase in the world price of oil. Assume the country is (i) an exporter of oil; (ii) an importer of oil.
   (b) An increase in the expected rate of inflation.
   (c) Technological progress which improves the productivity of capital.
   (d) A substantial reduction in income tax.

### Answers

1  (a) If exports cannot be loaded, sales of goods abroad will fall and this will tend to depress aggregate demand. However, if imports cannot be unloaded, some domestic consumers will turn to domestic substitutes and this will tend to increase aggregate demand. The effect of a dock strike on aggregate demand therefore depends partly on the volume of goods exported (the greater the volume of exports, the greater the fall in aggregate demand) and partly on the extent to which domestic demand rises as consumers turn to import substitutes.

   (b) An increase in the productivity of capital would tend to shift the short run and the long run aggregate supply curves outwards. It would not affect the position of the aggregate demand curve. However, as the aggregate supply curve shifts outwards, if all other things remain equal, the price level will fall and there will be a downward movement along the aggregate demand curve.

   (c) If all other things remain equal, an increase in the expected rate of inflation will cause an increase in aggregate demand because individual consumers and firms will bring forward expenditure plans before the real value of money balances falls. A decrease in the expected rate of inflation would reduce the incentive to bring forward expenditure plans and would therefore probably cause a relatively small reduction in aggregate demand.

   (d) A budget deficit would increase aggregate demand because, if all other things remain equal, it implies an increase in aggregate expenditure.

2  The real balance effect occurs when a change in the price level changes the real value of money balances. A rise in the price level will cause a reduction in the real value of money balances and vice versa. If the real balance effect is relatively weak then each change in the price level will have a relatively small effect on aggregate demand. If all other things remain equal, this implies that the aggregate demand curve will be less elastic when the real balance effect is relatively weak and more elastic when the real balance effect is relatively strong.

3  In the short run employment can rise above the natural rate, but such an increase is only temporary and can only be maintained at the cost of ever-increasing inflation. In the long run the maximum level of employment that can be achieved is that given by the natural rate.

4  The natural rate of output occurs when the economy is in equilibrium, that is, when the expected rate of inflation and the actual rate of inflation are equal. The economy cannot be in equilibrium under any other circumstances.

**5**

Figure 22.7   *The effect of an increase in aggregate demand on output and the price level in the short run and the long run*

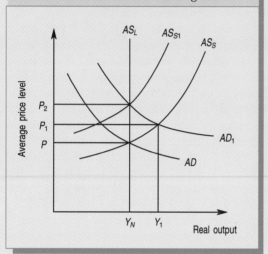

In Figure 22.7 aggregate demand is initially given by $AD$, short run aggregate supply is initially given by $ASs$ and $AS_L$ is the long run aggregate supply curve. The economy is initially in equilibrium with the price level at $P$ and output at the natural rate $Y_n$. An unanticipated increase in demand for exports shifts the aggregate demand curve to $AD_1$ and the economy establishes short run equilibrium at price level $P_1$ and output at $Y_1$. However the higher price level will lead to increases in costs of production, for example, when wage rates are renegotiated and in consequence the short run aggregate supply curve will shift to $AS_{S1}$ and long run equilibrium will be re-established at price level $P_2$ and output at the natural rate $Y_N$.

**6** (a) (i) If the country is an exporter of oil, an unanticipated increase in the price of oil will shift the aggregate demand curve outwards. This will pull the price level upwards.

(ii) If the country is an importer of oil the increase in the price of oil will tend to depress aggregate demand and therefore the price level will fall.

(b) An increase in the expected rate of inflation will cause an increase in aggregate demand because individual consumers and firms will bring forward expenditure plans before the real value of money balances falls. In consequence the price level will rise.

(c) An increase in the productivity of capital would tend to shift the short run and the long run aggregate supply curves outwards. It would not affect the position of the aggregate demand curve. However, as the aggregate supply curve shifts outwards, if all other things remain equal, the price level will fall.

(d) A substantial reduction in income tax will increase aggregate expenditure. As aggregate demand rises the price level will rise.

# CHAPTER 23

# MONEY AND THE CREATION OF BANK DEPOSITS

## Topic Summary

We all know what money is and most of us are only too aware that we do not have enough of it! Hardly a day goes by when we do not use it. We certainly have no difficulty in recognising it when we see it. Despite this, it is not easy to obtain a precise definition of exactly what money is. This, as we shall see on p. 144, is partly because there is no unique asset or small group of assets which can be thought of as money. In fact the only sensible way to define money is in terms of its functions. So what are the functions of money?

## The Functions of Money

### A Medium of Exchange

Without money how would trade be conducted? The answer to this question is through a system of **barter** where each individual bartered their output with other individuals. In such a world there would be little scope for division of labour and there would be greater concentration on **self-sufficiency**. Such a system would be hopelessly inefficient compared with using money. In the modern world money prices are assigned to commodities. Individuals sell their labour for money and specialise in different occupations. They then exchange the money they receive for the output they consume. Money is therefore the *medium* through which trade is conducted because it is the means through which payment is made.

### A Unit of Account

Money can be thought of as a **common denominator**. By expressing all goods and services in money terms it is easy to make comparisons and decisions about which goods and services to purchase in preference to others. For example, in the absence of money prices, we would need to know how many shirts a pair of shoes was worth, how many pairs of shoes a television was worth and so on.

### A Standard for Deferred Payments

Money provides a means whereby a price can be agreed today but payment *deferred* until some future date. Such agreements are possible without money, but they would be much more difficult to achieve. For example, if the alternative is payment in kind we cannot be certain about the quality of goods to be received in the future.

### A Store of Value

Money provides a means of **storing wealth**. For example, when we save we are storing our wealth in the form of money as opposed to consuming it. There are other assets, such as property, antiques and works of art, which can be used to store wealth. In some cases these are a better store of wealth because their value often rises, whereas the value of savings might fall because of inflation. Nevertheless, although money might not be the most effective store of wealth, it is certainly one form in which wealth is stored.

## The Creation of Bank Deposits

Bank deposits are created in two ways: when a customer deposits funds and when a bank makes a loan to a customer. In the former case, placing funds with a bank will clearly create a deposit. The size of the deposit will be equal to the amount of funds placed in it. However a deposit is also created when a bank makes a loan. Bank loans mainly take two forms: **advances** and **overdrafts**. In the former case a customer's account is credited with an agreed amount and in the latter case the bank agrees to lend various amounts up to an agreed limit. In this case funds are credited to the customer's account as and when required. In both cases the act of lending is carried out by creating a deposit on which funds can be withdrawn.

But, since the only funds banks possess are those deposited with them by their customers, it might be asked how they are able to make loans to anybody! After all, if funds are deposited with them, banks have an obligation to ensure that depositors can withdraw them as and when required. How can they do this if the same funds have been lent to other customers?

In fact banks are able to make loans because on average only a small proportion of the funds deposited with them will ever be withdrawn. There are many reasons for this, but an important one is that during the course of any particular day some customers will withdraw funds while other customers will deposit funds. As long as banks hold back sufficient funds to meet withdrawals by depositors, the rest can safely be lent to other customers.

## The Bank Deposit Multiplier

Banks are able to create deposits in excess of the funds deposited with them and this raises the interesting question about the existence of limits on their ability to make loans. In fact all banks are obliged to retain a portion of funds deposited with them to ensure that they are always able to meet withdrawals by customers and it is this which limits their ability to make loans. For example, let us assume that there is a demand for bank loans and that all banks maintain a reserve ratio of 20 per cent between deposits of cash and total lending. This implies that four-fifths of any funds deposited with a bank will be lent to customers.

Let us also assume that a bank, let us call it Bank A, receives a deposit of £1m. On the basis of our assumptions, £0.2m will be retained to meet withdrawals and £0.8m will be lent to other customers. These customers will spend their deposits and they will be paid into the accounts of various traders. These traders might hold their accounts at Bank A, but it is likely that at least some of them will hold their accounts at other banks. This is not important. All that matters is that 80 per cent of all funds which are deposited with a bank will be re-lent, and in this case this implies a further increase in lending of £0.64m, that is, 80 per cent of £0.8m. This process will continue until the entire £1m originally depos-

ited with Bank A is held to meet withdrawals by customers, in which case £1m will constitute one fifth of total bank deposits. In other words, following an initial deposit of £1m, total bank deposits will rise to £5m.

In fact, if we assume a constant ratio between the amount banks hold to meet withdrawals by customers and total deposits, we can easily calculate the *bank deposit multiplier* (sometimes referred to as the *credit multiplier* or the *money supply multiplier*) and, through this, the final increase in bank deposits following an initial deposit. The bank deposit multiplier is equal to

$$\frac{1}{\text{reserve ratio}}$$

In our example we have $1/0.2 = 5$. In other words an initial increase in total deposits of £1m will lead to a to a total increase in bank deposits of £1m $\times$ 5 = £5m.

## Common Mistakes to Avoid

The **bank deposit multiplier** and the **Keynesian income multiplier** are frequently confused in examinations. You must take great care to read the question carefully, since these are entirely different concepts. It is customary to refer to the Keynesian income multiplier as simply 'the multiplier'. Any reference to 'the multiplier' without further elaboration must therefore be taken as a reference to the Keynesian income multiplier. However, read all questions carefully to ensure that you have not missed a reference to bank deposits, the money supply or some other term that would indicate the bank deposit multiplier was being referred to.

Another problem is identifying exactly what constitutes money. Economists usually argue that anything which performs the functions of money is money. However money is ultimately the means of payment. Only those assets accepted in full and final settlement of a transaction can be regarded as money. Cash certainly fits into this definition and is quite clearly money. Sight bank deposits, that is, current account deposits which can be withdrawn on demand, are money. To settle a financial obligation all that is necessary is to transfer a bank deposit from one person to another person by means of a cheque.

However there are a range of other assets which perform some of the functions of money. Accounts which require notice of withdrawal (NOW accounts) are a store of value and over time can be converted into the means of payment. We shall see on p. 144 that economists use the terms **narrow money** and **broad money** to cope with these problems.

Another problem arises over the use of instruments of credit, and in particular credit cards. These are used to make purchases at the time goods and services are bought. However they are not regarded as money because final settlement of the financial obligation is made initially through the credit company, which reimburses the trader by transfer of bank deposits and subsequently by the credit card user who settles with the credit card company by transfer of a bank deposit.

## REVIEW QUESTIONS AND ANSWERS

### Questions

1  Why are banks able to lend a portion of any funds deposited with them?

2  Why are banks unable to lend sums in excess of the amount deposited with them?

3  Why are sight bank deposits money?

4  Are cheques money?

5  If all banks in a particular economy maintain a ratio of 12½ per cent cash to total deposits

   (i)   What is the size of the bank deposit multiplier?
   (ii)  What is the maximum increase in total deposits following an initial deposit of £1000?

### Answers

1  Banks are able to lend a portion of deposits because, on average, over any particular period of time, only a fraction of the funds deposited with them will be withdrawn. Individual customers might withdraw all, or nearly all, of their own deposit, but inflows are likely to at least match these outflows, leaving the average level of deposits little changed.

2  Banks cannot lend sums in excess of the amount deposited with them because once a loan is granted the customer will use the loan to finance purchases. No bank can guarantee that funds withdrawn to finance purchases will subsequently be deposited with the same bank. In other words, if a bank grants a loan in excess of its deposits, it might not be able to honour all these loans and it would certainly not be able to honour demands for funds from its depositors!

3  Sight bank deposits are usually regarded as money because they can be used for full and final settlement of any financial transaction.

4  Cheques are not money. They are simply the means by which funds are transferred from one bank deposit to another bank deposit. If a cheque cannot be honoured against a bank deposit it is worthless. Banks can refuse to honour cheques drawn against bank deposits with insufficient funds. In such cases a cheque is commonly said to 'bounce'.

5  In simple terms the bank deposit multiplier is equal to the inverse of the reserve ratio.

   (i) In this case we have $1/0.125 = 8$.
   (ii) If the bank deposit multiplier is 8, an increase in deposits of £1000 will make possible an ultimate increase in total deposits of $8 \times £1000 = £8000$.

CHAPTER 24

# THE MONETARY SECTOR

## Topic Summary

In the UK the monetary sector comprises all those institutions which together make up the sterling money market. This is a market where funds are deposited and borrowed for short periods ranging from *overnight to about one year*. In many of these borrowing and lending arrangements, securities, or IOUs, are issued. When these mature the holder receives the full face value of the security plus any interest due. However the sterling money market also provides an opportunity for those who wish to do so to sell their securities before maturity. It is useful to begin by looking at the main securities traded in the sterling money market.

## Securities Traded in the Money Market

### Treasury Bills

These are issued by the Bank of England to finance the government's short term borrowing requirements. Treasury bills are issued at a discount and normally mature 91 days after issue. They are pure discount securities, which implies that no rate of interest is paid to holders. Instead they are sold at less than their maturity value, the difference being the return to holders. Treasury bills are much sought after by participants in the money market because, being issued by the government, they are riskless securities in the sense that there is no risk of default by the borrower, that is, the government.

### Local Authority Bonds

These are securities issued by local authorities to finance their borrowing requirement. Unlike treasury bills, such bonds carry a rate of interest which guarantees their holder a fixed amount.

## Commercial Bills of Exchange

These are securities issued by traders. For example, a retailer might give a manufacturer a bill of exchange which will usually mature three months after issue. This gives the retailer a chance to sell output and so generate the funds with which to pay the manufacturer. This is obviously very convenient for the retailer but the manufacturer might need funds with which to finance further production. The sterling money market provides the manufacturer with the opportunity to sell the security and so obtain the required funds. Of course, unlike treasury bills, there is a risk of default. However for the holder of the bill this can be eliminated by having the bill *accepted* by an institution such as a bank. In this case the bank will accept, for a fee, the risk of default when the bill matures. After a bill has been accepted it can easily be sold at less than its maturity value on the money market. The difference is the return for holding the bill until maturity.

## Certificates of Deposit

These securities are issued mainly by banks and building societies when they require funds to exploit profitable lending opportunities. They are therefore simply IOU's which mature after a fixed period of time. They are issued at a fixed rate of interest for sums which usually range from £50 000 to £500 000, though there is no limit on the amount that can be raised if investors are willing to lend. Certificates of deposit are an extremely flexible instrument, since the length of time to maturity can be varied to fit in with the issuer's plans. One advantage to the organisation issuing a certificate of deposit is that, because they are issued at a fixed rate of interest, the issuing organisation knows in advance what the interest charge on the loan will be, irrespective of how market rates of interest change in the future.

## The Organisations which Participate in the Money Market

### The Discount Houses

The discount houses specialise in **discounting securities**. Securities are discounted when they are bought for less than their maturity value. The difference is profit for the discount house. There are currently nine discount houses and these institutions, which are unique to the UK, collectively form the London Discount Market Association (LDMA). The LDMA performs several important functions in the UK money market.

- The LDMA collectively submits a bid for the entire weekly issue of treasury bills which guarantees that the government's short term borrowing requirement will always be met. In fact the government sells treasury bills to the highest bidders and the LDMA simply takes up the remainder.
- By providing a ready market in short term securities the LDMA removes a possible obstacle which would prevent funds being channelled from lenders to borrowers. Few investors would buy securities if they could not immediately resell them if the need arose. The existence of the LDMA, by providing a ready market in short term securities, removes this possible problem.
- The banks and building societies in particular need to ensure that they are always in a position to meet demands from their customers for withdrawals. However they would wish to minimise the amount of cash kept on their premises because this would earn no interest. The problem can be solved by lending to the LDMA at **call and short notice**. Call money is particularly liquid because, if requested, it must be repaid by the LDMA within a few hours. A bank or building society which is running short of funds can therefore call in its loans to the discount market.
- The LDMA is the fulcrum through which the government implements its monetary policy, which is discussed on pp. 144–5.

### The Retail Banks

The best known retail banks in the UK are the clearing banks, such as Lloyds and Barclays. The main function of most retail banks is to make a profit for their shareholders, which they do by paying borrowers a lower rate of interest than they charge lenders. This is not unreasonable since it is the bank which indirectly brings borrowers and lenders into contact and it is the bank which accepts the risk of default by borrowers.

### The Bank of England

The Bank of England is the major participant in the monetary sector of the UK. The actions of all other participants in the monetary sector are heavily influenced by the actions of the Bank. As the central bank of the UK it performs several functions, which are summarised below.

**Banker to the Government**  A major function of any central bank is to act as banker to the government. Like any other institution, the government needs a bank to handle inflows and outflows of funds. In the case of central government the main inflows of funds are from tax remittances and sales of assets, as with the privatisation of an organisation. Outflows of funds stem from the spending plans of the various government departments, such as the Department of Education and Science, and the Department of Health and Social Security, along with other payments such as the upkeep of embassies abroad and interest payments on the national debt. As banker to the government, the Bank of England also has responsibility for handling the government's borrowing. It therefore issues securities, such as treasury bills, on behalf of the government and redeems them either on maturity or at an earlier date if it is convenient to do so.

**Implementation of Monetary Policy**  The Bank of England has responsibility for implementing the government's monetary policy as directed by the Treasury under the official control of the Chancellor of the Exchequer. The techniques of monetary policy are discussed on pp. 144–5.

**Banker to the Clearing Banks**  The Bank of England is also banker to the clearing banks, that is, those banks which operate the system through which cheques are cleared and any indebtedness between banks is settled. To facilitate this, clearing banks maintain **operational deposits** at the Bank of England and these are used to settle indebtedness between banks and indeed between the Bank of England and other banks.

**Lender of Last Resort**　The Bank gives assistance to the banking sector as lender of last resort. This assistance is provided through the discount market. Remember, banks (and other financial institutions) lend money *at call* to the discount market. If funds are short in the money market, these institutions will call in their loans to the discount market which, if it cannot obtain funds elsewhere, will be able to borrow from the Banks.

**Management of the Exchange Equalisation Account**　The Bank of England holds the nation's stock of gold and foreign currency reserves. As we shall see on pp. 195–6, the Bank of England can intervene in the foreign exchange market to influence the sterling exchange rate. It does this by buying and selling foreign currency and the account which records changes in the stock of foreign exchange reserves is the Exchange Equalisation Account.

**Supervision of the Financial System**　The Bank, since the 1987 Banking Act, has responsibility for supervision of the financial sector to reduce the risk of bank failure. There is no doubt that this has become an increasingly important function of the Bank. Bank failure can result in tens of thousands of private individuals and firms losing considerable sums and there is the possibility of a run on other banks as a result of the failure of one bank. To reduce the risk of failure the Bank has laid down guidelines relating to capital adequacy which are designed to ensure that banks have sufficient reserves to cover possible default by major creditors. The failure of the BCCI has vividly illustrated the need for supervision and reinforced the view that existing guidelines might not be adequate.

**Issue of Notes**　The Bank is the sole note issuing authority in England and Wales. The Bank withdraws old notes from circulation and issues new notes. With respect to the issue the Bank responds passively to changes in the public's demand for cash and makes no attempt to limit the supply of notes.

## The Eurocurrency Market

The discount market is a primary market but there are a number of other markets in the sterling money market which are referred to as **secondary markets**. The most important of these is undoubtedly the Eurocurrency market. This is simply a market in currencies held outside their country of issue. For example, if a trader in the UK accepts payment for exports in dollars, Deutschmarks or some currency other than sterling, and deposits this in a London bank, a Eurocurrency deposit will be created.

This market is completely outside the official control of the Bank of England, since banking regulations do not apply to it. However, as we shall see on pp. 144–5, the Bank has considerable power to influence interest rates. Since interest rate changes affect all institutions, by varying interest rates the Bank can exercise some control over the Eurocurrency market.

## Common Mistakes to Avoid

Sometimes there is confusion over the relationship between the Treasury and the Bank of England over which institution is responsible for the conduct of economic policy. In fact policy is decided by the Treasury and the Chancellor of the Exchequer, as first Lord of the Treasury, must defend the conduct of policy in the House of Commons. However, while the Bank of England receives directives from the Treasury over the conduct of economic policy and, under the 1946 Nationalisation Act, it must implement a Treasury directive, it does have considerable discretion over the way it acts so as to implement the government's monetary policy.

## REVIEW QUESTIONS AND ANSWERS

### Questions

1 What do the discount houses discount?

2 What do the accepting houses accept?

3 What is the inter-bank market, and why is it important?

4 Does the existence of a Euro-currency market make monetary control more difficult in the UK?

5 What is the purpose of the 'lender of last resort' facility?

6 Why is there a conflict between liquidity and profitability for the retail banks?

### Answers

1 The discount houses discount securities; that is, they purchase securities for less than their maturity value. A wide range of securities are discounted, including treasury bills, bills of exchange and certificates of deposit. Sometimes the discount houses hold these securities until maturity, at other times they simply resell them before maturity at a price which exceeds the amount they paid for them.

2 The accepting houses accept bills. This means they simply accept the risk of default so that, when the bill matures, if payment is not forthcoming to the holder of the bill, the acceptance house will honour the bill and then initiate action to reclaim the funds involved.

3 The inter-bank market is simply a market in which banks borrow from, and/or lend to, each other. It is important because it provides banks with an opportunity to match their assets with their liabilities. Banks which are short of funds are brought into contact with banks which have surplus funds.

4 The Eurocurrency market is unregulated by the UK authorities. However, since the mechanism used by the authorities for purposes of monetary control is to vary interest rates, and since interest rate changes affect all institutions in the money market, a large Eurocurrency market does not necessarily present a problem for the authorities.

5 The lender of last resort facility is designed to ensure that a bank can always obtain the funds it requires to meet withdrawals by customers. Usually lender of last resort facilities are provided to the discount market which will be short of funds whenever the banks have called in their loans. Before approaching the Bank for assistance, the discount market will try to obtain funds from other money market participants. Only when it is unsuccessful in obtaining funds from other sources will it approach the Bank, hence the term 'lender of last resort'.

6 In all of their dealings banks must constantly reconcile the conflicting aims of liquidity and profitability. Liquidity is necessary, as we have seen, to ensure that depositors can withdraw funds as and when required. Profitability is necessary to provide shareholders with a return. For banks, who are in the business of lending, the problem is that, the more liquid the loan, the lower its profitability. The development of certificates of deposit has alleviated the problem a little. While banks must still ensure that they can meet withdrawals by depositors, they know that they can create additional funds if necessary by issuing certificates of deposit.

# CHAPTER 25

# MONETARY CONTROL

## Topic Summary

### The Money Supply

As we have seen in Chapter 23, money is defined in terms of those assets which perform the functions of money. However, for practical purposes, a more formal definition of the money supply is necessary. Different countries use different assets in their definitions of the money supply, but all definitions include notes and coin in circulation with the public. Notes and coin are, after all, acceptable in full and final settlement of a financial transaction. The problem is that certain types of bank deposit are also acceptable in full and final settlement, while other types of bank deposit can be converted into the means of payment. It is because different types of bank deposit have **different degrees of liquidity** that there are different definitions of the money supply. Each definition represents a different measure of liquidity in the economy. The monetary aggregates currently monitored in the UK and their components are summarised below.

*M0* Notes and coin in circulation outside the Bank of England, plus bankers' operational deposits at the Bank of England.
*M2* Notes and coin in circulation with the non-bank private sector, plus private sector retail deposits[1] held with the banks and building societies.
*M4* Notes and coin in circulation with the public plus all sterling deposits (including certificates of deposit) held with banks and building societies by the non-bank non-building society private sector.

In April 1991, the government ceased to publish M4c and M5. These were replaced by a list of aspects referred to as *Liquid Assets Outside M4*. By far the larger component of Liquid Assets Outside *M4* is foreign currency deposits held either by UK banks and building societies or by UK offshore institutions.

M0 and M2 are referred to as **narrow money** because they include a narrower range of assets which correspond to the most liquid assets in the economy. For this reason M2 is sometimes referred to as a **measure of transactions balances**, that is, money which is used for making purchases. The M4 measure of the money supply, on the other hand, is referred to as **broad money** because it includes a broader range of assets that more accurately measure liquidity in the economy. There are several different money aggregates and while all are important the government might at times be more concerned with growth of certain of the monetary aggregates than with others depending on the way it conducts its monetary policy.

## Monetary Policy

### Open Market Operations

Open market operations are an important technique through which the Bank implements the government's monetary policy. Open market operations simply refer to sales and purchases of securities by the Bank of England. When the Bank carries out an open market sale of securities, payment is made by drawing a cheque against a bank deposit in favour of the Bank of England. When the cheque is presented for payment, bank deposits are transferred from the different commercial banks to the Bank of England. The effect will be to reduce the operational deposits of the commercial banks. The opposite happens when the Bank purchases securities in the open market.

---

[1]Retail deposits comprise all non-interest bearing deposits plus all sight or time deposits on which cheques can be drawn, regardless of maturity, plus other deposits (excluding certificates of deposit) of less than £100 000 and with less than one month to maturity.

## The Implementation of Policy

The government's monetary policy is concerned with controlling the growth of the money supply and the main instrument used to achieve this is varying the rate of interest. The Bank is particularly able to influence short term rates but, because changes in one rate of interest will generally affect other rates of interest, its influence is felt throughout the market. But how does the Bank operate to change interest rates and why does this affect the money supply?

The Bank, as lender of last resort, can vary the terms at which it lends to the discount market. If it wishes to raise interest rates throughout the economy it simply increases the rate at which it lends to the discount market. In turn the discount market will immediately raise its own rates in its transactions with banks and other financial intermediaries, who in turn will raise their own rates of interest and so on. The process works in reverse when the Bank cuts the rate at which it lends to the discount market.

This seems clear, but it might be asked how the Bank can change interest rates if the discount market does not need to borrow funds. In fact, the Bank can always ensure that the discount market is short of funds through its open market operations. If the Bank sells securities in the open market this will cause funds to be transferred from the retail banks to the Bank of England and operational deposits will fall as payment is made. In order to replenish their funds, the banks will call in their loans to the discount market and, since the open market sale of securities will have left all financial institutions short of funds, the discount market will be compelled to borrow from the Bank.

A change in interest rates does not have an immediate effect on the money supply but, over time, exerts a powerful influence. An increase in interest rates discourages borrowing and, in the absence of willing borrowers, banks lose the ability to create deposits. Since deposits are by far the main component of the money supply, a reduction in the demand for bank credit will reduce the growth of the money supply. The higher interest rates rise and the longer they are maintained at relatively high levels, the greater the reduction in money growth.

### Monetary Policy and Fiscal Policy

Monetary policy and fiscal policy are related in several ways but, in particular, as we shall see on p. 213, if the government has a budget deficit and finances this by borrowing from the banks, money growth will increase. They are also related because additional government borrowing implies increased sales of gilts. If all other things remain equal, this will cause a reduction in the price of gilts and therefore an increase in the rate of interest.

## Common Mistakes to Avoid

The effect of the bank's monetary policy on the supply of money in the economy is sometimes confused. It is sometimes alleged that the Bank operates so as to reduce the money supply or increase the money supply. In fact **the money supply is always increasing**. It is the rate at which the money supply grows, or money growth, which is important. Monetary policy changes the rate at which the *money supply grows* rather than the *stock of money*. Thus an expansionary monetary policy implies that the money supply grows more quickly and a contractionary monetary policy implies that the money supply grows less quickly.

It is sometimes alleged that when the Bank of England wishes to reduce the growth of the money supply it does so by open market sales of securities. It is further alleged that when payment is made to the Bank of England and the commercial banks' operational deposits fall, they will be forced to cut their lending. In fact open market operations are not directly used to influence money growth. Instead they are used to **support the Bank in the implementation of its interest rate policy**.

## Questions and Answers

### Questions

1 Which of the following activities of a commercial bank will lead directly to an increase in the supply of money?

 A  Paying out cash for a customer's cheque
 B  Buying Treasury Bills from discount houses
 C  Selling government securities to the public
 D  Buying government stock from the Bank of England
 E  Lending money to private customers

 ULEAC, June 1991

2 If the Bank of England buys gilt edged stock on the open market, all other things being equal, it will

A  increase the money supply and increase the national debt
B  increase the money supply and tend to lower interest rates
C  leave the money supply unaffected but raise interest rates
D  decrease the money supply and tend to raise interest rates

AEB, Nov 1989

## Answers

1  When cash is paid out of a bank against a cheque there is a reduction in sight deposits equal to the amount paid out in cash. However, since sight deposits and cash are both components of the money supply, the money supply is unaffected. Option A is therefore incorrect.

When Treasury bills are bought from the discount houses bank deposits are transferred from one account in the private sector to the discount houses' account which is also a private sector deposit. The money supply is therefore unaffected and so option B is incorrect.

When a bank sells government stock to the public there is a reduction in the bank's assets (securities are one of the bank's assets) and a reduction in the bank's deposits, that is, liabilities. Since bank deposits are included in measures of the money supply, the effect of this transaction will be to reduce the growth of the money supply. Option C is therefore incorrect.

When a bank buys government stock from the Bank of England it pays for the stock by creating a bank deposit. This bank deposit is then transferred by a reduction in operational deposits to the government's account at the Bank of England. Money supply growth therefore falls, so option D is incorrect.

When a bank makes a loan to a private customer it creates a bank deposit which, unless this deposit is used to buy securities from the Bank of England, implies an increase in the growth of the money supply. Option E is therefore correct.

The key is E.

2  If the Bank buys gilt edged stock on the open market money supply growth will increase as bank deposits are transferred to the operational balances of the commercial banks. However, since the national debt (see p. 213) is the total amount of government debt (securities) held outside the Bank of England, the national debt will fall. Option A is therefore incorrect.

The effect of an open market purchase of securities implies an increase in demand for securities and, if all other things remain equal, their price will rise. Since security prices and interest rates move in opposite directions, interest rates will fall. Option B is therefore correct.

Since option B is correct, options C and D are clearly incorrect because, as we have seen, the money supply will rise and interest rates will fall.

The key is therefore B.

## REVIEW QUESTIONS AND ANSWERS

### Questions

1  What is meant by the term 'arbitrage' and why is it important in explaining why the Bank's influence on interest rates is so pervasive?

2  What is meant by the term 'high-powered money'?

3  How will an open market purchase of securities by the government affect the supply of high-powered money?

4  If the government operated a system of monetary base control, that is, if it controlled the supply of high-powered money, how would this affect interest rates?

5  Why does the Bank of England act to influence short-term rather than long-term interest rates?

6  Why do sales of gilts to the non-bank private sector reduce money growth, whereas sales of gilts to the banking sector increase money growth?

7  In what ways are fiscal policy and monetary policy related?

## Answers

**1** Arbitrage occurs when there is a simultaneous purchase and sale of an asset in different markets in which there are price differences. Arbitrageurs aim to profit from the price difference and as they do so the difference is eliminated. There are many different instruments, or assets, in the money market and, since they are easily substituted for one another, a change in the price of one asset will lead to changes in the price of other assets until arbitrageurs see no further opportunity for profit. Arbitrage thus links asset prices in such a way that the Bank's influence is felt throughout the money market.

**2** High-powered money is the base money of the banking system. In the theory of the money supply multiplier, high-powered money is the reserve which supports the creation of bank deposits.

**3** If the Bank purchases securities in the open market it will pay for these by cheques drawn against itself. When these are presented for payment, funds will be transferred into the operational deposits of the banks. These are part of the stock of high-powered money and therefore the supply of high-powered money increases.

**4** If a system of monetary base control were used, the Bank could use open market operations to control the supply of high-powered money. Sales and purchases on the market would cause security prices to change and this, in turn, would cause interest rates to change (see p. 149). Because frequent intervention in the market would be necessary to control the supply of base money interest rates would appear quite volatile.

**5** The Bank has more control over short-term than over long-term rates. Interest rates at the short end of the market react immediately to any action by the Bank. The Bank's influence on longer-term rates occurs because of arbitrage.

**6** Sales of gilts to the banking sector result in an increase in the money supply because the banks pay for their purchases by creating a deposit against themselves in the way that they create a deposit when making any kind of loan. When the non-bank private sector purchase gilts, bank deposits are transferred to the government's account at the Bank of England. Since private sector deposits are part of the money supply, whereas public sector deposits are not, sales of gilts to the banking sector cause an increase in the money supply, whereas sales of gilts to the non-bank private sector cause a reduction in money growth.

**7** Fiscal policy and monetary policy are related in several ways but most obviously through the effect of government borrowing to finance its expenditure (fiscal policy) on interest rates and the money supply (monetary policy). Increased sales of gilts to finance government expenditure might cause security prices to fall and therefore interest rates to rise (see p. 149) and, depending on who buys the gilts, the money supply to rise (see answer to question 6).

# CHAPTER 26

# INTEREST RATES

## Topic Summary

Individual investors, the government and those involved in business, have a powerful incentive to forecast changes the rate of interest. To help do this it would be useful if we could formulate a theory of interest rate determination. In fact two theories are covered in this book. Unfortunately neither provides us with a complete theory of how interest rates are determined in the real world. Instead they each stress the importance of different factors which are relevant in determining interest rates.

## Loanable Funds Theory

In the loanable funds theory the rate of interest is fixed at the equilibrium level which equates supply of funds with demand for funds.

## Demand for Loanable Funds

In the loanable funds theory, the demand for money is given by the **demands of borrowers for funds**. Funds are demanded by all sectors of the economy and, while it is true that public sector investment is unlikely to be influenced by changes in the rate of interest, the same is not true of investment by firms and individuals. Firms demand funds **for investment purposes** and, as we have seen on p. 125, as the rate of interest falls the rate of private sector investment increases.

Individuals, or households, also demand funds for investment purposes. In particular investment in housing by private individuals is quite sensitive to changes in the rate of interest. The relatively high rates of interest in the early 1990s were partly responsible for a sizable reduction in the demand for housing. However households also demand funds to purchase consumer durables such as washing machines and dishwashers, along with many other goods and services bought on credit, often by using credit cards. Again such purchases are likely to be sensitive to changes in the rate of interest. The implication is that for the private sector the demand for loanable funds is *inversely related to the rate of interest*.

## Supply of Loanable Funds

In the loanable funds theory the supply of funds is determined by the **amount the community saves**. Many factors influence the amount the community saves, in particular the level of income. We have already seen in Chapter 19 that, as income rises, the marginal propensity to save rises. However, if all other things remain equal, it is assumed that as the rate of interest rises, households will save more because the higher rate of interest implies an increase in the opportunity cost of current consumption. However of more importance is the fact that, as the rate of interest rises, it becomes *more profitable for banks to increase their lending*. For both of these reasons it is assumed that the supply of loanable funds will rise as the rate of interest rises.

## The Equilibrium Rate of Interest

The equilibrium rate of interest is that rate which equates demand for loanable funds with supply of loanable funds as illustrated in Figure 26.1.

In Figure 26.1, demand for loanable funds is given by $DD$ and supply of loanable funds is given by $SS$. The equilibrium rate of interest is $r$. At any rate of interest above $r$ the supply of loanable funds exceeds the demand for loanable funds and so the rate of interest will tend to fall. At any rate of interest below $r$ the demand for loanable funds exceeds the supply of loanable funds and so the rate of interest will tend to rise. Only at $r$ is the rate of interest stable.

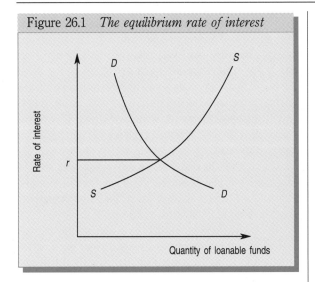

Figure 26.1 *The equilibrium rate of interest*

## The Liquidity Preference Theory

This theory of interest rate determination emphasises the importance of the **demand for money as an asset**. The term *liquidity preference* implies that we wish to focus on the circumstances in which the community prefers liquidity to other assets. This theory of interest rate determination is also known as the **monetary theory** or the **Keynesian theory**, after the English economist, Keynes, who put forward the theory in the 1930s.

### The Demand for Money

Three motives are identified for holding, or demanding, money. Each is considered in turn.

**The Transactions Demand for Money** This is simply money demanded to meet anticipated expenditures. Individuals might demand money to meet costs of travelling to work, or to purchase an item of clothing. Firms need working balances to meet suppliers' accounts that fall due for settlement and so on.

**Precautionary Demand for Money** This represents money demanded as a precaution against the possibility of some unanticipated expenditure. Firms hold petty cash to meet incidental items of expenditure and most individuals carry only the amount they need to meet *anticipated expenditures*. Most people allow for the possibility of finding some unanticipated item reduced for quick sale on a shopping trip!

**Asset Demand for Money** Keynes considered that the alternative to holding money was holding bonds. This might not necessarily be true for any individual, but for the community as a whole money that is placed on deposit with financial institutions might be used to purchase bonds. We therefore need to identify the circumstances when money will be preferred to bonds.

## Asset Prices and the Rate of Interest

It can be shown that the current market price of a bond and the rate of interest paid on that bond move in opposite directions. For example, let us consider a **consol**, which is a security issued by the UK government with no fixed redemption date. Let us assume that the *nominal price* of the bond is £100 and that it is issued at a rate of interest of 5 per cent. The holder of the consol receives £5 annually, irrespective of what happens to the *market price* of the bond. Let us consider two cases to illustrate the inverse relationship between bond prices and the yield, or market rate of interest ($I$) paid on the bond.

*Case 1* The market price of the bond rises to £125.

$$I = \frac{£5}{£125} \times 100 = 4 \text{ per cent.}$$

*Case 2* The market price of the security falls to £80.

$$I = \frac{£5}{£80} \times 100 = 6.25 \text{ per cent.}$$

Note that, as the market price of the consol rises, the market rate of interest falls and vice versa.

## Asset Prices and the Asset Demand for Money

Changes in bond prices, and therefore in the rate of interest, have an important bearing on the asset demand for money. If bond prices move upwards, holders of bonds make a capital gain. If bond prices fall, holders of bonds incur a capital loss. The inverse relationship between asset prices and the rate of interest is very important because, as asset prices rise, more and more investors will come to expect that the next change in asset prices will be downwards. They will therefore increasingly prefer to hold money in preference to bonds. Since the rate of interest falls as bond prices rise, this implies that the asset demand for money will rise as the rate of interest falls. The opposite happens if bond prices fall. Increasingly investors will come to expect the next change in bond prices to be upwards and therefore they will increasingly prefer bonds to money. In other words, as the rate of interest rises (bond prices fall) the asset demand for money will fall.

In fact it was argued that at any point in time there will exist in the minds of investors some rate of interest that is so high no-one expects the rate of interest to rise any further. This implies a minimum below which bond prices are not expected to fall. At this point all investors will prefer bonds to money, since the next expected change in bond prices will be upwards. In other words, there will be no asset demand for money. At the other extreme there is a rate of interest that is so low no-one expects it to fall any further. In other words the next expected change in the rate of interest will be upwards, that is the next expected change in bond prices will be down-wards and all investors will therefore prefer money to bonds. In these circumstances the asset demand for money will be infinite.

## The Liquidity Preference Curve

The demand for transactions balances and the demand for precautionary balances are unlikely to be significantly affected by changes in the rate of interest. In fact they are sometimes collectively referred to as the demand for **active balances** since they represent funds that are held with the intention of being actively used to purchase real output. Because of this the demand for active balances is interest rate inelastic.

However the same is not true of the asset demand for money. This represents funds held purely and simply because money is regarded as a better store of value than bonds. Because of this the asset demand for money is sometimes referred to as the demand for **idle balances**. The crucial point to note about the asset demand for money is that it is, as we have seen above, highly responsive to changes in the rate of interest.

Combining the demand for active balances and the demand for idle balances gives an overall demand for money function, that is, a liquidity preference curve. This is illustrated in Figure 26.2.

It can be seen in Figure 26.2 that at the highest rates of interest shown there is no asset demand for money and the total demand for money is given by the demand for active balances. As the rate of interest falls investors increasingly come to expect that the next change in interest rates will be upwards; that is, the next change in bond prices will be downwards. Because of this, liquidity pre-ference increases as interest rates fall. Note that at some low rate of interest the demand for money becomes *infinite* because everyone expects the next change in interest rates to be upwards, that is, everyone expects the next change in bond prices to be downwards.

## Determination of the Rate of Interest

In the liquidity preference theory the rate of interest is determined by the interaction of supply and demand for money. We have seen how the demand for money is determined. On any particular day the supply of money is assumed to be *fixed* by the

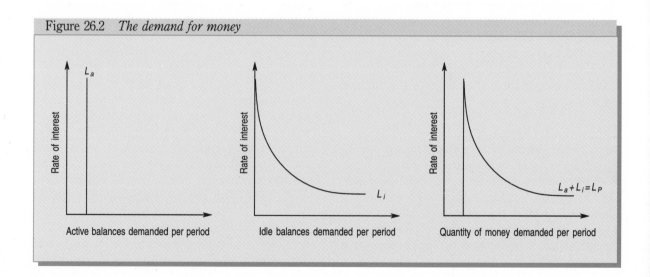

Figure 26.2    *The demand for money*

authorities as dictated by the government's monetary policy. Because of this it is unresponsive to changes in the rate of interest. In other words, it is *interest rate inelastic*. The determination of the rate of interest is illustrated in Figure 26.3

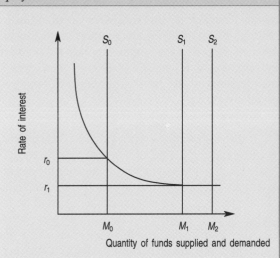

Figure 26.3 *The effect of a change in the money supply on the rate of interest in the liquidity preference model*

In Figure 26.3 $L_p$ is the liquidity preference curve and the supply of money is initially given by $S_0M_0$. The equilibrium rate of interest is therefore initially $r_0$. Now if the supply of money increases to $S_1M_1$, the rate of interest will fall to $r_1$. However, if the money supply now increases to $S_2M_2$, there is no change in the rate of interest, which remains at $r_1$. When the demand for money is infinite a change in the money supply has no effect on the rate of interest and therefore monetary policy is impotent. Because of this, the section of the demand for money curve which is infinitely elastic is referred to as the **liquidity trap**.

## Common Mistakes to Avoid

There is often some confusion over *what economists mean by the rate of interest*. Indeed in this chapter we have referred to the rate of interest as though there were only a single rate. In fact a passing glance in any bank or building society will confirm that there is more than one rate of interest. In the financial pages of the daily press several money market rates of interest are quoted. So what exactly do economists mean by the rate of interest? What economists believe is that

under normal circumstances all interest rates tend to move in the same direction. The rate of interest is therefore usually taken to refer to a single representative rate of interest. In other words movements in any single rate of interest are taken to represent movements in the general level of interest rates.

## Questions and Answers

### Questions

1

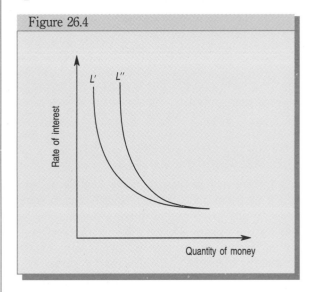

Figure 26.4

All other things being equal, a shift in the liquidity preference schedule from $L'$ to $L''$, as shown above, will be caused by

(1) an increase in money held for transactions
(2) an increase in the rate of interest
(3) an increase in money held as a precaution for unforeseen needs
(4) a fall in the supply of money

A  (1), (2) and (3) only are correct
B  (1) and (3) only are correct
C  (2) and (4) only are correct
D  (4) only is correct
E  (1) and (4) only are correct

JMB, June 1991

2  According to the liquidity preference theory, the rate of interest will

1  fall when the money supply is increased
2  rise when the community's liquidity preference is increased

3   fall when the marginal efficiency of capital
    rises
A   1,2 and 3 correct
B   1 and 2 only correct
C   2 and 3 only correct
D   1 only correct
E   3 only correct

ULEAC, Jan 1992

**3** The rate of interest paid on different financial
assets can vary because of

1   expectations of a rise in the rate of inflation
2   differences in liquidity
3   people's time preference
A   1,2 and 3 are correct
B   1 and 2 only are correct
C   2 and 3 only are correct
D   1 only is correct

AEB, June 1991

## Answers

**1** If there is an increase in money held for transactions purposes and all other things remain equal
then, at any given rate of interest, the demand for
money will increase. Option 1 is therefore correct.

An increase in the rate of interest can only be
caused by a change in the demand for money or a
change in the money supply. In other words, a
change in the rate of interest is the effect of a prior
change in either the demand for money or the supply
of money. It does not cause a change in the demand
for money. Option 2 is therefore incorrect.

As with option 1, if there is an increase in the
demand for precautionary balances and all other
things remain equal then, at any given rate of
interest, the demand for money will increase. Option
3 is therefore correct.

A fall in the money supply will cause a movement
along the liquidity preference curve with the result
that the rate of interest will rise. Option 4 is therefore
incorrect. The key is B.

**2** When there is an increase in the money supply
there is a downward movement along the liquidity
preference schedule, as in Figure 26.3 on p. 151. The
effect of an increase in the money supply is to pull
down the rate of interest. Option 1 is therefore correct.

An increase in liquidity preference implies an
outward movement of the liquidity preference schedule (as shown in Figure 26.4) and, if there is no
change in the money supply, the rate of interest will
rise. Option 2 is therefore correct.

When the marginal efficiency of capital rises, then
at any given rate of interest there will be an increase
in the rate of investment. An increase in investment
will, in turn, lead to an increase in the level of
income. At the higher level of income there will be
a higher demand for transactions balances to finance
the higher level of expenditure implied by the higher
level of income. This again implies an outward
movement of the liquidity preference schedule and
an increase in the rate of interest. Option 3 is
therefore correct.

The key is A.

**3** If the rate of inflation is expected to rise then we
would expect the rate of interest to rise because
lenders will require an additional amount to compen-
sate them for the expected reduction in the real value
of the sum lent. Borrowers would be prepared to pay
higher rates of interest to obtain funds because the
expected rise in prices implies an increase in the
return on funds invested. However the expectation of
a general increase in the rate of inflation will not
necessarily cause a difference in the rate of interest
on different financial assets. Option 1 is therefore
incorrect.

When assets vary in liquidity we would expect
this to be reflected in different rates of interest. If all
other things are equal, the more liquid the asset the
lower the rate of interest, because an investor will
find it easier to convert the asset back into the means
of payment. Option 2 is therefore correct.

All rational people have a time preference for
current consumption against the promise of future
consumption. The main reason for this is that
present utility derived from present consumption is
preferable to the same level of satisfaction in the
future. To persuade individuals and organisations to
forgo current consumption it is necessary to offer an
inducement in the form of a higher rate of interest.
The longer the period of time for which funds are
lent, the greater the compensation required. If other
things remain equal, this implies that the longer
funds are lent, the greater the rate of interest that
will be required. Option 3 is therefore correct.

The key is C.

## REVIEW QUESTIONS AND ANSWERS

### Questions

1  In what circumstances might a rise in the rate of interest persuade an individual to cut down on the amount of money saved per period of time?

2  From your own holdings of cash on a particular day, can you identify the proportion held for precautionary purposes?

3  Taking a bond with no fixed redemption date paying interest at the rate of 5 per cent p.a. and a nominal price of £100:

   (a)  What is the current rate of interest if the bond has a current market value of £110?

   (b)  What would be your answer if the current market price of the bond was £90?

   (c)  What would be the market price of the bond if the current market rate of interest is 5 per cent?

4  Can (i) the real rate of interest, (ii) the nominal rate of interest, ever be negative? Explain.

5  What does it mean to say the demand for money is interest inelastic?

6  If the community as a whole is holding less money than it desires at the current rate of interest, why will this lead to an increase in the rate of interest?

7  'UK money rates ease as inflation fears weaken.'

Money market rates were around $^1/_8$ to $^3/_{15}$ points lower in late trade as inflation fears faded slightly following today's lower than expected UK Retail Price Index.

A 0.4 per cent rise in the RPI for March giving an annual rate of 7.9 per cent was slightly below market expectations and compared with 7.8 per cent in February. The number eased fears of any immediate rise in base rates, dealers said, 'The market heaved a sigh of relief after today's figures', one money broker said, 'Everybody is certainly more optimistic and upward pressure on rates appears to be off at the moment.'

(a)  What is meant by the phrase 'Money market rates were around $^1/_8$ to $^3/_{15}$ points lower'?

(b)  Why are 'market expectations' important in the determination of nominal interest rates?

(c)  Use your knowledge of the Loanable Funds Theory to explain why a rise in the RPI below market expectations would cause a change in the demand for, and supply of, loanable funds which would cause a reduction in the rate of interest.

(d)  Does the influence of changes in the RPI on nominal interest rates imply that the Government is unable to control the rate of interest?

### Answers

1  If an individual wishes to save a fixed sum per period an increase in the rate of interest might lead this individual to save less because the extra interest income will make it possible to reach the target level of savings by saving less.

2  Make a list of all your anticipated expenditures such as bus fares, lunch and other purchases. Subtract this from your actual holding of cash. The amount left is precautionary balances on that day.

3  A 5 per cent bond with a nominal price of £100 will always earn for its owner £5 per year.

   (a)  If the current market price of the bond is £110, the current yield, or market rate of interest, is

$$\frac{£5}{£110} \times £100 = 4.5 \text{ per cent.}$$

   (b)  If the current market price of the bond is £90, the current yield is

$$\frac{£5}{£90} \times 100 = 5.5 \text{ per cent.}$$

   (c)  If the current yield on the bond is 5 per cent then the current market price must be equal to its nominal price of £100. We can easily verify this. If $P$ is the current market price of the bond, then

$$\frac{£5}{£P} \times 100 = \frac{£5}{£100} \times 100 = £5 \text{ per cent,}$$
$$\text{that is, } P = £100.$$

4  The nominal interest rate is simply the annual amount paid on a security expressed as a percentage of the current price of the security. The nominal rate of interest can never be negative because competition will always result in bor-

rowers offering some compensation to lenders for postponing consumption decisions. The real rate of interest is simply the nominal rate of interest less the rate of inflation. When the rate of inflation is greater than the nominal rate of interest the real rate of interest is negative.

**5** If the demand for money is interest inelastic, then changes in the rate of interest leave the quantity of money demanded unchanged.

**6** If the community as a whole is holding less money than it desires at the current rate of interest, then the community will increase its money balances. This implies an increase in the demand for money and, assuming the supply of money is unchanged, the rate of interest will rise.

**7** (a) The phrase 'Money market rates were around 1/8 to 3/15 points lower' implies that rates of interest in the money market were around 1/8 (0.125) of a percentage point to 3/15 (0.2) of a percentage point lower on the level earlier in the day.

(b) Lenders and borrowers are more interested in the real rate of interest than the nominal rate. If there is an expected increase in the rate of inflation then, if all other things remain equal, this implies an expected fall in the real rate of interest. To avoid this, lenders will require higher nominal rates of interest to persuade them to lend and borrowers, who also expect higher prices for the output they produce, will be prepared to pay higher nominal rates. Expectations are therefore very important in determining nominal rates of interest.

(c) In the loanable funds theory the rate of interest is determined by the supply of, and demand for, money. The supply of loanable funds varies directly with the rate of interest because as the rate of interest rises, more and more savers will be persuaded to overcome their time preference for current consumption. The demand for loanable funds, on the other hand, varies inversely with the price level. If all other things remain equal, at lower rates of interest it is less of a sacrifice to borrow funds and so we would expect a greater amount of funds to be demanded at lower rates of interest than at higher rates of interest. At any point in time the rate of interest which exists is that rate which brings supply and demand for funds into equilibrium.

If the rate of inflation as measured by the RPI (see p. 156) was less than the market had expected there would be downward pressure on interest rates. The main reason for this is that a lower rate of inflation implies that, at any given nominal rate of interest, lenders will now supply more funds because the lower rate of inflation implies that less will be required as compensation for expected inflation. Similarly there might be a reduction in demand for loanable funds. After all, if firms expect inflation to fall, they may expect their profits from production to fall, in which case they will cut back their demands for loanable funds. The effect of these changes will be to pull down the rate of interest.

(d) The RPI is an important influence on the rate of interest but, as we saw on p. 145, the Bank of England can intervene in the markets to determine rates of interest. However, if the Bank attempts to move interest rates in a way that runs against the tide of market sentiment, it will have great difficulty. The influence of the Bank therefore depends on its ability to interpret market sentiment and, to some extent, its ability to anticipate future changes in market sentiment.

# CHAPTER 27

# *MEASURING CHANGES IN THE VALUE OF MONEY*

## Topic Summary

Index numbers are used to measure changes in particular aggregates. In the UK the most widely quoted index is the Index of Retail Prices, which measures changes in the price of a basket of goods which are purchased by the average consumer. In order to ensure that the basket reflects the importance of the different items purchased, each item in the basket is assigned a *weight* which reflects the frequency with which that item is purchased. This is important because the effect of a price change depends, not only on the extent of the price change, but also on the frequency with which an item is purchased. If the price of a light bulb rises by 50 per cent, this is far less significant than a 10 per cent rise in the price of milk because most people buy milk daily, whereas light bulbs are bought far less frequently. If all other things are equal, the more frequently a good is bought, the higher will be its weight to reflect its greater importance in the average family's budget.

## Computing a Weighted Price Index

To compute the Retail Price Index (RPI) a representative group of households, some 10 000 in total,

provide detailed information on their expenditures. From this information the items to be included in the RPI and the weight of each item are derived. The actual statistical procedure for calculating the RPI is outside the scope of this book, but the basic principles are easy to understand. In the base period, year 1 or month 1, whenever the index is started, the prices of all items in the index are given an index number of 100. Price changes in subsequent periods are measured as percentage changes in prices in the base period. For each item, the index number is then multiplied by the appropriate weight to obtain a weighted index number. All weighted index numbers are then added together and the result is divided by the sum of the weights. This gives the value of the index for that period. This is illustrated in Table 27.1.

In Table 27.1, notice that in the base year each item in the index has an index number of 100 and that the index of prices also has a value of 100. Changes in the price of each item in the index in year 2 are then reflected in percentage changes in year 1 prices. Thus the price of good A rises by 10 per cent, so the index number for good A in year 2 rises to 110, and so on. Dividing by the sum of the weights in year 2 shows that expenditure on the three items in our index increased by 67 per cent in year 2 compared with year 1.

Table 27.1

| Good | Price (£) | Year 1 Index | Weight | Weighted Index | Price (£) | Year 2 Index | Weight | Weighted Index |
|------|-----------|--------------|--------|----------------|-----------|--------------|--------|----------------|
| A | 5.00 | 100 | 2 | 200 | 5.50 | 110 | 2 | 220 |
| B | 4.00 | 100 | 3 | 300 | 6.00 | 150 | 3 | 450 |
| C | 3.00 | 100 | 5 | 500 | 6.00 | 200 | 5 | 1000 |
|  |  |  |  | 1000 |  |  |  | 1670 |

## Measuring the Rate Inflation

Changes in the RPI are the most frequently quoted measure of changes in the rate of inflation. It is easy to calculate the rate of inflation from information about the value of the RPI. Between any two periods, such as a year, the rate of inflation can be calculated as

$$\frac{\text{RPI in year 2} - \text{RPI in year 1}}{\text{RPI in year 1}} \times 100$$

Thus, in the UK between 1989 and 1990, the RPI increased from 113.0 to 121.8 and therefore the rate of inflation over this period was

$$\frac{121.8 - 113.0}{113.0} \times 100 = 7.8 \text{ per cent.}$$

## Problems of Interpreting Changes in the RPI

### Different People Consume Different Goods and Services

One problem with interpreting changes in the RPI is that the weights will not accurately reflect the expenditure patterns of every member of society. For example, changes in the price of petrol have no direct effect on those who do not own a motor vehicle. Similarly students, pensioners and the unemployed have a different pattern of consumption from other households.

### Changing Patterns of Consumption

Over time patterns of consumption change and if the weights in the index are not revised frequently enough it will become less and less accurate. In fact the weights in the RPI are revised annually to minimise this problem, but because patterns of consumption change continuously throughout the year it is inevitable that there will be slight inaccuracies in the RPI.

### Different Retail Outlets

There is some problem over the way price changes are computed. After all, the same goods are often bought in more than one type of retail outlet. For example, food is purchased from small corner shops and in large supermarkets and the prices of the same items frequently vary. In fact, to minimise inaccuracies in the RPI, the prices of goods are recorded in different types of retail outlet and weighted according to the shopping habits of the population.

## Qualitative Changes

Over time there are changes in the quality and reliability of the different goods included in the index. For example, many foodstuffs are seasonal and if they are purchased in season they are generally of better quality than if they are grown out of season in artificial conditions. In other cases changes in design of some goods mean simple comparisons of price changes do not reflect the fact that the nature of the good has also changed. Because of this it is necessary to alter the base period of the index, otherwise changes in the nature of goods in the index will be such that we are measuring changes in the prices of different goods.

## Changes in the Mortgage Rate

In the UK, both changes in house prices and changes in the mortgage rate are included when calculating the RPI. The problem is that housing is regarded as investment rather than consumption and therefore there is a case for omitting it from the RPI altogether. Furthermore to include changes in the mortgage rate makes the RPI quite volatile at times, so that it can be quite a misleading indicator of the underlying rate of inflation.

This is a particular problem because, as we shall see on p. 161, changes in the rate of inflation have an important influence on pay demands. Furthermore other major European countries either omit housing costs altogether from their consumer price index or treat housing costs differently from the UK. This can result in misleading comparisons between the rate of inflation in UK, and the rate in other European countries. Again, this has implications in moves towards European Monetary Union (EMU), because a prerequisite is that countries moving to EMU should have achieved a similar rate of inflation.

## Common Mistakes to Avoid

In the UK there are several measures of inflation which are sometimes confused. Changes in the RPI are still the most widely quoted measure of inflation. However, because of the problems of interpreting changes in the RPI, it is now common to distinguish between **headline inflation** and **core inflation**. Changes in the RPI, are sometimes referred to as headline inflation. However the headline rate can sometimes give a misleading indication of what the underlying rate of inflation is. To give a more accurate picture, as well as the headline rate in the UK, the core rate is also measured. This removes the effect of changes in the mortgage rate, the council tax, and oil from the headline rate. Which measure of inflation is the most appropriate depends to some extent on the purpose for which the figures are to be used and there is no doubt that the debate about the proper way to measure inflation will continue for some time yet.

## Questions and Answers

### Questions

1 Table 27.2 shows data relating to the Index of Retail Prices (RPI) in the United Kingdom.

(a) Explain:
  (i) what is meant by the term 'weights in 1981'; (2 marks)
  (ii) why the weights in 1990 are different from those in 1981. (2 marks)
(b) With reference to the 'all items' index, examine three factors that may have influenced the rate of inflation over the period shown in the table. (3 marks)
(c) Suggest reasons why the rate of inflation for the following groups of spending differed from the rate of change of the 'all items' index of retail prices:
  (i) catering (meals bought and consumed outside the home);
  (ii) clothing and footwear;
  (iii) fuel and light. (6 marks)
(d) Why do rates of change in the RPI not completely measure changes in the purchasing power of:
  (i) all households; (3 marks)
  (ii) young people; (2 marks)
  (iii) old age pensioners? (2 marks)
ULEAC, Jan 1992

Table 27.2

| Retail Price Index | Weights in 1981 | Average annual percentage change in | | | | | | | | Weights in 1990 |
|---|---|---|---|---|---|---|---|---|---|---|---|
| | | 1981–2 | 1982–3 | 1983–4 | 1984–5 | 1985–6 | 1986–7 | 1987–8 | 1988–9 | 1989–90 | |
| All items | 1000 | 8.5 | 4.5 | 5.0 | 6.0 | 3.3 | 2.2 | 4.9 | 7.7 | 9.4 | 1000 |
| Food | 201 | 7.9 | 3.2 | 5.6 | 3.1 | 3.3 | 1.9 | 3.4 | 5.6 | 8.0 | 158 |
| Catering (meals bought and consumed outside the home) | 42 | 7.5 | 6.5 | 7.4 | 5.8 | 6.2 | 3.5 | 6.6 | 6.2 | 8.5 | 47 |
| Alcoholic drink | 79 | 11.3 | 7.5 | 5.8 | 6.2 | 4.4 | 2.3 | 5.1 | 5.6 | 9.6 | 77 |
| Tobacco | 36 | 15.4 | 6.7 | 10.9 | 8.8 | 9.8 | 3.0 | 3.2 | 2.9 | 6.7 | 34 |
| Housing | 135 | 12.6 | 2.5 | 9.1 | 12.7 | 5.7 | 5.0 | 8.9 | 20.2 | 21.0 | 185 |
| Fuel and light | 62 | 13.9 | 7.4 | 2.8 | 4.3 | 1.3 | 0.0 | 2.5 | 5.6 | 8.0 | 50 |
| Household goods (durable goods other than TV and radio, soap, detergents, stationary, etc.) | 78 | 4.2 | 3.8 | 4.2 | 4.8 | 2.6 | 0.2 | 3.7 | 3.9 | 4.8 | 71 |
| Household services (postage, telephone charges, shoe reparing, laundering, etc.) | 33 | 9.9 | 2.7 | 4.6 | 7.1 | 4.8 | 2.4 | 4.8 | 5.3 | 6.3 | 40 |
| Clothing and footware | 81 | 1.0 | 2.0 | –0.1 | 3.8 | 2.7 | 0.7 | 3.2 | 5.2 | 4.6 | 69 |
| Personal goods and services (medicines, toiletries, leather goods, hairdressing, etc.) | 27 | 8.8 | 5.8 | 5.0 | 7.6 | 5.1 | 2.5 | 4.8 | 6.8 | 7.5 | 39 |
| Motoring expenditure | 128 | 5.7 | 6.9 | 2.3 | 4.6 | –1.4 | 2.3 | 4.5 | 5.4 | 6.0 | 131 |
| Fares and other travel (includes cycles) | 24 | 13.4 | 5.4 | 1.5 | 4.6 | 6.6 | 3.3 | 5.9 | 7.1 | 7.1 | 21 |
| Leisure goods (radio, TV, books, newspaper, toys, sports goods, plants, etc.) | 48 | 6.5 | 4.7 | 3.5 | 4.6 | 1.8 | –0.1 | 2.5 | 3.0 | 4.6 | 48 |
| Leisure services (TV licences and video rentals, entertainment, etc.) | 26 | 10.3 | 3.0 | 2.7 | 5.9 | 4.7 | 1.1 | 6.3 | 6.4 | 8.1 | 30 |

*Source*: *Social Trends*, 20 HMSO, 1990.

**2** A retail price index is a direct measure of changes in

A  consumer patterns of expenditure
B  average standard of living
C  effective demand for consumer goods
D  average cost of living

AEB, Nov 1989

## Answers

**1** (a) (i) The Retail Price Index (RPI) measures the effect of changes in the price of a basket of goods and services bought by a representative family. There are two factors to consider: changes in the price of the different goods and services which make up the basket and the frequency with which each item is purchased. The weights in 1981 reflect the frequency with which each item in the basket was purchased by a representative family in 1981.

(ii) The weights in 1990 are different from the weights in 1981 because over the nine year period there will have been changes in the pattern of consumer spending. Some goods will be purchased less frequently or not at all, while other goods will be purchased more frequently. For example, food accounted for a smaller proportion of household expenditure in 1990 than it did in 1981, whereas housing accounted for more. The 1990 weights therefore reflect the changes in consumer spending which have occurred since 1981.

(b) In the 'all items' index, increases in the cost of housing clearly had a significant effect on inflation during the period covered and this reflects the relatively high rates of interest that have prevailed for much of this period. Fares and other travel costs also made a significant contribution to the rate of inflation. Many factors accounted for this, including fare increases on public transport. Changes in the prices of personal goods and services also contributed to inflation over the period. One important factor here was that prescription charges were increased several times during the 1980s.

(c) (i) For most of the period given the index for catering exceeded the 'all items' index, indicating the general rise in expenditure on catering as a result of rising living standards.

(ii) The clothing and footwear industries are highly competitive and consumers have access to a range of cheap imports. This accounts for the lower value of the index of this group of products than the 'all items' index.

(iii) The relatively low value of the index for fuel and light relative to the 'all items' index reflects the relatively low price of oil during the 1980s. World output of oil rose during the 1980s, whereas demand tended to fall as consumers became more energy conscious.

(d) (i) Changes in the RPI reflect the effect of price changes on a representative household. In fact many households will not correspond to this representative or average household. Some will be far wealthier than the average and many will be less wealthy. For households which differ markedly from the average household the weights assigned to the various categories in the index will be inappropriate and therefore the RPI will not accurately measure the effects of price changes on these households.

(ii) Young people are one group where the weights in the RPI are likely to be inaccurate. For young people housing and furniture are likely to be more important than for the average household. Food, on the other hand, is likely to be less important, since younger people, if they have children at all, will have younger children and so will spend less on food than the average household.

(iii) Old age pensioners are another group for whom the weights in the RPI are inappropriate. Pensioners will tend to spend very little on housing and food compared to the average household, but might spend considerably more on medicines and fuel and light because they tend to spend more time at home. The RPI is considered to be so inaccurate in reflecting the experiences of pensioners that a Pensioner Price Index is published monthly.

**2** The RPI takes account of patterns of expenditure in assigning weights to the different categories in the RPI, but it makes no attempt to measure patterns of expenditure. Option A is therefore incorrect.

The average standard of living is most commonly measured in terms of per capita income. The RPI does not measure this. Option B is therefore incorrect.

Effective demand for goods and services is measured by total expenditure on goods and services. Changes in prices might effect total expenditure on the different goods and services, but this would be reflected in the weights used to compute the RPI. Option C is therefore incorrect.

The RPI measures the effect of changes in the prices of those goods and services which are purchased by an average family. In other words, it measures changes in the average cost of living. Option D is correct.

The key is D.

# REVIEW QUESTIONS AND ANSWERS

## Questions

1  Why does a rise in the price level imply a fall in the value of money?

2  How accurately does the RPI measure the change in your own income?

3  What do the weights in the RPI reflect?

Question 4 is based on Table 27.4

4  (a)  Calculate a weighted index of prices for years 1 and 2.
   (b)  What is the percentage change in the weighted index over the period?
   (c)  What is the change in the value of money over the period?

Table 27.3  *Changes in prices and the value of money*

| Good | Year 1 | | | Year 2 | | |
| | Price (£) | Index | Weight | Price (£) | Index | Weight |
|---|---|---|---|---|---|---|
| A | 2.00 | 100 | 4 | 2.50 | 125 | 4 |
| B | 5.00 | 100 | 2 | 6.00 | 120 | 2 |
| C | 1.00 | 100 | 1 | 0.80 | 80 | 1 |
| D | 3.00 | 100 | 3 | 6.00 | 200 | 3 |

## Answers

1 When the price level rises a given amount of money will exchange for a smaller voume of goods and services. This implies that the value, or purchasing power, of money has fallen.

2 To answer this question you need to compute an index of prices over several months for the goods and services you buy. Compare the percentage change in your own index with the percentage changes in the RPI which is published monthly.

3 The weights in the RPI reflect the importance to the average household of the different items included in the basket of goods and services used to compute the RPI.

4 To calculate a weighted index we first multiply the index number for each good in the basket by its weight. The weighted index numbers thus obtained are then added together and the result is divided by the sum of the weights.

(a) The weighted index of prices for year 1 is 100, that is,

$$[4(100) + 2(100) + 1(100) + 3(100)] \div 10 = 100.$$

The weighted index of prices for year 2 is 142, that is,

$$[4(125) + 2(120) + 1(80) + 3(200)] \div 10 = 142.$$

(b) The percentage change in the weighted price index is 42 per cent, that is,

$$\frac{142 - 100}{100} \times 100.$$

(c) Between Year 1 and Year 2 there is a fall in the value of money of almost 30 per cent. Comparing the value of £100 in Year 1 with £100 in Year 2 we have

$$\frac{£100 \times \text{RPI in Year 1}}{\text{RPI in Year 2}} = \frac{£100 \times 100}{142} = £70.4,$$

that is, a fall in the value of money of almost 30 per cent

## CHAPTER 28
# *INFLATION*

## Topic Summary

Inflation is usually regarded as **a general rise in the price level** and this implies **a general reduction in the value of money**. After all, if the price level rises, a given amount of money will exchange for fewer goods and services. When inflation causes the price level to rise rapidly, economists refer to this as **hyperinflation**. No precise figure can be used to distinguish between a relatively high rate of inflation and hyperinflation but there is no doubt that the inflation rates of several hundred per cent per annum which have been experienced by Latin American countries such as Argentina, Brazil and Mexico in recent years are regarded as hyperinflation.

## The Quantity Theory of Money

The quantity theory of money is the **oldest theory of inflation**. It predicts that inflation can only be caused by an increase in the money supply and that an increase in the money supply will lead to an equiproportional increase in the price level. The quantity theory of money is based on the **equation of exchange**, which can be set as:

$$MV_t \equiv PT$$

where $M$ = the money supply,
$V_t$ = the transactions velocity of money, that is, the average number of times the money supply is used to make a transaction,
$P$ = the average price of each transaction, and
$T$ = the total number of transactions made.

This version of the quantity theory of money is referred to as the **transactions version**. However there is another version of the quantity theory of money which is referred to as the **income version**; this can be set out as:

$$MV_y \equiv PY$$

where $M$ = the money supply,
$V_t$ = the transactions velocity of money; that is, the average number of times the money supply is used to purchase final output,
$P$ = the average price of each unit of final output, and
$Y$ = the volume of final output.

The income version of the quantity theory of money is superior in some ways to the transactions version. In particular the transactions version includes all intermediate transactions as well as transactions in final output. This implies double-counting. The income version avoids this problem, since it focuses entirely on final output.

Whichever version of the equation of exchange we look at, it is simply a truism, that is, it is true by definition. For example, in the income version, $MV_y$ is total spending on final output in the economy and $PY$ is the value of final output produced. The two sides of the equation are therefore simply different ways of looking at the same thing! However it is alleged that $V_y$ changes only slowly over time and for simplicity it can be treated as a constant. It is further alleged that $Y$ tends towards an equilibrium natural rate in the long run. Again this long run equilibrium value changes only slowly over time. This implies that the money supply and the price level vary directly. Those economists known as *monetarists* argue that, whereas a rise in the money supply will cause a rise in the price level, there can be no change in the price level unless there has been a prior change in the money supply.

## The Keynesian View of Inflation

Keynesians have argued that there are two types of inflation, *demand pull* and *cost push*.

# Demand Pull Inflation

As the term suggests, demand pull inflation is caused by excess demand at the ruling price level. It is particularly associated with full employment because, when demand rises in these circumstances, domestic supply cannot respond. Inevitably demand pull inflation is also associated with a balance of payments deficit because exports are diverted to the home market and imports are sucked in.

In Keynesian models of the economy the aggregate supply curve is represented as relatively elastic until the economy approaches full employment. At very low levels of output it is argued that firms can obtain additional resources without any increase in the price of these. Consequently there is no reason why the price of final output should change. However, as the economy approaches full employment, competition for resources causes supply bottlenecks and the prices of inputs, including labour, are driven upwards. Firms will therefore require a higher price to supply additional output a when full employment is reached, no further increase in output is possible and the supply curve becomes perfectly inelastic. The effect of rising demand on output and the price level is illustrated in Figure 28.1.

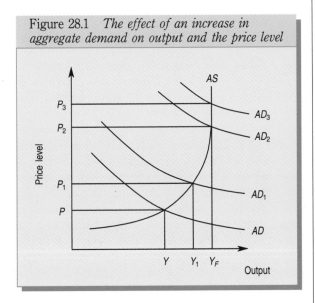

Figure 28.1 *The effect of an increase in aggregate demand on output and the price level*

In Figure 28.1, $AS$ is the aggregate supply curve and $AD$ is the original aggregate demand curve. The price level is initially $P$ and the level of output is initially $Y$. If aggregate demand rises to $AD_1$, the price level rises to $P_1$ and output rises to $Y_1$. If aggregate demand rises to $AD_2$, the price level rises to $P_2$ and output rises to the full employment level of

output, $Y_F$. Any further increase in aggregate demand at this point simply results in a higher price level. For example if aggregate demand rises to $AD_3$, output is unchanged at $Y_F$ but the price level rises to $P_3$.

# Cost Push Inflation

Keynesian economists also accept that pressure on costs might cause pressure on prices. For the economy as a whole, labour costs form the largest proportion of total costs and economists have coined the term **wage push inflation** to identify pressure on costs from this source. However, in the UK, with its dependence on imported raw materials, rising import prices because of a fall in the value of sterling against the dollar (most raw material imports are priced in dollars) has also been a cause of rising costs. Whatever the cause, if all other things remain equal, the effect of rising costs on final prices can be illustrated as in Figure 28.2.

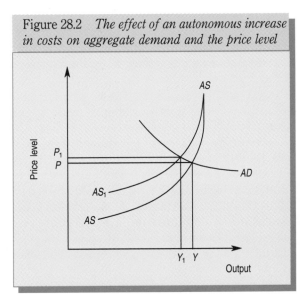

Figure 28.2 *The effect of an autonomous increase in costs on aggregate demand and the price level*

In Figure 28.2, aggregate supply and aggregate demand are initially given by $AS$ and $AD$, respectively. The economy is in equilibrium with the price level at $P$ and output at $Y$. Now if all other things remain equal and there is an autonomous increase in costs, for example because trade unions negotiate pay rises without any change in productivity, the aggregate supply schedule will shift to $AS_1$. The effect is to push prices up to $P_1$ and reduce output to $Y_1$.

## The Inflationary Spiral

We have analysed the effect on the price level of a rise in aggregate demand and a rise in costs if all other things remain equal. However, in each case, other things will not remain equal. For example, if the price level rises because there is an increase in aggregate demand, when wage contracts are renegotiated trade unions will demand pay increases to offset the fall in their members' real income. The effect will be to push costs up and, when the higher incomes are spent, there will be a further increase in aggregate demand. If the initiating cause of pressure on prices is a rise in costs, the price level rises but, as the higher incomes which are the counterpart of a rise in costs are spent, aggregate demand will rise, and so on. This process is referred to as the inflationary spiral.

## Criticisms of the Keynesian View of Inflation

A word of caution is necessary on the inflationary spiral outlined above, because it represents a particularly Keynesian interpretation of the inflationary process and would not be accepted by all economists. In particular, *monetarist economists* argue that a rise in costs cannot cause an increase in the price level unless there is an accommodating increase in the money supply. The argument is simple. Since the velocity of circulation and final output grow only slowly over time, if the money supply is constant, an increase in costs by one group which is passed on in the form of higher prices for some products must be accompanied by a reduction in the price of other products so as to leave the average price level unchanged. This reduction in the prices of other products occurs because, in order to pay the higher prices of those products which have increased in price, the demand for other products must fall at their existing price. Of course consumers might refuse to pay the higher prices in the first place, in which case higher costs will leave prices unchanged and output will initially fall until costs are bid down again.

## The Phillips Curve

The Phillips Curve hypothesises is a negative relationship between unemployment and the rate of inflation. The relationship was first discovered in

1958 and it formed the basis of policy in many countries for more than a decade after that. The Phillips Curve is illustrated in Figure 28.3.

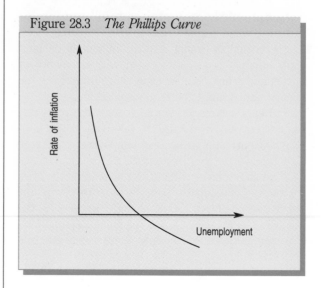

Figure 28.3    *The Phillips Curve*

In the original version, the Phillips Curve showed a negative relationship between wage rates and unemployment but, because wages form the bulk of total costs, it was soon discovered that the same general relationship existed between the rate of inflation and unemployment. One reason why the Phillips Curve attracted so much attention was that the relationship it illustrated seemed to have been relatively constant in the UK for almost a century. It was therefore assumed that it would remain relatively constant in the future.

The Phillips Curve appeared to explain why policy-makers had failed to achieve full employment without inflation. It offered policy-makers a range of alternatives. They could choose lower unemployment if they accepted higher inflation, but could only reduce inflation if they accepted higher unemployment. One variable could be traded off against the other. In fact this trade-off relationship ushered in the period of stop–go policy in the UK, though stop–go policy predates the discovery of the Phillips Curve. When policy-makers increased aggregate demand to reduce unemployment, inflation increased and inevitably led to a balance of payments deficit. When the balance of payments deficit became severe enough, aggregate demand was depressed. As a result inflation fell and the balance of payments deficit disappeared, but unemployment increased. When policy-makers became disturbed by rising unemployment, aggregate demand was increased and the cycle repeated itself.

## The Expectations-Augmented Phillips Curve

The expectations-augmented Phillips Curve reflects the view that in the long run there is no stable trade-off between inflation and unemployment. The origins of this view are grounded in the quantity theory of money. Since changes in the money supply ($M$) have no long run effect on real income ($Y$) and velocity changes only slowly over time, an increase in the money supply must be reflected in a rise in the price level. Any rise in real income will only be transitory or short term and in the long run the effect of an increase in the money supply will fall entirely on the price level.

The expectations-augmented Phillips Curve is based on the assumption that money illusion exists among the workforce, so that a change in the rate of inflation is not immediately perceived by the workforce. A difference between the expected rate of inflation and the actual rate of inflation can therefore exist until money illusion disappears and any change in the rate of inflation is clearly and accurately understood. The importance of this is explained in terms of Figure 28.4.

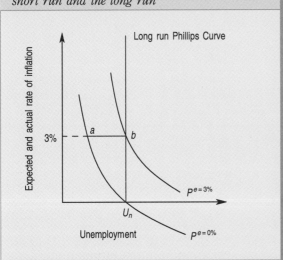

Figure 28.4 *The effect of an increase in money growth on unemployment and inflation in the short run and the long run*

In Figure 28.4 $P^{e=0}$ and $P^{e=3\%}$ represent two short run Phillips Curves where the expected rate of inflation is zero and 3 per cent respectively. The long run Phillips Curve is also illustrated and $U_n$ is the natural rate of unemployment. Assume the economy is initially in equilibrium so that unemployment is at the natural rate and the actual rate of inflation equals the expected rate of inflation. Assume the expected rate of inflation is zero and that the authorities attempt to reduce unemployment below the natural rate by a 3 per cent increase in money growth.

As money growth rises, aggregate demand will increase. Traders will experience an unplanned reduction in stocks and prices will begin to rise. The rise in prices implies an increase in real profits and firms will therefore expand output. To recruit additional workers they will offer higher nominal wages, though wages will initially rise by less than prices, otherwise the incentive to increase output disappears. Because the expected rate of inflation is zero, workers will perceive the higher nominal wages as higher real wages and will therefore accept offers of employment. The economy moves up the short run Phillips Curve $P^{e=0}$ until point $a$ is reached.

However this is not a long run equilibrium point because it is based on money illusion, that is, workers do not perceive rising prices and believe they have experienced a rise in real income. Once workers realise that, far from increasing, their real income has actually fallen, they will demand compensatory pay rises. However, when wages and prices have both increased by 3 per cent, real profits are reduced to the level that existed before the increase in money growth. The incentive for firms to produce a higher level of output therefore disappears and they will lay workers off. Workers who accepted jobs in the mistaken belief that the real wage had increased will also withdraw from the labour market.

Now it is important to realise that, while the economy moves up the short run Phillips Curve $P^{e=0\%}$, it does not move down the same short run Phillips Curve. After all, money growth is now 3 per cent higher, prices are rising by 3 per cent and the expected rate of inflation is now 3 per cent. If all other things remain equal, an increase in unemployment does not change this. The economy therefore moves to point $b$ and long run equilibrium is restored. The only way the authorities can reduce unemployment by varying monetary policy is to further increase money growth so that there is again a divergence between actual inflation and expected inflation. However, once money illusion disappears, unemployment will revert to the natural rate and the only affect of the authorities' action will be to increase inflation.

The same reasoning implies that the only way to reduce inflation is for the authorities to reduce money growth so that the actual rate of inflation is less than the expected rate of inflation. In these circumstances the mechanism outlined above operates in reverse. As prices fall, real profits fall and firms will cut back on production. Unemployment therefore rises above the natural rate. Once the fall in prices is perceived by workers, they will accept smaller pay rises, real profits will be restored and employment will revert to the natural rate.

## Common Mistakes to Avoid

Changes in the **price level**, are sometimes confused with changes in **the rate of inflation**. A change in the price level represents a once and for all adjustment from one price level to another. Inflation, on the other hand, is a continuous process. For example, if the rate of inflation is 4 per cent this implies that prices rise by 4 per cent annually. A change in the rate of inflation therefore implies that there has been a change in the rate at which prices are changing.

The terms **money growth** and **money supply** are sometimes confused. Money growth refers to the rate at which the money supply is changing. The money supply, on the other hand, is a stock concept.

Thus an increase in money growth implies that the money supply is rising at a faster rate, whereas it is possible for the money supply to increase even if money growth falls! For example, if money growth falls from 4 per cent per annum to 2 per cent per annum, this implies a 2 per cent increase in the money stock over the course of the year.

## Questions and Answers

### *Questions*

1  The diagram below (Figure 28.5) reproduces the curve plotted by A.W. Phillips showing the relationship between the annual rate of change of money wages and the percentage levels of annual unemployment in the UK over the period 1861–1913. (The curve is a statistical 'line of best fit' to a scatter diagram of data points.) Phillips argued that the plotted curve also fitted the data for the period 1919–57.

The annual data for price inflation and unemployment for the years 1972 to 1980 are depicted in Table 28.1 on the following page.

Figure 28.5

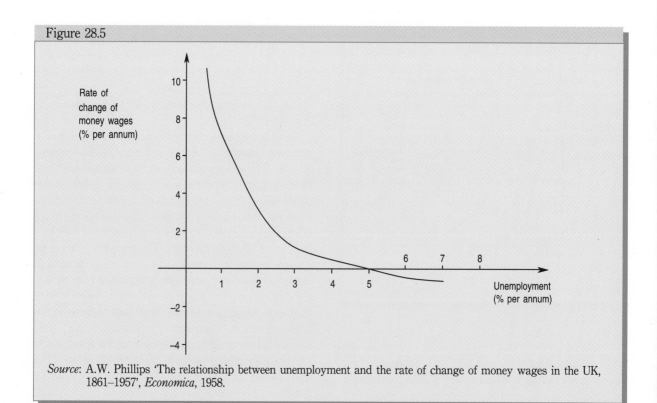

*Source*: A.W. Phillips 'The relationship between unemployment and the rate of change of money wages in the UK, 1861–1957', *Economica*, 1958.

Table 28.1

|  | Annual percentage change in prices | Unemployment (per cent) |
|---|---|---|
| 1972 | 10.3 | 3.7 |
| 1973 | 8.0 | 2.6 |
| 1974 | 16.9 | 2.6 |
| 1975 | 27.1 | 3.9 |
| 1976 | 13.9 | 5.3 |
| 1977 | 12.3 | 5.7 |
| 1978 | 11.5 | 5.7 |
| 1979 | 13.4 | 5.4 |
| 1980 | 18.1 | 6.4 |

*Source*: HMSO data.

Answer each of the following questions, explaining your reasons in each case.

(a) For what reasons could it be argued that the curve plotted by Phillips could be extended to show a relationship between commodity price inflation and unemployment? (3)

(b) What did the Phillips Curve imply for the 'demand-pull' versus 'cost-push' debate as to the main cause of inflation? (4)

(c) What implications did the Phillips Curve have for the formulation of government economic policy? (4)

(d) Examine the data for the period 1972 to 1980 and consider its consistency with the earlier relationship put forward by Phillips. (5)

(e) What factors might explain the differences in the data for the 1972–80 period compared with the earlier period studied by Phillips? (6)

(f) What are the implications of the data for the 1972–80 period for economic policy recommendations based on the Phillips Curve? (3)

WJEC, June 1991

2 Which of the following statements might represent the views of a monetarist economist?

1 Inflation is primarily the result of increases in the money supply which exceed the growth potential in the economy.

2 Monetary policy is a more effective way of controlling the economy than fiscal policy.

3 An increase in government expenditure financed by borrowing will be unsuccessful in reducing unemployment below the 'natural rate of unemployment' in the long run.

A 1, 2 and 3
B 1 and 2 only
C 2 and 3 only
D 1 only

AEB, Nov 1990

3 According to the quantity theory of money, a decrease in the stock of money will lead, other things being equal, to

A a decrease in the velocity of circulation of money.
B a decrease in the general level of prices.
C an increase in the general level of prices.
D an increase in the level of real output.

JMB, June 1990

## Answers

1 (a) For the economy as a whole labour costs are by far the most important element of total costs. In the UK they account for about 70 per cent of total costs. This implies that, if all other things remain equal, a 10 per cent rise in labour costs will increase total costs by 7 per cent. It is clear therefore that, after allowance is made for productivity changes, the relationship which Phillips identified between changes in wages and changes in unemployment can be generalised into a relationship between commodity prices and unemployment.

(b) It is generally argued that the Phillips Curve supports the 'demand pull' view of inflation. At low rates of unemployment there would be a high level of demand for labour. As labour shortages appeared employers would bid up the price of labour. At high levels of unemployment the opposite would be the case. The lower demand for labour and greater availability of workers implies downward pressure on wage increases. However the issue is not clear-cut and it could be argued that at low levels of unemployment the bargaining power of trade unions is increased, with the result that they are able to push for higher wages. Their bargaining power is considerably reduced at higher levels of unemployment.

(c) The existence of the Phillips Curve appeared to offer policy-makers a menu of options. They could choose lower unemployment if they were prepared to accept a higher rate of inflation or they could choose lower inflation if they were prepared to accept a higher rate of unemployment. In other words, the Phillips Curve implied that low inflation was not consistent with low unemployment and therefore policy-makers were obliged to trade off one policy aim against the other to attain the most acceptable position in terms of unemployment and inflation.

(d) The data for 1972–80 do not seem consistent with a stable Phillips Curve and even a cursory glance at the coordinates for 1972–80 shows that, for each of the years given, the economy was operating to the right of the point that would have been predicted by the original Phillips Curve. In other words, it seems that during the later period, any given rate of unemployment was associated with a higher rate of inflation than would have been predicted by the Phillips Curve. For example, the original Phillips Curve appears to indicate that a 5 per cent unemployment rate would be associated with stable prices. However we see from Table 28.1 that in 1979, when unemployment was 5.4 per cent, prices were rising by 13.4 per cent!

The data in the table indicate a further problem because they imply that inflation and unemployment sometimes moved in the same direction. For example, between 1974 and 1975 and between 1979 and 1980 there was an increase in the rate of inflation despite there being an increase in the rate of unemployment. Again this is completely at odds with the original Phillips Curve, which implied that unemployment and the rate of inflation moved in opposite directions.

(e) It has been argued that the relationship identified by Phillips was a short run relationship and that in the long run the Phillips Curve is vertical. Equilibrium exists when unemployment is at the natural rate. The natural rate of unemployment is sometimes referred to as the non-accelerating inflation rate of unemployment (NAIRU) because it is the only rate of unemployment associated with a stable rate of inflation. Figure 28.6 is used to provide a summary of the argument.

Let us assume that in Figure 28.6 unemployment is initially at the natural rate $U_n$ and that there is no inflation. Let us further assume that the economy has been here for some time and that no inflation is expected. Now if the government increases the money supply, say by 2 per cent, in order to reduce unemployment, aggregate demand will rise and prices will increase. Firms will therefore wish to expand output because the rise in prices implies higher profits. To attract additional workers they will offer higher nominal wages. Since workers are not expecting inflation they will not immediately perceive rising prices and will therefore mistake the increase in nominal wages as an increase in real wages. The economy will therefore move up the Phillips Curve $P^{e=0\%}$ and unemployment will fall

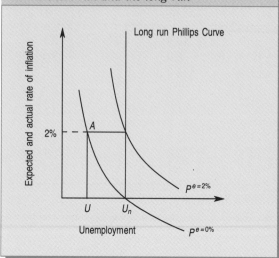

Figure 28.6   *The effect of an increase in money growth on the rate of inflation and unemployment in the short run and the long run*

to $U$. However, once point $A$ is reached and prices and wages have both increased by 2 per cent, real profits and real wages are both at the level that existed before the government increased the money supply. Firms will therefore cut back on production and will lay workers off. Unemployment will go on rising until it is again at the natural rate. However the economy will not move down the Phillips Curve $P^{e=0\%}$ because wages and prices are 2 per cent higher and the expected rate of inflation is now 2 per cent. Instead another short run Phillips Curve, $P^{e=2\%}$, will become the appropriate short run Phillips Curve. The only way for the government to reduce inflation is to reduce money growth, when the sequence will work in reverse.

This hypothesis would account for inflation and unemployment moving in the same direction. All that is happening is that in the long run the economy is moving up and down the vertical long run Phillips Curve.

(f) The data for 1972–80 imply that policy recommendations based on the original Phillips Curve will generate higher inflation than expected or higher unemployment. Indeed the analysis in section (e) above implies that policies to reduce unemployment by stimulating aggregate demand will simply result in a higher rate of inflation in the long run, with no change in the rate of unemployment. The authorities would be more successful in reducing unemployment without inflation if they concentrated on improving the efficiency with which the labour market operated, so as to reduce the natural rate of unemployment. This implies that the focus of attention should be measures to improve the mobility of labour, increased emphasis on training and some have even suggested a reduction in social security payments to the unemployed.

**2** The monetarist view of inflation is that it is caused entirely by an increase in money growth which exceed increases in productivity. Option 1 is therefore correct.

Monetarists argue that the economy is inherently stable and self-regulating. They argue that any attempt by the authorities to influence aggregate demand will destabilise the economy in the short run and cause inflation in the long run. This implies that in the long run the authorities can only influence the rate of inflation and they can do this most effectively by controlling the rate of money growth. Option 2 is therefore correct.

To some extent whether option 3 is correct depends on what is financed through government expenditure! If it is used to finance an extensive training programme this might lead to a reduction in the natural rate of unemployment. However, since we assume that all other things remain equal, an increase in government expenditure on goods and services implies an increase in aggregate demand which will have no long run effect on the natural rate of unemployment. Option 3 is therefore correct.

The key is A.

**3** The quantity theory of money assumes that the velocity of circulation is determined by institutional factors such as whether income is received weekly or monthly. It is unaffected by changes in the stock of money and so option A is incorrect.

The main prediction of the quantity theory of money is that, if all other things remain equal, a change in the stock of money will lead to a proportional change in the price level. Option B is therefore correct.

The quantity theory predicts that changes in the stock of money cause prices to change in the same direction. Option C is therefore incorrect.

The quantity theory of money assumes that the level of real output is determined by institutional factors such as changes in technology and is unaffected by changes in stock of money. Option D is therefore incorrect.

## REVIEW QUESTIONS AND ANSWERS

### Questions

**1** If prices rise by 10 per cent, by how much does the value of money fall?

**2** How does inflation affect the efficiency with which money fulfils its functions?

**3** Are the problems of inflation greater if the rate of inflation is variable?

**4** What is the prediction made by the quantity theory of money?

**5** Why is it often difficult to distinguish between cost push and demand pull inflation?

**6** What is meant by the term 'money illusion'?

**7** Why is the existence of money illusion important to the derivation of the short run Phillips Curve?

**8** What is 'natural' about the natural rate of unemployment?

**9** Does the existence of a natural rate of unemployment imply that the government is powerless to influence the level of unemployment?

### Answers

**1** The fall in the value of money can be calculated in the following way:

$$\frac{110 - 100}{100} \times 100 = 9.1 \text{ per cent.}$$

**2** Inflation impairs the efficiency with which money performs its functions. In particular money becomes less useful as a unit of account because its real value is less certain, especially if inflation is variable and unpredictable. For this reason it also becomes less acceptable as a medium of exchange. Uncertainty over the value of money will prevent it providing a standard for deferred payments and it will most certainly fail to provide a store of value, since inflation implies that the value of money falls.

**3** Inflation is a major cause of resource misallocation. Producers and sellers cannot distinguish between an increase in price caused by an increase in demand for their product and a general increase in prices caused by inflation. Because of this they sometimes increase output in the mistaken belief that a price rise implies an increase in demand for their product. Even when inflation is predictable not all prices rise by the same amount or at the same time. Indeed some prices fall even during periods of quite rapid inflation. As we have seen in the answer to question 2 above, inflation, even when it is predictable, also impairs the ability of money to perform its functions. Inflation is therefore a major problem for the economy whether it is variable or not. On the other hand, when inflation is predictable, some groups in society might be able to insure themselves against its effect. For example, lenders can negotiate a more appropriate rate of interest rather than being locked into contracts they would not have found acceptable had they correctly anticipated the rate of inflation.

**4** The traditional version of the quantity theory of money predicts that a rise in the money supply will lead to a proportional increase in the price level.

**5** It is difficult to distinguish between cost push and demand pull inflation because, once inflation is under way, nominal incomes will be bid up to preserve their real value and as nominal incomes rise demand for real output will rise.

**6** Money illusion exists when an increase in prices is not fully perceived. In these circumstances, a rise in nominal income is perceived to be an increase in real income, even if prices have risen by a greater percentage than nominal income, so that real income has actually fallen.

**7** If all other things remain equal, an increase in prices implies an increase in real profits. To attract additional workers firms will therefore be prepared to offer higher nominal wages. In the short run workers will not perceive rising prices and an increase in nominal wages will be perceived as an increase in real income. Workers will therefore accept job offers in the mistaken belief that the higher nominal wage implies a higher real wage. This is why unemployment falls as inflation increases. Once the workforce are aware that real wages are unchanged and firms are aware that real profits are unchanged, unemployment will rise back to the natural rate.

**8** The natural rate of unemployment is the equilibrium rate of unemployment. In this sense the economy has a natural tendency to settle at this level of unemployment.

**9** The existence of a natural rate of unemployment implies that an increase in aggregate demand, whether engineered through an increase in monetary policy or fiscal policy, will only reduce unemployment temporarily and in the long run will simply result in a higher rate of inflation. This implies that the government cannot reduce unemployment in the long term through an active policy of demand management. However it does not imply that the government is powerless to influence the level of unemployment since it can implement policies designed to reduce the natural rate. Such policies might include measures to improve the mobility of labour, increased emphasis on training, measures to curb the power of trade unions, increased privatisation and deregulation of markets, an end to subsidies, lower rates of income tax and so on.

CHAPTER 29

# RATIONAL EXPECTATIONS IN ECONOMICS

## Topic Summary

The way in which expectations are formed is crucial to an understanding of the way the economy operates. Firms, individuals and the government base their decisions about their future courses of action partly on the basis of what they expect to happen to the relevant economic variables. There are two approaches to the formation of expectations: **adaptive** and **rational**. Let us consider each in turn.

### Adaptive expectations

One way in which expectations might be formed about the future value of some economic variable, such as the rate of inflation, is by reference to the *past behaviour*, and in particular the *recent behaviour*, of that variable. When expectations are formed in this way they are said to be **adaptive**. However economic variables are affected by many factors and past behaviour has not always proved to be a reliable guide to future behaviour.

### Rational expectations

Expectations are said to be **rational** when they are formed by considering all relevant information. Of course rational expectations will not always turn out to be correct. However, because all relevant information is considered in forecasting the future value of some economic variable, if a forecast turns out to be incorrect, then rational expectations implies that the model used to forecast that variable will be changed so as to improve its predictive accuracy in the future.

Sooner or later, by a process of continuous adjustment, rational expectations will enable firms, individuals and so on to correctly forecast the future value of any economic variable. The only source of inaccuracy is random events which, by their very nature, cannot be forecast.

This raises an interesting possibility with respect to the effect of government policy on the economy. If the outcome of government policy is correctly anticipated it will be much more difficult for the authorities to influence key aggregates such as the level of unemployment by varying economic policy. In fact proponents of the rational expectations hypothesis refer to the likelihood of policy-ineffectiveness to indicate the impotence of the authorities to influence real aggregates in the economy.

For example, if the authorities announce an increase in money growth to stimulate the economy, the quantity theory of money predicts that the only long run effect of this will be an increase in the rate of inflation. The argument is that rational expectations will lead this end result to be widely anticipated at the time money growth is increased. It is claimed that this will lead workers to renegotiate their wages in anticipation of higher prices, and firms to adjust prices in anticipation of a general increase in demand. The implication is that an anticipated increase in money growth has no effect on output and employment. It simply leads immediately to a higher price.

In practice, this prediction of the rational expectations approach is unlikely to be fulfilled because it is often difficult for workers to renegotiate their wages. However, in those markets where contracts are continually being agreed, such as the financial markets, rational expectations might be more relevant in explaining the formation of expectations.

## REVIEW QUESTIONS AND ANSWERS

### Questions

1 What is 'rational' about rational expectations?

2 What are 'adaptive expectations'? Are they ever rational?

3 Why might the labour market not adjust instantaneously to new information?

4 If the authorities bring about a random change in the money supply this will have a short run effect on output and employment, but if they vary the money supply systematically it will have no effect on output and employment. Why is this?

5 Are forecasts based on rational expectations always correct?

6 Why might the theory of rational expectations be more relevant in explaining the behaviour of financial markets than the effect of monetary policy on the level of output and employment?

### Answers

1 Rational expectations are rational in the sense that all available information about the behaviour of a particular variable is taken into account when forming an expectation about that variable's future value.

2 Adaptive expectations are expectations about the future value of a variable which are based on a weighted average of its past values. Adaptive expectations may be rational if little is known, apart from its past behaviour, about the determinants of a particular variable.

3 In the labour market many wage contracts are negotiated annually and, once agreed, are not subject to revision until one year later. Once a contract is agreed, it cannot be revised in the light of new information and so instantaneous adjustment of the labour market to new information is not possible.

4 A random change in the money supply that is completely unanticipated will create a divergence between the expected rate of inflation and the actual rate of inflation. Money illusion will therefore exist and there will be short run effects on output and employment. However, if the money supply is varied systematically changes in money growth will come to be accurately anticipated and these effects will therefore be discounted when contracts are agreed.

5 Forecasts based on rational expectations take account of all available information. Economic agents might not possess all of the relevant information to enable them to forecast with complete accuracy the behaviour of an economic variable. However, because it considers all available information about the behaviour of a particular variable, a rational expectations forecast represents the best available forecast of that variable. Over time, as more information becomes available, the only errors that are possible in a rational expectations forecast are those which arise because of random events which, by their very nature, cannot be forecast.

6 Financial markets can adjust instantaneously to new information, whereas the labour and goods markets cannot. On the financial markets new contracts are negotiated throughout the day. Wage contracts, as we have seen in the answer to question 3 above, are negotiated annually and contracts to produce or deliver goods are often agreed many months in advance. Buyers are often given several months to pay for goods. In such circumstances new information has no effect on existing contracts.

# CHAPTER 30

# INTERNATIONAL TRADE

## Topic Summary

Countries engage in international trade for many reasons. Sometimes the main reason is political rather than economic. Sometimes certain countries are the only suppliers of particular goods. Most of the world's coffee is grown in Brazil, Chile is the world's main supplier of nitrates; and so on. However, with modern technology, many countries are capable of producing the same goods and yet they choose to obtain goods they could produce themselves from abroad. Economists have traditionally explained this in terms of the gains from specialisation. In other words, countries **specialise** in the production of those goods where they are **most efficient**.

## Absolute Advantage

A country is said to have an **absolute advantage** when, with a **given amount of resources**, it can produce more of a particular good than another country. To illustrate, let us consider a simple model where there are only two countries, A and B, and only two goods, tractors and wheat, are produced. Let us further assume that each country has a total of $X$ resources and can produce tractors and wheat, as illustrated in Table 30.1

Table 30.1 shows that country A has an absolute advantage in the production of wheat because, with a

**Table 30.1**

| | Number of tractors that can be produced using X resources | Tonnes of wheat that can be produced using X resources |
|---|---|---|
| Country A | 10 | 50 |
| Country B | 20 | 40 |

given amount of resources, it can produce more wheat than country B. On the other hand, country B has an absolute advantage in the production of tractors because, with a given amount of resources, it can produce more tractors than country A.

If we assume that each country has 10X resources and there are constant returns to scale as output increases, it is easy to show that specialisation will lead to a higher level of output than could otherwise be achieved. For simplicity we assume that before specialisation each country devotes half of its resources to the production of wheat and half of its resources to the production of tractors. When each country specialises it devotes its entire stock of resources to the production of that good where it has an absolute advantage. The gains from specialisation are now illustrated in Table 30.2.

**Table 30.2**

| | Before specialisation | |
|---|---|---|
| | Number of tractors | Tonnes of wheat |
| Country A | 50 | 250 |
| Country B | 100 | 200 |
| Total combined output | 150 | 450 |
| | After specialisation | |
| | Number of tractors | Tonnes of wheat |
| Country A | — | 500 |
| Country B | 200 | — |
| Total combined output | 200 | 500 |

It is clear that total combined output is greater after each country specialises than when each country produces both goods. However, although total combined output is greater when each country specialises, it does not necessarily follow that both countries gain from specialisation. It depends on the terms of trade, that is, the rate at which one good exchanges against the other good. In fact, for specialisation and trade to be mutually beneficial, the terms of trade must lie somewhere between the **domestic opportunity cost ratios**.

The domestic opportunity cost ratio is simply the amount of one good that must be given up in order to produce a given amount of the other good. In our example the domestic opportunity cost ratio in country A is 1 tractor : 5 tonnes of wheat, and the domestic opportunity cost ratio in country B is 1 tractor : 2 tonnes of wheat. If the terms of trade lie somewhere between these two ratios, both countries will gain from specialisation and trade. For example, if the terms of trade are 1 tractor : 3 tonnes of wheat, country A will gain from specialisation and trade because to produce 1 tractor domestically it must give up 5 tonnes of wheat. Country B will also gain from specialisation and trade because for each tractor it gives up it can only produce 2 tonnes of wheat whereas through trade it can obtain three tonnes of wheat for each tractor given up.

## Comparative Advantage

It is easy to understand the gains from trade when each country has an absolute advantage in the production of one good. However it is also possible for countries to gain from specialisation and trade even when one country has an absolute advantage in the production of all goods compared with another country as long as each country has a **comparative advantage** in the production of at least one good. A country is said to have a comparative advantage when the domestic opportunity cost of producing a good is lower in one country than in another country. In other words, in terms of the domestic opportunity cost, one country is relatively more efficient in the production of a particular good than another country. Again we can illustrate (Table 30.3) the principle of comparative advantage using a simple numerical example in which there are two countries, producing two goods (tractors and wheat) and there are constant returns to scale.

Table 30.3 shows that country A has an absolute advantage in the production of both goods. However, if we compare the domestic opportunity cost ratios, it is clear that each country has a comparative advantage. Thus in country A, the domestic opportunity cost ratio is 1 tractor : 5 tonnes of wheat, whereas in

| Table 30.3 | | |
|---|---|---|
| | *Number of tractors that can be produced using X resources* | *Tonnes of wheat that can be produced using X resources* |
| Country A | 12 | 60 |
| Country B | 10 | 40 |

country B, the domestic opportunity cost ratio is 1 tractor : 4 tonnes of wheat. Country A therefore has a comparative advantage (as well as an absolute advantage) in the production of wheat because each tractor it gives up makes possible the production of 5 tonnes of wheat, compared with only 4 tonnes of wheat in country B. Country B, on the other hand, has a comparative advantage in the production of tractors (despite country A's absolute advantage) because each tractor produced involves a sacrifice of only 4 tonnes of wheat compared with a sacrifice of 5 tonnes of wheat in country A.

Again if we assume each country has a total of 10X resources we can demonstrate the gains from specialisation and trade. However, in this case, because country A has an absolute advantage in the production of both goods, to demonstrate the gains from specialisation it is necessary for country A to *partially specialise* in the production of the good where it has a comparative advantage and for country B to *fully specialise* where it has a comparative advantage. For example, if country A devotes 9X resources to the production of wheat, while country B devotes 10X resources to the production of tractors, we can compare this with the total amount that can be produced when each country devotes half of its resources to the production of both goods. This is shown in Table 30.4.

Again, although specialisation leads to an increase in the combined output of both goods, for specialisation and trade to be mutually beneficial the terms of trade must lie somewhere between the domestic opportunity cost ratios. In our example, the domestic opportunity cost ratios are 1 tractor : 5 tonnes of wheat in country A and 1 tractor : 4 tonnes of wheat in country B. For example, if the terms of trade are 1 tractor : 4.5 tonnes of wheat, both countries can gain from specialisation and trade. Country A will gain because, if it produces tractors domestically, it will have to sacrifice 5 tonnes of wheat for each tractor produced. However, country B also gains because, if it produces wheat domestically, for each tractor given up it gains only 4 tonnes of wheat.

Table 30.4

| Before specialisation | Number of tractors | Tonnes of wheat |
|---|---|---|
| Country A | 60 | 300 |
| Country B | 50 | 200 |
| Total combined output | 110 | 500 |

| After specialisation | Number of tractors | Tonnes of wheat |
|---|---|---|
| Country A | 12 | 540 |
| Country B | 100 | — |
| Total combined output | 112 | 540 |

## Problems with Theories of Specialisation

The principles of absolute and comparative advantage are clearly important in explaining why countries specialise in the production of certain goods and services. However our discussion of the principles of absolute and comparative advantage as outlined in this chapter is a little simplistic and is based on certain assumptions which might not always be met in the real world. These assumptions are briefly summarised.

### Constant Costs

Throughout our discussion we have assumed the existence of **constant returns to scale** as output changes. However, in the real world, we know from p. 41 that, as output expands, firms may experience diseconomies of scale. If this is the case, then as output increases the domestic opportunity cost ratio will increase. What appears to be an absolute or comparative advantage at low levels of output may then disappear at higher levels of output.

### Full Employment

Our analysis of the gains from specialisation assumes there is **full employment of resources**. If there is less than full employment then the opportunity cost of increasing the production of a good is zero.

### Perfect Factor Mobility

It has been assumed that resources are equally well suited to the production of different goods and that there are no barriers to mobility so that resources can move easily from the production of one good to the production of another. In the real world resources are not equally well suited to the production of different goods and there are **barriers to mobility**. Both of these might limit the ability of nations to specialise.

### Trading Costs

There are **costs of trading internationally** which our analysis of the gains from specialisation has ignored. For example, there are costs of transporting goods across frontiers which do not arise in domestic trade. Transport costs might be higher and there are costs associated with converting one currency into another. There is also a risk that the terms of trade might change because of a change in exchange rates, thus reducing the real gains from trade.

### Protection

In the real world there are barriers to trade such as **tariffs** and **quotas** (see p. 179) which will reduce or even eliminate the gains from specialisation.

## The Terms of Trade

Thus far the terms of trade have been defined as the rate at which tractors exchange for wheat. More generally the terms of trade are defined as the rate at which a nation's exports exchange against its imports. However, because countries export and import vast amounts of different products, it is impossible in the real world to calculate the terms of trade as so much of this good for so much of that good and so on. Instead the terms of trade are computed as an index, in the following way:

$$\frac{\text{Index of export prices}}{\text{Index of import prices}} \times 100$$

When the terms of trade rise, this implies that a given quantity of exports now exchanges for a greater volume of imports. This is referred to as a **favourable movement** in the terms of trade because it implies that a given amount of exports now exchanges for a greater volume of imports. The converse is also true. When the terms of trade index falls, this is referred to as an **unfavourable movement** in the terms of trade because a given volume of exports now exchanges for a smaller volume of imports.

A favourable movement in the terms of trade occurs when:

- export prices rise and import prices fall, or
- export prices rise faster than import prices, or
- export prices fall by less than import prices fall.

## Common Mistakes to Avoid

One obvious area of confusion is the distinction between **absolute advantage** and **comparative advantage**. An absolute advantage exists when one country can produce more of a good than another country by using the same quantity of resources. A comparative advantage exists when one country has a lower domestic opportunity cost ratio in the production of a particular good than another country. It is, of course, possible for a country to have an absolute *and* a comparative advantage in the production of a good while another country has an absolute disadvantage and a comparative advantage in the production of a different good.

Another common mistake is in the *identification* of absolute or comparative advantage. The problem is illustrated in Tables 30.5 and 30.6.

### Table 30.5

|  | Number of tractors that can be produced using X resources | Tonnes of wheat that can be produced using X resources |
|---|---|---|
| Country A | 10 | 60 |
| Country B | 20 | 40 |

In Table 30.5 it is clear that country A has an absolute advantage in the production of wheat because it can produce more wheat than country B with the same resources. The corollary is that country B has an absolute advantage in the production of tractors because it can produce more tractors than country A with the same resources. Now compare Table 30.5 with Table 30.6. Which country has the absolute advantage in which product now?

In fact Table 30.6 gives exactly the same information as Table 30.5! We can see from Table 30.5 that the domestic opportunity cost ratio in country A is 1

### Table 30.6

|  | Units of resources required to produce 1 tractor | Units of resources required to produce 1 tonne of wheat |
|---|---|---|
| Country A | 6 | 1 |
| Country B | 2 | 1 |

tractor : 6 tonnes of wheat. In other words country A requires six times more resources to produce a tractor than it requires to produce a tonne of wheat. Table 30.5 also shows that in country B the domestic opportunity cost ratio is 1 tractor : 2 tonnes of wheat. In other words country B requires twice as many resources to produce a tractor than it requires to produce a tonne of wheat. Table 30.5 and Table 30.6 are therefore different ways of presenting the same information. However, referring to Table 30.6, the tendency is often to suggest that country A has an absolute advantage in the production of tractors and country B has an absolute advantage in the production of wheat.

Another possible source of confusion is over the interpretation of the term **favourable movement in the terms of trade**. Remember, a favourable movement in the terms of trade implies that the price of exports has risen relative to the price of imports. This implies that a given volume of exports now exchanges for a greater volume of imports. The price movements are therefore favourable. However the effect on the economy of these favourable price movements might actually be *unfavourable*. For example, if the price of exports rises while import prices remain unchanged, there will be a favourable movement in the terms of trade. But if, as a result of higher export prices, fewer exports are sold and more imports are purchased, the balance of payments on current account (see pp. 186–7) will deteriorate and unemployment will rise. The consequences of a favourable movement in the terms of trade might therefore be very unfavourable for the economy as a whole.

## Questions and Answers

### Questions

1  The table shows the domestic prices of two products X and Y produced in the United Kingdom and the United States of America

|  | Good X | Good Y |
|---|---|---|
| United Kingdom | £1 | £2 |
| United States of America | $2 | $5 |

If transport costs are zero and there are constant returns to scale in both countries, which exchange rate would result in an exchange of goods?

A  £1 = $1.00
B  £1 = $2.00
C  £1 = $2.25
D  £1 = $5.00

AEB, Nov 1989

**2** Two countries, X and Y, can produce cars and computers according to the following table.

| Commodity | Costs of production | |
|---|---|---|
|  | Country X | Country Y |
| 1 car | 4 labour-days | 7 labour-days |
| 1 computer | 6 labour-days | 8 labour days |

A  X will export cars and import computers.
B  X will export both cars and computers.
C  X will import both cars and computers
D  X will neither import nor export cars or computers.
E  The pattern of trade cannot be determined from the information given.

ULEAC, June 1990

**3** In 1982, the base year, the terms of trade of a country were 100. In 1983 export prices rose by 8% and import prices rose by 10%. The terms of trade for 1983 were therefore

A  137½
B  120
C  118
D  108
E  102

ULEAC, January 1991

## Answers

**1** Note that the data in this question give money prices rather than real costs. The domestic opportunity cost ratios are therefore 1 : 0.5 for the UK and 1 : 0.4 for the USA. This tells us that the UK has a comparative advantage in good Y and the USA has a comparative advantage in good X. However in this case, for trade to be mutually beneficial, the exchange rate must lie somewhere between the domestic price ratios, that is, somewhere between the ratio 1 : 0.5 and the ratio 1 : 0.4. The only exchange rate which satisfies this condition is C. However, before

we conclude that C is the key, let us check whether any other exchange rate will facilitate mutually beneficial trade.

If the exchange rate is £1 = $1.00, the UK will need to export one unit of good Y for each unit of good X it imports. But when it undertakes domestic production, the UK gains 2 units of X for each unit of Y given up. At £1 = $1, country A does not therefore benefit from international trade.

If the exchange ratio is £1 = $2.00, the UK will need to export one unit of Y for each 2 units of X it imports. However the UK can produce good X domestically in exactly the same ratio. The UK does not therefore gain from trade when the exchange rate is £1 = $2.

If the rate of exchange is £1 = $2.25, for each unit of Y the UK exports, it can import 2.25Y. This exceeds the amount of X that can be produced domestically for each unit of Y given up. The UK therefore gains from trade when the exchange rate is £1 = £2.25. However the USA also gains from trade at this exchange rate. For each 2 units of X it exports it gains 1 unit of Y. If it produces Y domestically, for each 2 units of X it gives up it gains only 0.8 units of Y.

If the exchange rate is £1 = $5 for each unit of X the USA exports it gains 0.4Y, exactly the same as it obtains if it produces Y domestically. When the rate of exchange is £1 = $5 the USA does not therefore gain from trade.

The key is C.

**2** The domestic opportunity cost ratios are 1 computer : 1.5 cars in country X and 1 computer : 1.14 cars in country Y. Country X therefore has a comparative advantage in the production of cars and country Y has a comparative advantage in the production of computers. For trade to be mutually beneficial, therefore, country X must specialise in the production of cars and country Y must specialise in the production of computers. A further requirement is that the terms of trade lie somewhere between these domestic opportunity cost ratios. Since we are given no information on the terms of trade we cannot determine what each country will produce.

The key is therefore E.

**3** The terms of trade can be calculated from the formula:

$$\frac{\text{Index of export prices}}{\text{Index of import prices}} \times 100$$

Substitution in this formula gives:

$$\frac{108}{90} \times 100 = 102$$

The key is therefore E.

## REVIEW QUESTIONS AND ANSWERS

### Questions

Question 1 is based on the following extract.

*Côte d'Ivoire*

Major exports: Cocoa-beans and derivatives 27%, coffee and extracts 17%, wood 9%, petroleum products 8%, cotton 5% (1989)

Agriculture and forestry: Agriculture provided employment for 79% of the labour force and accounted 30% of GDP and three quarters of export revenues in 1983. The country is the world's leading producer of cocoa and the fifth largest producer of coffee. With cocoa and coffee accounting for 27% and 17% of exports respectively, price movements in these commodities have a major impact on the economy. Crops are sold to the Caisse de Stabilisation et de Soutien des Prix des Productions Agricoles (CSSPA), the government marketing agency, at state regulated prices. The subsequent lowering of these in 1989 may have had an adverse long term impact on production.

In an effort to diversify export crops, the production of cotton, which now acounts for only 5% of exports, palm oil, tropical fruits and rubber is being developed. Self sufficiency remains a major objective. The increase in food crops has made it possible to cut some imports, including rice and wheat. The export of wood, which acounts for 9% of exports, is declining as a result of the progressive depletion of forestry reserves.

*Source*: Barclays Bank.

1   Consider the extract above:

   (a) Which hypothesis of specialisation can best account for the observed pattern of crop production?

   (b) Why do you think the Côte d'Ivoire is seeking to diversify its exports? To what extent is this likely to be compatible with the stated aim of self-sufficiency?

Question 2 is based on Table 30.7.

Table 30.7  *Value added per worker and wage rate, developed and developing countries*

| | Value added per worker (1980 dollars) | | Average wage rate (1980 dollars) | |
|---|---|---|---|---|
| | South | North | South | North |
| Food products | 7,546 | 28,790 | 2,054 | 10,268 |
| Beverages | 19,831 | 47,428 | 4,126 | 13,100 |
| Tobacco products | 9,263 | 74,987 | 1,622 | 14,057 |
| Textiles | 4,913 | 17,334 | 1,824 | 8,164 |
| Wearing apparel | 5,961 | 13,722 | 2,456 | 6,946 |
| Leather and fur products | 6,450 | 17,161 | 2,186 | 7,856 |
| Footwear | 6,985 | 13,558 | 2,513 | 6,629 |
| Wood and wood products | 5,174 | 21,422 | 1,823 | 10,037 |
| Furniture and fixtures | 6,560 | 19,916 | 2,161 | 9,761 |
| Paper and paper products | 12,716 | 34,660 | 3,494 | 14,446 |
| Printing and publishing | 9,210 | 31,258 | 3,334 | 14,191 |
| Industrial chemicals | 20,624 | 49,968 | 4,277 | 16,875 |
| Other chemical products | 15,877 | 48,084 | 4,076 | 14,696 |
| Petroleum refineries | 86,262 | 188,437 | 8,638 | 19,971 |
| Miscellaneous petroleum and coal products | 23,074 | 50,703 | 3,464 | 13,291 |
| Rubber products | 9,794 | 27,029 | 2,804 | 12,956 |
| Plastic products | 10,456 | 26,535 | 2,953 | 11,711 |
| Pottery, china and earthenware | 6,428 | 19,672 | 2,292 | 9,485 |
| Glass and glass products | 9,904 | 26,790 | 3,220 | 11,860 |
| Other non-metal mineral products | 9,408 | 29,589 | 2,752 | 11,418 |
| Iron and steel | 11,544 | 32,938 | 3,423 | 15,244 |
| Non-ferrous metals | 17,717 | 37,308 | 4,077 | 15,291 |
| Metal products | 9,377 | 25,561 | 3,305 | 12,278 |
| Non-electrical machinery | 10,815 | 29,606 | 3,820 | 14,002 |
| Electrical machinery | 10,366 | 28,500 | 3,251 | 13,183 |
| Transport equipment | 11,948 | 29,685 | 4,129 | 15,286 |
| Professional and scientific equipment | 8,968 | 33,524 | 3,243 | 3,852 |
| Other industries | 7,897 | 23,041 | 2,407 | 9,812 |

*Source*: UNIDO.

The data in Table 30.7 refer to developed countries ('North') and developing countries ('South').

(a) Calculate for each product the ratio of unit labour costs (South divided by North)

(b) On the basis of this calculation select **six** industries in which South countries would be likely to have:
  (i) a comparative advantage;
  (ii) a comparative disadvantage.

(c) Consult available World Bank and United Nations trade data sources to see to what extent actual trade patterns confirm your prediction.

3 In what circumstances will a country have a comparative advantage in producing a particular good despite having an absolute disadvantage in producing that good?

4 Why might nations not wish to specialise even when they have a comparative advantage in the production of some goods compared with other countries?

## Answers

**1** (a) The text indicates that the Côte d'Ivoire enjoys an absolute and comparative advantage in the production of cocoa. We are told it is the world's largest producer of cocoa. However it also enjoys a comparative advantage in coffee, being the world's fifth largest producer. The size of the agricultural and forestry sector, accounting for 75 per cent of export revenue, also indicates a comparative advantage in this area.

**(b)** Exports from the Côte d'Ivoire are primary products. In general these products have a low price elasticity of demand, which causes large fluctuations in price, and therefore in the incomes of exporters, when there are changes in supply, which can be frequent when production depends on the weather. They also tend to have a low income elasticity of demand, which implies that, as incomes grow in the importing countries, exports and income in the Côte d'Ivoire will not grow to the same extent. The aim of diversifying production is to reduce the impact of price fluctuations on domestic incomes and to encourage production of those products with a more income elastic demand.

Export diversification is not incompatible with self-sufficiency. Self-sufficiency does not imply that a country ceases to be an exporter. It might mean that export revenues are sufficient to cover import expenditures without recourse to borrowing. Diversifying exports might very well help to achieve this. In any case, if export revenues raise national income and this generates resources for increased investment, the prospects for self-sufficiency will actually be improved.

**2** (a)

Table 3.8 *Ratio of unit labour costs*

| | |
|---|---|
| Food products | 0.20 |
| Beverages | 0.31 |
| Tobacco products | 0.12 |
| Textiles | 0.22 |
| Wearing apparel | 0.35 |
| Leather and fur products | 0.28 |
| Footwear | 0.38 |
| Wood and wood products | 0.18 |
| Furniture and fixtures | 0.22 |
| Paper and paper products | 0.24 |
| Printing and publishing | 0.23 |
| Industrial chemicals | 0.25 |
| Other chemical products | 0.28 |
| Petroleum refineries | 0.43 |
| Miscellaneous petroleum and coal products | 0.26 |
| Rubber products | 0.21 |
| Plastic products | 0.25 |
| Pottery, china and earthenware | 0.20 |
| Glass and glass products | 0.27 |
| Other non-metal mineral products | 0.24 |
| Iron and steel | 0.22 |

(b) On the basis of the above calculation, the South would appear to have a comparative advantage and a comparative disadvantage, as detailed below:

| *Comparative advantage* | *Comparative disadvantage* |
|---|---|
| Food products | Beverages |
| Tobacco products | Wearing apparel |
| Wood and wood products | Leather and fur products |
| Furniture and fixtures | Footwear |
| Rubber products | Other chemical products |
| Petroleum refineries | |
| Pottery china and earthenware | |

(c) Data are not available to show categorically that the South has a comparative or absolute advantage in the product groups noted above.

However supportive information is easily obtained if export data are consulted.

**3** A country will have a comparative advantage in the production of a good whenever it has a lower domestic opportunity cost ratio than another country. This is irrespective of whether it has an absolute disadvantage or not.

**4** One reason why countries might not wish to specialise in the production of certain goods is that this might leave them dependent on other countries for goods which might be considered strategic, such as food. Another reason is that specialisation might lead to the closure of an industry in an area of high unemployment and politicians might wish to avoid this. (See motives for protection on pp. 179–80.)

# CHAPTER 31

# *FREE TRADE AND PROTECTION*

## Topic Summary

We have seen in Chapter 30 that there are gains from specialisation and trade. However, for these gains to materialise, it is important that countries can trade freely. In the real world this is not always the case and countries sometimes adopt a range of measures designed to restrict imports. These measures are sometimes referred to as protection because their aim is to **protect** domestic markets from foreign competition.

### Forms of Protection

Protective measures can take a variety of different forms. These are easily summarised.

### Tariffs

A tariff is **a tax on imports**. Since at least part of the tax will be passed on to domestic consumers in the form of higher prices, the effect will be to reduce competition for domestic substitutes. In other words, the higher price will discourage consumption of imports and tend to increase sales of domestic products above the level that might otherwise be achieved.

### Quotas

Quotas are **a volume restriction on imports** and represent a very powerful protective measure. When a quota is imposed only a particular amount of a product can be imported within a particular period and once this limit is reached no further imports of the restricted product are permitted until the next period.

Despite this, quotas have not always been as successful at restricting expenditure on imports as

might be expected. One reason for this is that, if a quota is placed on a particular good, such as cars, producers have an incentive to concentrate on selling those models which have the highest profit margin and this inevitably means the more expensive models.

### Exchange Controls

Exchange controls are probably the most complete barrier to trade. In most cases imports must be paid for *in foreign currency*. This can only be obtained from the central bank and if the authorities refuse to release foreign currency would-be importers will be unable to pay for imports. By specifying the range of goods and services that foreign currency will be released to pay for, governments can exercise a high degree of control over import expenditure and the nature of the goods imported.

### Voluntary Export Restraints

These are a relatively new protective measure and represent an agreement between two countries that one country will voluntarily limit the amount it exports to the other. VERs are now quite widespread and limit international trade in a variety of products. Since they are voluntary agreements, countries are under no obligation to honour them but there is no doubt that in many cases they foreshadow stiffer measures if they are not adhered to. It is difficult to measure the extent to which international trade has been affected by VERs, but there is no doubt that their existence has limited the growth of trade in certain products.

### Arguments For and Against Protection

The economic motives for protection are considered in detail in the answer to question 1 on pp. 182–3.

Here we simply provide a brief summary of the main points.

## To Counter the Effects of a Recession

It is argued that, if domestic industry is protected against foreign competition, demand for domestic products will rise and the economy will be lifted out of recession. One problem with this argument is that it reflects a Keynesian view of how the economy works. Instead, if there is a natural rate of unemployment, the long run effect of protection will be to increase the natural rate of unemployment because protection will divert resources to less efficient uses. This implies a long run increase in the rate of unemployment.

## To Remove a Balance of Payments Deficit

Sometimes it is suggested that protection might reduce a balance of payments deficit. Here again, if protection encourages inefficiency, it is likely to worsen any balance of payments problem. The problem could be exacerbated if other countries retaliated with their own protective measures. In any case, balance of payments deficits are caused by a relatively high rate of inflation and protection deals with the symptom of the problem, not the cause.

## To Reduce Structural Unemployment

Again the argument is that, if demand is transferred away from imports in favour of domestic output, structural unemployment can be reduced. However, it has been argued above that in the long run protection simply increases inefficiency and, to the extent that this is the case, unemployment will rise. Protection might nevertheless reduce unemployment in the short run as demand is transferred away from foreign producers in favour of domestic firms.

## To Protect an Infant Industry

A popular argument for protection is that it is necessary to protect an infant industry. However this argument assumes that a potentially successful industry can be recognised more easily by the authorities than by entrepreneurs. This is a highly dubious argument and again protection might simply increase inefficiency.

## Strategic Reasons

Sometimes it is argued that an industry should be protected to ensure its survival in the long run because it is of strategic importance. Agriculture is a case in point. If a country is self-sufficient in the production of food then other countries cannot threaten it with a food embargo for some political reason. There is no economic case against protection for strategic reasons, though it might be difficult to define criteria with which to assess whether an industry is strategically important!

## The General Case Against Protection

A general problem with protection is that it implies a lower real income for domestic residents. Consumers are obliged to pay higher prices and resources are diverted into areas where they are used inefficiently. In addition, by removing the spur to competition, protection reduces the incentive for firms to increase productive efficiency. The implication is that protection will reduce the growth of output in the long run compared with the rate of growth that might otherwise have been achieved, living standards will be adversely affected and unemployment will be higher.

## The General Agreement on Tariffs and Trade (GATT)

Gatt was set up in 1947 with the aim of encouraging trade liberalisation and a return to the protectionist measures which characterised the 1920s. Agreements are negotiated between GATT members on a reciprocal basis and then, through GATT's most favoured nation clause, any concession granted to one country is then available to all GATT members.

GATT negotiations are referred to as rounds. In general GATT has achieved considerable success in bringing about a reduction in tariffs in the industrialised world, especially for manufacturing output. However the current Uruguay Round has met with considerable problems and, despite negotiations which began in 1986, no agreement has yet been reached.

## The Uruguay Round

The Uruguay Round has tried to be more ambitious than other rounds by including non-tariff barriers, as well as tariff barriers, in the negotiations. However this is an item that has been carried over from the previous Tokyo Round and is non-controversial. Other areas are more controversial. The issues which are new to GATT are **trade in intellectual property rights, trade related investment measures** and **trade in services**.

Trade in intellectual property rights is important because a great deal of copying is undertaken by developing countries which might reduce sales of firms in the developed world. For example, copies of Gucci watches and Lacoste T-shirts are readily available from third world producers. Such copying is illegal in the country of origin because of patent laws, copyright laws and so on but there is little that can be done outside the country of origin. Agreement on the protection of intellectual property rights will be difficult to reach since they generate employment and are an important source of foreign currency for the developing countries.

Trade-related investment measures refers to investments carried out by multinational firms where the host countries imposes restrictions such as the purchase of a certain proportion of inputs from the domestic economy. This has implications for trade because it reduces exports from those countries who would otherwise have supplied inputs.

Trade in services is becoming increasingly important. The EC and the USA who have a comparative advantage in the provision of services in general, particularly in the provision of financial services, have argued strongly that trade in services should be no more subject to restrictions on trade than trade in goods. This is not a view shared by all countries.

Despite the growing importance of trade in intellectual property rights, trade related investment measures and trade in services, it is widely recognised that these issues are unlikely to be resolved in the Uruguay Round. Indeed they have only recently been added to the agenda. The area of most current controversy is undoubtedly agriculture.

Many countries, including the EC, support agriculture. However it is well known that agricultural support causes **trade distortion** since the protecting countries have no comparative advantage in agriculture. If they had such an advantage protection would be unnecessary. The scale of the problem is great and, although most tariffs have fallen substantially since GATT began its operations in 1947, agricultural tariffs have fallen by only 4.6 per cent. Furthermore agricultural support has increased in most countries in recent years. Agricultural support hits those countries in the temperate zone such as the USA, New Zealand, Canada and Argentina, as well as many developing countries with their relatively large agricultural sector. The greatest friction exists between the USA and the EC. A 30 per cent reduction in agricultural support was proposed by the EC and rejected. It remains to be seen if the current reforms to the Common Agricultural Policy (CAP) (see pp. 204–5) offer a basis for agreement.

## Common Mistakes to Avoid

The effect of a **tariff** and a **quota** are sometimes confused. Like a quota, a tariff, if severe enough, can be used to limit the volume of a particular product. In addition a quota, like a tariff, might result in higher prices. If, as a result of a quota, supply of a product falls, prices might well be forced upwards. Because of this, a quota might also raise revenue for the government because higher prices imply higher VAT yields.

The way in which a tariff affects foreign currency expenditure is sometimes a source of confusion. A tariff has no effect on the foreign currency price of imports. It raises the domestic price only. For example, if the rate of exchange is £1 = $2, a good costing $20 000 in the USA costs £10 000 in the UK. Now if the UK government imposes a 20 per cent tariff on imports from the USA, the price of this good in the UK rises to £12 000, though its price in the USA is unchanged at $20 000. Because the foreign price is unchanged, any reduction in the quantity of imports purchased from the USA will reduce total dollar expenditure.

## Questions and Answers

### Questions

1  (a)  How may a country try to restrict imports?

(8)

(b)  Explain and evaluate the economic reasons for trying to restrict imports. (17)

UCLES, Nov 1991

2  Figure 31.1 (on following page) represents a domestic market for motor cars. *DD* and *SS* are, respectively, the domestic demand and supply for cars. *W* and $W_1$ show the world price for cars before and after the imposition of a tariff on cars. The tax revenue which

Figure 31.1 *The effect of a tariff on the price of cars and the quantity imported*

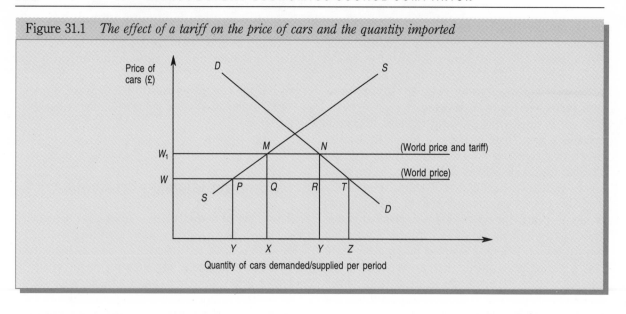

accrues to the government after the imposition of the tariff is shown by the area

A PMNT
B XMNY
C PMQ
D QMNR
E PMXV

ULEAC, Jan 1990

## Answers

**1** It is sometimes suggested that protective measures can counter a recession. The argument is that, if competition from imports is restricted, demand for domestic products will increase. This in turn, it is alleged, will encourage domestic production, increase domestic employment, and, through the multiplier, generate economic recovery. However this argument has little support. Some economists argue that the supply side of the economy is self-regulating and that any attempt to increase domestic aggregate demand will only generate increased inflation in the long run. It is also argued that protection, by diverting resources into areas where they are used less efficiently, is likely to lead to an increase in unemployment in the long run.

Even those economists who favour a policy of demand management may not support a policy of import controls. Such a policy may encourage retaliation from other countries, with the result that international trade is adversely affected, so that all countries are penalised and there are no gainers.

Furthermore, it is also possible that exports will be diverted to the home market or, because imports normally sold in the home market will be diverted to other markets where they will displace exports from the home country. There may also be income effects. If the home country imports fewer goods, incomes abroad will fall and foreigners will have less to spend on the home country's exports. For all of these reasons protection is unlikely to lift an economy out of recession.

It has been suggested that one way to eliminate a balance of payments deficit is to restrict imports and protect domestic industry. However we have already argued that if barriers to imports are erected, other countries may retaliate, which would hamper exports. Similarly exports will fall if they are diverted to the protected home market or if income effects abroad lead to falling demand for the home country's exports. In the long run protection will lead to inefficiency in the allocation of resources and this will reduce the competitiveness of domestic industry.

A balance of payments deficit reflects a basic lack of competitiveness due to inefficiency. Protecting domestic industries and reducing competition from imports is likely to encourage further inefficiency and exacerbate the balance of payments problem. The solution lies in restoring competitiveness and the official view is that this can most effectively be achieved by restricting money growth so as to control inflation.

It is sometimes claimed that protection can be used selectively to reduce structural unemployment. Structural unemployment has many causes but a major factor is **changes in the competitiveness** of imports. As imports of a particular type of good increase and domestic production is displaced, workers in the domestic industry become unemployed. The problem may be particularly acute when the industry is highly localised so that regional unemployment may rise well above the national average and unemployed workers will have little prospect of obtaining employment in the area where they live. It is alleged that, if the domestic industry is protected, demand will be diverted away from imports and domestic employment will safeguarded.

The problem is that, when an industry is thrown into decline because of increased foreign competition, unless foreign competitiveness is based on subsidies, this indicates a change in comparative advantage. To protect domestic industry in these circumstances therefore implies a **misallocation of resources** because resources will be diverted to industries which use them inefficiently. If the industry is protected from competition it will simply go on operating inefficiently. In the long run this will increase unemployment. It is argued that workers could more effectively protect their jobs if they accepted lower wages and adopted working practices that would increase productivity. It is further argued that, rather than protecting an inefficient industry, governments might offer workers retraining to increase their employment prospects in other industries.

It is sometimes suggested that infant industries require protection. An infant industry is a newly formed industry in the early stages of growth. Where there are significant economies of scale established, foreign producers have a considerable advantage over an infant industry. It is argued that, if the infant industry is protected against foreign competition, it will grow and compete with other international firms. One problem with this argument is that it is necessary to recognise an industry which will grow and compete successfully. This is the function of the capital market. Entrepreneurs provide venture capital for this very purpose. They bear the risk of production and are likely to be more able to assess the long term prospects of an emerging industry than government officials. A further problem, as argued above, is that if an industry is protected from competition it has no incentive to increase efficiency and reduce costs. In addition it is often argued that once protection is granted it is difficult to remove. Even if an infant industry was recognised there is no guarantee that protection would not be extended beyond the point at which the firm is able to compete internationally. Here again this implies inefficiency in the allocation of resources.

The arguments for protecting domestic industry against foreign competition are many and varied but none can be supported by economic reasoning. In fact economic reasoning predicts that protection is harmful to domestic industry and in the long run simply leads to increased inefficiency.

**2** When the tariff is imposed the price of imports in the domestic economy rises to $W_1$. The quantity of imports consumed is $XY$ ($OX$ represents the quantity of domestic output consumed) and total expenditure on imports is $XMNY$. The tax revenue raised by the tariff is therefore $QMNR$.

The key is D.

## REVIEW QUESTIONS AND ANSWERS

### Questions

1  If trade liberalisation is in a country's own interest, why is protectionism increasing?

2  Some countries impose a 'dubbing tax' on foreign language films. Examine the economic arguments for and against this.

3  When might a country prefer to impose quotas on imports rather than levy a tariff?

4  If the Uruguay Round succeeds, some countries will suffer. Why is this?

5  In what circumstances will the imposition of a quota lead to an increase in import expenditures?

### Answers

1  There is no doubt that trade liberalisation is in the best interests of global efficiency. However countries might protect certain industries for strategic reasons. They might also protect them for political reasons and this is potentially more serious. For example, protection might be given to particular industries because they are a powerful political lobby or because an industry which is localised is declining as a result of foreign competition. In times of recession, the transitional costs of reallocating resources away from declining industries might be severe. Sometimes protectionist measures are adopted as a short run measure. However, once granted, they are difficult to remove and have an adverse effect on the allocation of resources.

2  A dubbing tax can be used to raise revenue for governments and/or to cut down import expenditure by raising the domestic price of imports. Like most protective measures, it reduces efficiency in the allocation of resources and, by increasing the price consumers pay, it reduces the real income of consumers.

3  Quotas are a physical limit on the amount of a good that can be imported, whereas a tariff is a tax on imports. A quota might be preferable to a tariff when it is considered important to restrict the amount of a particular good imported or the amount spent on imports.

4  If the Uruguay Round succeeds in reducing trade barriers, all countries will gain in the long run. However there may be short run adjustment costs which will be borne by those countries whose industry has been protected against foreign competition. In the short run these countries will suffer if the Uruguay Round succeeds. Of course which countries gain and which countries initially suffer depends on the degree of success of the Uruguay Round.

5  A quota places a limit on the amount of a product that can be imported within any given period. If a quota is imposed, foreign producers have an incentive to concentrate on the most expensive models in the restricted range of products because these will usually confer the highest profit per unit sold. In these circumstances imposing a quota might result in an increase in import expenditure though this does not necessarily imply that the quota has failed. If the aim is simply to restrict the quantity of a product imported the quota will succeed.

# CHAPTER 32

# THE BALANCE OF PAYMENTS

## Topic Summary

### Recording International Transactions

The balance of payments is a set of accounts showing one nation's international transactions with the rest of the world over the course of a year. The balance of payments accounts therefore record sales of goods and services (exports) and purchases of goods and services (imports). The balance of payments accounts also record purely financial transactions, such as the purchase or sale of treasury bills, as well as remittances sent home by expatriates and donations of aid from one country to another.

Balance of payments accounts are based on the principle of **double-entry bookkeeping**. Each transaction is therefore recorded twice. For example, if the UK exports cars, the shipment of cars is a debit entry in the balance of payments accounts and receipt of payment for the cars is the credit entry. Since credit entries are recorded with a positive sign and debit entries with a negative sign, it follows that in total the balance of payments must always balance.

### Balance of Payments Surpluses and Deficits

If the balance of payments always balances, how can a nation have a balance of payments deficit or a balance of payments surplus? The answer is that certain transactions are **autonomous**, that is, they reflect **voluntary decisions** to buy, sell, lend, borrow or donate, while other transactions are **accommodating**, that is, they are **necessary** because autonomous credits are greater than or less than autonomous debits.

Strictly, a balance of payments deficit or surplus exists when accommodating transactions are carried out by the authorities. For example, if autonomous debits exceed autonomous credits and the difference is not accommodated by borrowing abroad, the authorities will be obliged to exchange domestic currency (sterling in the UK) for foreign currency, so that debit accounts can be settled. The amount of currency exchanged by the authorities is the balance of payments deficit. A balance of payments surplus occurs in exactly the opposite circumstances.

Despite this, the focus of attention is now the difference between sales of goods and services abroad and purchases of goods and services from abroad. The reason for this is that the authorities have limited reserves of foreign currency which can be used to finance a deficit in autonomous transactions. However, by increasing the rate of interest, they can always attract additional flows of foreign currency but, higher rates of interest depress the domestic economy, for example, causing a fall in investment. Countries are therefore concerned that autonomous credits should, over time, broadly equal autonomous debits and this implies that sales of goods and services abroad should, over time, broadly match purchases of goods and services from abroad. Because of this, the difference between the value of sales of goods and services abroad and purchases of goods and services from abroad is often thought of as the balance of payments deficit or surplus.

### The Structure of the UK Balance of Payments Accounts

The overall balance of payments accounts are made up of a series of accounts each recording different types of international transaction. Let us summarise the different accounts maintained by the UK authorities.

# The Current Account

The current account records visible trade (trade in goods) and invisible trade (trade in services and other items, such as remittances home by expatriate workers, interest, profit and dividends from investments overseas and so on).

In the official statistics sales and purchases of goods are recorded as exports and imports respectively. Table 32.1 shows that the visible balance (sometimes known as the balance of trade or simply the trade balance) was −£10 119m in 1991. The magnitude of the visible deficit is a cause of concern because it implies a manufacturing sector which is uncompetitive and which is of declining importance relative to the manufacturing sector in the rest of the world.

Table 32.1 also shows that there was a surplus on invisibles of £5720m. Traditionally the UK has a surplus on the invisible account and this is important because of the weak manufacturing sector.

Adding the visible balance to the invisible balance gives the current balance. Table 32.1 shows that, in 1991, the UK had a current account deficit of −£4399m. This must be financed by borrowing from abroad, by net foreign investment in UK industry or by running down the official reserves of foreign currency. Table 32.1 provides the appropriate information.

| Table 32.1 *The UK balance of payments in 1991 (£m)* | | |
|---|---:|---:|
| *Current account* | | |
| Exports | 103 704 | |
| Imports | 113 823 | |
| Visible balance | | −10 119 |
| Invisible credits | 117 381 | |
| Invisible debits | 111 661 | |
| Invisible balance | | 5 720 |
| Current balance | | −4 399 |
| *Transactions in assets and liabilities* | | |
| Transactions in assets | | |
| Investment | | −38 880 |
| Change in the official reserves | | −2 662 |
| Other | | 22 414 |
| | | −19 128 |
| Transactions in liabilities | | |
| Investment | 31 467 | |
| Other | −3 519 | |
| | 27 948 | |
| Net transactions in assets and liabilities | | 8 820 |
| Balancing item | | −4 421 |

# Transactions in Assets and Liabilities

In Table 32.1, 'Transactions in assets and liabilities' shows how the current account deficit was financed. Note that if we add the current account deficit to transactions in assets and transactions in liabilities, excluding the 'Change in official reserves', there is an overall balance of payments surplus of £2662m. In keeping with the principle of double entry bookkeeping, to ensure that the balance of payments balances, the addition of £2662m to the official reserves has a negative sign. If it did not the surplus of £2662m would be counted twice! The opposite is also true. In the case of an overall balance of payments deficit, the deficit has a positive sign in the official statistics.

# The Balancing Item

The balancing item is not, as might be expected, included to ensure that the balance of payments always balances. Instead it is an estimate of all errors and omissions. In any one year there are many millions of individual transactions between the UK and the rest of the world. When such magnitudes are estimated there are bound to be errors and omissions and the balancing item is included to account for these. It is regarded as an accurate estimate because the Bank of England records the sum of all flows of currency, though it cannot account for each individual transaction.

## Balance of Payments Problems

Earlier we distinguished between autonomous transactions and accommodating transactions. In the case of a balance of payments deficit, accommodating transactions consist of either **borrowing abroad**, **sales of assets abroad** or a **reduction in the official reserves**. None of these options can be carried on indefinitely.

Borrowing abroad implies higher domestic rates of interest in order to attract foreign funds and in consequence domestic industry will cut back on its investment. Sales of assets abroad can take many forms but might imply a foreign takeover of domestic firms which will lead to an outflow of property income (interest, profit and dividends) in subsequent years; or they might involve the sale of art treasures abroad which will reduce the nation's cultural heritage, and so on. Reducing the reserves is not a practical option in the long term since there is a limit on the reserves the nation holds.

A 'balance of payments problem' is therefore an inability to match autonomous credits with autonomous debits, particularly in the current account. It is a particular problem for deficit countries because a deficit cannot be sustained indefinitely. The existence of a persistent deficit on the current account therefore implies that action must be taken by the authorities to eliminate the cause of the deficit. We consider what courses of action are open to the authorities in Chapter 36.

## Common Mistakes to Avoid

A common mistake is to confuse the **balance of trade** with the **terms of trade**. As we have seen on p. 186, the balance of trade is simply the net value of exports minus imports. In a developed country like the UK, a deterioration in the balance of trade reflects a declining manufacturing sector and this has implications for employment in manufacturing and, where industry is highly localised, the prosperity of particular regions.

The terms of trade, on the other hand, is simply the ratio of export prices to import prices. An improvement in the terms of trade implies that export prices have risen relative to import prices. However the consequences of this might be very unfavourable since it implies that exports have become less competitive and imports have become more competitive. An improvement in the terms of trade might very well cause a deterioration in the balance of trade and in the overall current account.

## Questions and Answers

### Questions

1   'Is Britain's trade deficit simply the temporary result of the consumer boom, or the consequence of a steady decline in British competitiveness and a steady increase in import penetration?

In the case of consumer goods, imports appear to offer both price and non-price advantages. More fundamentally, imports are rising because, often, there is no British product available.

In 1979, Britain had a trade surplus in engineering of £2 billion. In 1988, according to the Engineering Employers' Federation, the deficit will be about £8.5 billion, and in 1989 nearly £310 billion.

"The biggest reason of all for this is the recession of the early 1980s", said Mr Ian Thompson, economic adviser to the EEF. "If we hadn't had North Sea oil and the strong pound in the early 1980s many more engineering companies would have remained in business."

"There are two messages in the present situation. The first is that nothing can be done to produce more export growth and import substitution in the short term. The second is that it is inconceivable that the gap left by North Sea oil can be closed without a major contribution from industries like engineering."

In other words, industry not only has to slow down the process of import penetration, but it must start clawing back the home market from foreign firms, while maintaining a strong export performance.'

*Source:* Adapted from D. Smith, 'The darker side of Britain's boom', *The Times*, 17 October 1988.

(a)   Examine possible reasons for the deterioration of Britain's trade performance in engineering from a surplus of £2 billion in 1979 to a deficit in 1988. (5 marks)

(b)   Do you agree that 'nothing can be done to produce more export growth and import substitution in the short term' (lines 22–4)? Explain your views. (5 marks)

(c)   Examine the proposition that it is 'inconceivable that the gap left by North Sea oil can be closed without a major contribution from industries like engineering' (lines 25–7). (5 marks)

(d)   Examine measures that might have corrected this trade deficit in engineering. (5 marks)

ULEAC, Jan 1992

2   The following table gives information about the visible trade of a certain country.

|  | Exports | | Imports | |
| --- | --- | --- | --- | --- |
|  | Price per unit | Number of units | Price per unit | Number of units |
| Year 1 | £100 | 1000 | £500 | 400 |
| Year 2 | £200 | 600 | £800 | 300 |

What changes have taken place in the balance of visible trade and the terms of trade?

|  | Balance of trade | Terms of trade |
| --- | --- | --- |
| A | Improved | Improved |
| B | Improved | Worsened |
| C | Worsened | Improved |
| D | Worsened | Worsened |

AEB, Nov 1991

3  Which of the following is regarded as an invisible import for the United Kingdom?

A  UK expenditure on supporting the British army overseas

B  Spending in the UK by American tourists

C  Expenditure by foreign governments on maintaining embassies in the UK

D  The purchase of a UK treasury bill by an American citizen

E  The purchase of Deutschmarks by a UK bank from another UK bank in the foreign exchange market

## Answers

**1** (a) The information we are given suggests that Britain's trade performance in engineering has deteriorated because of the recession in the 1980s. The implication is that the recession depressed domestic demand and as demand fell many engineering firms were forced to close. When the economy recovered and domestic demand rose, the smaller number of engineering firms were unable to satisfy domestic demand and the shortfall was made good by imports of engineering products.

We are also told that the pound was strong in the early 1980s because of North Sea oil. A strong pound implies that UK exports are relatively expensive while imports into the UK will be relatively cheap. Again this would have handicapped the engineering industry. Exports of engineering products would fall and imports would rise, with the inevitable result that there would be a trade deficit in engineering. Moreover, as markets were lost to foreign competition, the number of firms in engineering fell, so that when demand for engineering products rose the UK was unable to respond.

More generally the UK engineering industry may have declined because other countries now have a comparative advantage in this area. There is no reason why a country should always have a trade surplus in some products and a trade deficit in others. The decline in the engineering industry may simply reflect the fact that productivity growth in UK engineering firms did not match productivity growth in foreign firms. Non-price factors such as poor design, late delivery or poor after-sales service may also account for the loss of a comparative advantage in engineering.

(b) In the short term one option that might stimulate export demand and encourage import substitution is to devalue sterling against other currencies. Until recently the authorities have not had an entirely free hand which would allow them to do this because sterling was a member of the exchange rate mechanism of the EMS. However, since the UK's withdrawl from the ERM sterling has been devalued and the effect will be to increase the price of imports in the UK and to reduce the price of exports abroad. If the demand for exports and imports are both elastic then export earnings will increase and there will be a significant shift away from imports in favour of domestic substitutes.

However, in the UK, balance of payments difficulties have usually been caused by a rate of inflation above that of our major competitors. In these circumstances devaluing sterling will have no long term effect on the problem. The higher rate of inflation in the UK will continue to erode competitiveness until the effect of devaluation is wiped out. Instead, a sustained anti-inflationary policy will offer a solution. As inflation falls exports will become more competitive and imports less competitive. In consequence export demand will increase and import demand will fall as consumers turn to domestic substitutes. Depending on how quickly inflation falls it is conceivable that such a policy will be successful in the short term as well as the long term.

(c) The gap in the trade balance created by the decline in North Sea oil can only be filled by an increase in the output of those sectors where the UK has a comparative advantage compared with foreign firms. If the UK had a comparative advantage in engineering it is unlikely that the recession would have been associated with a decline of the engineering industry. After all, in the current recession some sectors of the economy, such as financial services, are net exporters and are making a significant contribution to the balance of payments.

The UK is not dependent on any particular industry for foreign currency earnings and therefore the statement that it is 'inconceivable that the gap left by North Sea oil can be closed without a major contribution from industries like engineering' is misleading. An increase in net export earnings (export earnings minus import expenditure) by any industry will help close the gap. Traditionally the UK balance of trade is in deficit whereas the invisible account is in surplus. If the trade deficit worsens, all that is necessary to avoid a balance of payments problem is for the invisible account to improve. There is certainly no requirement that industries like engineering make an increased contribution.

(d) If a balance of trade deficit reflects a loss of comparative advantage then the solution to the problem is long term. In the long term the problem will be self-correcting and will require a reallocation of resources away from the declining sectors into the expanding sectors where the UK has a comparative advantage. Because of structural rigidities in the economy this process will be long and drawn-out, and will impose substantial adjustment costs on the economy.

It might be argued by some that the solution is to encourage exports of engineering products, for example by the use of subsidies. The lower price of UK products might lead to increased exports. Simultaneously imports could be discouraged by imposing protective measures such as a tariff on engineering imports. The higher price of imported engineering products would no doubt divert domestic demand away from foreign output in favour of UK products. The combined effect would be to improve the trade balance in engineering. Furthermore some might argue that the increased demand will encourage investment in engineering by UK firms and, in time, as efficiency and output increase, protection could be withdrawn.

This is a dubious argument. After all, the information we are given tells us that there is no shortage of demand for engineering products. On the contrary, there are too few UK firms to satisfy the demand. If the long term prospects for engineering firms were good, entrepreneurs would supply funds for expansion through the capital market. Protection against foreign competition and export subsidies are more likely to increase inefficiency in the long run. However, it remains true that in the short run protection will reduce the deficit in engineering.

**2** In year 1 the balance of trade was $(£100 \times 1000) - (£500 \times 400) = -£100\,000$. In year 2 the balance of trade was $(£200 \times 600) - (£800 \times 300) = -£120\,000$. The balance of trade has therefore worsened.

Between year 1 and year 2 export prices rise by 100 per cent, while import prices rose by only 60 per cent. The terms of trade have therefore improved.

The key is C.

**3** When the UK government finances an army overseas, the expenditure incurred is an inflow of funds to some other country. Such expenditure is therefore an invisible import. In the official statistics it is included in 'General government expenditure abroad'. Option A is therefore correct.

When foreign tourists visit the UK, their expenditure in the UK is a receipt from abroad. Such expenditure is therefore an invisible export. In the official statistics it is recorded under 'Tourism'. Option B is therefore incorrect.

Expenditure by foreign governments maintaining their embassies in the UK is an inflow of funds to the UK and is therefore an invisible export. In the official statistics it is recorded under 'General government receipts from abroad'. Option C is therefore incorrect.

When an American citizen purchases a UK treasury bill there is an inflow of investment to the UK. However it is a short term capital inflow and it will therefore be recorded in *Transactions in Assets and Liabilities*. Within this section of the accounts it will appear under 'Portfolio investment in the UK'. Option D is therefore incorrect.

The purchase of foreign currency by a UK bank from another UK bank has no net effect on the overall balance of payments. Option E is therefore incorrect.

The key is A.

## REVIEW QUESTIONS AND ANSWERS

### Questions

1 Consider the following data:

|  | Money values |
|---|---|
| Visible imports | 4000 |
| Balance of trade | 200 |
| Invisible imports | 3800 |
| Invisible exports | 2000 |
| Net long term capital | −2100 |
| Change in foreign exchange reserves | 200 |
| Balancing item | nil |

(a) On the basis of the data calculate the value of:
  (i) visible exports
  (ii) the invisible balance
  (iii) the current balance
  (iv) net short-term capital

(b) If the country in question has a GNP of 10,000 comment on the significance of its balance of payments situation.

Question 2 is based on the information in Figure 32.1.

2 How are the types of developments in the motor car industry described above likely to affect the UK's balance of payments in the 1990s:

(a) On the visible account?
(b) On the invisible account?
(c) In transactions in assets and liabilities?

3 Distinguish between the *terms of trade* **and the** *balance of trade*.

4 Why does the balance of payments always balance?

5 Study the information on the following page, which relates to the economies of Italy and Norway, and then answer the questions that follow.

Figure 32.1   *UK motor industry trade deficit cut*

# UK motor industry cuts trade deficit

Andrew Cornellus
Business Editor

THE motor industry, which last year accounted for £6 billion of the UK's $20 billion trade deficit, improved its trading performance in the first quarter of this year, but still showed a £1.4 billion deficit in its trade with the rest of the world.

Figures from the Society of Motor Manufacturers and Traders published this morning reveal that the industry's first quarter deficit was £151 million down on the first quarter of 1989, making it the second successive quarter when the industry's trading position has improved.

The figures will hearten ministers who have made the issue of improving the UK's motor industry trading deficit a priority.

This has been done largely by encouraging Japanese manufactures like Nissan, Toyota and Honda to produce cars in Britain for export to the rest of Europe.

According to the SMMT, the improved first quarter trading position was helped by a 9 per cent fall in car imports to the UK, reflecting the overall slowdown in the British car market.

Motor industry exports were also up by 12 per cent at £2.24 billion in the first quarter, helped by stronger sales of car components, heavy trucks and specialist vehicles like tractors and dumper trucks.

The most buoyant markets for the UK exporters were the European Community, particularly France, and on a smaller scale, Japan where the government is slowly relaxing the rules which prevent overseas companies penetrating the Japanese market.

The SMMT says the figures show that Britain's motor industry has continued to play a positive part towards reducing the national trade deficit.

*Source: Guardian* (12 June 1990).

## ITALY

'Despite the problems caused by comparatively high inflation . . . Italy has been one of the fastest growing economies in Europe. In 1990 growth is likely to be maintained at around 3%, broadly in line with the European average. Domestic demand growth has slackened . . . Although international competitiveness has deteriorated, Italy should benefit from the trade stimulus of developments in Germany and Eastern Europe.'

| A. Domestic Economy | Average | | Forecast | |
|---|---|---|---|---|
| (% Annual changes) | 1981–88 1987 | 1988 | 1989 | 1990 |
| Real GDP | 2.2  3.0 | 3.9 | 3.0 | 3.0 |
| Private consumption | 2.5  3.9 | 3.8 | 3.6 | 3.3 |
| Public consumption | 3.0  3.6 | 3.0 | 2.5 | 2.0 |
| Fixed investment | 1.2  6.8 | 4.9 | 5.4 | 5.0 |
| Total domestic demand | 2.2  4.6 | 4.7 | 3.0 | 3.4 |
| Consumer prices | 10.6  4.7 | 5.0 | 6.6 | 6.0 |
| Money supply | 11.2  8.7 | 8.5 | 11.0 | 9.0 |
| Unemployment (%) | 10.3  12.0 | 12.0 | 12.0 | 12.0 |
| B. External | | | | |
| Export volume (% change) | 3.9  2.0 | 5.2 | 9.2 | 8.0 |
| Import volume (% change) | 3.9  9.5 | 6.9 | 8.7 | 8.5 |
| Trade balance (US $bn) | −4.0  −0.1 | −0.8 | −1.8 | −2.7 |
| Current account (US $bn) | −3.0  −1.5 | −5.2 | −11.0 | −13.0 |

*Source*: Barclay's Country Report (1990).

## NORWAY

'The last three years have seen Norway pass through a difficult period of adjustment following the 1986 oil market collapse (resulting in proportionally the largest current account deficit of any OECD country) . . . Weaker domestic demand, assisted by firmer energy prices, has succeeded in returning the current account to surplus. Inflation is also now at, or below, the level of Norway's major competitors.

Prospects for the next few years are favourable, with moderate inflation and a growing current account surplus.'

| A. Domestic Economy | Average | | Forecast | |
|---|---|---|---|---|
| (% Annual changes) | 1981–88 1987 | 1988 | 1989 | 1990 |
| Real GDP | 2.9  0.9 | 1.1 | 2.5 | 1.5 |
| Private consumption | 2.4  −0.8 | −2.3 | −2.0 | 1.5 |
| Public consumption | 3.4  4.5 | 0.1 | 3.0 | 2.5 |
| Fixed investment | 2.9  −0.6 | 4.0 | −3.0 | −5.0 |
| Total domestic demand | 2.6  −1.0 | −0.5 | −3.0 | 0.4 |
| Consumer prices | 8.5  8.7 | 6.7 | 4.5 | 4.5 |
| Money supply | 12.2  11.2 | 13.0 | 6.5 | 7.0 |
| Unemployment (%) | 2.6  2.1 | 3.2 | 3.8 | 4.0 |
| B. External | | | | |
| Export volume (% change) | 4.8  8.4 | 6.5 | 12.0 | 6.0 |
| Import volume (% change) | 3.7  −2.0 | −2.5 | −2.5 | 2.5 |
| Trade balance (US $bn) | 1.8  −1.2 | −0.7 | 4.6 | 5.2 |
| Current account (US $bn) | −0.2  −4.2 | −3.7 | 1.5 | 2.2 |

*Source*: Barclay's Country Report (1989).

(a) For the period 1987 to 1990, compare the balance of payments of the two countries.

(b) What factors might account for their different balance of payments performance?

(c) Determine, and give possible reasons for, Italy's declining invisible balance.

(d) What extra data would you require to determine which country had the sounder overall balance of payments position in the period 1987–90?

## Answers

**1** (a) (i) Since visible imports are 4000 and the balance of trade is 200, it follows that visible exports must be 4200.

(ii) The invisible balance is simply invisible exports minus invisible imports, which in this case is equal to −1800.

(iii) The current balance is the balance of trade plus the invisible balance, which is equal to −1600.

(iv) Net short term capital must be equal to the current balance plus net long term capital plus the change in the reserves, that is, $-1600 -2100 + 200 = -3500$. This must be so, otherwise the balance of payments would not balance.

(b) If GNP is 10 000 this country has a serious balance of payments problem, partly due to the size of its invisible deficit which is equal to almost a fifth of GNP, and partly due to the relatively high level of long term investment overseas. The current account deficit and the deficit on long term capital are financed by a net inflow of short term funds, or hot money. This can only be sustained if interest rates in this country compare very favourably with interest rates abroad. In the short term this might cause recession in the domestic economy and a cutback on investment which might hamper the growth of productivity.

**2** (a) The developments in the trading performance of the motor industry outlined in the information we are given implies that trade in motor vehicles will contribute to an improvement in the visible balance.

(b) Since the improvement in visible trade in motor vehicles is due to investment by Japan, in the longer term there will be an adverse effect on the invisible account because of an increase in property income repatriated to the parent companies in Japan. (See also the answer to part (c) below.)

(c) Since the favourable effect on the visible balance will almost certainly exceed the unfavourable effect on the invisible balance there is likely to be increased investment abroad or additions to the reserves as a result of increased Japanese investment. If there is increased investment abroad this will result in an inflow of property income which might equal or exceed the outflow mentioned in (b) above.

**3** The terms of trade are simply the ratio of export prices to import prices. The balance of trade is the difference between the aggregate value of exports and the aggregate value of imports.

**4** The balance of payments always balances because double entry bookkeeping ensures that each entry appears twice: once as a positive entry and once as a negative entry.

**5** (a) For most of the period 1987–90, export volume has grown faster in Norway than in Italy. Conversely import volume has grown faster in Italy than in Norway. The results of this are reflected in the trade balance and in the current account generally. Norway has turned a deficit into a surplus on both accounts, while Italy has recorded a persistent deficit on both accounts. The Italian current account is particularly weak.

(b) A current account deficit is often a sign of a growing economy. Rising home demand draws in imports and rising production often requires imported raw materials. The data we are given shows that, from 1987 onwards, GDP has risen faster in Italy than in Norway. Domestic demand in the Italian economy has shown strong growth throughout the period whereas it has fallen in Norway for most of the period and has only started to rise in 1990. Indeed we are told that in Norway 'weaker domestic demand, assisted by firmer energy prices, has succeeded in returning the current account to surplus'. We are also told that in Italy inflation is 'comparatively high' and that 'international competitiveness has deteriorated'. In Norway 'inflation is now at, or below, the level of Norway's major competitors'.

(c) In Italy the current account is deteriorating faster than the trade balance. This implies a worsening of the invisible balance. The deterioration of invisible trade in Italy might be due to any number of reasons. Given the higher rate of inflation in Italy it is likely that tourism, a major invisible export from Italy, has deteriorated. Higher Italian prices will discourage tourists from visiting Italy but may also encourage Italians to take holidays abroad.

(d) To judge which country had the sounder balance of payments position over the period under review we would need to know what restrictions, if any, were placed on imports and what inducements, if any, were granted to exporters.

It would be useful to have information on changes in the official reserves of both countries and on the nature of external capital flows. In the case of Italy a persistent and substantial reduction in the reserves would indicate a weakening balance of payments situation. On the other hand, if the deficit is financed by a substantial inflow of long term capital, this implies a relatively stable balance of payments position. However, if the Italian current account deficit is largely financed by an inflow of short term funds, this indicates a weak position. How weak could be partly judged by interest rates in Italy compared with other countries.

# CHAPTER 33

# EXCHANGE RATE SYSTEMS

## Topic Summary

### The Foreign Exchange Market

An exchange rate is simply the rate at which one currency can be exchanged for another currency. For example, if the rate of exchange between sterling and the Deutschmark is £1 = DM2.95, this tells us that each pound sterling we give up 'purchases' 2.95 Deutschmarks. But what determines the exchange rate? The answer depends on the type of exchange rate system. If exchange rates **float freely**, the rate of exchange is determined by market forces and it fluctuates in response to changes in supply and demand conditions. On the other hand, if the rate of exchange is **fixed**, its value is determined by the authorities and they intervene to preserve the agreed parity.

When we say the exchange rate is determined by supply and demand this implies the existence of a foreign exchange market. Similarly, when we say the authorities intervene to preserve the agreed exchange rate, intervention is carried out in the foreign exchange market. In fact the foreign exchange market is large and complex. Technological advances and the removal of many government regulations (deregulation) during the 1980s have led to the emergence of a global foreign exchange market. In other words, it is now possible for a dealer in foreign exchange to participate in one of the world's markets 24 hours a day!

However the foreign exchange market is not housed in a particular building. Indeed all of the major banks and other foreign exchange dealers have their own dealing rooms from where they transact their business of buying and selling different currencies on behalf of clients from other dealers via the telecommunications network. If you have ever taken a holiday abroad, no doubt you took some foreign currency along with you. This, along with many other requests for small amounts of the same currency, will have been acquired by a dealer through the foreign exchange market.

### Floating Exchange Rates

When an exchange rate floats freely its value on the foreign exchange market is **determined freely by supply and demand**. Let us consider the exchange rate for sterling against the US dollar as a hypothetical example.

### Demand for Sterling

The demand for any currency on the foreign exchange market stems from the desire of residents in one country to **carry out transactions in another currency**. For example, if residents of the USA wish to purchase British goods or services, or if they wish to invest in British firms or to purchase securities they will demand sterling to finance their transactions. For simplicity we assume that the demand for sterling on the foreign exchange market is inversely related to its price. This might not be an unrealistic assumption. For example, if we consider a rate of exchange of £1 = $1.80, a good costing £10 000 in the UK costs an importer in the USA $18 000. However, if the rate of exchange is $1.70, the same good now costs an importer in the USA $17 000. In other words, as the sterling exchange rate depreciates, exports from the UK become cheaper. At the lower price it is reasonable to assume that a greater amount will be purchased and, assuming demand for UK exports is elastic, this implies an increase in the demand for sterling.

### Supply of Sterling

The supply of any currency to the foreign exchange market stems from the demands of domestic residents to **finance transactions in some foreign**

**currency**. For example, if a UK car dealer purchases cars from America, payment will normally be made in US dollars. To obtain US dollars the dealer will instruct his (her) bank to exchange sterling for dollars. The bank, on behalf of its client, will buy dollars and in so doing will supply sterling to the foreign exchange market. Again it is convenient to assume that the supply curve of sterling to the foreign exchange market is the normal shape. The basis for this is that, as the sterling exchange rate depreciates, the sterling price of imports rises. For example, if the exchange rate is £1 = $1.80, a good costing $36 000 in the USA costs a UK resident £20 000. If the exchange rate depreciates to £1 = $1.60, the same good now costs an importer in the UK £22 500. As the sterling price of imports rises, fewer imports will be demanded and therefore the supply of sterling to the foreign exchange market will fall.

## The Equilibrium Rate of Exchange

In all markets where the forces of supply and demand operate freely, price and quantity traded will eventually settle at the equilibrium. The foreign exchange market is no exception. Figure 33.1 shows the equilibrium rate of exchange in a free market.

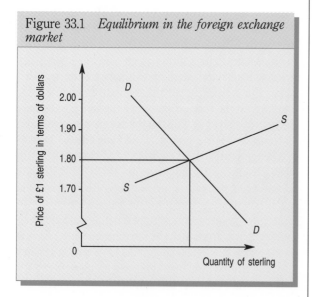

Figure 33.1   *Equilibrium in the foreign exchange market*

In Figure 33.1, *DD* and *SS* are the demand and supply curves for sterling and £1 = $1.80 is the equilibrium rate of exchange. Unless there is a change in the conditions of demand or the conditions of supply, no other rate of exchange is

sustainable. At any rate of exchange above £1 = $1.80, supply of sterling exceeds demand and in a free market the rate of exchange will fall, that is, sterling will depreciate. At any rate of exchange below £1 = $1.80, demand for sterling exceeds supply of sterling and the rate of exchange will rise, that is, sterling will appreciate.

## A Change in the Equilibrium Rate of Exchange

Once the equilibrium rate of exchange for a particular currency is established, there can be no change in a free market unless there is a change in the conditions of demand for that currency or the conditions of supply of that currency. Figure 33.2 is used as a basis for explanation.

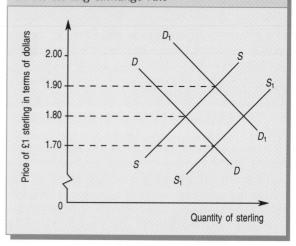

Figure 33.2   *The effect of a change in demand for sterling and a change in the supply of sterling on the sterling exchange rate*

In Figure 33.2 *DD* and *SS* are the original demand and supply curves for sterling on the foreign exchange market and the exchange rate is initially £1 = $1.80. Subsequently, if there is an increase in demand for sterling to $D_1D_1$ and all other things remain equal, sterling will *appreciate* against the dollar from £1 = $1.80 to £1 = £1.90. A decrease in demand for sterling will have exactly the opposite effect. For example, if $D_1D_1$ is now the original demand curve and *SS* is the original supply curve, the rate of exchange will initially be £1 = $1.90. Subsequently, if the demand for sterling falls to *DD* and all other things remain equal, the rate of exchange will *depreciate* to £1 = $1.80.

We can also examine the effect of a change in the conditions of supply. Returning to the original situation with supply and demand represented by $SS$ and $DD$ and the exchange rate at £1 = $1.80, if there is an increase in supply of sterling to the foreign exchange market from $SS$ to $S_1S_1$ and all other things remain equal, sterling will depreciate against the dollar to £1 = $1.70. A decrease in the supply of sterling will have exactly the opposite effect. With supply and demand initially represented by $S_1S_1$ and $DD$ and the exchange rate initially in equilibrium at £1 = $1.70, a decrease in the supply of sterling to $SS$ will cause sterling to appreciate against the dollar to £1 = $1.80.

## Factors Causing a Change in the Exchange Rate

In the real world many factors influence the rate of exchange. In this section we analyse the most important factors but it is important to remember that we assume all other things remain equal in each case.

**Relative Inflation Rates**  In the long run there is no doubt that relative rates of inflation are the most important determinant of a country's rate of exchange. If one country has a higher rate of inflation than its trading partners then, at any given rate of exchange, its exports will become more competitive and its imports will become less competitive. In consequence demand for its currency will fall on the foreign exchange market as export demand falls, and supply of its currency will increase as import demand rises. This will cause the rate of exchange to depreciate against all other currencies.

**Relative Interest Rates**  In the modern world funds are highly mobile between currencies and therefore, if all other things remain equal, an increase in the rate of interest in one country relative to interest rates in other countries will cause the exchange rate to appreciate. (Indeed funds are so mobile and information so quickly transmitted that the merest hint that interest rates are about to change can sometimes cause exchange rates to change.) The reason is simple. A rise in interest rates in one country relative to other countries implies a higher return on funds invested in that country. In consequence, if one country increases its rate of interest and all other things remain equal, demand for that country's currency will increase as foreigners take advantage of the higher return. There might also be a reduction in supply of currency as domestic residents now invest at home rather than abroad. The combined effect will be to force the exchange rate upwards.

**The Current Account**  Changes in the state of the current account will also cause a change in the exchange rate. When the current account deficit worsens, the gap between import expenditure and export earnings widens. For the deficit country this implies an increase in supply of its currency and a reduction in demand for its currency, with the inevitable result that its currency depreciates.

**Expectations**  When a currency is expected to appreciate, holders of that currency make a capital gain if their expectation is correct. For example, if the sterling exchange rate is initially £1 = $1.80 then an investor with $1.80m who expects sterling to appreciate can convert this into £1m. If this expectation proves to be correct and sterling appreciates to £1 = $1.90, then, after appreciation, £1m can be converted into $1.90m – a capital gain of over 5 per cent!

Many factors can influence expectations and investors will act upon any new information that becomes available which influences their expectation of future exchange rates. In this sense expectations about the factors discussed above will influence the exchange rate as investors seek to make a capital gain. Thus an expected change in the rate of inflation, an expected change in the rate of interest or an expected change in the size of the current account deficit (surplus) will cause a change in the exchange rate.

## Fixed Exchange Rates

A fixed exchange rate exists when the authorities **stipulate the rate** at which their currency will exchange against other currencies. The central bank then intervenes as and when necessary as buyer or seller to maintain the specified exchange rate. The object of intervention is to neutralise changes in supply or demand for currency on the foreign exchange market so that the exchange rate neither appreciates nor depreciates against other currencies. Figure 33.3 is used to explain how intervention stabilises the exchange rate.

In Figure 33.3, if $DD$ and $SS$ are the original demand and supply curves for sterling on the foreign exchange market and the exchange rate is

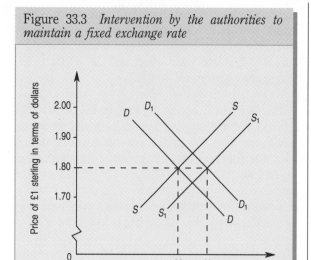

Figure 33.3 *Intervention by the authorities to maintain a fixed exchange rate*

initially £1 = $1.80. Assume £1 = $1.80 is the agreed fixed parity of sterling against the US dollar. The foreign exchange market is therefore initially in equilibrium. Subsequently, if there is an increase in supply of sterling the supply curve will shift to $S_1S_1$. In a free market the exchange rate would depreciate. However, if the authorities are committed to maintaining the rate of exchange at £1 = $1.80, to avoid depreciation they will be compelled to purchase the excess supply of sterling, $MN$, on the foreign exchange market at this rate of exchange. The demand curve for sterling therefore shifts to $D_1D_1$ and downward pressure on sterling is averted. When there is upward pressure on a currency the authorities act in the opposite way to avoid appreciation.

It is important to realise that, when the authorities intervene to prevent a currency from depreciating, they are drawing on the official reserves of foreign currency. In terms of Figure 33.3, the reserves of foreign currency fall by $MN$. Such a policy cannot continue indefinitely because the nation only possesses a limited amount of reserves. In the longer run action will be necessary to remove the need for intervention.

The appropriate response of the authorities depends on the cause of downward pressure on the exchange rate. In the long run the main cause of downward pressure on the exchange rate is a higher rate of inflation than that experienced in competing economies. To remove downward pressure on the exchange rate in the long run, the authorities must therefore gear monetary policy to reducing the rate of inflation. One obvious policy measure open to the

authorities is to raise the domestic rate of interest. As we have seen on p. 195, this will attract a capital inflow and will reduce a capital outflow. If the rate of interest is increased high enough it will therefore eliminate the need for direct intervention in the foreign exchange market by the authorities. In the longer run the higher rate of interest will tend to reduce domestic inflation and when this happens interest rates will fall because the cause of downward pressure on the exchange rate will have disappeared.

## Advantages of Floating Exchange Rates

### Automatic Adjustment in the Balance of Payments

It is sometimes alleged that the major advantage of floating exchange rates is that they guarantee that the foreign exchange market is in continuous equilibrium and therefore the authorities do not need to gear domestic policy to achieving a stable exchange rate. For example, if the UK has a higher rate of inflation than its trading partners, this will simply lead to depreciation of the sterling exchange rate without the need for any kind of policy to be adopted in the domestic economy. As sterling depreciates export prices *abroad* will fall and import prices in the *domestic economy* will rise. As consumers respond to these price changes, supply and demand for sterling on the foreign exchange market will change so as to ensure that the foreign exchange market, and therefore the balance of payments, are in continuous equilibrium. The opposite will happen if UK inflation is below that in other countries. Here the sterling exchange rate will appreciate so as to preserve equilibrium in the foreign exchange market and avoid a surplus in the balance of payments.

Despite this bold claim, floating exchange rates do not always eliminate balance of payments surpluses and deficits as smoothly as implied here, since the effect of depreciation depends on such factors as the elasticity of demand for exports and imports, the elasticity of supply of exports, and so on.

### Greater Freedom to Pursue Domestic Policy Goals

It is alleged that, because floating exchange rates ensure equilibrium in the balance of payments, the authorities have greater freedom to direct domestic policy to achieving other goals, such as full employment. The argument is that, when governments boost aggregate demand to increase employment, inflation rises and the balance of payments moves into deficit. Since the deficit is self-correcting when exchange rates float, there is no reason to reverse policy. In fact, inflation imposes many costs on the economy and governments would wish to avoid these costs even if floating exchange rates did guarantee that balance of payments deficits were self-correcting! The real problem is that unstable exchange rates make it difficult for firms to plan and encourage inefficiency in the allocation of resources. Because of this it is alleged that floating rates lead to higher, rather than lower, unemployment.

## Economy in the Size of Reserves

It is argued that under a system of floating exchange rates the authorities will not require such large holdings of foreign exchange reserves, since they will not be required for intervention in the foreign exchange market. The point is that holding reserves imposes an opportunity cost on society because these reserves could otherwise be spent. Here again this is not a strong argument because, if domestic inflation is kept in line with that of a country's trading partners, its exchange rate will be stable and therefore reserves will not be required for intervention purposes.

## Advantages of Fixed Exchange Rates

### Reduced Uncertainty

A major advantage of fixed exchange rates is that they reduce uncertainty about costs and returns for those involved in international trade. When export orders are received the exporter knows how much will be received when the contract is fulfilled. Similarly importers know in advance the cost they will incur when entering into particular agreements. If exchange rates float freely then it is much more difficult for the exporter to predict how much will be received from a particular contract because this will vary with the exchange rate. If the domestic exchange rate appreciates, exporters will receive a windfall gain. However, if the domestic exchange rate depreciates, exporters will incur an unanticipated reduction in revenue.

There is equal uncertainty for importers. The cost of imports to domestic buyers will change if the exchange rate changes between the time the contract is agreed and the time the contract is fulfilled. For example, if the sterling exchange rate is £1 = \$1.80 when an import contract for 1000 units of a particular commodity at \$1000 per unit is agreed, the anticipated cost to the importer is £555 555.6. However, if the exchange rate at the time payment is made is £1 = \$1.70, the actual cost to the importer is £588 235. When firms import raw materials the cost of final output will be similarly affected by changes in the exchange rate. The higher price might jeopardise sales in the domestic economy and therefore adds to the risks of production.

Of course firms can eliminate risk through the **forward market** but this adds to their costs. Indeed for many small and medium sized firms the cost of forward cover is prohibitive. The reduction in uncertainty that is implied by fixed exchange rates makes it easy for firms to plan their output and investment decisions. This encourages greater efficiency in the allocation of resources and greater productive efficiency in the way firms use resources.

## Control of Inflation

It has been suggested that a major advantage of fixed exchange rates is that they remove from governments the power to vary money growth for short term political aims. We have seen on p. 163 that the effect of increased money growth in the long run is an increase in the rate of inflation with no effect on real variables such as employment or output. When exchange rates are fixed, economic policy must be directed towards ensuring that inflation is broadly in line with that in other countries. It is suggested that, under a system of fixed exchange rates, inflation in many countries will be lower and therefore the costs of inflation (see pp. 167–8) will be reduced or eliminated altogether.

## A Note on Speculation

It has been suggested that floating exchange rates deter destabilising speculative capital flows because there is a risk of capital loss, as well as the possibility of capital gain, under floating rates. Under a fixed exchange rate system speculators have a one-way option. Thus, if a currency is weak against other currencies and the authorities have failed to deal with the cause, then **devaluation**, that is, a reduction in the exchange rate to a lower fixed parity, looks increasingly likely.

Under these circumstances investors can move their funds out of the domestic currency into a foreign currency, wait for devaluation, and then move their funds back into the domestic currency, thus realising a speculative gain if their expectation proves correct. If their expectation is incorrect they can move back into the domestic currency without loss, apart from any transactions costs incurred. It is argued that, since there is no risk of loss from speculating on currency devaluation, a weak currency will be further weakened as funds are transferred to another currency and this might precipitate a devaluation that would otherwise not have occurred.

However, a country's currency weakens against other currencies only because it has a higher rate of inflation or, if all other things are equal, a lower rate of interest. It makes no difference whether an exchange rate is fixed or floating; the same factors are at work and therefore speculators are able to recognise a weak currency whatever exchange rate regime is operational. In the case of floating exchange rates it is most unlikely that, if economic indicators are pointing to currency depreciation, the exchange rate will actually appreciate. Speculators therefore have the same one way option under floating exchange rates that they have under fixed exchange rates!

# Common Mistakes to Avoid

A major source of confusion concerning exchange rates is the **effect of depreciation on export prices and import prices**. When a currency depreciates this changes the *foreign price of exports* and the *domestic price of imports*. For example, if the exchange rate for sterling depreciates from £1 = $1.80 to £1 = $1.70, a good exported from the UK which costs £1000 in the domestic market will cost $1800 before depreciation and $1700 after depreciation. The domestic price is unchanged. It is the **dollar price** which has fallen. An import, on the other hand, which costs $1080 in the USA costs £600 in the UK before depreciation and £635.3 after depreciation. The dollar price is unchanged. It is the **sterling price** which has increased.

Note that, because depreciation changes the domestic price of imports, if there is any reduction in the *volume of imports* consumed, total foreign currency expenditure on imports will fall.

# Questions and Answers

## Questions

1  The following is an abstract of an article by Professor Milton Friedman, published in the *Financial Times* on 18 December 1989.

Study the passage carefully, then answer *each* of the questions which follow, explaining your reasoning in *each* case.

*The Case for Floating Exchange Rates*
Discussions of the prospects for a monetary union within the Common Market have generally ignored the difference between two superficially similar but basically very different exchange rate arrangements.

One arrangement is a unified currency, the pound sterling in Scotland, England and Wales. Further back in time essentially the same arrangement applied in the late 19th century when pound, dollar, franc, etc., were simply different names for specified fixed amounts of gold. A truly unified currency would make a great deal of sense.

An alternative arrangement is a system of exchange rates between national currencies pegged at agreed values to be maintained by the separate national central banks by altering domestic monetary policy appropriately.

Many proponents of a common European currency regard such a system of pegged exchange rates (the EMS) as a step towards a unified currency. I believe that is a grave mistake. In my opinion, a system of pegged exchange rates among national currencies is worse than either extreme, a truly unified currency, or national currencies linked by freely floating exchange rates. The reason is that the national central banks will not, under modern conditions, be permitted to shape their policies with an eye solely to keeping the exchange rates of their currencies at the agreed level. Pressure to use monetary policy for domestic purposes will from time to time be irresistible. And when that occurs the exchange rate becomes unstable. That was certainly the experience under Bretton Woods. Even in its heyday, exchange rate changes were numerous and when they came often massive.

Experience since then has strengthened my confidence in a system of freely floating exchange rates, though it has also made me far more sceptical that such a system is politically feasible. Central banks will meddle, always of course with the best of intentions. None the less, even dirty floating exchange rates seem to me preferable to pegged rates, though not necessarily to a unified currency.

(a) Why did the author assert that in effect a unified currency arrangement applied worldwide in the late nineteenth century? (5)

(b) What reasons might justify the author's assertion that a truly unified European currency would 'make a great deal of sense'? (5)

(c) Why does the maintenance of pegged exchange rates between national currencies involve separate national central banks 'altering domestic monetary policy appropriately'? (5)

(d) What did the author mean when he argued that 'pressure to use monetary policy for domestic purposes will from time to time be irresistible'? (5)

(e) For what reasons could monetary policy used for domestic purposes cause the exchange rate to become 'unstable'? (5)

WJEC, June 1991

2 Faced with speculative pressure against the pound sterling on the foreign exchange market, a suitable short term counter-measure which could be taken by the authorities would be:

A sell pounds
B buy government bonds
C increase interest rates
D reduce import duties

AEB, Nov 1991

3 A fall in the foreign exchange value of the pound sterling will benefit the UK balance of payments position when:

A UK imports have low price elasticity of demand.
B UK exports have high income elasticity of demand.
C UK interest rates are low.
D UK exports have high price elasticity of demand.

JMB, June 1991

## Answers

1 (a) In the late nineteenth century the gold standard operated. The currency of a country on the gold standard was convertible into a specific quantity of gold per unit of currency. Any currency on the gold standard could therefore be converted into any other currency on the gold standard at a fixed and immutable rate. For example, if gold was priced at \$20 per fine ounce in the USA and at £5 per fine ounce in the UK then the sterling/dollar exchange rate would be fixed at £1 = \$5. In fact, because all currencies which were on the gold standard were convertible at a fixed rate, effectively a unified currency arrangement existed.

(b) A single European currency might confer considerable benefits on participating countries. First, the risk of exchange rate changes would be removed forever. Secondly, there would be savings because it would no longer be necessary to convert one currency into another to facilitate international payments. Thirdly, competition would increase because price differences in different parts of Europe would be easily observable.

(c) Maintenance of a pegged exchange rate requires countries to have a similar rate of inflation. If they have different rates of inflation this inevitably leads to those countries with the highest rates of inflation experiencing a balance of payments deficit, and those countries with the lowest rates of inflation experiencing a balance of payments surplus. Ultimately falling competitiveness can only be restored by devaluation of the weakest currencies and unless inflation is brought under control further devaluations will follow. Only by altering domestic monetary policy so as to achieve a rate of inflation compatible with its trading partners can a currency be maintained at some pegged rate.

(d) It is argued that in the long run an increase in money growth leads only to an increase in prices. However, in the short run, an expansionary monetary policy might lead to an increase in real variables such as real income and employment. At certain times, such as the run-up to an election, politicians might find the urge to achieve short term economic success irresistible. They might therefore engineer an increase in money growth because of its short run benefits, even though in the long run it leads only to an increase in prices.

(e) In the long run, an expansionary monetary policy will lead to higher inflation. If some of the world's major countries expand their money growth rates in an attempt to increase real income and employment in their own economy, world inflation will rise. Over time this will increase the nominal value of surpluses and deficits. If reserves do not rise in line with deficits the growth of international trade will be restricted because there will be insufficient liquidity to finance deficits. This was a major source of instability with the Bretton Woods system.

In addition, an expansionary monetary policy because of its effect on the expected rate of inflation, might motivate speculative capital flows which could destabilise exchange rates. In the longer run, as actual prices increase above prices in other countries, imports will become increasingly competitive and exports will become increasingly uncompetitive. Inevitably the balance of payments on current account will move into deficit and again this will lead to downward pressure on the exchange rate.

Unless the deficit countries reduce money growth to levels compatible with the surplus countries, devaluation will be necessary to restore competitiveness. However this can also be a source of instability for the exchange rate system. Devaluation will cause an immediate change in relative prices but the authorities have no way of knowing what the free market equilibrium will be. They are forced to estimate this and adjust exchange rates accordingly. If their estimate is inaccurate, instability will remain and further adjustments will be necessary. In the long run, the only way to remove instability is to reduce money growth so that inflation in deficit countries is broadly similar to inflation in surplus countries.

**2** If there is speculative pressure against the pound and the authorities sell sterling they will simply add to the supply of sterling on the foreign exchange market. This would signal to the market their intention to let sterling fall further. The result would be further speculative pressure against sterling. Option A is incorrect.

If the authorities in the UK buy bonds on the open market they will drive up bond prices and force interest rates down. Again this would increase speculative pressure against sterling. Option B is incorrect.

If the authorities increase the rate of interest in the UK, sterling will become a more attractive currency to hold and capital flows will be attracted. In other words speculative pressure against sterling would subside. Option C is correct.

A reduction in import duties is not a short term measure but in any case it will tend to increase imports in the long run and will therefore tend to increase the size of the balance of payments deficit in the long run. The expectation that this would cause downward pressure on sterling would lead to increased speculative pressure against sterling. Option D is incorrect.

The key is C.

**3** A fall in the sterling exchange rate will increase the sterling price of imports and the foreign price of exports. If UK imports have a low price elasticity of demand, a fall in the sterling exchange rate will have relatively little effect on foreign currency expenditure on imports. Although there will be some reduction and therefore some benefit to the UK balance of payments, it will be relatively small and therefore we must treat option A as incorrect.

A fall in the sterling exchange rate will tend to reduce incomes abroad as demand for UK exports increases. Option B is incorrect.

If UK interest rates are low then, as the sterling exchange rate falls, this will tend to encourage a capital outflow. Option C is incorrect.

If UK exports have a high price elasticity of demand then, as the sterling exchange rate falls, UK exports will become cheaper abroad. With an elastic demand, this implies that foreign currency earnings from exports will increase. This will be a major benefit to the UK balance of payments. Option D is therefore correct.

## REVIEW QUESTIONS AND ANSWERS

### Questions

**1** Assume the following exchange rates are quoted on a particular day: £1 = 3DM, £1 = $1.8 and $1 = 4DM. How can an investor with £1m make a riskless gain by buying and selling currency on the foreign exchanges?

**2** If the forward rate of exchange is at a discount, what does this tell you about the expected future spot rate?

**3** Why does a country require reserves of foreign currency when exchange rates are fixed but not when they are floating?

**4** When exchange rates are fixed, is the purchasing power parity theory irrelevant?

**5** Distinguish between *depreciation* **and** *devaluation.*

**6** Does speculation stabilise or destabilise exchange rates?

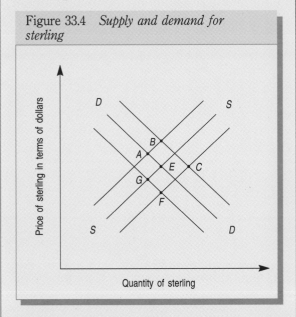

Figure 33.4　*Supply and demand for sterling*

Figure 33.4 shows supply and demand for sterling. *SS* and *DD* represent the original supply and demand conditions. In Questions 7–11 begin with the original equilibrium point *E* and identify the new equilibrium point in each case. Assume that all other things remain equal

**7** The rate of interest in the UK rises.

**8** The UK restricts the import of cars.

**9** Inflation in the UK falls.

**10** Inflation abroad rises.

**11** There is a sharp increase in the price of oil on world markets.

**12** To what extent can the SDR be regarded as money?

### Answers

**1** Exchange £1m for $1.8m. Convert $1.8m into DM7.2m and then convert Deutschmarks into sterling to obtain £2.4m.

**2** If the forward rate of a currency is at a discount this tells us that the spot rate for that currency is expected to depreciate.

**3** Reserves of foreign currency are used for intervention purposes to stabilise the domestic exchange rate. When exchange rates float freely there is no intervention by the authorities and therefore strictly no need for reserves. In practice exchange rates are seldom allowed to float freely and even under a floating exchange rate regime there is likely to be some intervention by the authorities, if only to smooth out random fluctuations.

**4** The purchasing power parity theory predicts that a higher rate of inflation in one country relative to other countries will be offset by an equivalent depreciation of the exchange rate. If exchange rates are fixed the authorities might intervene directly or increase interest rates to shore up the exchange rate. In these circumstances full purchasing power parity will be maintained in the short run. However, in the long run, if inflation in one country is persistently above that in other countries it will be necessary to devalue the exchange rate. To the extent that devaluation restores purchasing power parity the theory holds.

**5** Depreciation is simply a reduction in the external value of a currency through the operation of free market forces. Devaluation, on the other hand, is an administered change in the exchange rate from one fixed parity to a lower fixed parity.

**6** On the one hand it is possible to argue that speculation, by changing supply and demand for different currencies, might destabilise exchange rates. On the other hand, since speculators buy when they feel a currency is undervalued they increase demand for that currency and thus limit the extent of any depreciation. Furthermore they sell when they feel a currency is overvalued and thus limit the extent of any appreciation of that currency. In this way it is possible to argue that speculation actually stabilises currencies.

**7 B**, because the higher rate of interest in the UK will reduce the supply of funds to the foreign exchange market as more domestic residents invest at home, and will increase the demand for sterling as more foreign investors place their funds in the UK to take advantage of the higher rate of interest.

**8 A**, because restricting the volume of car imports will reduce expenditure on foreign cars so the supply of sterling to the foreign exchange market will fall.

**9 B**, because the lower rate of inflation in the UK will encourage domestic consumers to purchase goods in the home market, thereby reducing the supply of sterling to the foreign exchange market, and it will encourage more foreigners to buy UK goods thus increasing demand for sterling on the foreign exchange market.

**10 B**, since a rise in inflation abroad has exactly the same effect as a reduction in the domestic rate of inflation.

**11 F**, because the UK is now a net importer of oil. Higher oil prices would therefore imply an increase in supply of sterling on the foreign exchange market and, as foreigners face higher oil prices, they are likely to cut their demand for UK products.

**12** The SDR performs some, but not all, of the functions of money. It is a unit of account and a standard for deferred payments, but there are limits on its acceptability in settlement of a debt. The SDR cannot therefore function as a universal medium of exchange.

# CHAPTER 34

# EUROPE'S ECONOMIC COMMUNITY

## Topic Summary

### Introduction

The European Community or, as it is more simply known, the EC, currently has twelve members. These are Germany, France, Luxembourg, the Netherlands, Belgium, the UK, Denmark, Portugal, Spain, Greece, Italy and Ireland. These countries have adopted a common external tariff against imports into the EC and certain common policies in certain key areas such as regional policy, transport policy and policy with respect to the movement of labour and capital. Two important policies are summarised below, but first we consider the static and dynamic effects of abandoning trade restrictions within the EC.

## Static effects

The static effects of abandoning restrictions on trade refer to **trade creation**. Trade creation occurs when the removal of restrictions on trade permits greater specialisation by countries in areas where they have a comparative advantage. The result is that higher cost suppliers are replaced by lower cost suppliers. The effect on real income benefits all member states.

## Dynamic effects

The dynamic effects of abandoning trade restrictions occur over time and take the form of **increased efficiency**. One factor that will promote increased efficiency is that the larger market will create greater scope for economies of scale. Increased trade might also lead to improvements in the infrastructure, such as improved road and rail networks. The removal of barriers to trade will also encourage greater competition between firms in the EC.

## The Common Agricultural Policy (CAP)

### Aims of the CAP

The Common Agricultural Policy of Europe has several aims:

- To increase farm yields.
- To stabilise farm incomes so that independent farming communities survive.
- To stabilise agricultural prices which in free markets are subject to wide fluctuations.
- To ensure adequate supplies of food within the Community.

### Operation of the CAP

To achieve these aims farmers are guaranteed minimum prices for their produce and, where necessary, intervention takes place through the *Agricultural Guidance and Guarantee Fund* to ensure these guaranteed prices are achieved. To avoid competition from abroad a variable import levy is imposed on food imports to ensure that the price of such imports is at least equal to EC farm prices. Figure 34.1 is used as a basis for explanation.

In Figure 34.1, $SS$ and $DD$ represent the initial supply and demand conditions of an agricultural commodity in a particular year. The equilibrium price of this commodity is $P_G$ and let us assume that this is also the guaranteed minimum price. In the following year the supply curve of this commodity increases to $S_1S_1$ and in a free market the equilibrium price will fall to $P$. However, since $P_G$ is the guaranteed minimum price, there will be a surplus of $QQ_1$ and the authorities will be compelled to purchase this surplus in order to maintain the guaranteed minimum price. In years when supply

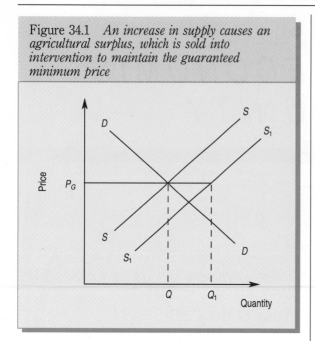

Figure 34.1   *An increase in supply causes an agricultural surplus, which is sold into intervention to maintain the guaranteed minimum price*

falls, if the surplus has been stored, it can be sold to avoid a sharp rise in price. In other cases, the surplus is sold on world markets outside the EC at subsidised prices.

## Problems with the CAP

**Effects on other countries**   A major problem with the CAP is that it **prevents** those countries with a comparative advantage in the production of food from fully exploiting that comparative advantage. The variable levy on imports of foods protects Community agriculture from competition from lower cost suppliers. This involves a **serious misallocation of global resources**. A further problem is that agricultural surpluses are often sold on world markets at **subsidised prices**. This again reduces the gains from trade for those with a comparative advantage in the production of food and implies **trade diversion**. This has brought the EC into sharp conflict with the USA in particular, and with GATT in general.

Sales of food surpluses to third world countries have also caused a **decline in agricultural production** in those countries to the extent that when drought occurs their already inefficient agricultural sector cannot produce sufficient food to feed the population. The result is that pressure is put on the EC to donate food to countries where the population is starving partly because of EC agricultural policy. In other words the CAP is contributing

to inefficiency in third world agriculture, which exacerbates the effect of a drought.

**Agricultural Surpluses**   Another problem with the CAP is that the guaranteed prices have encouraged **overproduction** of many commodities, with the result that huge 'mountains and lakes', the term used to describe stocks which are sold into intervention and stored, appear. These mountains and lakes are a problem for two reasons. Their increasing size implies that the EC incurs increasingly heavy storage and intervention costs. These costs are financed through the Community's budget, and this in turn is financed by taxpayers in all Community countries.

**Misallocation of Resources**   There is no specific formula that links the guaranteed price farmers receive and the free market equilibrium price. It is suggested that in some cases the guaranteed price is significantly above the free market equilibrium, while in other cases it approximates more closely to the free market equilibrium. The effect is to **distort** the allocation of resources within the agricultural sector.

**Increased Inequality of Farm Incomes**   Larger farms produce a greater output than smaller farms and therefore benefit from the higher farm prices under the CAP to a greater extent than smaller farms. The effect is to increase inequality in farm incomes.

**Increased General Inequality**   Since the CAP involves maintaining relatively high food prices it discriminates against the poorer people in the Community. Its effects are therefore regressive.

## Reform of the CAP

On 21 May 1992, EC ministers agreed to a reform of the CAP. The reforms, which are to be implemented in July 1993, are summarised below.

**Reduction in Guaranteed Prices**   The guaranteed price at which grain can be sold into intervention is to be reduced by 29 per cent. In 1992, there were 26m tonnes of surplus grain in EC stocks and this figure is expected to rise to 40m tonnes by May 1993. Farmers are to receive compensation of about £36 per tonne on their 1992 output provided they 'set aside', that is, withdraw, 15 per cent of their arable land from production.

The guaranteed price of beef is to be reduced by 15 per cent with the aim of reducing the 800 000 tonnes of frozen beef which were in store in 1992. Similarly the price of butter is to be cut by 5 per cent over two years with the aim of reducing the 800 000 tonnes butter mountain that existed in 1992.

**Reduction in Export Subsidies** Export subsidies, which have been a source of contention in the international community, are to be reduced but are not to be phased out altogether. The effect will be to keep EC export prices at competitive levels in world markets

## Effects of Reform

It may seem that the reduction in grain prices will offer a solution to overproduction of grain. However farmers will undoubtedly set aside the least productive sections of land and this, added to expected productivity increases on the larger farms (20 per cent of farmers produce 80 per cent of EC output), has led to estimates that, by the end of the century, wheat production could rise to 100m tonnes, 25 per cent more than in 1991!

The payment of subsidies will also leave unresolved the problem of inequality between larger farm incomes and smaller farm incomes. Since all farmers receive subsidy at the **same rate** the problem will be perpetuated and if, as expected, productivity continues to rise on the larger farms, inequality will continue to increase in the future.

Because export subsidies will maintain EC prices at competitive levels in world markets there is little doubt that these subsidies will remain a problem for the EC *vis à vis* the international community. In particular, the subsidies will continue to result in **trade diversion** and will do little to encourage efficiency in third world countries. If pressure grows, for example from GATT, further reductions in the export subsidy may well be necessary.

## The European Monetary System (EMS)

The EMS has three components: The Exchange Rate Mechanism (ERM), the European Currency Unit (ECU) and European Monetary Cooperation Fund (EMCF).

## The Exchange Rate Mechanism

The ERM is an agreement to maintain fixed exchange rates among participating currencies which float against non-participating currencies. Within the ERM, currencies are allowed to diverge from the fixed parity by agreed limits. Currently the limits of fluctuation are ± 6 per cent for currencies in the wide band of the ERM, and ± 2.25 per cent for currencies in the narrow band of the ERM. When a currency approaches its limits in the ERM, the authorities intervene in the way described on p. 196 to ensure that the margins of fluctuation are not breached. If there is persistent downward pressure on a currency in the ERM the most likely short term course of action will be for the authorities to increase the rate of interest.

## The European Currency Unit (ECU)

The ECU is a **basket currency** or weighted average of all EMS currencies. It consists of a fixed amount of all participating currencies, each weighted according to its importance in the EC. A major function of the ECU is to act as a **unit of account** and an increasing amount of borrowing and lending is carried out in ECUs which can, if necessary, then be converted into any EMS currency.

## The European Monetary Cooperation Fund (EMCF)

The functions of the EMCF are to be taken over by the European Central Bank once this is established, possibly in 1995. One of the main functions of the EMCF within the EMS is to provide short term assistance when a country is faced with downward pressure on its currency within the ERM and requires credit for intervention purposes.

## Benefits of ERM Membership

The UK joined the EMS when it was created in 1978 but did not participate in the ERM. It joined the **wide band** of the ERM in October 1990 but withdrew from the ERM in September 1992. Since then there has been considerable discussion about whether the UK has gained from ERM membership.

**Lower Inflation** There is no doubt that ERM membership was a major factor in achieving lower inflation in the UK. ERM discipline might work in a number of ways. One argument is that the need to maintain the fixed exchange rate within its agreed band forced the authorities to exercise tight control of money growth. In the absence of ERM membership, monetary policy might not have been so tight and inflation might therefore have been higher.

**Lower Cost of Reducing Inflation**  It has also been argued that inflation was reduced at a lower cost in terms of unemployment than might otherwise have occurred. The argument is that those involved in fixing wages and prices were aware of the government's commitment to the fixed exchange rate and therefore, because this implied a tight monetary policy, they realised that relatively high wages could not be passed on in higher prices. Instead it was argued that relatively high wage awards would result in job losses. The result was that wage awards fell and more jobs were preserved than might otherwise have been the case.

It is clear that inflation fell after the UK joined the ERM but it is by no means agreed that ERM membership caused inflation to fall. Since 1990, world inflation has fallen and, as a result, inflation has fallen in all ERM countries. It has also been argued that a major factor in reducing UK inflation has been the depth of the recession in the UK. Again recession has been a global phenomenon, but it has been particularly severe in the UK where interest rates were maintained at a relatively high level to preserve the value of sterling in the ERM. The suggestion has been made that the depth of the recession in the UK has been due to the fact that the UK joined the ERM at an uncompetitive rate, that is, sterling was overvalued in the ERM. If this is the case it would certainly increase the severity of the recession in the UK because it would reduce the competitiveness of UK exports in the European market and increase the competitveness of European imports in the UK market. It is impossible to test this proposition conclusively but supportive evidence is provided by the size of the UK balance of payments deficit with Europe when the UK was in the ERM which might indicate an overvalued exchange rate.

## *Economic and Monetary Union (EMU)*

Strictly **economic union** and **monetary union** are different concepts. Economic union implies the creation of a single market without artificial barriers to trade, a community-wide competition policy, a common regional policy and the coordination of macro-economic policy-making. Monetary union implies economic union but also involves agreeing to irrevocably fixed exchange rates and the eventual creation of a single currency.

## Advantages of Economic and Monetary Union

There are many possible advantages of economic and monetary union. It is important to be clear at the outset that there is no disagreement about the benefits of economic union. The issue is whether the EC should proceed to full monetary union. The advantages of EMU are summarised below.

**Increased Competition**  In an economic union there will be an increase in competition because of the elimination of restrictions on trade. However monetary union will further increase competition because price differences between goods sold in different parts of the Community will be more obvious to consumers.

**Elimination of Exchange Rate Risk**  In a full EMU there is no possibility of exchange rate changes. It is argued that this will encourage even greater specialisation and trade.

**Real Resource Savings**  EMU will lead to real resource savings for the Community as a whole. One source of such savings is that it will no longer be necessary to convert one currency into another to settle international indebtedness. Another source of savings is the reduction in the provision of those instruments such as swaps, futures and options which are designed to provide a hedge against exchange rate changes.

**Increased Efficiency in the Allocation of Resources**  There are many ways in which EMU will encourage efficiency in the allocation of resources. Perhaps the most important way is that capital will be free to move to where returns are greatest.

## Disadvantages of EMU

There are two major disadvantages with EMU and again these are summarised below.

**Loss of Policy Sovereignty**  Any country which joins an EMU surrenders control of its monetary policy. In other words an individual country cannot pursue an independent monetary policy. Monetary policy is dictated from the centre and, since changes in monetary policy can impose costs on a country, the possibility will always exist that certain countries could have achieved a better result outside the union than has been achieved inside the union. Given the success of the Bundesbank in controlling inflation, German reservations about surrendering control of monetary policy are understandable!

**Loss of Exchange Rate Sovereignty** Countries which agree to EMU surrender the ability to vary the exchange rate. Changes in the exchange rate have often been the major means through which price and cost differences between different countries are offset. This adjustment mechanism is surrendered in a monetary union: if a country experiences a balance of payments deficit with other countries the costs of adjustment will be borne by the domestic economy and will take the form of falling real income and rising unemployment. The situation can be illustrated by the trading relationship between Scotland and England. The economic situation in Scotland might well be improved if it were possible to devalue the Scottish currency against sterling.

## Common Mistakes to Avoid

With respect to economic groupings such as the EC, it is important to distinguish between a **customs union** and a **common market**. A customs union is simply a loose grouping of countries with the aim of establishing free trade within the union. A common external tariff is applied to all imports into the union but there is no adoption of any other common policy. Members pursue their own independent domestic polices. Neither is there any intention to adopt a fixed exchange rate or to adopt a common currency between members and there are no political aspirations. A common market is a more formal arrangement whereby countries adopt a common external tariff against imports outside the common market and remove barriers to trade within the common market. However a common market also requires common policies. In particular it requires the free movement of capital and labour within the common market and common regional and transport policies. The EC now satisfies these criteria.

## Questions and Answers

### Questions

1  (a)  Explain why the European Community needs a policy for agriculture.          (10)
   (b)  Discuss the economic reasons why reform of the Common Agricultural Policy (CAP) has been advocated.          (15)

UCLES, June 1992

2  The European Monetary System could benefit a member country because:

   1  it becomes more difficult for a single government to cause inflation at home by increasing domestic demand too rapidly
   2  it reduces uncertainty and so helps to stimulate trade between members of the European Community
   3  when the inflation rates of European Community Members differ balance of payments disequilibria are less likely to result
   A  1, 2 and 3 are correct
   B  1 and 2 only are correct
   C  2 and 3 only are correct
   D  1 only is correct

AEB, Nov 1991

3  The main aim of the European Monetary System (EMS) is to

   A  stabilise exchange rates between Community members
   B  stabilise Community exchange rates against the dollar
   C  encourage the creation of a common currency in member states
   D  eliminate destabilising capital flows in the Community
   E  provide funds for member states with balance of payments deficits

### Answers

1  (a)  There are many reasons why the European Community has adopted a common policy on agriculture. One reason is to guarantee adequate supplies of food within the Community. Other reasons are to stabilise agricultural prices and farm incomes.

Very basically the CAP is a system of guaranteed minimum prices for agricultural produce and its operation is explained in terms of Figure 34.2

In Figure 34.2, $SS$ and $DD$ are the original supply and demand curves for some agricultural commodity. The equilibrium price is $P_G$ and for simplicity we assume this is the guaranteed minimum price. Assume that supply now increases to $S_1S_1$. At the guaranteed minimum there is now a surplus and in a free market price would fall. To avoid this the authorities buy up the surplus which they will either store for release onto the market when supply falls, or sell outside the EC on world markets.

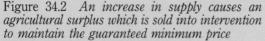

Figure 34.2 *An increase in supply causes an agricultural surplus which is sold into intervention to maintain the guaranteed minimum price*

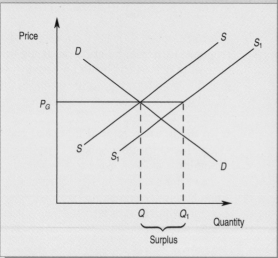

The operation of the guaranteed minimum price will clearly encourage production and so guarantee adequate supplies of food. It will also avoid fluctuations in the supply of agricultural products which characterise some markets where the cobweb theorem operates. In fact, in the EC, the CAP has been so successful in achieving this aim that surpluses have appeared in many products, including beef and butter.

In agriculture price fluctuations are a particular problem because supply can be disrupted by random factors such as changes in the weather which affect the annual harvest. However the problem is exacerbated because the price elasticity of demand for agricultural products is relatively low. Because of this relatively small changes in supply can cause relatively large fluctuations in price.

There is another problem because the income elasticity of demand for agricultural products is also relatively low. Therefore, as real incomes rise, demand for food does not rise in proportion. Individuals tend to consume different foodstuffs, better cuts of meat for example, but the total demand for food changes very little. This has an important effect on the growth of farm incomes because it implies that, as real national income rises, farm incomes will rise by a smaller amount. Those who work in agriculture will therefore experience a slower growth in real income than those who work in other sectors. Guaranteed minimum prices for agricultural produce do not give farm workers a guaranteed minimum income. However, they almost certainly

guarantee less fluctuation in farm incomes than would occur in an unregulated market.

(b) The CAP clearly works to the benefit of the European agricultural sector but its operation has caused many problems. A major problem with the CAP is that it prevents those countries with a comparative advantage in the production of food from fully exploiting that comparative advantage. The variable levy on imports of foods protects Community agriculture from competition from lower cost suppliers in the temperate zones, such the USA, Canada and Australia. The USA has been particularly critical of the CAP because it increases the imported price of agricultural crops from the USA in the EC. In addition sales of agricultural products from the EC at subsidised prices on world markets have reduced farm incomes in the USA.

Reform of the CAP has been high on the agenda in the Uruguay Round of the GATT negotiations. Its operation distorts world markets and causes a serious misallocation of resources. The gains from specialisation and trade are well known and when countries are prevented from exploiting a comparative advantage because of protectionist policies there will be a misallocation of resources. In the case of agriculture, resources could be more optimally allocated if protection for the agricultural sector in the EC was reduced.

Sales of exports from the EC at subsidised prices have also caused problems for many third world countries. In such countries the availability of relatively cheap food has depressed agricultural prices and discouraged agricultural production. Investment in agriculture has fallen, with the result that in times of drought serious food shortages have developed and the agricultural sector is too inefficient to respond.

Another problem with the CAP is that the guaranteed prices have encouraged overproduction of many commodities, with the result that huge surpluses of many products have appeared. To preserve the guaranteed price these stocks have been sold into intervention and, where possible, stored. However the growing size of the surpluses has presented a problem for the authorities because of the increasing cost of intervention purchases and storage. These costs are financed through the Community's budget, and this in turn is financed by taxpayers in all Community countries. Tax revenues spent on intervention have an opportunity cost and this is borne by the Community as a whole.

A further problem is that there is no specific formula which links the guaranteed price farmers receive and the free market equilibrium price. It has been suggested that in some cases the guaranteed price is significantly above the free market equilibrium, while in other cases it approximates more closely to the free market equilibrium. The effect is to distort the allocation of resources within the agricultural sector by encouraging farmers to concentrate on production of those crops which offer the highest return.

A source of contention within the agricultural community is the fact that the larger farms, because they produce a greater output than smaller farms, benefit from the higher farm prices under the CAP to a greater extent than smaller farms. The effect is to increase inequality in farm incomes and to encourage the trend towards larger farms. The disappearance of smaller farms might lead to the elimination of small farm communities – something the CAP was designed to avoid.

Whatever the reasoning behind the operation of the CAP, it implies a high food price policy. Consumer real income has therefore been adversely affected as a result of the CAP's operation. Since the same higher food prices are experienced by all consumers regardless of their real incomes, the CAP discriminates against the lower income groups, pensioners, the unemployed, those in low wage occupations and so on. Its effect is therefore regressive.

It is clear that there are many economic reasons why reform of the CAP has been advocated. It has had an adverse effect on the allocation of resources within the agricultural sector. It has also increased inequality within the EC's own agricultural sector and, because of the higher food prices its operation has involved, for the community as a whole.

**2** For countries which participate in the EMS the overriding obligation is to gear domestic macroeconomic policy towards ensuring stability in the foreign exchange market. Any country that allows demand to rise at a relatively rapid rate will soon find its currency depreciating against other EMS currencies and will be obliged to reign back aggre-

gate demand. To the extent that inflation is also reigned back, a country will benefit from EMS membership. Option 1 is correct.

It is widely agreed that fixed exchange rates will reduce uncertainty and as a result specialisation and trade will increase for countries which participate fully in the EMS. Option 2 is correct.

When inflation rates diverge between trading partners, balance of payments surpluses and deficits appear. The EMS can do nothing to avoid these. Option 3 is incorrect.

The key is B.

**3** At its inception the main aim of the EMS was declared to be the 'creation of a zone of monetary stability'. This can only be achieved if exchange rates are stable. Option A is therefore correct.

There is no attempt to stabilise Community exchange rates against the dollar – or any other non-EMS currency. Option B is incorrect.

There is no doubt that, as the EMS has evolved, the creation of a common currency has become a definite possibility. Furthermore if a common currency is to be created it will be necessary to eliminate fluctuations in EMS exchange rates. However, the main aim of the EMS is not to encourage the creation of a common currency – though it might well have this effect. Option C is incorrect.

An important feature of the EMS is that there are no controls on capital flows between member states. It is likely that the EMS will eliminate destabilising capital flows because the need to maintain the fixed exchange rate will lead to changes in the rate of interest when a currency is under pressure in the EMS. However this is not the aim of the EMS. Option D is incorrect.

As part of the EMS arrangements funds are provided for those countries which require them for intervention to stabilise their exchange rate in the EMS. However, again, this is not an aim of the EMS. It is simply an integral part of the EMS arrangements. Option E is incorrect.

The key is A

## REVIEW QUESTIONS AND ANSWERS

### Questions

1  What is 'common' in a common market?

2  Why is free competition in transport important in stabilising a single market?

3  Why will the development of the single market by 1992 lead to an increase in cross border mergers?

4  Is full economic union in Europe possible without monetary union?

5  Since their respective inceptions, EFTA has contracted and lost membership while the EC has expanded and gained membership. What political and economic reasons can you think of to account for this?

6  If you were a Japanese business manager how would you view the likely development of the EC in the 1990s? How would you be likely to respond?

7  Which UK industries do you consider most likely to benefit from the 1992 changes, and which could be adversely affected? Explain your answers.

8  Prepare a case for the siting of a future European Central Bank in London rather than Frankfurt, Paris or some other continental financial centre.

9  What do we mean by the terms 'trade creation' and 'trade diversion'? Examine these concepts in the context of the EC.

10  Why was the UK slow to become a full member of the EMS, and why has it been resisting the idea of European monetary union?

11  What UK professions are likely to experience increased opportunities on the Continent as a result of the 1992 measures aimed at 'freeing' the labour market? How might your likely chosen profession be affected?

### Answers

1  A common market is a market in which member governments adopt certain common policies and accept certain common regulations relating to industry and commerce. In particular a common exchange rate policy is required, along with common external tariffs and common policies in industries where subsidies are widely used, such as agriculture and transport. There is also free movement of the factors of production.

2  A single market cannot exist unless there is free competition in transport. If different countries adopt different regulations with respect to transport, this will restrict competition between goods produced in different countries.

3  Cross-border mergers increased as the Single Market neared completion. One reason for this is that firms outside the EC wish to gain access to the larger European market. Increased intra-EC merger activity also suggested that firms in the EC wished to expand and take advantage of the increased availability of economies of scale.

4  Whether full economic union is possible without monetary union is a controversial issue. Strictly economic union and monetary union are different but it is increasingly argued that, in order to realise the full benefits of economic union, monetary union will be necessary. It is argued that one reason for this is that without a common currency the need to exchange one currency for another will reduce competition by raising costs and by concealing price differences in different parts of the community.

5  EFTA is simply a free trade area without political ties between members. It does not therefore have the same authority in the international world as the EC. This is particularly important with the world becoming polarised into powerful trading blocs. A major problem with EFTA is that it has no common external tariff against imports. There is simply free trade between members. One

problem with this is that imports can enter the country with the lowest tariff and can then be sold in other member countries without incurring any other tariff payments. The EC is a customs union with a common external tariff against imports so that it is impossible to evade the tariff of any particular country. The EC also has many common policies towards industry and commerce and the free movement of the factors of production. In these circumstances the potential for efficiency in the allocation of resources is far greater than in a free trade area. Hence the rise of the EC and the decline of EFTA.

**6** The creation of the Single Market will make possible vast economies of scale for EC firms, which will increase their ability to compete in world markets. In some sectors this represents a threat to Japanese producers. A logical response of Japanese firms to the creation of the Single Market is to locate subsidiaries inside the EC so that the cost disadvantages associated with the common external tariff will be avoided.

**7** One area where the UK is expected to do well as a result of the 1992 measures is pharmaceuticals. In fact the UK pharmaceutical industry is the most profitable in Europe. The UK also seems to have a comparative advantage in the food sector, where value added per worker is twice that in France and Germany. In medical and surgical equipment the UK has a considerable comparative advantage. London's pre-eminence in financial services and especially in the provision of insurance implies that this sector will gain after 1992. Similarly UK airlines are relatively efficient.

In certain areas of the manufacturing sector the 1992 measures might result in a loss of market share. The UK motor industry is likely to face even stiffer competition. In the production of many consumer durables the UK appears relatively weak. Increasingly dishwashers and washing machines are imported from Europe. The same is true of machine tools.

**8** London has a long history of financial expertise. At one time London was the largest financial centre in the world and even today it remains the third largest. It is considerably larger than Paris or Frankfurt. In the financial world, where funds are highly mobile, such a position represents a continuing comparative advantage over most other countries. The ability of London to operate effectively as a financial centre is indicated by the relatively large share of the ECU bond market which London has captured.

**9** Trade creation takes place when a high cost source of production is replaced by a low cost source of production owing to the removal of some restriction on trade such as a tariff. In the case of the EC, the completion of the internal market has generated increased efficiency through greater economies of scale and this has resulted in trade creation. Trade diversion occurs when a low cost supplier is replaced by a high cost supplier because some barrier to trade has been erected. The CAP diverts trade to EC countries away from lower cost suppliers of agricultural produce.

**10** Membership of the EMS implies some loss of policy sovereignty. In particular with respect to the EMS, monetary policy must be geared towards maintaining the exchange rate within the agreed band. This was the major reason why the UK did not join the ERM of the EMS before 1991 and is a major reason for the UK's withdrawl from the system in 1992. Since EMU implies irrevocably fixed exchange rates and eventually the creation of a common currency, it is the main reason why many UK politicians are resisting pressure to move towards EMU.

**11** Most professions will experience increased opportunities on the Continent after 1992 for talented and qualified personnel because qualifications gained in one country will be recognised by all countries. Thus a GP who qualified in the UK will be able to practise anywhere in Europe. It is generally considered that there will be greater opportunities for solicitors, accountants, medical practitioners and nurses, among others.

## CHAPTER 35

# PUBLIC FINANCE AND TAXATION

## Topic Summary

Public finance and taxation are concerned with government expenditure and the way in which funds are raised to finance these expenditures.

## The Government's Expenditure Plans

As from 1993 the Chancellor will present a macro-economic statement to parliament in which the government's expenditure plans for the coming years are outlined. This macroeconomic statement will also be the occasion when the Chancellor presents the government's annual Budget which contains the government's plans for raising revenue to meet its planned expenditures.

Since the 1980s the level of government expenditure has received considerable attention and efforts have been made to limit its growth. The major reason for this is the view that an increase in government expenditure will crowd out an equivalent amount of private sector expenditure. The argument is that, since private sector organisations are compelled to make a profit in order to survive, the private sector will use resources more efficiently than the public sector, where there are no profitability requirements. The implication is that a reduction in government expenditure will increase efficiency in the economy. This view is examined more fully on p. 224. Here we simply consider the basic reasons for government expenditure and these are easily summarised.

## Public Goods and Merit Goods

We have seen on p. 20 that in a free market certain goods would be underproduced or underconsumed in relation to the optimum level. The government undertakes to ensure a minimum level of provision of street-lighting, education, health-care and so on, so as to improve the allocation of resources.

## Redistribution of Income

A major item of government expenditure takes the form of **transfer payments** to the unemployed, the retired, students in full-time higher education and so on. These transfer payments are made entirely for redistributional purposes and their effect is to reduce inequality in the distribution of income.

## Regional Assistance

Certain regions such as the north-east, Scotland and South Wales have experienced a fall in prosperity and a rise in unemployment owing to the decline of a localised industry such as ship-building or coal-mining. To attract industry back to these regions the government offers financial assistance to firms which create or safeguard additional jobs in the regions.

## Interest Payments on the National Debt

To meet its expenditures the government sometimes borrows and therefore adds to the national debt. Annual interest payments on the national debt are now about 9 per cent of total annual government expenditure.

## The Budget

From 1993, the Budget will form part of the Chancellor's macroeconomic statement which is presented to parliament each year in December. When revenue from taxation is less than expenditure, a budget deficit exists and the government is compelled to finance the deficit by borrowing. The opposite is true when expenditure is less than tax revenue and in this case the surplus can be used to redeem part of the national debt.

The Budget attracts considerable interest among economists because of the effect of changes in taxation and government borrowing on the economy. For example, a change in taxation will have a direct impact on aggregate demand and therefore may effect the level of national income, the rate of inflation and unemployment. This view is examined on pp. 219–20. Here we concentrate on the effect of government borrowing.

## The Budget Deficit and the PSBR

The Public Sector Borrowing Requirement is the **sum of all anticipated borrowing by the public sector** over the course of the coming year. It therefore consists of the Central Government Borrowing Requirement, the Local Authorities Borrowing Requirement and the Public Corporations Borrowing Requirement. However, since part of the Central Government Borrowing Requirement is on-lent to other parts of the public sector, attention focuses on borrowing by the central government and, since the vast majority of government borrowing stems from the Budget deficit, this explains economists' interest in the Budget.

The effect of the PSBR on money growth depends on the size of the PSBR and the way in which it is financed. If all other things remain equal, the larger the PSBR, the greater the effect on money growth. However all other things might not remain equal and differences in the way the PSBR is financed might have a different effect on money growth.

If the PSBR is financed by borrowing from the non-bank private sector, money growth is unaffected. All that happens is that private sector deposits are transferred to the public sector and then, when the public sector spends these deposits, they are returned to the private sector. The effect on money growth is therefore neutral. However the same is not true if the PSBR is financed by borrowing from the banking sector. Here the banks lend to the public sector by creating a deposit which, when spent, will increase private sector bank deposits. In consequence money growth will rise. Money growth also rises if the government borrows overseas. Funds are paid into the government's account at the Bank of England and, when these are spent, private sector deposits will rise.

## The National Debt

The National Debt is the **total of all outstanding central government debt**. It currently stands at over £200bn. Most of the debt is held by UK residents but part is held by foreign nationals living abroad, the result of financing the PSBR by borrowing abroad. However it is not the size of the National Debt which attracts attention, it is whether the existence of the debt imposes a financial burden on the community. There are two strands to the argument. One strand is that, if one generation borrows funds and a different generation repays them, a burden has been transferred from one generation to another generation. The second strand of the argument is that the present generation pays taxes to meet interest payments on the debt.

In fact it is not possible to transfer a burden from one generation to another in the way suggested above. For the most part payment of taxes and receipt of interest or debt repayment simply represent a redistribution of income within the community. The same generation which pays taxes receives interest and repayment when debt is redeemed. To this extent, the community as a whole is neither better off nor worse off as a result of the debt. Nevertheless we might argue that the existence of the National Debt does impose some kind of burden on the community, for the reasons examined below.

### External Debt

If the government borrows abroad then at the time the debt is incurred the community can import more than it exports, the difference being financed by borrowing overseas. However, when the debt is redeemed, a future generation must export more than it imports. This implies a cut in domestic living standards and therefore the imposition of a burden on the generation that redeems the debt.

### Disincentive Effects

It is sometimes argued that higher rates of taxation have a disincentive effect on effort and initiative and that this reduces real national income below the level that might otherwise have been achieved. If this is correct it implies a lower standard of living for the community as a whole and hence the imposition of a burden on society.

## Costs of Administering the Debt

Administering the debt involves a financial cost that would otherwise not exist. The resources used in administering the debt have an alternative use and so there is an opportunity cost, the output that might otherwise have been produced, which represents a burden on society. Again the costs of administration are financed by the taxpayer, which might contribute to any disincentive effect.

## Some Taxes Levied in the UK

### Direct Taxes

Direct taxes are levied on incomes, capital gains, or transfers of wealth. The main direct taxes levied in the UK at present are summarised below.

**Personal Income Tax**   This is tax levied on taxable incomes; that is, gross income less certain non-taxable allowances, from employment and self-employment, as well as unearned income such as interest income on savings. It is by far **the most important tax** in terms of the amount raised in revenue, accounting for almost 25 per cent of total tax revenue in 1991/92. Income tax is progressive in its effect. A tax is progressive when the marginal rate of tax exceeds the average rate of tax. In the UK in 1992/3, the following rates of tax were levied on taxable earned income.

| Rate of tax (%) | Taxable income (£) |
|---|---|
| 20 | 2 000 |
| 25 | 20 700 |
| 40 | Over 20 700 |

The rate of tax is therefore 20 per cent on the first £2000 of taxable income, 25 per cent on the next £18 700 of taxable income and so on.

One problem with personal income tax is the possibility of a **disincentive effect** on effort and initiative. As incomes rise tax liability rises and this might reduce mobility of labour as individuals are discouraged from moving to better paid occupations. Similarly it might discourage effort because higher incomes paid as a reward for higher productivity might be taxed at a higher rate.

**National Insurance Contributions**   These are levied on personal incomes and are used to finance expenditure on the National Health Service and certain transfer payments such as state pensions. Revenue from national insurance contributions does not cover the full cost of the expenditure on the items it is used to fund and the difference is made up from revenue from other sources.

**Corporation Tax**   This tax is levied on company profits. It is levied at the rate of 25 per cent for small companies with profits up to £250 000. For larger companies with profits in excess of this the rate of corporation tax is 33 per cent.

### Indirect Taxes

Indirect taxes are collected by the Customs and Excise Department in the UK. The most important indirect tax levied in the UK is **Value Added Tax** (VAT). This is levied on most goods and services at the constant rate of 17.5 per cent. Some expenditures, such as medicines and children's clothing, are completely exempt from VAT.

One problem with VAT is that all consumers pay the same rate of tax on their purchases, regardless of their personal circumstances. The effect of VAT is therefore regressive since it bears more heavily on the lower income groups than the higher income groups, that is, for any given purchase VAT payments constitute a higher proportion of the income of lower income groups than of higher income groups.

## Common Mistakes to Avoid

Sometimes there is confusion over whether the existence of the National Debt imposes a burden on the community. This argument was examined in the text, but to emphasise the point, remember that, if the government borrows from domestic residents and this is used to finance transfer payments, there is simply a redistribution of income within the community. Similarly when debt is redeemed there is simply a redistribution of income within the community. Even when domestic borrowing is used to finance real expenditures, such as an increase in road building or the construction of hospitals, it is impossible to transfer any kind of burden from one generation to the next. In these circumstances resources are transferred from the private sector to the public sector at the time construction takes place. It is at this time that any burden is borne by the community because of the opportunity cost involved in increasing the output of the public sector.

The operation of a progressive tax can also be a source of confusion. As taxable income rises it is only the amount in the higher taxable band which is subject to the higher rate. The higher rate does not apply to total taxable income. Thus in the UK in 1992/93, higher income earners paid tax at three different rates. For example, an individual with taxable income of £40 000 would pay tax at the following rates:

| Rate of tax (%) | Taxable income (£) | Amount of tax paid (£) |
|---|---|---|
| 20 | 2 000 | 400 |
| 25 | 20 700 | 4 675 |
| 40 | Over 20 700 | 7 720 |
| | Total | 12 795 |

## Questions and Answers

### Questions

1 In 1978 the standard rate of income tax in the UK was 33% and the top rate was 83%; in 1990 the standard rate was 25% and the top rate was 40%. Examine the likely economic consequences of these changes.

ULEAC, June 1992

Questions 2 and 3 are based on Figure 35.1, which shows how the proportion of income paid in tax varies with income in different situations.

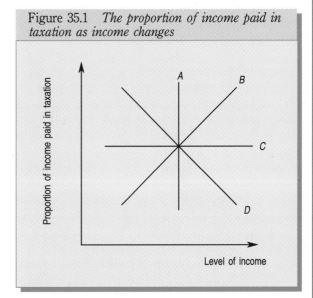

Figure 35.1 *The proportion of income paid in taxation as income changes*

2 Which curve illustrates a tax which is regressive in its effect?

3 Which curve illustrates a tax which is proportional in its effect?

4 The government would increase the 'poverty trap' if it lowered

A unemployment pay
B child benefits
C the standard rate of income tax
D income tax thresholds

AEB, Nov 1990

### Answers

1 Income tax is a tax levied on the taxable incomes of individuals. Taxable income is simply gross income from employment and self-employment as well as income from other sources such as interest paid on savings, minus certain tax-free allowances.

In the UK, income tax is progressive and therefore the marginal rate of tax exceeds the average rate of tax. This simply means that there are tax thresholds and, as taxable income rises, a higher rate is applied to income above each threshold. In the UK in 1978, the standard rate of tax was 33 per cent. Those with income above the tax-free allowance but below the next tax threshold would only pay income tax at the standard rate. The highest taxable incomes were subject to a marginal rate of 83 per cent. By 1990 the standard rate of tax had fallen to 25 per cent and the top rate of income tax was down to 40 per cent.

The main reason for the reduction in income tax rates is the belief that higher rates of taxation have a powerful disincentive effect which impairs the allocation of resources and discourages effort and initiative. The belief is that, if individuals are allowed to keep more of the income they earn, the disincentive effect will be reduced or even eliminated altogether.

Disincentive effects might take many forms, but a great deal of attention has focused on the effect of disincentives on the efficiency with which the labour market operates. The disincentive effect might be particularly acute for those caught in the poverty trap or the unemployment trap. The former refers to individuals with relatively low incomes and who are in receipt of supplementary benefit and who qualify for other forms of state aid, such as free school meals for children, free medical prescriptions and so on. In many cases such individuals have little incentive to accept paid employment since they tend to be unskilled and would earn relatively low wages. Their wages from employment would nevertheless often become liable for taxation and at the same time they would lose their entitlement to state benefits. This implies an effective marginal rate of taxation well in excess of the standard rate, which would leave many individuals little better off in employment than they would be out of employment. In such circumstances there is little incentive to seek paid employment.

The unemployment trap operates in a similar way but is more acute. Here individuals are trapped because the tax and benefit systems operate in such a way that they are actually better off out of work than when they are employed. This, added to the disutility and expense, such as travel to and from work, of accepting employment, actively discourages unemployed workers from seeking employment.

It is argued that higher rates of taxation increase the numbers caught in the poverty and unemployment traps and that lower rates of taxation, by allowing individuals to retain more of their earnings, provide a means of reducing the extent of these traps. If this is correct the greater number of workers accepting employment will reduce the unemployment total, increase tax revenue for the government and cut down government expenditure on the provision of benefits. It will also increase real national income as unemployed workers add to the flow of output. Belief in this view of the way the labour market works clearly provides governments with a powerful incentive to reduce the standard rate of taxation.

The disincentive effect might also manifest itself in other ways. In particular, higher rates of taxation will reduce the incentive of workers to move to different parts of the country where vacancies exist and/or to change their occupation to obtain employment. Lower mobility as a result of higher rates of taxation will affect workers in different occupations and different income groups. By increasing after-tax income, lower rates of taxation might increase mobility of labour for all groups and so increase the efficiency with which the labour market allocates resources. Again the effects will be widespread. Allocative efficiency will increase because supply will be more responsive to changes in demand. Other benefits will include those outlined above, such as a reduction in unemployment and an increase in real income.

There is also some evidence that higher rates of taxation persuaded the most talented individuals to move to countries where taxes were lower. If this is correct higher rates of taxation would again adversely affect the productive potential of the economy. If lower rates of taxation remove the incentive to move

to other countries then the existence of better managerial and research talent will improve productivity in the economy, which will confer benefits on all.

Despite this, disincentive effects are not confined to the labour market. It is possible that high rates of taxation will reduce the incentive and ability of individuals to save and invest. Higher rates of income tax, by reducing disposable income, clearly reduce the ability of individuals to save. However, since interest income is also subject to taxation, the incentive to save also falls. If all other things remain equal this might reduce the flow of funds available for investment.

However investment will also be adversely effected by higher rates of income tax because dividends paid to shareholders are affected by the rate of tax shareholders pay. Higher rate taxpayers receive a lower rate of dividend than lower rate taxpayers because income tax is effectively deducted at source. Since those on higher incomes are more likely to invest in companies it follows that higher rates of taxation might well reduce the flow of investment funds to firms. Lower rates of taxation might encourage savings in investment in industry and this may have been a factor behind the reduction of income tax rates. If investment is encouraged as a result of reducing income tax rates this will certainly be consistent with the aim of the Conservative government in power when tax rates were reduced of widening share ownership in industry.

It might also be argued that higher rates of taxation dissuade individuals from declaring the full extent of their taxable income. The growth of the black economy in the UK is evidence of tax avoidance. The lower rates of taxation introduced in the 1980s and 1990s may have reduced the incidence of tax avoidance by reducing the gain from such illegal behaviour. If this is the case it is possible that tax receipts have increased despite the lower rate of taxation.

In general lower rates of income tax are widely believed to have increased a whole range of incentives. If this is correct the effect will be to improve the efficiency with which the labour market allocates resources. This in turn implies a lower rate of unemployment and a higher standard of living than might otherwise have been achieved. If employment has increased there will also have been a reduction in the payment of benefits to the unemployed and this, along with increased tax payments, will have reduced the need for governments to borrow. Since an increase in government borrowing will lead to an increase in money growth, and an increase in money growth will cause higher inflation, it follows that the lower rate of taxation may have been a contributory factor in achieving the lower rate of inflation which the UK has experienced in the 1980s and 1990s compared with earlier decades.

**2** A regressive tax is one where a declining proportion of income is paid in taxation. The correct option is therefore D.

**3** A proportional tax is one where the proportion of income paid in taxation is constant as income changes. The correct option is therefore C.

**4** The poverty trap exists when the tax and benefit system operate in such a way as to trap an individual in relative poverty. When an unemployed person accepts employment, tax liability increases while benefit entitlement falls. The result is that, when a person accepts employment, they might very well face an effective marginal rate of tax which is close to 100 per cent.

If the government lowered unemployment pay this would reduce the poverty trap (though it might increase actual poverty) by reducing the effective marginal rate of tax when a person accepts employment. Option A is incorrect.

The same applies if child benefits are reduced. The loss of benefit after a job is accepted falls and this reduces the effective marginal rate of tax. Again, although this would reduce the poverty trap, it might increase actual poverty. Option B is incorrect.

If the standard rate of income tax is reduced this will increase disposable income from employment and will reduce the poverty trap. Option C is incorrect.

If tax thresholds are reduced then the level of income at which an individual becomes liable for income tax falls. The effect of reducing tax thresholds would therefore be to reduce after-tax incomes, which would most certainly increase the poverty trap. Option D is correct

The key is D.

## REVIEW QUESTIONS AND ANSWERS

### Questions

**1** Summarise the arguments for and against the proposition that progressive taxes have disincentive effects.

**2** What is the 'poverty trap'?

**3** Using supply and demand curves, show how the incidence of an indirect tax is shared between producers and consumers when the *impact* **is initially on** *consumers*.

**4** The UK tax system discriminates heavily against earned income, but leaves wealth relatively untouched. Why is this?

**5** Is the National Debt a debt the nation owes itself?

**6** How is the PSBR related to the Budget deficit?

### Answers

**1** Taxes are progressive when the marginal rate of tax exceeds the average rate of tax so that, as incomes rise, the amount paid in tax rises more than proportionately. The main argument in favour of progressive taxation is that, as income increases, the marginal utility of each additional pound falls. To ensure equality of sacrifice it is therefore essential that, as income rises, the amount paid in tax should increase more than proportionately. The main disadvantage of progressive taxation is that it might have powerful disincentive effects on effort and initiative on the part of individuals. It might also discourage investment.

**2** The tax and benefit system sometimes works in such a way that when a person accepts work the tax they pay on earned income, combined with their loss of benefit entitlement, leaves little, if any, improvement in their real income. They are therefore caught in a trap which condemns them to relatively low real income whether they are in employment or unemployed.

**3** In Figure 35.2, *SS* and *DD* are the original supply and demand curves for a particular commodity. The equilibrium price is initially *P*. If a flat rate tax is now imposed on this commodity the supply curve will shift to $S_1S_1$ and the equilibrium price will rise to $P_1$. The impact of the tax falls on producers because they are responsible for payment of the tax to the authorities. However the incidence of the tax is partly borne by consumers and partly by producers. The total amount paid in tax is shown by the area

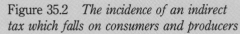

Figure 35.2  *The incidence of an indirect tax which falls on consumers and producers*

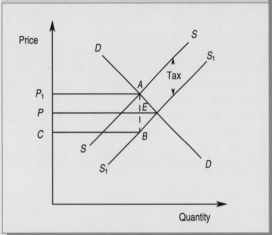

$P_1ABC$. Since price has increased from $P$ to $P_1$, the area $PP_1AF$ is the incidence of the tax which falls on the consumer and the area $PFBC$ is the incidence of the tax which falls on the producer.

4 There are problems with attempts to tax wealth. A major problem is defining what consti-tutes wealth and even if a definition can be agreed there are problems of valuing wealth for purposes of taxation. It would be extremely difficult to collect a tax on wealth. If wealth owners were forced to sell off some of their wealth this might depress asset prices and would make it extremely difficult to assess tax liability. A wealth tax would also be difficult to administer and expensive to collect. Taxing earned income avoids all of these problems.

5 To a large extent the National Debt is a debt the nation owes itself since the present generation are holders of the debt. However, part of the National Debt, roughly 10 per cent, is held by foreigners and this part of the National Debt is not a debt the nation owes itself.

6 The PSBR is comprised of the Central Govern-ment Borrowing Requirement, the Local Authority Borrowing Requirement and the Public Corpora-tions Borrowing Requirement. By far the largest of these is the Central Government Borrowing Requirement and the main component here is the central government's budget deficit.

## CHAPTER 36

# *STABILISATION POLICY*

## Topic Summary

Stabilisation policy involves **government intervention in the economy** to offset the fluctuations that occur as a result of the trade cycle. All economies seem to have an in-built tendency to fluctuate between **periods of boom** and **periods of recession**. During the boom phase economic activity is buoyant so that output and employment are relatively low but the rate of inflation is relatively high and the current account tends to move into deficit. During the recession phase of the cycle economic activity is depressed so that employment, output and the rate of inflation are relatively low and the current account deficit falls or moves into surplus.

## *The Aims of Stabilisation Policy*

The aims of stabilisation policy are easily summarised:

## A High Level of Employment

A major aim of all governments is to achieve a relatively high and stable level of employment. Unemployment is regarded as a waste of economic resources and imposes costs on the taxpayer to finance the provision of supplementary benefits.

## A low Rate of Inflation

We have seen in Chapter 28 that inflation imposes very severe costs on society. To achieve and maintain a low rate of inflation is the main macroeconomic goal of all governments.

## Economic Growth

This can be defined as an increase in real national income and faster economic growth is an important objective of all governments because, if all other things remain equal, as output rises the standard of living rises.

## Income Redistribution

Income in the UK is unevenly distributed and in the last decade the level of inequality has increased. Nevertheless this does not imply that governments do not aim to promote a certain amount of equality. Income tax is levied at a progressive rate primarily for reasons of equality. The point to emphasise is that, however uneven the distribution of income is, it is certainly a good deal more even than it would be without the government's redistributional policies.

## *Techniques of Stabilisation Policy*

The aim of stabilisation policy is to **alter aggregate demand** in a counter-cyclical way so as to maintain output and employment at a high level while avoiding the problems of inflation and a deficit in the current account. It has to be admitted at the outset that there is considerable doubt about whether governments have achieved much success in stabilising aggregate demand so as to achieve the aims mentioned above. The current view is that in the long run the economy tends towards a stable equilibrium and that attempts to manipulate aggregate demand bring about changes in money growth which cause changes in the rate of inflation and actually destabilise the economy.

The techniques of demand management are particularly associated with a **Keynesian view** of the economy. The main instrument of demand management is the government's **annual budget** which is used to implement its fiscal policy, that is, the **deliberate manipulation of taxation** and **government expenditure**. As the economy moves into recession, stabilisation policy implies that the government aims for a budget deficit; that is, government expenditure exceeds revenue from taxation.

The implication is that, as net injections increase, a multiplier effect will be generated and the economy will be lifted out of recession. As part of its overall strategy the government might also cut interest rates to stimulate investment and consumer spending. However, in the traditional Keynesian view, monetary policy is comparatively insignificant and slow to take effect. Fiscal policy, on the other hand, is considered capable of bringing about major changes in aggregate demand and produces more rapid results than monetary policy. During the boom phase of the cycle, aggregate demand management implies the opposite policy prescription. A budget surplus increases net leakages and, as aggregate demand falls, inflation falls and the current account improves.

Stabilisation policy clearly implies a Keynesian view of income determination and links changes in all other macroeconomic variables to changes in national income. However, the effects of stabilisation policy are not inconsistent with a **monetarist** view of the economy. During the boom phase of the cycle a budget deficit will result in a reduction in money growth so that inflation will fall and during the recession phase of the cycle the budget deficit implies an increase in money growth and a rise in the rate of inflation.

## The Causes and Consequences of Economic Growth

## The Causes of Economic Growth

The causes of economic growth are many and varied. In some cases they are specific to a particular country. For example, the Gulf States have achieved economic growth by exploiting their oil reserves. Such natural factor endowments are not transferrable from one country to another and in this section we focus on more general factors that promote growth.

**Capital : Labour Ratio**  One of the most important factors encouraging economic growth is the ratio of capital to labour. When capital is substituted for labour there is usually a substantial increase in productivity. However, for many of the world's poorer countries where population growth is rapid, it is difficult to achieve even *capital widening*; that is, to ensure that the capital stock grows at the same rate as the population. *Capital deepening*, that is, accumulating capital at a faster rate than the labour

force is rising, is an important source of growth for most countries.

**Technological Progress**  Capital deepening will increase economic growth but another major factor is the *quality of capital*. Where technological progress leads to improvements in the type of capital equipment available to firms, and if all other things remain equal, this will encourage greater economic growth. Technological progress is of course the result of investment in research and development and greater expenditure on this can therefore be an important engine of economic growth.

**Labour**  The quantity and quality of labour available is an important source of economic growth. In densely populated countries labour tends to be relatively cheap and this gives those countries an advantage in the production of certain goods. Frequently the availability of relatively cheap labour input will attract investment by large multinational corporations. On the other hand, a relatively large labour force does not guarantee economic growth since it is important that workers are gainfully employed.

As well as the quantity of labour, the quality of labour is an important factor promoting economic growth. Other things equal, an increase in the skills possessed by the labour force through training will result in an increase in economic growth. Skills are important because they promote mobility and adaptability to changing conditions and patterns of demand. However, entrepreneurship is also important in generating economic growth and though it is impossible to train entrepreneurs it is true that the more 'enterprising' an economy's population, the greater the prospects for economic growth.

**Reallocation of Resources**  One way to increase economic growth is to reallocate resources from low productivity industries to high productivity industries. However, this is not always possible since countries often face stiff competition in international producers who exploit a comparative advantage. For example, in the UK it might seem that economic growth could be increased if resources were transferred from the production of fabrics, where value added per worker is low, to the production of cars, where value added per worker is higher. The problem is that the UK does not have a comparative advantage in the production of cars and such a transfer would therefore not be economically viable. There are far greater prospects for improved living standards in transferring resources from the production of armaments to the production of other goods and services.

## Consequences of Economic Growth

**Improved Living Standards**   The major benefit of economic growth is that it makes possible an improvement in the standard of living. Greater economic growth implies an increase in the real volume of output a nation produces and, as output rises faster than population, this implies an increase in real income per head. For developed countries, such as the UK, with an ageing population the benefit is obvious. As people grow older and withdraw from the labour market they cease to be producers but continue as consumers. The working population must provide output for the non-working population and, if output per head is constant, this implies a fall in living standards for the population as the number of dependants increases. On the other hand, if output rises faster than total population, it is possible for all groups to experience a rise in living standards – even though the number of dependants is increasing.

Greater economic growth also makes possible increased investment without necessarily reducing the total volume available for consumption. This is important because investment provides the potential for even greater growth in the future and will also make possible an increase in funds available for research and development. In the medical world this has led to the development of vaccines which have eliminated many fatal diseases which were once rife. It has also led to improved methods of treatment and has had a profound effect on the quality of life.

**Environmental Effects**   Attention often focuses on the adverse environmental effects of economic growth. The exploitation of natural resources often causes environmental damage and imposes negative externalities on the community. The loss of clean air because of production or consumption, for example through the use of motor cars, is an example, while industry is often blamed for loss of clean water because they sometimes dump waste material into the waterways. In recent years acid rain and the greenhouse effect have attracted considerable attention. The destruction of the Amazon rain forest, as well as other rain forests across Asia, has been carried out to increase economic growth in many of the world's poorer countries but has undoubtedly contributed in a major way to the greenhouse effect. Motor cars and coal-fired power stations have also contributed to the greenhouse effect and have been a cause of acid rain which has resulted in dead lakes and forests. Such environmental devastation is regarded by many as a high price to pay for economic growth and must be set against any improvements in material welfare as a result of increased output.

However, it could be argued that greater economic growth also provides the resources to combat negative externalities. We have the means to clean up dirty rivers and re-landscape areas which have been devastated by industrial pollution. Despite this, it remains true that a great deal of environmental damage is irreversible. Areas of natural beauty, once destroyed, cannot be recreated. Some of the damage caused by the greenhouse effect may be irreversible.

## Questions and Answers

### Questions

1 According to Keynesian theory, domestic economic activity could be stimulated by

    1  a fall in the exchange rate
    2  reduced levels of taxation
    3  increased government spending
    A  1,2 and 3 correct
    B  1 and 2 only correct
    C  2 and 3 only correct
    D  1 only correct

    AEB, Nov 1991

2 Which of the folowing is (are) regarded as an automatic stabiliser?

    1  Tax revenue
    2  Social security
    3  Exports earnings
    A  1, 2 and 3
    B  1 and 2 only
    C  2 and 3 only
    D  1 only
    E  3 only

### Answers

**1** If the exchange rate is reduced exports will become cheaper abroad and imports will become more expensive in the domestic economy. A reduction in the exchange rate would therefore tend to stimulate aggregate demand and so option 1 is correct.

A reduction in taxation will tend to reduce leakages from the circular flow of income and, since at least part of the implied increase in disposable income will be spent, aggregate demand will tend to rise. Option 2 is correct.

If the government increases its own expenditure injections will tend to rise either directly, because the government is spending more on goods and services, or indirectly as households spend additional transfer payments. Option 3 is correct.

The key is A.

**2** An automatic stabiliser functions to reduce the extent of fluctuations in the level of nominal national income. To function as an automatic stabiliser a leakage must vary directly with national income whereas an injection must vary inversely as national income. In other words a leakage must fall as national income falls and rise as national income rises, while an injection must fall as national income rises and rise as national income falls. On this criteria tax revenue and social security payments are both automatic stabilisers whereas exports are not.

The key is B.

## REVIEW QUESTIONS AND ANSWERS

### Questions

**1** Are high interest rates an effective anti-inflationary policy, or do they cause inflation?

**2** If a government wishes to increase taxes to reduce inflation, which would be the more effective: income tax or Value Added Tax? Justify your answer.

**3** Is it realistic to expect governments to achieve the aims of macroeconomic policy? Discuss the proposition that governments should neither be praised for all successes, nor blamed for all failures.

**4** Do demand management policies ignore the supply side of the economy?

### Answers

**1** In the short run high interest rates might add to inflation by raising the cost of borrowing. In particular, since mortgage costs are included in the RPI, any increase in mortgage rates will be reflected in an increase in the RPI. However, in the long run, there is no doubt that maintaining interest rates at a relatively high level will depress investment and discourage consumption. It may also keep the exchange rate at an overvalued level, thus reducing exports and increasing imports. The effect will be a reduction in the rate of inflation as output falls and unemployment rises.

**2** One view of the economy is that in the long run it is money growth which causes inflation and so it makes no difference whether the government increases direct taxes or indirect taxes. They will both reduce the extent of government borrowing and will therefore have the same effect on money growth and the rate of inflation.

However there may be other factors to consider. An increase in VAT will be reflected in an immediate rise in the price level and to that extent may have a short run inflationary bias. In the long run the effect of higher prices will be to reduce demand and so to reduce inflation. A rise in direct taxes, on the other hand, implies an immediate reduction in disposable income which will more quickly be reflected in a fall in demand and a fall in inflation.

In the longer run, if direct taxes have more of a disincentive effect than indirect taxes, higher direct taxes will reduce the efficiency with which the supply side of the economy operates. This implies an increase in the natural rate of unemployment and a lower standard of living.

**3** Governments clearly believe in their ability to achieve macroeconomic objectives and therefore it is realistic to expect them to achieve those which they aim to achieve. What seems unrealistic is that governments can achieve all objectives at all times. All economies are subject to random shocks and so it is probably correct that governments should neither be praised for all success nor blamed for all failures.

**4** Demand-side policies are based on the assumption that the supply side of the economy simply responds passively to changes in aggregate demand. In other words an important assumption of demand side models is that supply is determined by demand! To this extent demand side models ignore the supply side of the economy.

## CHAPTER 37

# *SUPPLY-SIDE POLICIES IN THE UK*

## Topic Summary

Demand-side policies were first introduced in the UK after 1945 and continued to be the main approach to macroeconomic management until well into the 1970s. However, even by the 1960s it was becoming clear that the ability of demand-side policies to deliver macroeconomic success was limited. During the **boom phase** of the cycle inflation was reaching higher and higher levels and current account deficits were becoming more severe. During the **recession phase** of the cycle unemployment reached higher and higher levels and in general the rate of economic growth in the UK lagged well behind that of other developed countries. Despite this it was not until the 1980s that emphasis shifted from demand-side policies to supply-side policies.

Basically supply-side policies involve the **removal of barriers to competition in markets**, the **return of assets from the public sector to the private sector** and the **provision of incentives to increase efficiency**. The aim is to increase real national output whilst avoiding the problems of inflation. The effect of a successful supply-side strategy is illustrated in Figure 37.1.

In Figure 37.1 $AS_s$ is the initial short run aggregate supply curve, $AS_L$ is the initial long run aggregate supply curve and $AD$ is the aggregate demand curve. The price level is initially $P$ and real income is initially $Y_N$. Subsequently, if efficiency in the supply side of economy increases, the short run aggregate supply curve will shift to $AS_{s1}$ and the long run aggregate supply curve will shift to $AS_{L1}$. The effect is to increase the equilibrium level of real income to $Y_{N1}$ and to pull down the price level to $P_1$. It is impossible to illustrate the attraction of supply-side policies more vividly than this!

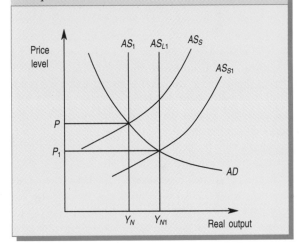

Figure 37.1 *The effect of improved efficiency in the supply side of the economy on real output and the price level*

## *Supply-Side Policies in the UK*

### Taxation

An important strand of the supply-side approach is to **improve incentives** by reducing the burden of taxation and to **improve the allocation of resources** by reducing tax distortion. To improve incentives, successive Conservative governments have reduced the rate of income tax for all income earners. In particular the highest rate of income tax has been reduced from 83 per cent to 40 per cent and the lowest rate has been reduced from 34 per cent to 20 per cent. This is designed to encourage effort and initiative in the labour market. It provides greater incentive for workers to move to different jobs or different parts of the country and is likely to have a favourable effect on the *poverty* and *unemployment traps*. Similarly corporation tax has been reduced from 52 per cent to 25 per cent. This is designed to encourage investment in industry.

Measures have also been implemented to reduce *tax distortion*. For example, tax allowances on mortgages have been reduced from £30 000 per person in the late 1980s to £30 000 per dwelling. The aim is to reduce the attractiveness of investment in property and thereby to increase the attractiveness of investment in industry. Similarly tax relief on life insurance premiums was abolished in 1984 to encourage investment in company equities.

## The Labour Market

The aim of supply-side policies in the labour market is to **increase efficiency** by creating a flexible labour market and by improving mobility. Flexibility has been encouraged by widening the gap between the incomes of those in employment and the incomes of the unemployed. This has been achieved partly by changes in the taxation of incomes, as outlined above. However it has also been achieved by reducing the real value of benefits received by the unemployed relative to the real wage received by those in employment.

Successive Conservative governments have also curbed the power of trade unions by a series of Acts which have outlawed secondary picketing, so that only those workers in dispute with their employer may picket their place of work, and have reduced the maximum number of pickets to six. Unions are now obliged to hold a secret ballot before calling a strike. Closed shops can no longer be enforced and an individual cannot be dismissed for refusing to join a trade union.

Training and Enterprise Councils (TECs) have also been set up to improve the quality of training in local areas and to ease the transition from education to work. Similarly the Technical and Vocational Educational Initiative (TVEI) aims to ensure that educational provision in schools is geared more towards the demands of employers. The aim is to increase the stock of skills possessed by the UK labour force.

## Competition

The **privatisation programme** is also an integral part of the supply-side strategy and reflects a view that private sector organisations operate more effi-

ciently than public sector organisations. There may be many reasons for this. One important reason is that, to survive in the private sector, firms must be profitable. They must therefore aim at increased efficiency to keep costs down. In addition, if shareholders are dissatisfied with company performance they can vote to change the board of directors. Even if shareholders take no action, a poor company performance will be reflected in relatively low share prices and this could encourage a takeover and a managerial shake-out as the new owners seek to improve efficiency. This gives the board a powerful incentive to ensure that a company operates efficiently.

**Deregulating markets** has also been an important strand of the supply-side approach. By removing legal barriers to entry it is hoped that competition in deregulated markets will increase. It is widely believed that competition will provide a powerful incentive for firms to increase their operating efficiency and will result in lower prices as firms attempt to win consumers. In particular there has been a marked increase in competition in the bus and coach industry following deregulation. The capital market has also been reformed and deregulated, one immediate effect of which was a narrowing of the bid–offer spread, that is, the rate at which dealers will buy or sell shares, and a reduction in commissions. The intended effect is to encourage an increase in the number of small investors, thus giving more people an interest in the efficiency of the business sector.

## Common Mistakes to Avoid

An emphasis on supply-side policies does not imply that there is no role for other macroeconomic policies. For example, in the UK in recent years, emphasis on improving the supply side of the economy has been accompanied by quite a severe disinflationary policy. The main instrument of disinflation has been relatively high interest rates to curb aggregate demand and reign back inflation. Emphasis on the supply side simply implies a belief that in the long run the performance of the domestic economy will be enhanced if the supply side operates more efficiently.

## Questions and Answers

### Questions

1  (a)  What do the aggregate demand and aggregate supply curves represent?                (8)

(b) Explain what is meant by the term 'supply-side economics' and outline the effect that 'supply-side policies' may have on the aggregate supply curve.  (7)

(c) How might policies such as tax reform, privatisation and measures to improve the workings of the factor markets, strengthen the supply side of the economy?  (10)

NISEAC May 1991

**2** A 'supply-side' economist would argue that a reduction in direct tax rates could eventually increase government revenue because

1   incentives to work would increase
2   tax avoidance would fall
3   the propensity to save would fall
A   1,2 and 3 correct
B   1 and 2 only correct
C   2 and 3 only correct
D   1 only correct

AEB, Nov 1991

## Answers

**1** (a) An aggregate demand curve simply shows the level of real output that will be demanded at each and every price level. As the price level falls the volume of real output will increase. One reason for this is the real balance effect, that is, as prices fall, the real value of money balances will rise and this will encourage an increase in expenditure. In addition, as the price level falls, exports will become more competitive in world markets and imports will become less competitive in the domestic market. Expenditure may also rise as the price level falls because, as the price level falls, the rate of interest will fall. This might stimulate investment and consumption expenditures. The inverse relationship between the price level and the demand for real output is illustrated in Figure 37.2.

An aggregate supply curve shows the different levels of output that will be supplied at different price levels. In the long run the aggregate supply curve is vertical at the natural rate of output. In other words, in the long run changes in the price level have no effect on the level of output. However, in the short run, as the price level rises, aggregate supply will rise. Firms incur costs in anticipation of a particular rate of profit. If the price level rises then the actual rate of profit will exceed the anticipated rate of profit and this will encourage further production.

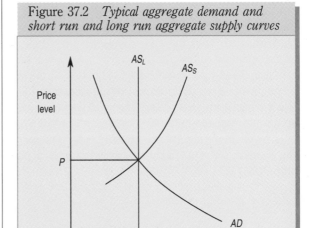

Figure 37.2  *Typical aggregate demand and short run and long run aggregate supply curves*

In Figure 37.2 *AD* is the aggregate demand curve, $AS_S$ is the short run aggregate supply curve and $AS_L$ is the long run aggregate supply curve. The economy illustrated in Figure 37.2 is in long run equilibrium, with price level $P$ and real output $Y_N$.

(b) 'Supply-side economics' is the term used to describe measures introduced by the government to improve the efficiency with which the supply side of the economy operates. In other words, supply-side economics refers to those policies designed to increase productivity and to encourage competition.

If supply-side policies are successful and productivity does increase then the short run and the long run aggregate supply curves will shift outwards to the right. This indicates that in the short run a greater level of output will now be supplied at any given price level. An increase in productivity implies that a given input of resources will now produce a greater output than previously. In other words the average cost of producing any given level of output will fall, and therefore the expected profitability of any given output will rise. This will encourage firms to increase the amount they supply at any given price level; that is, the short run aggregate supply curve will shift outwards to the right. This is illustrated in Figure 37.3, with the short run aggregate supply curve initially given by $AS_S$ and by $AS_{S1}$ after the increase in productivity.

Increased competition might also encourage firms to cut costs in order to keep their products competitive with those of rival firms. Again, if costs fall, the expected profitability from production at any given price level will increase and the aggregate supply curve will shift outwards to the right.

In the long run, if supply-side policies are effective, the increased efficiency with which resources are used will also shift the long run aggregate supply curve outwards to the right. As a result there will be a fall in the natural rate of unemployment. In other words, long run equilibrium will be associated with a lower level of unemployment. Figure 37.3 shows the shift in the aggregate supply curve from $AS_L$ to $AS_{L1}$ as a result of an improvement in the supply side of the economy. The new long run equilibrium level of output is $Y_{N1}$.

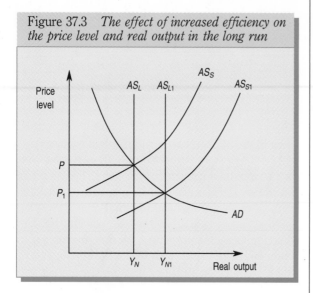

Figure 37.3   *The effect of increased efficiency on the price level and real output in the long run*

(c) In the UK, tax reform has been a major supply-side measure. In particular income tax has been reduced so that those in employment are allowed to retain a greater amount of their earnings. The aim is to increase incentives in the labour market so that unemployed workers have a greater incentive to obtain employment, to increase mobility of labour and to encourage workers already in employment to increase their efforts. In all cases the result will be higher productivity of labour. Corporation tax has also been reduced so that firms pay less tax on their profits, thus releasing greater funds for investment and increasing the return to shareholders. If investment does increase, the effect will be to increase productivity and thus strengthen the supply side of the economy.

Privatisation is the transfer of assets from state ownership to private ownership. It is designed to increase the efficiency with which enterprises are run and in this way strengthen the supply side of the economy. It is argued that private sector organisations are more responsive to changes in consumer preferences than public sector organisations because

of the need to earn a profit. For the same reason they are likely to be more cost conscious and therefore more efficient than state-run enterprises. Another major advantage is that, if an organisation in the private sector is not run efficiently, its share prices will fall and this will make it vulnerable to takeover. This gives management a powerful incentive to operate efficiently because, if they do not, they will almost certainly lose their jobs, either because the company is taken over or because shareholders vote to change the board of directors and a managerial 'shake-out' ensues.

Supply-side policies also include measures designed to increase efficiency in the factor markets. In the UK, capital controls have been abolished so that funds are now free to move to where the best combination of risk and return can be obtained. In addition the capital market has been reformed to increase competition. Fixed commissions by brokers who buy and sell shares on behalf of others have been abolished and full ownership of Stock Exchange firms by non-members is now permissible.

Far-reaching reforms have also been introduced into the labour market. It is now illegal to compel an individual to join a closed shop and the number of individuals allowed to picket their place of work is limited to six. Secondary picketing is illegal and unions must hold a secret ballot before taking industrial action. As a result of reducing the power of trade unions and strengthening the rights of individuals it is anticipated that productivity and mobility will both increase. Measures have also been introduced to increase training opportunities for those out of work. In particular Training and Enterprise Councils (TECs) have been established to ensure training is more directly related to local needs. The aim is to make sure that the local labour force possesses those skills required by the local economy so that the labour market is more responsive to the demands of employers.

**2** It is widely believed that relatively high direct taxes reduce incentives in the labour market to the extent that many people caught in the unemployment trap or the poverty trap have little incentive to accept paid employment. When direct taxes are reduced, disposable income from employment increases and therefore the incentive to accept paid employment increases. Option 1 is correct.

A reduction in direct taxes reduces the gain from tax avoidance. This view is particularly associated with the supply-side view of the economy since a demand-side view assumes a reduction in taxes stimulates aggregate demand. If tax avoidance is widespread a reduction in taxation will have less impact. Option 2 is correct.

A supply-side view of the economy does not postulate any relationship between a change in direct tax rates and the propensity to save. Note also that a reduction in tax rates may change the average propensity to save but it will not necessarily change the marginal propensity to save. Option 3 is incorrect.

The key is B.

## REVIEW QUESTIONS AND ANSWERS

### Questions

1  Distinguish between demand-side and supply-side policies.

2  How might supply-side policies affect (i) economic growth, (ii) the balance of payments?

3  Has deregulation increased the number of 'contestable markets' in the UK?

4  'Since privatisation simply transfers monopolies from the public sector to the private sector it has no effect on efficiency'. Do you agree with this statement?

### Answers

1  Demand-side policies aim to achieve the targets of economic policy (low inflation, high employment and so on) by varying aggregate demand. They are based on the assumption that the supply side of the economy responds to variations in aggregate demand. Supply-side policies aim to achieve the targets of macroeconomic policy by improving the efficiency with which the supply side of the economy operates. It is assumed that variations in aggregate demand have only a transitory effect on macroeconomic variables such as output and employment. It is further assumed that changes in money growth lead only to changes in the price level in the long run and only by improving the supply side can the government hope to reduce unemployment and increase output.

2  (i) If supply-side policies improve the efficiency with which the supply side operates economic growth will undoubtedly increase. Increased efficiency implies that a given amount of input will produce a greater amount of output.

(ii) Similarly supply-side policies might have a favourable effect on the balance of payments for a number of reasons. If resources are used more efficiently then any given level of employment will be associated with a lower rate of inflation. This will reduce the pressure on governments to reflate the economy in order to reduce unemployment and, to the extent that inflation is lower as a result, the current account will improve. In addition, greater efficiency implies an increase in domestic output and, to the extent that more substitutes will be available for imported goods, the current account may improve. Increased efficiency might improve delivery dates and this might have a favourable effect on exports.

3  Strictly a market is contestable when the costs of entry and exit are low. Since public provision of a good or service through a state monopoly is the most complete barrier to entry we might expect privatisation to increase contestability. In practice the public sector monopolies are natural monopolies where the costs of entry are substantial. Contestability might not therefore change as a result of privatisation. On the other hand, by removing an important barrier to entry, markets which were previously uncontestable might now be contestable. Telecommunications is a case in point. Before privatisation there were no competitors for BT. Since privatisation Mercury, though much smaller than BT, has offered some competition and, as the cost of telecommunications falls, this is likely to increase, with Mercury vying for a greater share of the market and other suppliers entering the market.

4  There is a view that public sector monopolies are less efficient than private sector monopolies because the profit motive has less relevance in the public sector. In the private sector if shareholders do not receive a satisfactory rate of return on their shareholdings they will vote to change the board of directors. In addition, if profits and dividends fall, share prices are likely to fall. In such cases a company might become the victim of a hostile takeover. Corporate raiders are always on the look-out for companies whose shares are undervalued because of incompetent management and after the takeover it is the existing management who usually lose their jobs. This provides organisations which have been privatised with a powerful incentive to improve efficiency.

# CHAPTER 38

# DEVELOPMENT AND THE PROBLEMS OF THE LESS DEVELOPED COUNTRIES

## Topic Summary

The developing countries, or less developed countries (LDCs) as they are sometimes called, have a diverse range of characteristics. Nevertheless most developing countries are characterised by certain common features, which we consider below.

## Characteristics of Developing Countries

### Low Per Capita Income

A developing country is a country where **real per capita income is low** compared with developed countries such as those in Western Europe or Japan. In developing countries infant mortality is high compared with the developed countries and the majority of people have poor health, a low level of literacy, inadequate accommodation and a diet that leaves millions starving. Probably the only thing that all developing countries have in common is their low level of real per capita income. In many, though not all, developing countries there is economic stagnation in the sense that the relatively low level of real per capita income is either constant or falling.

### Dominant Agricultural Sector

Another characteristic feature of developing countries is that a large proportion of the population is engaged in **subsistence agriculture**. In other words they raise their own crops to provide themselves with food. They also provide their own clothing and shelter so that there is limited scope for specialisation and exchange – the very activities which characterise the developed countries and which are responsible for the relatively high rates of productivity. In the developed world only a relatively small proportion of the population is employed in agriculture. The situation is exacerbated in developing countries where many people engaged in agricultural production exist in a situation of **disguised unemployment**; that is, their marginal product is zero. This implies a waste of resources since those workers whose marginal product is zero could be employed elsewhere with no reduction in agricultural output.

### Rapid Population Growth

Many developing countries have rapid rates of population growth. In the poorer countries of Asia, Africa and South America population growth has been 2.5 per cent per annum. At this rate of growth a country's population will **double** in less than thirty years. Such growth rates impose a strain on resources since greater and greater amounts must be devoted to providing health-care and education. If all other things remain equal it also implies an increase in the dependency ratio. In such cases ever-increasing amounts must be devoted to current consumption simply to maintain living standards. In many developed countries population growth is less than 1 per cent and in some cases population is projected to fall in the future.

### Vicious Circle of Poverty

In many developing countries, particularly where population growth is rapid, there is a little saving, which reduces the resources available for investment. Such countries are caught in the **vicious circle of poverty**. Because income is relatively low it is devoted almost entirely to current consumption and therefore savings are relatively low. Because of this investment is relatively low and therefore income is perpetuated at a relatively low level. Left to their own devices countries often find it impossible to break out of this vicious circle of poverty. The vicious circle of poverty is illustrated in Figure 38.1.

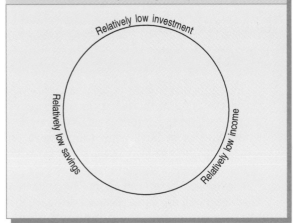

Figure 38.1    *The vicious circle of poverty which condemns many of the world's poorer countries to a continuation of their poverty*

## Development Strategies

There is no simple solution to the problem of development. Economists are not even agreed on the causes of lack of development and there is no guarantee that a strategy to increase development which works in one country will work in other countries. Nevertheless for many countries it is clear that a **policy on population is an essential ingredient** of any development strategy and this is considered below, along with some of the more commonly suggested economic strategies.

## The Population Problem

Population growth in the developing countries is caused by high birth rates and a falling death rate due to the transfer of medical advances from the developed countries. In many developing countries life expectancy has increased by almost one hundred per cent in less than three decades, but the birth rate is little changed. The problem for many people in developing countries is the absence of any form of benefit system, so that a large family provides a means of supporting elderly relatives. However, for countries where population growth is large, what is good for the individual is not good for the nation as a whole and rapid population growth simply depresses

per capita income. For some countries, whatever policy is adopted to promote development, the best that can be hoped for is limited success unless a policy to reduce population growth is also adopted.

## Greater Industrialisation

It is sometimes suggested that a major problem of many of the world's developing countries is their heavy reliance on agriculture. The implication is that, if resources could be transferred to the manufacturing sector, where productivity is greater, this would increase development. However it is not easy to transfer resources from one sector to another and in any case the result of moving people from the land is urban population growth on such a scale that there is overcrowding in the towns and cities. Many people live in slum dwellings and even squatter camps, where disease is rife. The real problem is lack of investment in the infrastructure and in industry. However, as we have seen earlier, many countries are trapped in a vicious circle of poverty and it is not easy for such countries to increase their rate of investment.

## Increased International Trade

A dilemma sometimes exists for countries aiming to increase development: is **self-sufficency** a better strategy than **specialisation and trade**? Self-sufficency implies a policy of encouraging the growth of industries which produce import substitutes, whereas specialisation and trade implies that additional exports should be generated to pay for the increase in imports that development entails. Self-sufficency initially looks to be an attractive option since development is not jeopardised by shocks from the international economy. However, developing import substitute industries implies protecting domestic industry from foreign competition and we have seen (p. 180) that this encourages inefficiency in production and in the allocation of resources. We have also seen, in Chapter 30, that countries gain from specialising in the production of those goods and services where they have a comparative advantage compared with other nations. The rise of the 'Asian dragons' (Singapore, Hong Kong, Taiwan and South Korea) in recent years bears testimony to the benefits of growth through trade.

Despite this, full specialisation where a country has a comparative advantage might not be a wise strategy if it implies concentrating on a narrow range of products. The problem is particularly acute for countries which supply commodities which have low income elasticity of demand and low price elasticity of demand. The low income elasticity of demand implies that growth in the developed countries will exceed growth in their demand for commodities from developing countries so that it will be difficult for the developing countries to grow at the same rate as the developed countries. The low price elasticity of demand implies that changes in supply will cause relatively large changes in price and therefore relatively large changes in the incomes of producers.

## Property Rights and Entrepreneurship

It is now widely recognised that markets provide the most efficient means of allocating resources. By encouraging the ownership of private property and allowing the profit motive to guide producers, many developing countries have experienced an increase in economic growth. State regulation of the economy stifles initiative, reduces the incentive to increase productivity and prevents resources moving to where they can be used most productively. Deregulation is therefore rapidly becoming an integral part of development strategy in the 1990s.

## The Debt Problem

For countries trapped in the vicious circle of poverty one possibility is **greater international borrowing** to finance investment. Developing countries have adopted this strategy for decades but in the 1970s and 1980s borrowing increased dramatically. The term 'debt crisis' emerged in the 1980s when, as a result of rising world interest rates and falling demand for exports from the developing countries, many debtor countries defaulted on the interest payments on their debt.

The problems of the debtor countries would undoubtedly have been lessened if borrowed funds had been invested in industries likely to promote growth. This is precisely what happened in some countries such as Singapore, which has had no problem in meeting debt service charges or in redeeming its debts. However, in some cases it appears that funds were used to increase domestic consumption. In brief the response of the developed countries to the debt problem has been:

- to cut back on lending to the debtor countries;
- to write off a certain amount of debt;
- to reschedule the majority of debt repayments, that is, to allow the debtor countries longer to meet interest payments and final redemption of the debt;
- to negotiate lower debt service charges; that is, to reduce the interest payable by debtor countries.

## Questions and Answers

### Questions

1  Coffee and cocoa prices – which have this year collapsed along with their commodity agreements – are set to fall further in 1990, according to the Economist Intelligence Unit. And a big question mark remains over the possible revival of the two commodity agreements.

The rubber agreement is the only international pact still operating. But stabilising rubber prices is made easier by the presence of synthetic rubber, which gains market share if natural rubber prices move too high, according to the Unit's latest report on food, feedstuffs and beverages.

The task of stabilising the price of tree crops is inherently difficult because smallholders – who dominate both the coffee and cocoa industries – are all too likely to expand production when prices are high, but much less likely to cut production when prices fall.

Once the cost of establishing the crop has been borne, prices have to 'fall a very long way indeed before they are lower than the opportunity cost of picking the crop with unpaid family labour' according to the EIU.

Therefore very strong agreements are needed to keep cocoa and coffee prices in an agreed range. The EIU believes the producers' inability to agree on the distribution of export quotas is the key to the coffee agreement's problems. Brazil, the world's biggest coffee producer, was at least as much to blame for the collapse of the pact as the US, the biggest consumer, which is generally hostile to all agreements.

The cocoa agreement has succumbed to a difficulty common to all cartels – the thrusting newcomer who remains outside, says the report.

Malaysia, with its low production costs and tenfold increase in output in 10 years, has led to a structural change in the market, making supplies far less vulnerable to disruption in Africa and Brazil, the two traditional growing areas.

Malaysian producers are against their country's membership of the International Cocoa Organisation because it could lead to restricted exports and threaten the financial viability of their expansion plans.

*Source*: D. Blackwell, 'Bleak future for commodity pacts and prices', *Financial Times*, 8 December 1989.

(a) (i) Explain the meaning of the view that 'prices have to fall a very long way indeed before they are lower than the opportunity cost of picking the crop with unpaid family labour'.　(4 marks)

　　(ii) What does this indicate about the economic rent received by cocoa and coffee producers?　(2 marks)

(b) The author of the article suggests that stabilising rubber prices is easier than is the case with cocoa and coffee. Explain why this may be so.　(2 marks)

(c) Why does Malaysia pose a problem for other cocoa producers in their attempt to stabilise prices?　(6 marks)

(d) The income elasticity of demand for cocoa in the United States has been estimated to be +0.43*. What relevance has this figure for cocoa producers?　(5 marks)

(* The International Cocoa Organisation, London)

ULEAC, June 1992

**2** Third World countries aiming to increase economic growth will be hindered by

1　fluctuating primary product prices
2　lack of capital
3　poor infrastructure
A　1,2 and 3 correct
B　1 and 2 only correct
C　2 and 3 only correct
D　1 only correct

AEB, June 1990

## Answers

**1** (a) (i) The bulk of the cost involved in coffee or cocoa production is the fixed cost of establishing the crop, that is, planting and rearing of trees. Once these costs have been met, production will be profitable as long as price is greater than the variable cost of production. In the case of coffee and cocoa we are

told that unpaid family labour is used to pick the crop. In this case production will still take place even at very low prices because of the very low variable cost. Hence the phrase 'prices have to fall a very long way indeed before they are lower than the opportunity cost of picking the crop with unpaid family labour'.

　　(ii) Economic rent is a surplus over transfer earnings. The transfer earnings for unpaid family labour are likely to be very low indeed, otherwise workers would move to where rewards are greatest. This implies that the majority of the earnings of cocoa and coffee workers are economic rent.

(b) It is easier to stabilise rubber prices because the supply of synthetic rubber can respond to changes in the market demand for rubber. In other words, when the demand for rubber increases manufacturers can increase production of synthetic rubber. This implies an increase in the supply of rubber in response to the higher demand and this limits the effect on the price of rubber of the increase in demand. Conversely, when the demand for rubber falls, the implied fall in the price of rubber will encourage a cut-back in the production of synthetic rubber. This mitigates the effect of the fall in demand on the price of rubber. The production of synthetic rubber therefore acts as a buffer stock mechanism which reduces fluctuations in price. However coffee and cocoa are grown on trees and cannot be produced by any other process. Any change in demand or supply will therefore result in price fluctuations which cannot be stabilised in the way that rubber prices can.

(c) With the exception of Malaysia, cocoa producers belong to a cartel. This is a formal agreement between producers to market their product jointly. This implies that individual producers control supply so as to achieve a monopoly position. Individual producers accept a quota on the amount they supply, the aim being to limit the total supply of cocoa so as to drive up the price of cocoa and thus increase cartel profits above that which could be achieved if cartel members competed against each other in world markets.

Malaysia poses a problem for the established cartel because it is not a member and is not therefore bound by the cartel agreement to limit the supply of cocoa. On the contrary Malaysia has increased its output of cocoa tenfold in ten years. This has clearly had a powerful impact on market supply because we are told that there has been 'a structural change in the market, making supplies far less vulnerable to disruption in Africa and Brazil, the two traditional growing areas'. We are also told that

Malaysia is a low cost producer and this, combined with the increase in the supply of cocoa from Malaysia, will exert downward pressure on cocoa prices in world markets. Since Malaysia is not part of the cartel agreement, it will be difficult for cartel members to stabilise cocoa prices.

(d) The income elasticity of demand at 0.43 implies that for each 1 per cent growth in national income in the USA, the demand for cocoa will increase by only 0.43 per cent. For those countries which are major exporters of cocoa this implies that it will be difficult if not impossible to achieve a rate of growth equal to that of the USA. More generally, if the income elasticity of demand for cocoa in the USA has a similar value to that in other developed countries, the implication is that it will be extremely difficult for the cocoa exporting countries to close the development gap between themselves and the developed world.

2 Many developing countries are producers of primary products. The prices of primary products often fluctuate widely because they tend to have a low price elasticity of demand and are prone to fluctuations in supply. Fluctuating primary product prices imply fluctuating incomes for primary producers. In some cases this might represent a formidable barrier to economic growth. Option 1 is correct.

Another major problem developing countries face is a lack of capital equipment. In many cases they tend to rely on low cost labour. However capital is much more productive than labour and the absence of an adequate capital stock represents a barrier to growth. Option 2 is correct.

An essential prerequisite for growth in the world's poorer countries is a well-developed infrastructure so that raw materials can be transported to the place of production and finished products can be transported to market. Option 3 is correct.

The key is therefore A.

## REVIEW QUESTIONS AND ANSWERS

### Questions

1 Why is an efficient banking sector important for developing countries?

2 Why is unemployment 'disguised' when a worker's marginal product is zero?

3 Who is responsible for the international debt crisis, and what should be done about it?

4 'Successful aid depends upon liberal trade'. Do you agree with this statement?.

5 With reference to a particular country, examine the economic and social effects of underdevelopment.

6 Could emigration help solve the problem of economic underdevelopment?

7 Examine the role of Third World pressure groups such as 'UNCTAD'.

8 What criteria and data would you use to decide if:

(a) Hong Kong (b) Russia, were developed or developing countries?

9 Is there a 'Third World'?

10 Why might it be in the interest of creditor countries to reduce the debt burden of developing countries?

11 Do all developing countries face similar problems in seeking to achieve economic development?

12 Both Mexico and the United States have a high level of foreign debt: why is this more of a problem for the former than for the latter?

13 'With every mouth God sends a pair of hands'. How relevant is this comment to the economic effects of population expansion in developing countries?.

### Answers

1 An efficient banking sector is essential so that a nation's savings can be made available to industry to finance investment programmes.

2 When marginal product is zero the last worker contributes nothing to output. It follows that if the last worker was made redundant, total output would remain unchanged. In these circumstances unemployment is 'disguised'.

3 To some extent borrowers and lenders are both responsible for the debt crisis: borrowers because they have often not put funds to the most productive uses and have not directed policies towards ensuring they can service their

debts; lenders because they allowed borrowers to overextend themselves and borrow too heavily. However there are many other factors to consider. We might blame the industrialised countries for inflating and driving up interest rates to levels beyond that which the developing countries could afford. We might blame the oil rich countries for driving up oil prices and forcing the developing countries to borrow to finance their current account deficits. Strictly speaking it is not possible to apportion blame for the debt crisis.

Neither is it possible to provide a definitive answer as to what should be done about the debt crisis. One possibility is to write the debts off. However this seems an unlikely solution and would be unfair on those countries which have made sacrifices to redeem their debts. The only viable course of action is to go on rescheduling debts so as to give the poorer countries sufficient time to repay them.

4 One argument for providing aid to developing countries is to provide them with capital. However increased investment is pointless if the additional output that is produced cannot be sold on world markets because of protectionist policies. Aid can be very successful in alleviating a crisis in the short term, for example, by providing food to people who are starving. However, in the long term, liberalisation of trade will provide the conditions for production to become profitable in developing countries. This is regarded as the key to successful development.

5 Many factors could be considered here, depending on which country we look at. In many of the world's poorer places poverty leads to starvation and poor housing conditions where disease is rife. Malnourishment can cause problems in the physical and mental development of children. In some countries, for example Brazil, poverty is associated with an explosion in the crime rate. Another problem is that an increasing amount of resources is devoted to dealing with the problems of poverty, so that in many developing countries it is impossible for the population to save, there is little investment and the future prospects are bleak. In an effort to increase investment the Brazilian Government has hewn down large sections of the Amazon Jungle and the timber has been sold for hard currency. This might well help finance investment but it is also likely to increase the greenhouse effect.

In Brazil, as in many poorer countries, there are vast inequalities in the distribution of income. In many towns and cities luxury residences, where the wealthier people live, overlook shanty towns, where the poorer people live. A growing number of people are homeless, and among the poorer groups literacy rates are low and disease is rife.

6 To have any effect on population size, emigration would need to be on a quite massive scale. Even if this were possible it is the young and the skilled who are most likely to move and this would seriously reduce the development prospects of a country, since it would reduce the incentive of firms to invest.

7 The role of any pressure group is to inform and persuade. Only if we know about a problem can we adopt policies to solve that problem.

8 The basic criterion to compare countries is GNP per capita. However in Hong Kong there is a greater degree of inequality than in Russia, so it would be useful to compare the number of people in different income brackets. Other criteria are literacy rates, number of doctors per head of population and availability of medical care. The majority of people in Russia probably have greater access to medical care than in Hong Kong, where medical care is provided through the private sector.

9 'Third World' is the term used to describe all the underdeveloped nations of the world. In this sense there is very clearly a third world.

10 It might be in the interests of creditor countries to reduce the debt burden on debtor countries because this might encourage debtor countries to make greater efforts to meet interest payments and to redeem the debt. Lower debt charges might also enhance the prospects for trade, and developed countries would benefit from this.

11 Many developing countries face similar problems such as high population growth and high debt/GDP ratios. Many countries are also caught in the vicious circle of poverty. This simply means income is low and devoted mainly to consumption. Because of this savings are low and hence investment is low. Low investment implies low growth of income and so the circle is complete. The more rapid the population growth the more difficult it becomes to break out of the circle. Despite this, there are differences between countries, since the

severity of the problems facing developing countries varies.

**12** The ratio of debt/GDP is much lower in the USA than in Mexico. The USA therefore has a far greater ability to service its debt charges and to redeem the debt than Mexico.

**13** The statement implies that every individual is both a producer and a consumer. However other resources besides labour are required for production, in particular capital equipment. Without sufficient capital many workers simply exist as disguised unemployment. As well as resources, developing countries also need access to markets. In other words, although increased population implies more pairs of hands, people might not always be able to use their hands productively!

# INDEX